ethernet networks

Fourth Edition

- Design
- Implementation
- Operation
- Management

GILBERT HELD

4-Degree Consulting, Macon, Georgia, USA

JOHN WILEY & SONS, LTD

Other Wiley Editorial Offices

John Wiley & Sons Inc., 111 River Street, Hoboken, NJ 07030, USA

Jossey-Bass, 989 Market Street, San Francisco, CA 94103-1741, USA

Wiley-VCH Verlag GmbH, Boschstr. 12, D-69469 Weinheim, Germany

John Wiley & Sons Australia Ltd, 33 Park Road, Milton, Queensland 4064, Australia

John Wiley & Sons (Asia) Pte Ltd, 2 Clementi Loop #02-01, Jin Xing Distripark,
Singapore 129809

John Wiley & Sons Canada Ltd, 22 Worcester Road, Etobicoke, Ontario, Canada M9W 1L1

British Library Cataloguing in Publication Data

A catalogue record for this book is available from the British Library

ISBN 0-470-84476-0

Typeset in 10.5/13pt Melior by Laserwords Private Limited, Chennai, India
Printed and bound in Great Britain by Biddles Ltd, Guildford and King's Lynn
This book is printed on acid-free paper responsibly manufactured from sustainable forestry
in which at least two trees are planted for each one used for paper production.

For the past decade I have been most fortunate in being able to teach graduate courses that were truly enjoyable to teach. In doing so I have been able to tailor my presentation of technical information covering LAN performance and other data communications topics, providing a two-way learning facility and enhancing my presentation skills. Thus, I would be remiss if I did not thank the students at Georgia College and State University as well as Dr Harvey Glover for providing me with the opportunity to teach. In doing so I would like to dedicate this book to those who pursue higher education.

contents

preface

In a prior edition of this book the preface commenced with the paraphrase of an old adage in an era of evolving local area networking technology: Ethernet is dead — long live Ethernet!

Although advances in communications technology continue to occur at a rapid pace, that paraphrase continues to be valid. Within the past decade, the bandwidth of 10 Mbps Ethernet was advanced by a factor of one thousand with the introduction of a series of enhancements to the original Ethernet specification. First, Fast Ethernet resulted in the bandwidth of Ethernet increasing by a factor of 10 to 100 Mbps. The introduction of Gigabit Ethernet resulted in another order of magnitude increase in bandwidth to 1 Gbps. Although many persons felt that a transmission capacity of 1 Gbps would be more than sufficient for the foreseeable future, another adage states that many applications will grow to use all available bandwidth. While most organizations may be hard pressed to use 1 Gbps of bandwidth, other organizations, including Internet Service Providers and corporations and universities with large backbone LANs, were able to literally fill the 1 Gbps pipe, resulting in the development of 10 Gbps Ethernet. Thus, over the past decade Ethernet's 10 Mbps operation has increased by a factor of 1000 to 10 Gbps.

This new edition provides a significant amount of additional material to most of the chapters of this book's previous edition. New information added includes coverage of the transmission of Gigabit over copper conductors, the evolution of cabling standards that facilitate support of higher Ethernet operating rates, and the manner by which LAN switches operate on Ethernet frames transporting information at higher layers in the Open System Interconnection Reference Model.

Recognizing the importance of networking without wires, a new chapter is focused upon wireless Ethernet. This chapter describes and discusses the series of IEEE 802.11 standards and provides practical information concerning the setup and operation of a wireless LAN. Recognizing the importance of security in the modern era of networking resulted in the movement of most security related topics to a new chapter focused on this topic. This chapter considerably expands the prior disparate coverage of security by adding information covering the use of firewalls in both a wired and wireless environment. In addition, information concerning the use of router access lists is considerably expanded, while new information covering authentication, authorization and accounting has been added to the chapter.

Other topics that have been added or significantly revised in this new edition include the operation of new versions of Windows on Ethernet LANs, the operation and utilization of LAN switches above layer 2 in the ISO Reference Model, new gateway methods you can consider to connect workstation users to mainframes, and the use of both copper and fiber optic to transport high-speed Ethernet. Thus, the scope and depth of material have been significantly revised and updated to continue to provide you with detailed information concerning the design, implementation, operation and management of different types of Ethernet networks.

This book incorporates into one reference source the material you will need to understand how Ethernet networks operate, the constraints and performance issues that affect their design and implementation, and how their growth and use can be managed both locally and as part of an enterprise network. Assuming readers have varied backgrounds in communications terms and technology, the first two chapters were written to provide a common foundation of knowledge. Those chapters cover networking concepts and network standards—two topics on which material in succeeding chapters is based. Succeeding chapters examine Ethernet concepts: frame operations; network construction; the use of bridges, routers, hubs, switches, and gateways; Internet connectivity; network backbone construction; Wireless Ethernet; Security; and the management of Ethernet networks.

In writing this book, my primary goal was to incorporate practical information you can readily use in designing, operating, implementing, and managing an Ethernet network. Although Ethernet had its origins in the 1970s and can be considered a relatively "old" technology, in reality, the technology is anything but old. Only a few years ago, the standardization of what is now known as 10BASE-T (a twisted-wire version of Ethernet) resulted in a considerable expansion in the use of this type of local area network. By 1994 the use of intelligent switches greatly enhanced the operational capability of 10BASE-T networks, providing multiple simultaneous 10 Mbps connectivity. During 1995 high-speed Ethernet technology in the form of Fast Ethernet products provided users with the ability to upgrade their Ethernet networks to satisfy emerging multimedia requirements. Within a few years industry realized that emerging applications, as well as the growth in the use of the Internet, required higher-speed backbone LANs as a mechanism to support Internet access and similar high-speed networking requirements. This realization resulted in the deployment of Gigabit Ethernet hubs and switches during

1997, which was quickly followed by 10 Gbps operations a few years later. Thus, Ethernet technology can be expected to continue to evolve to satisfy the communications requirements of business, government, and academia.

For over 30 years I have worked as a network manager responsible for the design, operation, and management of an enterprise network in which local area networks throughout the United States are interconnected through the use of different wide area network transmission facilities. This challenging position has provided me with the opportunity to obtain practical experience in designing, operating, and interconnecting Ethernet networks to Token-Ring, SNA, the Internet, and other types of networks — experience which I have attempted to share with you. This book will help you consider the practicality of different types of routing protocols, LAN switches, and gateway methods. These and other network design issues are crucial to the efficient and effective expansion of a local Ethernet so that users on that network can access resources on other networks.

As a professional author, I very much value readers' comments. Those comments provide me with feedback necessary to revise future editions so that they better reflect the information requirements of readers. I look forward to receiving your comments, as well as suggestions for information you would like to see in a future edition of this book. You can write to me directly or through my publisher, whose address you can find on page 4 of this book or communicate with me directly via electronic mail at gil_held@yahoo.com.

Gilbert Held
Macon, GA

acknowledgments

This book would not have been possible without the work of two people whose foresight and pioneering efforts were instrumental in the development of the technology upon which Ethernet is based.

One of the key concepts behind Ethernet — that of allocating the use of a shared channel — can be traced to the pioneering efforts of Dr Norman Abramson and his colleagues at the University of Hawaii during the early 1970s. The actual development of Ethernet is due to the foresight of Dr Robert Metcalfe. Working at the Xerox Palo Alto Research Center in Palo Alto, California, Dr Metcalfe headed a development team that interconnected over 100 computers on a 1-km cable using a carrier sense multiple access collision detection (CSMA/CD) protocol. In addition to pioneering the technical development of Ethernet, Dr Metcalfe coined its name, after the luminiferous ether through which electromagnetic radiation was once thought to propagate. I would be remiss if I did not thank Dr Abramson, Dr Metcalfe, and their colleagues for their visionary efforts in developing the technology through which hundreds of millions of people now communicate.

Writing and producing a book about technology requires not only the technology itself, but also the efforts of many individuals. First and foremost, I would like to thank my family for their understanding for the nights and weekends I disappeared to write this book. Once again, I am indebted to Mrs Linda Hayes and Mrs Susan Corbitt for taking my notes and drawings and converting them into a manuscript. Last, but not least, I would like to thank Birgit Gruber and Ann-Marie Halligan as well as the production staff at John Wiley & Sons for backing the new edition of this book, as well as in facilitating the conversion of my manuscript into the book you are reading.

chapter one

Introduction to Networking Concepts

One of the most logical assumptions an author can make is that readers will have diverse backgrounds of knowledge and experience. Making this book as valuable as possible to persons with different backgrounds requires an introductory chapter that covers basic networking concepts. Unfortunately, basic concepts for one person may not be the same as basic concepts for another person, which presents an interesting challenge for an author.

To meet this challenge, this book takes two courses of action. First, it assumes that some readers will have limited knowledge about the different types of communications systems available for transporting information, the relationship between wide area networks (WANs) and local area networks (LANs), and the relationships among different types of local area networks. Thus, this introductory chapter was written to provide those readers with a basic level of knowledge concerning these important topics. Secondly, readers who are already familiar with these basic concepts may wish to consult individual chapters separately, rather than reading through the entire book. To satisfy those readers, each chapter was written to be as independent as possible from preceding and succeeding chapters. Thus, readers who are familiar with wide and local area networking concepts, as well as the technical characteristics of LANs, may elect to skim or bypass this chapter. For other readers, information contained in this chapter will provide a level of knowledge that will make succeeding chapters more meaningful.

In this introductory chapter, we will first focus our attention on the key concepts behind the construction of wide area networks and local area networks. In doing so, we will examine each type of network to obtain an understanding of its primary design goal. Next, we will compare and contrast their operations and utilizations to obtain an appreciation for the rationale behind the use of different types of local area networks.

Although this book is about Ethernet networks, there are other types of local area networks that provide a viable data transportation highway for millions of users. By reviewing the technological characteristics of different types of LANs, we will obtain an appreciation for the governing characteristics behind the use of different local area networks. In addition, because many local area networks are connected to other LANs and WANs, we will conclude this chapter by focusing on the technological characteristics of local area networks. This will form a foundation for discussing a variety of Ethernet networking issues in succeeding chapters of this book.

1.1 Wide Area Networks

The evolution of wide area networks can be considered to have originated in the mid- to late 1950s, commensurate with the development of the first generation of computers. Based on the use of vacuum tube technology, the first generation of computers were large, power-hungry devices whose placement resulted in a focal point for data processing and the coinage of the term *data center*.

Computer-Communications Evolution

Originally, access to the computational capability of first-generation computers was through the use of punched cards. After an employee of the organization used a keypunch to create a deck of cards, that card deck was submitted to a window in the data center, typically labeled input/output (I/O) control. An employee behind the window would accept the card deck and complete a form that contained instructions for running the submitted job. The card deck and instructions would then be sent to a person in production control, who would schedule the job and turn it over to operations for execution at a predefined time. Once the job was completed, the card deck and any resulting output would be sent back to I/O control, enabling the job originator to return to the window in the data center to retrieve his or her card deck and the resulting output. With a little bit of luck, programmers might see the results of their efforts on the same day that they submitted their jobs.

Because the computer represented a considerable financial investment for most organizations, it was understandable that these organizations would be receptive to the possibility of extending their computers' accessibility. By the mid-1960s, several computer manufacturers had added remote access capabilities to one or more of their computers.

Remote Batch Transmission

One method of providing remote access was the installation of a batch terminal at a remote location. That terminal was connected via a telephone company–supplied analog leased line and a pair of modems to the computer in the corporate data center.

The first type of batch terminal developed to communicate with a data center computer contained a card reader, a printer, a serial communications adapter, and hard-wired logic in one common housing. The serial communications adapter converted the parallel bits of each internal byte read from the card reader into a serial data stream for transmission. Similarly, the adapter performed a reverse conversion process, converting a sequence of received serial bits into an appropriate number of parallel bits to represent a character internally within the batch terminal. Because the batch terminal was located remotely from the data center, it was often referred to as a *remote batch terminal*, while the process of transmitting data was referred to as *remote batch transmission*. In addition, the use of a remote terminal as a mechanism for grouping card decks of individual jobs, all executed at the remote data center, resulted in the term *remote job entry terminal* being used as a name for this device.

Figure 1.1 illustrates in schematic form the relationships between a batch terminal, transmission line, modems, and the data center computer. Because the transmission line connects a remote batch terminal in one geographic area to a computer located in a different geographic area, Figure 1.1 represents one of the earliest types of wide area data communications networks.

Paralleling the introduction of remote batch terminals was the development of a series of terminal devices, control units, and specialized communications equipment, which resulted in the rapid expansion of interactive computer applications. One of the most prominent collections of products was introduced by the IBM Corporation under the trade name *3270 Information Display System*.

Figure 1.1 Remote batch transmission. The transmission of data from a remote batch terminal represents one of the first examples of wide area data communications networks.

IBM 3270 Information Display System

The IBM 3270 Information Display System was a term originally used to describe a collection of products ranging from interactive terminals that communicate with a computer, referred to as *display stations*, through several types of control units and communications controllers. Later, through the introduction of additional communications products from IBM and numerous third-party vendors and the replacement of previously introduced products, the IBM 3270 Information Display System became more of a networking architecture and strategy rather than a simple collection of products.

First introduced in 1971, the IBM 3270 Information Display System was designed to extend the processing power of the data center computer to remote locations. Because the data center computer typically represented the organization's main computer, the term *mainframe* was coined to refer to a computer with a large processing capability. As the mainframe was primarily designed for data processing, its utilization for supporting communications degraded its performance.

Communications Controller

To offload communications functions from the mainframe, IBM and other computer manufacturers developed hardware to sample communications lines for incoming bits, group bits into bytes, and pass a group of bytes to the mainframe for processing. This hardware also performed a reverse function for data destined from the mainframe to remote devices. When first introduced, such hardware was designed using fixed logic circuitry, and the resulting device was referred to as a *communications controller*. Later, minicomputers were developed to execute communications programs, with the ability to change the functionality of communications support by the modification of software—a considerable enhancement to the capabilities of this series of products. Because both hard-wired communications controllers and programmed minicomputers performing communications offloaded communications processing from the mainframe, the term *front-end processor* evolved to refer to this category of communications equipment. Although most vendors refer to a minicomputer used to offload communications processing from the mainframe as a front-end processor, IBM has retained the term *communications controller*, even though their fixed logic hardware products were replaced over 20 years ago by programmable minicomputers.

Control Units

To reduce the number of controller ports required to support terminals, as well as the amount of cabling between controller ports and terminals, IBM developed *poll and select* software to support its 3270 Information Display System. This software enabled the communications controller to transmit messages from one port to one or more terminals in a predefined group of devices. To share the communications controller port, IBM developed a product called a *control unit*, which acts as an interface between the communications controller and a group of terminals.

In general terms, the communications controller transmits a message to the control unit. The control unit examines the terminal address and retransmits the message to the appropriate terminal. Thus, control units are devices that reduce the number of lines required to link display stations to mainframe computers. Both local and remote control units are available; the key differences between them are the method of attachment to the mainframe computer and the use of intermediate devices between the control unit and the mainframe.

Local control units are usually attached to a channel on the mainframe, whereas remote control units are connected to the mainframe's front-end processor, which is also known as a communications controller in the IBM environment. Because a local control unit is within a limited distance of the mainframe, no intermediate communications devices, such as modems or data service units, are required to connect a local control unit to the mainframe. In comparison, a remote control unit can be located in another building or in a different city; it normally requires the utilization of intermediate communications devices, such as a pair of modems or a pair of data service units, for communications to occur between the control unit and the communications controller. The relationship of local and remote control units to display stations, mainframes, and a communications controller is illustrated in Figure 1.2.

Network Construction

To provide batch and interactive access to the corporate mainframe from remote locations, organizations began to build sophisticated networks. At first, communications equipment such as modems and transmission lines was obtainable only from AT&T and other telephone companies. Beginning in 1974 in the United States with the well-known Carterphone decision, competitive non−telephone company sources for the supply of communications equipment became available. The divestiture of AT&T during the 1980s and

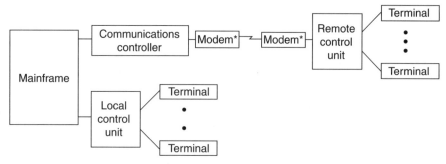

*Note: Modems replaced by data service units when a digital transmission facility used.

Figure 1.2 Relationship of 3270 information display products.

the emergence of many local and long-distance communications carriers paved the way for networking personnel to be able to select from among several or even hundreds of vendors for transmission lines and communications equipment.

As organizations began to link additional remote locations to their mainframes, the cost of providing communications began to escalate rapidly. This, in turn, provided the rationale for the development of a series of line-sharing products referred to as *multiplexers* and *concentrators*. Although most organizations operated separate data and voice networks, in the mid-1980s communications carriers began to make available for commercial use high-capacity circuits known as T1 in North America and E1 in Europe. Through the development of T1 and E1 multiplexers, voice, data, and video transmission can share the use of common high-speed circuits. Because the interconnection of corporate offices with communications equipment and facilities normally covers a wide geographical area outside the boundary of one metropolitan area, the resulting network is known as a *wide area network* (WAN).

Figure 1.3 shows an example of a wide area network spanning the continental United States. In this example, regional offices in San Francisco and New York are connected with the corporate headquarters, located in Atlanta, via T1 multiplexers and T1 transmission lines operating at 1.544 Mbps. Assuming that each T1 multiplexer is capable of supporting the direct attachment of a *private branch exchange (PBX)*, both voice and data are carried by the T1 circuits between the two regional offices and corporate headquarters. The three T1 circuits can be considered the primary data highway, or *backbone*, of the corporate network.

Figure 1.3 Wide area network example. A WAN uses telecommunications lines obtained from one or more communications carriers to connect geographically dispersed locations.

In addition to the three major corporate sites that require the ability to route voice calls and data between locations, let us assume that the corporation also has three smaller area offices located in Sacramento, California; Macon, Georgia; and New Haven, Connecticut. If these locations only require data terminals to access the corporate network for routing to the computers located in San Francisco and New York, one possible mechanism to provide network support is obtained through the use of tail circuits. These tail circuits could be used to connect a *statistical time division multiplexer (STDM)* in each area office, each serving a group of data terminals to the nearest T1 multiplexer, using either analog or digital circuits. The T1 multiplexer would then be configured to route data terminal traffic over the corporate backbone portion of the network to its destination.

Network Characteristics

There are certain characteristics we can associate with wide area networks. First, the WAN is typically designed to connect two or more geographical areas. This connection is accomplished by the lease of transmission facilities from one or more communications vendors. Secondly, most WAN transmission occurs at or under a data rate of 1.544 Mbps or 2.048 Mbps, which are the operating rates of T1 and E1 transmission facilities.

A third characteristic of WANs concerns the regulation of the transmission facilities used for their construction. Most, if not all, transmission facilities marketed by communications carriers are subject to a degree of regulation at the federal, state, and possibly local government levels. Even though we now live in an era of deregulation, carriers must seek approval for many offerings before making new facilities available for use. In addition, although many of the regulatory controls governing the pricing of services were removed, the communications market is still not a truly free market. Thus, regulatory agencies at the federal, state, and local levels still maintain a degree of control over both the offering and pricing of new services and the pricing of existing services.

1.2 Local Area Networks

The origin of local area networks can be traced, in part, to IBM terminal equipment introduced in 1974. At that time, IBM introduced a series of terminal devices designed for use in transaction-processing applications for banking and retailing. What was unique about those terminals was their method of connection: a common cable that formed a loop provided a communications path within a localized geographical area. Unfortunately, limitations in the data transfer rate, incompatibility between individual IBM loop systems, and other problems precluded the widespread adoption of this method of networking. The economics of media sharing and the ability to provide common access to a centralized resource were, however, key advantages, and they resulted in IBM and other vendors investigating the use of different techniques to provide a localized communications capability between different devices. In 1977, Datapoint Corporation began selling its Attached Resource Computer Network (ARCNet), considered by most people to be the first commercial local area networking product. Since then, hundreds of companies have developed local area networking products, and the installed base of terminal devices connected to such networks has increased exponentially. They now number in the hundreds of millions.

Comparison to WANs

Local area networks can be distinguished from wide area networks by geographic area of coverage, data transmission and error rates, ownership, government regulation, and data routing—and, in many instances, by the type of information transmitted over the network.

Geographic Area

The name of each network provides a general indication of the scope of the geographic area in which it can support the interconnection of devices. As its name implies, a LAN is a communications network that covers a relatively small local area. This area can range in scope from a department located on a portion of a floor in an office building, to the corporate staff located on several floors in the building, to several buildings on the campus of a university.

Regardless of the LAN's area of coverage, its geographic boundary will be restricted by the physical transmission limitations of the local area network. These limitations include the cable distance between devices connected to the LAN and the total length of the LAN cable. In comparison, a wide area network can provide communications support to an area ranging in size from a town or city to a state, country, or even a good portion of the entire world. Here, the major factor governing transmission is the availability of communications facilities at different geographic areas that can be interconnected to route data from one location to another.

To better grasp the differences between LANs and WANs, today we can view the LAN as being analogous to our local telephone company, while the WAN can be compared with the long-distance communications carrier. However, this may not be true in the future when local telephone companies obtain permission to offer long-distance service and long-distance communications carriers obtain regulatory approval to offer local telephone service. However, for the present we will presume that telephone support in different cities is provided by the local telephone company in each city. Thus, for calls between cities, the local telephone companies must connect to the long-distance carrier. Similarly, we can have separate LANs in different cities or within different buildings in the same city; however, to interconnect those LANs we would normally require a wide area network.

Until the turn of the millennium these differences between LANs and WANs with the respect to geographic area of coverage were distinct and easy to recognize. However, within the past two years a new role has been proposed for Gigabit Ethernet that could enable this technology to function as a miniature WAN. As we will note later in this book, the ability to transmit Gigabit Ethernet over optical fiber makes it possible to transmit this technology over extended distances. In fact, by the time you read this book Gigabit Ethernet may provide a low-cost alternative to synchronous optical networking (SONET) transmission.

Data Transmission and Error Rates

Two additional areas that differentiate LANs from WANs and explain the physical limitation of the LAN geographic area of coverage are the data transmission rate and error rate for each type of network. Older LANs, such as the original version of Ethernet and Token-Ring, normally operate at a low megabit-per-second rate, typically ranging from 4 Mbps to 16 Mbps. More modern high-speed Ethernet networks, such as Fast Ethernet that operates at 100 Mbps, Gigabit Ethernet and 10 Gigabit Ethernet provide transmission rates of 1 Gbps and 10 Gbps, respectively. In comparison, the communications facilities used to construct a major portion of most WANs provide a data transmission rate at or under the T1 and E1 data rates of 1.544 Mbps and 2.048 Mbps.

Although some readers may have encountered references to WAN transmission rates of 10 and 40 Gbps in various trade literature, the use of optical carriers (OCs) at those data rates is primarily by communications carriers whose transmission facilities are shared by tens of thousands to millions of users. Thus, in considering the data transmission rate with respect to LANs and WANs on a non-communications carrier basis, we can say that LANs provide a transmission capacity up to 10 Gbps while WANs are limited to a low Mbps data rate.

Because LAN cabling is primarily within a building or over a small geographical area, it is relatively safe from natural phenomena, such as thunderstorms and lightning. This safety enables transmission at a relatively high data rate, resulting in a relatively low error rate. In comparison, because wide area networks are based on the use of communications facilities that are much farther apart and always exposed to the elements, they have a much higher probability of being disturbed by changes in the weather, electronic emissions generated by equipment, or such unforeseen problems as construction workers accidentally causing harm to a communications cable. Because of these factors, the error rate on WANs is considerably higher than the rate experienced on LANs. On most WANs you can expect to experience an error rate between 1 in a million and 1 in 10 million (1×10^6 to 1×10^7) bits. In comparison, the error rate on a typical LAN may exceed that range by one or more orders of magnitude, resulting in an error rate from 1 in 10 million to 1 in 100 million bits.

Ownership

The construction of a wide area network requires the leasing of transmission facilities from one or more communications carriers. Although your organization can elect to purchase or lease communications equipment, the transmission facilities used to connect diverse geographical locations are owned by the communications carrier. In comparison, an organization that installs a local area network normally owns all of the components used to form the network, including the cabling used to form the transmission path between devices.

Regulation

Because wide area networks require transmission facilities that may cross local, state, and national boundaries, they may be subject to a number of governmental regulations at the local, state, and national levels. Most of those regulations govern the services that communications carriers can provide customers and the rates (*tariff*) they can charge for those services. In comparison, regulations affecting local area networks are primarily in the areas of building codes. Such codes regulate the type of wiring that can be installed in a building and whether the wiring must run in a conduit.

Data Routing and Topology

In a local area network data is routed along a path that defines the network. That path is normally a bus, ring, tree, or star structure, and data always flows on that structure. The topology of a wide area network can be much more complex. In fact, many wide area networks resemble a mesh structure, including equipment to reroute data in the event of communications circuit failure or excessive traffic between two locations. Thus, the data flow on a wide area network can change, while the data flow on a local area network primarily follows a single basic route.

Type of Information Carried

The last major difference between local and wide area networks is the type of information carried by each network. Many wide area networks support the simultaneous transmission of voice, data, and video information. In comparison, most local area networks are currently limited to carrying data. In addition, although all wide area networks can be expanded to transport voice, data, and video, many local area networks are restricted by design to the transportation of data. An exception to the preceding is asynchronous transfer mode (ATM), which can provide both a local and wide area network transmission capability. Asynchronous transfer mode was designed to support voice, data, and video from end-to-end, enabling different types of data to be transported from one LAN to another via an ATM WAN. Unfortunately, the cost of ATM network adapters considerably exceeded the cost of other types of LAN equipment used to include different types of Ethernet adapters. As the base of Ethernet expanded, the cost associated with establishing an Ethernet infrastructure decreased, widening the price gap between ATM and Ethernet, making it difficult for asynchronous transfer mode to establish a viable market for local area networking. Today the vast majority of ATM equipment is used by communications carriers in the wide area network. Table 1.1 summarizes the similarities and differences between local and wide area networks.

Utilization Benefits

In its simplest form, a local area network is a cable that provides an electronic highway for the transportation of information to and from different devices connected to the network. Because a LAN provides the capability to route data between devices connected to a common network within a relatively limited distance, numerous benefits can accrue to users of the network. These can include the ability to share the use of peripheral devices, thus obtaining common access to data files and programs, the ability to communicate with other people on the LAN by electronic mail, and the ability to access the larger processing capability of mainframes through common gateways that link a local area network to larger computer systems. Here, the gateway can be directly cabled to the mainframe if it resides at the same location, or it may be connected remotely via a corporate wide area network.

TABLE 1.1   Comparing LANs and WANs

Characteristic	Local Area Network	Wide Area Network
Geographic area of coverage	Localized to a building, group of buildings, or campus	Can span an area ranging in size from a city to the globe
Data transmission rate	Typically 4 Mbps to 16 Mbps, with high-speed Ethernet and fiber optic-based networks operating at 100 Mbps and 1 and 10 Gbps	Normally operate at or below T1 and E1 transmission rates of 1.544 Mbps and 2.048 Mbps
Error rate	1 in 10^7 to 1 in 10^8	1 in 10^6 to 1 in 10^7
Ownership	Usually with the implementor	Communications carrier retains ownership of line facilities
Data routing	Normally follows fixed route	Switching capability of network allows dynamic alteration of data flow
Topology	Usually limited to bus, ring, tree, or star	Virtually unlimited design capability
Type of information carried	Primarily data	Voice, data, and video commonly integrated

Peripheral sharing allows network users to access color laser printers, CD-ROM jukebox systems, and other devices that may be needed only a small portion of the time a workstation is in operation. Thus, users of a LAN can obtain access to resources that would probably be too expensive to justify for each individual workstation user.

The ability to access data files and programs from multiple workstations can substantially reduce the cost of software. In addition, shared access to database information allows network users to obtain access to updated files on a real-time basis.

One popular type of application program used on LANs enables users to transfer messages electronically. Commonly referred to as *electronic mail* or *e-mail*, this type of application program can be used to supplement and, in many cases, eliminate the need for paper memoranda.

For organizations with a mainframe, a local area network gateway can provide a common method of access. Without the use of a LAN gateway, each personal computer requiring access to a mainframe would require a separate method of access. This might increase both the complexity and the cost of providing access.

Perhaps the most popular evolving use of LANs is to provide a group of computer users with economical access to the Internet. Instead of having a large number of employees obtain individual modem dial-up or ISDN dial access accounts with an Internet service provider (ISP), it is often more economical to connect an organizational LAN to the Internet via a single connection to an ISP. In addition, the connection to the Internet will usually provide a higher transmission capability than obtainable on an individual user basis. Later in this book we will turn our attention to methods that can be used to connect organizational LANs to the Internet, as well as the use of different products to protect organizational computer facilities from Internet users that have no business accessing those facilities.

Technological Characteristics

Although a local area network is a limited distance transmission system, the variety of options available for constructing such networks is anything but limited. Many of the options available for the construction of local area networks are based on the technological characteristics that govern their operation. These characteristics include different topologies, signaling methods, transmission media, access methods used to transmit data on the network, and the hardware and software required to make the network operate.

Topology

The *topology* of a local area network is the structure or geometric layout of the cable used to connect stations on the network. Unlike conventional data communications networks, which can be configured in a variety of ways with the addition of hardware and software, most local area networks are designed to operate based on the interconnection of stations that follow a specific topology. The most common topologies used in LANs include the loop, bus, ring, star, and tree, as illustrated in Figure 1.4.

Loop   As previously mentioned in this chapter, IBM introduced a series of transaction-processing terminals in 1974 that communicated through the use of a common controller on a cable formed into a loop. This type of topology is illustrated at the top of Figure 1.4.

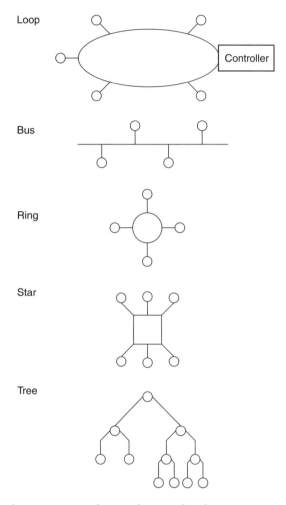

Figure 1.4 Local area network topology. The five most common geometric layouts of LAN cabling form a loop, bus, ring, star, or tree structure.

Because the controller employed a poll-and-select access method, terminal devices connected to the loop required a minimum of intelligence. Although this reduced the cost of terminals connected to the loop, the controller lacked the intelligence to distribute the data flow evenly among terminals. A lengthy exchange between two terminal devices or between the controller and a terminal would thus tend to bog down this type of network structure. A second problem associated with this network structure was the centralized placement of network control in the controller. If the controller failed, the entire network would become inoperative. Due to these problems, the use of loop systems is restricted to several niche areas, and they are essentially considered a derivative of a local area network.

Bus   In a bus topology structure, a cable is usually laid out as one long branch, onto which other branches are used to connect each station on the network to the main data highway. Although this type of structure permits any station on the network to talk to any other station, rules are required for recovering from such situations as when two stations attempt to communicate at the same time. Later in this chapter, we will examine the relationships among the network topology, the method employed to access the network, and the transmission medium employed in building the network.

Ring   In a ring topology, a single cable that forms the main data highway is shaped into a ring. As with the bus topology, branches are used to connect stations to one another via the ring. A ring topology can thus be considered to be a looped bus. Typically, the access method employed in a ring topology requires data to circulate around the ring, with a special set of rules governing when each station connected to the network can transmit data.

Star   The fourth major local area network topology is the star structure, illustrated in the lower portion of Figure 1.4. In a star network, each station on the network is connected to a network controller. Then, access from any one station on the network to any other station can be accomplished through the network controller. Here, the network controller functions like a telephone switchboard, because access from one station to another station on the network can occur only through the central device. In fact, you can consider a telephone switchboard or PBX as representing a star-structured LAN whose trunks provide connections to the wide area network telephone infrastructure.

Tree   A tree network structure represents a complex bus. In this topology, the common point of communications at the top of the structure is known as the *headend*. From the headend, feeder cables radiate outward to nodes, which in turn provide workstations with access to the network. There may also be a feeder cable route to additional nodes, from which workstations gain access to the network. One common example of a tree structure topology is the cable TV network many readers use on a daily basis. With the upgrade of many cable TV systems to two-way amplifiers and the support of digital transmission, the local cable TV infrastructure can be considered to represent an evolving type of tree-structured local area network.

Mixed Topologies   Some networks are a mixture of topologies. For example, as previously discussed, a tree structure can be viewed as a series of inter-connected buses. Another example of the mixture of topologies is a type of Ethernet known as 10BASE-T, which is described in detail in Chapter 3. That network can actually be considered a *star-bus* topology, because up to 16 or 24 devices known as *stations* are first connected to a common device known as a *hub*, which in turn can be connected to other hubs to expand the network.

Comparison of Topologies

Although there are close relationships among the topology of the network, its transmission media, and the method used to access the network, we can examine topology as a separate entity and make several generalized observations. First, in a star network, the failure of the network controller will render the entire network inoperative. This is because all data flow on the network must pass through the network controller. On the positive side, the star topology normally consists of telephone wires routed to a LAN switch. A local area network that can use in-place twisted-pair telephone wires in this way is simple to implement and usually very economical.

In a ring network, the failure of any node connected to the ring normally inhibits data flow around the ring. Due to the fact that data travels in a circular path on a ring network, any cable break has the same effect as the failure of the network controller in a star-structured network. Because each network station is connected to the next network station, it is usually easy to install the cable for a ring network. In comparison, a star network may require cabling each section to the network controller if existing telephone wires are not available, and this can result in the installation of very long cable runs.

In a bus-structured network, data is normally transmitted from a single station to all other stations located on the network, with a destination address included within each transmitted data block. As part of the access protocol, only the station with the destination address in the transmitted data block will respond to the data. This transmission concept means that a break in the bus affects only network stations on one side of the break that wish to communicate with stations on the other side of the break. Thus, unless a network station functioning as the primary network storage device becomes inoperative, a failure in a bus-structured network is usually less serious than a failure in a ring network. However, some local area networks, such as Token-Ring and FDDI, were designed to overcome the effect of certain types of cable failures. Token-Ring networks include a backup path which, when manually placed into operation, may be able to overcome the effect of a cable failure between hubs (referred to as *multistation access units* or *MAUs*). In an FDDI network, a second ring can be activated automatically as part of a self-healing process to overcome the effect of a cable break.

A tree-structured network is similar to a star-structured network in that all signals flow through a common point. In the tree-structured network, the common signal point is the headend. Failure of the headend renders the network inoperative. This network structure requires the transmission of information over relatively long distances. For example, communications between two stations located at opposite ends of the network would require a signal to propagate twice the length of the longest network segment. Due to the propagation delay associated with the transmission of any signal, the use of a tree structure may result in a response time delay for transmissions between the nodes that are most distant from the headend.

Although the first type of Ethernet network was based on a bus-structured topology, other types of Ethernet networks incorporate the use of different topologies. Today you can select bus-based, star-bus, or tree-structured Ethernet networks. Thus, you can select a particular type of Ethernet network to meet a particular topology requirement.

Signaling Methods

The *signaling method* used by a local area network refers to both the way data is encoded for transmission and the frequency spectrum of the media. To a large degree, the signaling method is related to the use of the frequency spectrum of the media.

Broadband versus Baseband

Two signaling methods used by LANs are broadband and baseband. In *broadband signaling*, the bandwidth of the transmission medium is subdivided by frequency to form two or more subchannels, with each subchannel permitting data transfer to occur independently of data transfer on another subchannel. In *baseband signaling*, only one signal is transmitted on the medium at any point in time.

Broadband is more complex than baseband, because it requires information to be transmitted via the modulation of a carrier signal, thus requiring the use of special types of modems, as discussed later in this chapter.

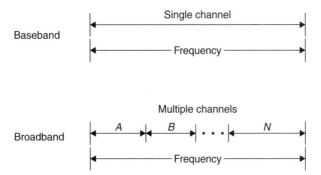

Figure 1.5 Baseband versus broadband signaling. In baseband signaling the entire frequency bandwidth is used for one channel. In comparison, in broadband signaling the channel is subdivided by frequency into many subchannels.

Figure 1.5 illustrates the difference between baseband and broadband signaling with respect to channel capacity. It should be noted that although a twisted-pair wire system can be used to transmit both voice and data, the data transmission is baseband, because only one channel is normally used for data. In comparison, a broadband system on coaxial cable can be designed to carry voice and several subchannels of data, as well as fax and video transmission.

Broadband Signaling   A broadband local area network uses analog technology, in which high-frequency (HF) modems operating at or above 4 kHz place carrier signals onto the transmission medium. The carrier signals are then modified—a process known as *modulation*, which impresses information onto the carrier. Other modems connected to a broadband LAN reconvert the analog signal block into its original digital format—a process known as *demodulation*.

Figure 1.6 illustrates the three primary methods of data encoding used by broadband analog systems: amplitude, frequency, and phase modulation. The most common modulation method used on broadband LANs is *frequency shift keying (FSK)*, in which two different frequencies are used, one to represent a binary 1 and another frequency to represent a binary 0.

Another popular modulation method uses a combination of amplitude and phase shift changes to represent pairs of bits. Referred to as *amplitude modulation phase shift keying (AM PSK)*, this method of analog signaling is also known as *duobinary signaling* because each analog signal represents a pair of digital bits.

Because it is not economically feasible to design amplifiers that boost signal strength to operate in both directions, broadband LANs are unidirectional.

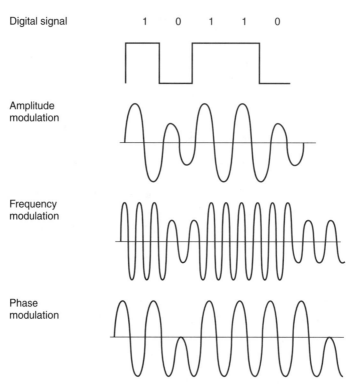

Figure 1.6 Modulation methods. Baseband signaling uses amplitude, frequency, or phase modulation, or a combination of modulation techniques to represent digital information.

To provide a bidirectional information transfer capability, a broadband LAN uses one channel for inbound traffic and another channel for outbound traffic. These channels can be defined by differing frequencies or obtained by the use of a dual cable.

Baseband Signaling In comparison to broadband local area networks, which use analog signaling, baseband LANs use digital signaling to convey information.

To understand the digital signaling methods used by most baseband LANs, let us first review the method of digital signaling used by computers and terminal devices. In that signaling method, a positive voltage is used to represent a binary 1, while the absence of voltage (0 volts) is used to represent a binary 0. If two successive 1 bits or 0 bits occur, two successive bit positions then have a similar positive voltage level or a similar zero voltage level.

Because the signal goes from 0 to some positive voltage and does not return to 0 between successive binary 1s, it is referred to as a *unipolar nonreturn to zero signal (NRZ)*. This signaling technique is illustrated at the top of Figure 1.7.

Although unipolar NRZ signaling is easy to implement, its use for transmission has several disadvantages. One of the major disadvantages associated with this signaling method involves determining where one bit ends and another begins. For example, if you examine the top portion of Figure 1.7 you will note that the bit sequences "00" and "111" remain at distinct voltage levels. Thus, the ability to recognize that a sequence of two or more pulses of the same value occurred requires synchronization between a transmitter and receiver by the use of clocking circuitry, which can be relatively expensive.

To overcome the need for clocking, baseband LANs use *Manchester* or *Differential Manchester encoding.* In Manchester encoding, a timing transition always occurs in the middle of each bit, while an equal amount of positive and negative voltage is used to represent each bit. This coding technique provides a good timing signal for clock recovery from received data, due to its timing transitions. In addition, because the Manchester code always maintains an equal amount of positive and negative voltage, it prevents direct current (DC) voltage buildup, enabling repeaters to be spaced farther apart from one another.

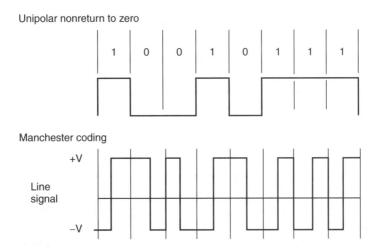

Figure 1.7 Unipolar nonreturn to zero signaling and Manchester coding. In Manchester coding, a timing transition occurs in the middle of each bit and the line code maintains an equal amount of positive and negative voltage.

The lower portion of Figure 1.7 illustrates an example of Manchester coding. Note that a low to high voltage transition represents a binary 1, while a high to low voltage transition represents a binary 0. A second type of Manchester coding is referred to as Differential Manchester encoding. Under Differential Manchester encoding, the voltage transition is used only to provide clocking. The encoding of a binary 0 or 1 is represented by the presence or absence of a transition at the beginning of each bit period. Refer to Chapter 4 for specific information concerning Manchester encoding on different types of Ethernet networks.

Along with providing users with a choice of topologies, Ethernet also provides a choice of signaling methods. Although most types of Ethernet networks use baseband signaling, a broadband Ethernet is also available. In fact, you can connect baseband- and broadband-based Ethernet networks to satisfy different organizational requirements. Refer to Chapter 3 for specific information concerning the signaling methods used by different Ethernet networks and the hardware components used to construct and interconnect such networks.

Transmission Medium

The transmission medium used in a local area network can range in scope from twisted-pair wire, such as is used in conventional telephone lines, to coaxial cable, fiber-optic cable, and electromagnetic waves such as those used by FM radio and infrared. Each transmission medium has a number of advantages and disadvantages. The primary differences between media are their cost and ease of installation; the bandwidth of the cable, which may or may not permit several transmission sessions to occur simultaneously; the maximum speed of communications permitted; and the geographic scope of the network that the medium supports.

Twisted-Pair Wire

In addition to being the most inexpensive medium available for LAN installations, twisted-pair wire is very easy to install. Since this wiring uses the same RJ11 and RJ45 modular connectors as a telephone system, once a wire is cut and a connector fastened, the attachment of the connector to network devices is extremely simple. Normally, a screwdriver and perhaps a pocket knife are the only tools required for the installation of twisted-pair wire. Anyone who has hooked up a pair of speakers to a stereo set has the ability to install this transmission medium.

Although inexpensive and easy to install, unshielded twisted-pair (UTP) wire is very susceptible to noise generated by fluorescent light ballasts and electrical machinery. In addition, a length of twisted-pair wire acts as an antenna; however, the twists serve as a mechanism to partially counteract this antenna effect. Unfortunately, due to the law of physics, the longer the wire length, the greater the noise it gathers. At a certain length, the received noise will obliterate the signal, which attenuates or decreases in strength as it propagates along the length of the wire. This noise can affect the error rate of data transmitted on the network, although lead-shielded twisted-pair (STP) cable can be employed to provide the cable with a high degree of immunity to the line noise and enable extended transmission distances. In Chapter 3 we will examine a building cabling standard and the various categories of twisted-pair that can support different transmission rates which, in turn, enable different types of Ethernet networks to be supported.

Because the bandwidth of twisted-pair cable is considerably less than coaxial or fiber-optic cable, normally only one signal is transmitted on this cable at a time. As previously explained, this signaling technique is known as baseband signaling and should be compared with the broadband signaling capability of coaxial and fiber-optic cable.

Although a twisted-pair wire system can be used to transmit both voice and data, the data transmission is baseband because only one channel is normally used for data. In comparison, a broadband system on coaxial or fiber-optic cable can be designed to carry voice and several subchannels of data, as well as fax and video transmission. Other constraints of unshielded twisted-pair wire are the rate at which data can flow on the network and the distance it can flow. Although data rates up to 1 gigabit per second (Gbps) can be achieved, normally local area networks employing UTP wiring operate at a lower data rate. In addition, UTP systems normally cover a limited distance, measured in terms of several hundred to a few thousand feet, while coaxial and fiber-optic cable—based systems may be limited in terms of miles. Extending transmission distances over twisted-pair wire requires the periodic insertion of repeaters into the cable. A repeater receives a digital signal and then regenerates it; hence, it is also known as a *data regenerator*.

Coaxial Cable

At the center of a coaxial cable is a copper wire, which is covered by an insulator known as a *dielectric*. An overlapping woven copper mesh surrounds the dielectric, and the mesh, in turn, is covered by a protective jacket consisting of polyethylene or aluminum. Figure 1.8 illustrates the

Protective polyethylene jacket

Polyethylene dielectric

Steel strength member

Overlapped-seam copper outer conductor

Copper inner conductor

Figure 1.8   Coaxial cable.

composition of a typical coaxial cable; however, it should be noted that over 100 types of coaxial cable are currently marketed. The key differences between such cables involve the number of conductors contained in the cable, the dielectric employed, and the type of protective jacket and material used to provide strength to the cable so it can be pulled through conduits without breaking.

Two basic types of coaxial cable are used in local area networks. The type of cable used is based on the transmission technique employed: baseband or broadband signaling. Both cable types are much more expensive than twisted-pair wire; however, the greater frequency bandwidth of coaxial cable permits higher data rates for longer distances than you can obtain over twisted-pair wire.

Normally, 50-ohm coaxial cable is used in baseband networks, while 75-ohm cable is used in broadband networks. The latter coaxial is identical to that used in cable television (CATV) applications, including the coaxial cable used in a home. Data rates on baseband networks using coaxial cable range from 50 to 100 Mbps. With broadband transmissions, data rates up to and including 400 Mbps are obtainable.

A coaxial cable with a polyethylene jacket is normally used for baseband signaling. Data is transmitted from stations on the network to the baseband cable in a digital format, and the connection from each station to the cable is accomplished by the use of a simple coaxial T-connector. Because data on a baseband network travels in a digital form, those signals can be easily regenerated by the use of a device known as a *line driver* or *data regenerator*. The line driver or data regenerator is a low-cost device that is constructed to look for a pulse rise, and upon detecting the occurrence of the rise, it will disregard the entire pulse and regenerate an entirely new pulse. Thus, you can install low-cost line drivers into a baseband coaxial network to extend the distance over which transmission can occur on the cable. Typically, a coaxial cable baseband system can cover an area of several miles, and may contain hundreds to thousands of stations on the network.

Obtaining independent subchannels defined by separate frequencies on coaxial cable broadband transmission requires the translation of the digital signals from workstations into appropriate frequencies. This translation process is accomplished by the use of radio-frequency (RF) modems, which modulate the digital data into analog signals and then convert or demodulate received analog signals into digital signals. Because signals are transmitted at one frequency and received at a different frequency, a headend or frequency translator is also required for broadband transmission on coaxial cable. This device is also known as a *remodulator*, as it simply converts the signals from one subchannel to another subchannel.

Fiber-Optic Cable

Fiber-optic cable is a transmission medium for light energy, and as such, provides a very high bandwidth, permitting data rates ranging up to billions of bits per second. The fiber-optic cable has a thin core of glass or plastic, which is surrounded by a protective shield. Several of these shielded fibers are bundled in a jacket, with a central member of aluminum or steel employed for tensile strength.

Digital data represented by electrical energy must be converted into light energy for transmission on a fiber-optic cable. This is normally accomplished by a low-power laser, or through the use of a light-emitting diode and appropriate circuitry. At the receiver, light energy must be reconverted into electrical energy. Normally, a device known as a *photo detector*, as well as appropriate circuitry to regenerate the digital pulses and an amplifier, are used to convert the received light energy into its original digital format.

Figure 1.9 provides an illustration of the cross section of a single-strand fiber cable. The cladding that surrounds the core of the fiber can be considered to represent a cylindrical mirror whose job is to ensure light stays in the core as it flows along the fiber. The kevlar fibers add strength to the cable, while the

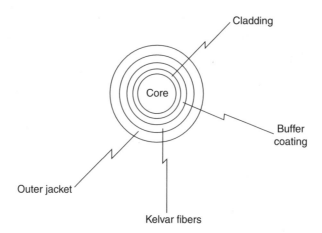

Figure 1.9 Horizontal cross section of a single-strand fiber cable.

outer jacket, which is commonly colored orange, represents a polymer-based shield that protects the cable from the elements.

There are two key factors that govern the manner by which light flows through a fiber-optic cable. Those factors are the diameter of the core and the light source. The first type of fiber-optic cable developed had a relatively large diameter that ranged from 50 to 140 microns, where a micron is a millionth of a meter. The original light source used to transmit information was a light-emitting diode (LED). The coupling of an LED to a large-diameter optical fiber results in photons flowing along multiple paths through the optical fiber, resulting in the transmission referred to as multimode, which is also the same name used to reference the type of optical fiber.

There are two types of multimode fiber, referred to as step-index and graded-index. A step-index fiber has a core with a uniform refractive index, resulting in the different components of a light signal in the form of modes or rays flowing in a non-uniform manner through the optical cable. The top portion of Figure 1.10 illustrates the flow of light through a step-index, multimode fiber.

In a graded-index multimode fiber, the refractive index is varied from the center to the edge of the core to minimize modal dispersion. The middle portion of Figure 1.10 illustrates the flow of light through a graded-index, multimode fiber. This type of fiber minimizes model dispersion and supports higher data rates than a step-index multimode optical fiber.

A third type of optical fiber has a relatively small core diameter, typically between 7 and 12 microns (10^{-6} meters). This type of optical fiber permits only one path for the flow of light due to the small diameter of the core. As

Step–index, multimode

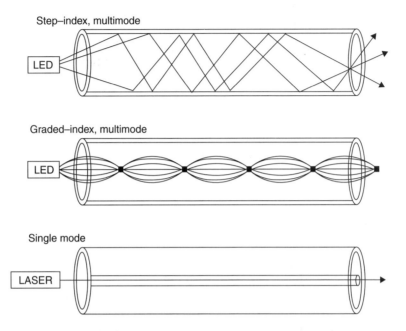

Graded–index, multimode

Single mode

Figure 1.10   Light flow in multimode and single-mode optical fiber.

a result of the lack of modal dispersion, single mode supports a much higher data rate than multimode fiber. Because of the small diameter of single-mode fiber, lasers are used as the light source instead of LEDs.

Both the core thickness and the cladding of an optical fiber are measured in microns. The three major core thicknesses used in optical fiber are 50, 62 and 100 microns. The associated claddings for those core diameters are 125, 125 and 140 microns, respectively. Table 1.2 summarizes the relationships between core and cladding diameters for single-mode and multimode fiber.

In trade literature you will note what appears as a ratio in the form of x/y when the metrics associated with an optical fiber are referenced. In actuality, this is not a ratio but instead references the core and the cladding thickness of an optical fiber in microns. Thus, 50/125 would, for example, reference an optical fiber whose core diameter is 50 microns and whose cladding diameter is 125 microns.

In addition to their high bandwidth, fiber-optic cables offer users several additional advantages over conventional transmission media. Because data travels in the form of light, it is immune to electrical interference and to the building codes that often require expensive conduits for conventional cables.

TABLE 1.2 Common Core and Cladding Diameters of Optical Fiber in Microns

Mode	Glass Core Diameter	Glass Cladding
Single-mode	2–8	20
Multimode	50	125
	62	125
	100	140

Similarly, fiber-optic cable can be installed through areas where the flow of electricity could be dangerous.

Because most fibers provide only a single, unidirectional transmission path, a minimum of two cables is normally required to connect all transmitters to all receivers on a network built using fiber-optic cable. Due to the higher cost of fiber-optic cable, the dual cable requirement of fiber cables can make them relatively expensive in comparison with other types of cable. In addition, until recently it was very difficult to splice fiber-optic cable, and sophisticated equipment and skilled installers were required to implement a fiber-optic-based network. Similarly, once this type of network was installed, until recently it was difficult to modify the network. Recent advances in fiber transmission through the use of wavelength division multiplexing enables two or more transmission paths separated by the frequency of light to be carried on a common optical cable. Although wavelength division multiplexing is being used in the long-distance fiber backbones of communications carriers to increase the transmission capacity of their infrastructure, the cost of electro-optical transmitter receivers to support this technology usually precludes its use with local area networks.

Currently, the cost of the cable and the degree of difficulty of installation and modification make the utilization of fiber-optic-based local area networks impractical for many commercial applications. Today, the primary use of fiber-optic cable is to extend the distance between stations on a network or to connect two distant networks to one another. The device used to connect a length of fiber-optic cable into the LAN or between LANs is a *fiber-optic repeater*. The repeater converts the electrical energy of signals flowing on the LAN into light energy for transmission on the fiber-optic cable. At the end of the fiber-optic cable, a second repeater converts light energy back into electrical energy. A key exception to the preceding involves Gigabit Ethernet, whose data rate normally requires the use of optical fiber as a transport medium. Although Gigabit Ethernet can operate on copper conductors, its transmission distance is limited in comparison to when optical fiber is used. With the declining cost of the fiber-optic cable and fiber-optic components, and the continued introduction of improvements that simplify the installation and modification of networks using this type of cable, the next few years may bring a profound movement toward the utilization of fiber optics throughout local area networks.

Ethernet can be categorized as a network for everyone, because of its support of multiple topologies, signaling methods, and transmission media. In addition to twisted-pair and coaxial cable-based Ethernet networks, you can also extend the transmission distance of such networks by the use of fiber-optic cable. Thus, the old adage from a presidential campaign, "a choice not an echo," is highly relevant to Ethernet networks.

Access Method

If the topology of a local area network can be compared with a data highway, then the access method might be viewed as the set of rules that enable data from one workstation to successfully reach its destination via the data highway. Without such rules, it is quite possible for two messages sent by two different workstations to collide, with the result that neither message reaches its destination. The three access methods primarily employed in local area networks are carrier-sense multiple access/collision detection (CSMA/CD), carrier-sense multiple access/collision avoidance (CSMA/CA), and token passing. Each of these access methods is uniquely structured to address the previously mentioned collision and data-destination problems. A fourth access method, referred to as *demand priority*, is applicable to a high-speed Ethernet network referred to as 100VG-AnyLAN. Through the use of a demand-priority access method you can support either existing Ethernet CSMA/CD or token passing networks at 100 Mbps.

Before discussing how access methods work, let us first examine the two basic types of devices that can be attached to a local area network to gain an appreciation for the work that the access method must accomplish.

Listeners and Talkers

We can categorize each device by its operating mode as being a *listener* or a *talker*. Some devices, like printers, only receive data, and thus operate only as listeners. Other devices, such as personal computers, can either transmit or receive data and are capable of operating in both modes. In a baseband signaling environment where only one channel exists, or on an individual channel on a broadband system, if several talkers wish to communicate at the same time, a collision will occur. Therefore, a scheme must be employed to define when each device can talk and, in the event of a collision, what must be done to keep it from happening again.

For data to reach its destination correctly, each listener must have a unique address, and its network equipment must be designed to respond to a message on the net only when it recognizes its address. The primary goals in the design of an access method are to minimize the potential for data collision, to provide a mechanism for corrective action when data does collide, and to ensure that an addressing scheme is employed to enable messages to reach their destinations.

Carrier-Sense Multiple Access with Collision Detection (CSMA/CD)

CSMA/CD can be categorized as a *listen-then-send* access method. CSMA/CD is one of the earliest developed access techniques and is the technique used in Ethernet. Ethernet represents a local area network developed by Xerox Corporation; its technology is now licensed to many companies, and was standardized by the Institute of Electrical and Electronics Engineers (IEEE) under its 802.3 standard.

Under the CSMA/CD concept, when a station has data to send, it first listens to determine whether any other station on the network is talking. The fact that the channel is idle is determined in one of two ways, based on whether the network is broadband or baseband.

In a broadband network, the fact that a channel is idle is determined by *carrier sensing*, or noting the absence of a carrier tone on the cable.

Ethernet, like other baseband systems, uses one channel for data transmission and does not employ a carrier. Instead, Ethernet encodes data using a Manchester code, in which a timing transition always occurs in the middle of each bit, as previously illustrated in Figure 1.7. Although Ethernet does not transmit data via a carrier, the continuous transitions of the Manchester code can be considered as equivalent to a carrier signal. Carrier sensing on a baseband network is thus performed by monitoring the line for activity. Manchester coding is used by Ethernet at data rates up to 10 Mbps. At operating rates above 10 Mbps, different encoding techniques are used, which provide a higher level of efficiency than Manchester's 50-percent level of efficiency.

In a CSMA/CD network, if the channel is busy, the station will wait until it becomes idle before transmitting data. Because it is possible for two stations to listen at the same time and discover an idle channel, it is also possible that the two stations could then transmit at the same time. When this situation arises, a collision will occur. Upon sensing that a collision has occurred, a delay scheme will be employed to prevent a repetition of the collision. Typically, each station will use either a randomly generated or a predefined time-out period before attempting to retransmit the message that collided. Because this access method requires hardware capable of detecting the occurrence of a collision, additional circuitry required to perform collision detection adds to the cost of such hardware.

Figure 1.11 illustrates a CSMA/CD bus-based local area network. Each workstation is attached to the transmission medium, such as coaxial cable, by a device known as a *bus interface unit (BIU)*. To obtain an overview of the operation of a CSMA/CD network, assume that station A is currently using the channel and stations C and D wish to transmit. The BIUs connecting stations C and D to the network listen to the channel and note that it is busy. Once station A completes its transmission, stations C and D attempt to gain access to the channel. Because station A's signal takes longer to propagate down the cable to station D than to station C, C's BIU notices that the channel is free slightly before station D's BIU. However, as station C gets ready to transmit, station D now assumes that the channel is free. Within an infinitesimal period of time, C starts transmission, followed by D, resulting in a collision. Here, the collision is a function of the propagation delay of the signal and the distance between two competing stations. CSMA/CD networks therefore work better as the main cable length decreases.

The CSMA/CD access technique is best suited for networks with intermittent transmission, because an increase in traffic volume causes a corresponding increase in the probability of the cable being occupied when a station wishes

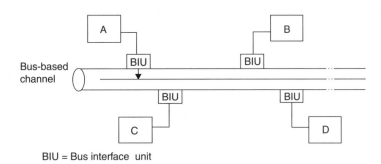

BIU = Bus interface unit

Figure 1.11 CSMA/CD network operation. In a CSMA/CD network, as the distance between workstations increases, the resulting increase in propagation delay time increases the probability of collisions.

to talk. In addition, as traffic volume builds under CSMA/CD, throughput may decline, because there will be longer waits to gain access to the network, as well as additional time-outs required to resolve collisions that occur. In spite of the lower level of throughput, as we will note later in this book CSMA/CA is used as the access method supported by many types of wireless LANs including several types of wireless Ethernet LANs.

Carrier-Sense Multiple Access with Collision Avoidance (CSMA/CA)

CSMA/CA represents a modified version of the CSMA/CD access technique. Under the CSMA/CA access technique, each of the hardware devices attached to the talkers on the network estimates when a collision is likely to occur and avoids transmission during those times. Because this technique eliminates the requirement for collision-detection hardware, the cost of hardware to implement this access technique is usually less than CSMA/CD hardware. Unfortunately, time delays associated with collision avoidance usually result in a lower level of throughput than that obtainable with CSMA/CD-based networks, and this limitation has made CSMA/CA-based networks less popular.

Token Passing

In a *token-passing* access method, each time the network is turned on, a token is generated. The token, consisting of a unique bit pattern, travels the length of the network, either around a ring or along the length of a bus. When a station on the network has data to transmit, it must first seize a free token. On a Token-Ring network, the token is then transformed to indicate that it is in use. Information is added to produce a frame, which represents data being transmitted from one station to another. During the time the token is in use, other stations on the network remain idle, eliminating the possibility of collisions. Once the transmission is completed, the token is converted back into its original form by the station that transmitted the frame, and becomes available for use by the next station on the network.

Figure 1.12 illustrates the general operation of a token-passing Token-Ring network using a ring topology. Because a station on the network can only transmit when it has a free token, token passing eliminates the requirement for collision detection hardware. Due to the dependence of the network on the token, the loss of a station can bring the entire network down. To avoid this, the design characteristics of Token-Ring networks include circuitry that automatically removes a failed or failing station from the network, as well as other self-healing features. This additional capability is costly: a Token-Ring

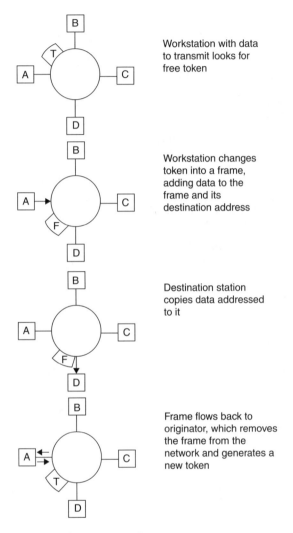

Workstation with data
to transmit looks for
free token

Workstation changes
token into a frame,
adding data to the
frame and its
destination address

Destination station
copies data addressed
to it

Frame flows back to
originator, which removes
the frame from the
network and generates a
new token

Figure 1.12   Token-Ring operation.

adapter card is typically priced at two to three times the cost of an Ethernet adapter card.

Due to the variety of transmission media, network structures, and access methods, there is no one best network for all users. Table 1.3 provides a generalized comparison of the advantages and disadvantages of the technical characteristics of local area networks, using the transmission medium as a frame of reference.

TABLE 1.3   Technical Characteristics of LANs

Characteristic	Transmission Medium			
	Twisted-pair wire	Baseband coaxial cable	Baseband coaxial cable	Fiber-optic cable
Topology	Bus, star, or ring	Bus or ring	Bus or ring	Bus, star, or ring
Channels	Single channel	Single channel	Multichannel	Single, multichannel
Data rate	Normally 4 to 16 Mbps; up to 1000 Mbps obtainable	Normally 2 to 10 Mbps; up to 100 Mbps obtainable	Up to 400 Mbps	Up to 40 Gbps
Maximum nodes on net	Usually <255	Usually <1024	Several thousand	Several thousand
Geographical coverage	Thousands of feet	Miles	Tens of miles	Tens of miles
Major advantages	Low cost; may be able to use existing wiring	Low cost; simple to install	Supports voice, data, video applications simultaneously	Supports voice, data, video applications simultaneously
Major disadvantages	Limited bandwidth; requires conduits; low immunity to noise	Low immunity to noise	High cost; difficult to install; requires RF modems and headend	Cable cost; difficult to splice

1.3 Why Ethernet

After reviewing the basic characteristics of various local area networks, you will note that they present a considerable range of technological characteristics. You can select a network based on its topology, access method, signaling method, and/or support of a particular type of transmission medium. Although there is no one best network for all users, Ethernet represents a diverse mixture of technological characteristics. As such, it provides many more potential networking solutions to user communications requirements than other types of local area networks.

In addition to supporting a broad range of technological characteristics, Ethernet is a declining-cost network. Due to economies of manufacture, as well as the recent support of twisted-pair wiring, Ethernet networks can be established for a fraction of the cost of other types of local area networks. In fact, by late 2002, adapter cards supporting 10 Mbps Ethernet that were designed for use in IBM PCs and compatible personal computers could be obtained for under $20, while 10/100 Mbps adapter cards could be obtained for under $50. In addition, several notebook and laptop computer vendors, as well as vendors of many business desktop systems, were incorporating Ethernet chip sets into their computers, enabling computer users who want to transfer files to other computers and printers connected to the network to simply plug their computer into a telephone jack upon returning to the office.

Although the previously mentioned reasons are significant, the scalability of Ethernet and the product development effort of industry provide two additional reasons to use Ethernet. Concerning scalability, you can obtain interoperable Ethernet equipment that enables you to operate a network originally at 10 Mbps and have the option of using a variety of vendor products to upgrade your network to 100 Mbps or even 1 or 10 Gbps. Concerning product development, over the past decade a large number of products reached the market that enable Ethernet users to boost the performance and management of their networks. Perhaps the most versatile product is actually a series of Ethernet switches that enable multiple cross-connections between workstations and servers to occur simultaneously, as well as enable the transmission on multiple ports to be aggregated, a technique referred to as a *fat pipe*. Over the past five years the capability of LAN switches has been significantly enhanced. Today many LAN switch manufacturers support switching not only directly at the LAN frame layer but, in addition, at higher layers in the International Standards Organization (ISO) Open System Interconnection (OSI) Reference Model, which is described in Chapter 2.

Although your organization may not currently require the ability to transmit data at 100 Mbps or 1 or 10 Gbps nor require the ability to aggregate multiple paths at those data rates, the capability is there if you should need it in the future. For other organizations such as Internet Service Providers that use a local area network as a gateway for subscribers to access the Internet, the ability to upgrade to 1 or 10 Gbps can be a significant benefit. Due to this capability Ethernet is truly a "people's network," able to satisfy the networking requirements of the small business, large corporation, university, and government.

chapter two

Networking Standards

Standards can be viewed as the "glue" that binds hardware and software from different vendors so they can operate together. The importance of standards and the work of standards organizations have proved essential for the growth of both local and worldwide communications. In the United States and many other countries, national standards organizations have defined physical and operational characteristics that enable vendors to manufacture equipment compatible with line facilities provided by communications carriers, as well as equipment produced by other vendors. At the international level, standards organizations have promulgated several series of communications-related recommendations. These recommendations, while not mandatory, have become highly influential on a worldwide basis for the development of equipment and facilities, and have been adopted by hundreds of public companies and communications carriers.

In addition to national and international standards, a series of de facto standards has evolved through the licensing of technology among companies. These de facto standards have facilitated, for example, the development of communications software for use on personal computers. Today, communications software can control modems manufactured by hundreds of vendors, because most modems are now constructed to respond to a core set of uniform control codes.

2.1 Standards Organizations

In this chapter, we will first focus our attention on two national and two international standards organizations. The national standards organizations we will briefly discuss in this section are the American National Standards Institute (ANSI) and the Institute of Electrical and Electronics Engineers (IEEE). The work of both organizations has been a guiding force in the rapid expansion in the use of local area networks due to a series of standards they have developed. Due to the importance of the work of the IEEE in developing LAN standards, we will examine those standards as a separate entity in the next section in this chapter. In the international arena, we will discuss the role of the International Telecommunications Union (ITU), formerly known as the Consultative Committee for International Telephone and Telegraph (CCITT), and the International Standards Organization (ISO), both of which have developed numerous standards to facilitate the operation of local and wide area networks.

Because of the importance of the ISO's Open Systems Interconnection (OSI) Reference Model and the IEEE's 802 Committee lower layer standards, we will examine each as a separate entity in this chapter. Because a series of Internet standards define the manner by which the TCP/IP protocol suite can transport data between LANs and WANs, we will also discuss what are referred to as Requests For Comments (RFCs). Because we must understand the OSI Reference Model before examining the effect of the efforts of the IEEE and ANSI upon the lower layers of that model and the role of RFCs, we will look at the OSI Reference Model before examining the role of other standards.

National Standards Organizations

The two national standards organizations we will briefly discuss are the American National Standards Institute and the Institute of Electrical and Electronics Engineers. In the area of local area networking standards, both ANSI and the IEEE work in conjunction with the ISO to standardize LAN technology.

The ISO delegated the standardization of local area networking technology to ANSI. The American National Standards Institute, in turn, delegated lower-speed LAN standards — initially defined as operating rates at and below 50 Mbps — to the IEEE. This resulted in ANSI's developing standards for the 100-Mbps fiber distributed data interface (FDDI), while the IEEE developed standards for Ethernet, Token-Ring, and other LANs. Because the IEEE developed standards for 10-Mbps Ethernet, that organization was tasked with the responsibility for modifications to that LAN technology. This resulted in the IEEE becoming responsible for the standardization of high-speed Ethernet to include isoENET, 100BASE-T, and 100VG-AnyLAN, the latter two representing 100-Mbps LAN operating rates. Another series of IEEE standards beginning with the prefix of 1000 defines the operation of Gigabit Ethernet over different types of copper and optical fiber media. In addition, when this book revision occurred the IEEE was in the process of finalizing a standard for 10 Gbps Ethernet.

Once the IEEE develops and approves a standard, that standard is sent to ANSI for review. If ANSI approves the standard, it is then sent to the ISO. Then, the ISO solicits comments from all member countries to ensure that the standard will work at the international level, resulting in an IEEE- or ANSI-developed standard becoming an ISO standard.

ANSI

The principal standards-forming body in the United States is the American National Standards Institute (ANSI). Located in New York City, this nonprofit, nongovernmental organization was founded in 1918 and functions as the representative of the United States to the ISO.

American National Standards Institute standards are developed through the work of its approximately 300 Standards Committees, and from the efforts of associated groups such as the Electronic Industry Association (EIA). Recognizing the importance of the computer industry, ANSI established its X3 Standards Committee in 1960. That committee consists of 25 technical committees, each assigned to develop standards for a specific technical area. One of those technical committees is the X3S3 committee, more formally known as the Data Communications Technical Committee. This committee was responsible for the ANSI X3T9.5 standard that governs FDDI operations, and that is now recognized as the ISO 9314 standard.

IEEE

The Institute of Electrical and Electronics Engineers (IEEE) is a U.S.-based engineering society that is very active in the development of data communications standards. In fact, the most prominent developer of local area networking standards is the IEEE, whose subcommittee 802 began its work in 1980 before they had even established a viable market for the technology.

The IEEE Project 802 efforts are concentrated on the physical interface between network devices and the procedures and functions required to establish, maintain, and release connections among them. These procedures include defining data formats, error control procedures, and other control activities governing the flow of information. This focus of the IEEE actually represents the lowest two layers of the ISO model, physical and link, which are discussed later in this chapter.

International Standards Organizations

Two important international standards organizations are the International Telecommunications Union (ITU), formerly known as the Consultative

Committee for International Telephone and Telegraph (CCITT), and the International Standards Organization (ISO). The ITU can be considered a governmental body, because it functions under the auspices of an agency of the United Nations. Although the ISO is a nongovernmental agency, its work in the field of data communications is well recognized.

ITU

The International Telecommunications Union (ITU) is a specialized agency of the United Nations headquartered in Geneva, Switzerland. The ITU has direct responsibility for developing data communications standards and consists of 15 study groups, each with a specific area of responsibility. Although the CCITT was renamed as the ITU in 1994, it periodically continues to be recognized by its former mnemonic. Thus, the remainder of this book will refer to this standards organization by its new set of commonly recognized initials.

The work of the ITU is performed on a four-year cycle known as a study period. At the conclusion of each study period, a plenary session occurs. During the plenary session, the work of the ITU during the previous four years is reviewed, proposed recommendations are considered for adoption, and items to be investigated during the next four-year cycle are considered.

The ITU's eleventh plenary session met in 1996 and its twelfth session occurred during 2000. Although approval of recommended standards is not intended to be mandatory, ITU recommendations have the effect of law in some Western European countries, and many of its recommendations have been adopted by communications carriers and vendors in the United States. Perhaps the best-known set of ITU recommendations is its V-series, which describes the operation of many different modem features — for example, data compression and transmission error detection and correction.

ISO

The International Standards Organization (ISO) is a nongovernmental entity that has consultative status within the UN Economic and Social Council. The goal of the ISO is to "promote the development of standards in the world with a view to facilitating international exchange of goods and services."

The membership of the ISO consists of the national standards organizations of most countries. There are approximately 100 countries currently participating in its work.

Perhaps the most notable achievement of the ISO in the field of communications is its development of the seven-layer Open Systems Interconnection (OSI) Reference Model.

2.2 The ISO Reference Model

The International Standards Organization (ISO) established a framework for standardizing communications systems called the Open Systems Interconnection (OSI) Reference Model. The OSI architecture defines the communications process as a set of seven layers, with specific functions isolated and associated with each layer. Each layer, as illustrated in Figure 2.1, covers lower layer processes, effectively isolating them from higher layer functions. In this way, each layer performs a set of functions necessary to provide a set of services to the layer above it.

Layer isolation permits the characteristics of a given layer to change without impacting the remainder of the model, provided that the supporting services remain the same. One major advantage of this layered approach is that users can mix and match OSI-conforming communications products, and thus tailor their communications systems to satisfy particular networking requirements.

The OSI Reference Model, while not completely viable with many current network architectures, offers the potential to connect networks and networking devices together to form integrated networks, while using equipment from different vendors. This interconnectivity potential will be of substantial benefit to both users and vendors. For users, interconnectivity will remove the shackles that in many instances tie them to a particular vendor. For vendors, the ability to easily interconnect their products will provide them with access to a larger market. The importance of the OSI model is such that it was adopted by the ITU as Recommendation X.200.

Layered Architecture

As previously discussed, the OSI Reference Model is based on the establishment of a layered, or partitioned, architecture. This partitioning effort is

Application	Layer 7
Presentation	Layer 6
Session	Layer 5
Transport	Layer 4
Network	Layer 3
Data Link	Layer 2
Physical	Layer 1

Figure 2.1   ISO Reference Model.

derived from the scientific process, in which complex problems are subdivided into several simpler tasks.

As a result of the application of a partitioning approach to communications network architecture, the communications process was subdivided into seven distinct partitions, called *layers*. Each layer consists of a set of functions designed to provide a defined series of services. For example, the functions associated with the physical connection of equipment to a network are referred to as the *physical layer*.

With the exception of layers 1 and 7, each layer is bounded by the layers above and below it. Layer 1, the physical layer, is bound below by the interconnecting medium over which transmission flows, while layer 7 is the upper layer and has no upper boundary. Within each layer is a group of functions that provide a set of defined services to the layer above it, resulting in layer n using the services of layer $n-1$. Thus, the design of a layered architecture enables the characteristics of a particular layer to change without affecting the rest of the system, assuming that the services provided by the layer do not change.

OSI Layers

The best way to gain an understanding of the OSI layers is to examine a network structure that illustrates the components of a typical wide area network. Figure 2.2 illustrates a network structure that is typical only in the sense that it will be used for a discussion of the components upon which networks are constructed.

The circles in Figure 2.2 represent nodes, which are points where data enters or exits a network or is switched between two networks connected by

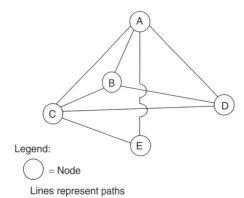

Legend:

◯ = Node

Lines represent paths

Figure 2.2   Generic network structure.

one or more paths. Nodes are connected to other nodes via communications cables or circuits and can be established on any type of communications medium, such as cable, microwave, or radio.

From a physical perspective, a node can be based on any of several types of computers, including a personal computer, minicomputer, mainframe computer, or specialized computer, such as a front-end processor. Connections to network nodes into a wide area network can occur via terminal devices, such as PCs and fixed logic devices, directly connected to computers, terminals connected to a node via one or more intermediate communications devices, or paths linking one network to another network. In fact, a workstation on an Ethernet local area network that provides access into a wide area network can be considered a network node. In this situation, the workstation can be a bridge, router, or gateway, and provides a connectivity mechanism between other stations on the Ethernet local area network and the wide area network.

The routes between two nodes — such as C-E-A, C-D-A, C-A, and C-B-A, all of which can be used to route data between nodes A and C — are *information paths*. Due to the variability in the flow of information through a wide area network, the shortest path between nodes may not be available for use, or may be inefficient in comparison to other possible paths. A temporary connection between two nodes that is based on such parameters as current network activity is known as a *logical connection*. This logical connection represents the use of physical facilities, including paths and temporary node-switching capability.

The major functions of each of the seven OSI layers are described in the following seven paragraphs.

Layer 1 — The Physical Layer

At the lowest or most basic level, the physical layer (level 1) is a set of rules that specifies the electrical and physical connection between devices. This level specifies the cable connections and the electrical rules necessary to transfer data between devices. Typically, the physical link corresponds to previously established interface standards, such as the RS-232/V.24 interface. This interface governs the attachment of data terminal equipment, such as the serial port of personal computers, to data communications equipment, such as modems.

Layer 2 — The Data Link Layer

The next layer, which is known as the data link layer (level 2), denotes how a device gains access to the medium specified in the physical layer.

It also defines data formats, including the framing of data within transmitted messages, error control procedures, and other link control activities. Because it defines data formats, including procedures to correct transmission errors, this layer becomes responsible for the reliable delivery of information. An example of a data link control protocol that can reside at this layer is the ITU's High-Level Data Link Control (HDLC).

Because the development of OSI layers was originally targeted toward wide area networking, its applicability to local area networks required a degree of modification. Under the IEEE 802 standards, the data link layer was initially divided into two sublayers: *logical link control (LLC)* and *media access control (MAC)*. The LLC layer is responsible for generating and interpreting commands that control the flow of data and perform recovery operations in the event of errors. In comparison, the MAC layer is responsible for providing access to the local area network, which enables a station on the network to transmit information.

With the development of high-speed local area networks designed to operate on a variety of different types of media, an additional degree of OSI layer subdivision was required. First, the data link layer required the addition of a reconciliation layer (RL) to reconcile a medium-independent interface (MII) signal added to a version of high-speed Ethernet, commonly referred to as Fast Ethernet. Next, the physical layer used for Fast Ethernet required a subdivision into three sublayers. One sublayer, known as the *physical coding sublayer (PCS)* performs data encoding. A *physical medium attachment* sublayer (PMA) maps messages from the physical coding sublayer to the transmission media, while a *medium-dependent interface (MDI)* specifies the connector for the media used. Similarly, Gigabit Ethernet implements a gigabit media-independent interface (GMII), which enables different encoding and decoding methods to be supported that are used with different types of media. Later in this chapter, we will examine the IEEE 802 subdivision of the data link and physical layers, as well as the operation of each resulting sublayer.

Layer 3 — The Network Layer

The network layer (level 3) is responsible for arranging a logical connection between the source and destination nodes on the network. This responsibility includes the selection and management of a route for the flow of information between source and destination, based on the available data paths in the network. Services provided by this layer are associated with the movement of data packets through a network, including addressing, routing, switching, sequencing, and flow control procedures. In a complex network, the source and destination may not be directly connected by a single path, but instead require a path that consists of many subpaths. Thus, routing data through the network onto the correct paths is an important feature of this layer.

Several protocols have been defined for layer 3, including the ITU X.25 packet switching protocol and the ITU X.75 gateway protocol. X.25 governs the flow of information through a packet network, while X.75 governs the flow of information between packet networks. Other popular examples of layer 3 protocols include the Internet Protocol (IP) and Novell's Internet Packet Exchange (IPX), both of which represent layers in their respective protocol suites that were defined before the ISO Reference Model was developed. In an Ethernet environment the transport unit is a frame. As we will note later in this book when we examine Ethernet frame formats in Chapter 4, the frame on a local area network is used as the transport facility to deliver such layer 3 protocols as IP and IPX, which in turn represent the vehicles for delivering higher-layer protocols in the IP and IPX protocol suites.

Layer 4 — The Transport Layer

The transport layer (level 4) is responsible for guaranteeing that the transfer of information occurs correctly after a route has been established through the network by the network level protocol. Thus, the primary function of this layer is to control the communications session between network nodes once a path has been established by the network control layer. Error control, sequence checking, and other end-to-end data reliability factors are the primary concern of this layer, and they enable the transport layer to provide a reliable end-to-end data transfer capability. Examples of popular transport layer protocols include the Transmission Control Protocol (TCP) and the User Datagram Protocol (UDP), both of which are part of the TCP/IP protocol suite, and Novell's Sequence Packet Exchange (SPX).

Layer 5 — The Session Layer

The session layer (level 5) provides a set of rules for establishing and terminating data streams between nodes in a network. The services that this session layer can provide include establishing and terminating node connections, message flow control, dialogue control, and end-to-end data control.

Layer 6 — The Presentation Layer

The presentation layer (level 6) services are concerned with data transformation, formatting, and syntax. One of the primary functions performed by the presentation layer is the conversion of transmitted data into a display format appropriate for a receiving device. This can include any necessary conversion between ASCII and EBCDIC codes. Data encryption/decryption and data compression/decompression are additional examples of the data transformation that can be handled by this layer.

Layer 7 — The Application Layer

Finally, the application layer (level 7) acts as a window through which the application gains access to all of the services provided by the model. Examples of functions performed at this level include file transfers, resource sharing, and database access. While the first four layers are fairly well defined, the top three layers may vary considerably, depending on the network protocol used. For example, the TCP/IP protocol, which predates the OSI Reference Model, groups layer 5 through layer 7 functions into a single application layer. In Chapter 5 when we examine Internet connectivity, we will also examine the relationship of the TCP/IP protocol stack to the seven-layer OSI Reference Model.

Figure 2.3 illustrates the OSI model in schematic format, showing the various levels of the model with respect to a terminal device, such as a personal computer accessing an application on a host computer system. Although Figure 2.3 shows communications occurring via a modem connection on a wide area network, the OSI model schematic is also applicable to local area networks. Thus, the terminal shown in the figure could be replaced by a workstation on an Ethernet network while the front-end processor (FEP) would, via a connection to that network, become a participant on that network.

Data Flow

As data flows within an ISO network, each layer appends appropriate heading information to frames of information flowing within the network, while removing the heading information added by a lower layer. In this manner, layer n interacts with layer $n - 1$ as data flows through an ISO network.

Figure 2.4 illustrates the appending and removal of frame header information as data flows through a network constructed according to the ISO Reference Model. Because each higher level removes the header appended by a lower level, the frame traversing the network arrives in its original form at its destination.

As you will surmise from the previous illustrations, the ISO Reference Model is designed to simplify the construction of data networks. This simplification is due to the potential standardization of methods and procedures

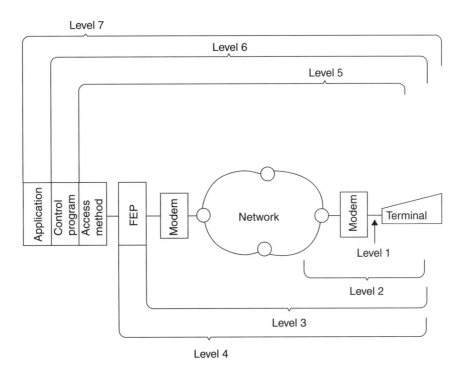

Figure 2.3   OSI model schematic.

Legend:
DH, NH, TH, SH, PH and AH are appropriate headers Data Link, Network header,
Transport header, Session header, Presentation header and Application header
added to data as the data flows through an ISO Reference model network

Figure 2.4   Appending and removal of frame header information.

to append appropriate heading information to frames flowing through a network, permitting data to be routed to its appropriate destination following a uniform procedure.

2.3 IEEE 802 Standards

The Institute of Electrical and Electronics Engineers (IEEE) Project 802 was formed at the beginning of the 1980s to develop standards for emerging technologies. The IEEE fostered the development of local area networking equipment from different vendors that can work together. In addition, IEEE LAN standards provided a common design goal for vendors to access a relatively larger market than if proprietary equipment were developed. This, in turn, enabled economies of scale to lower the cost of products developed for larger markets.

The actual committee tasked with the IEEE Project 802 is referred to as the IEEE Local and Metropolitan Area Network (LAN/WAN) Standards Committee. Its basic charter is to create, maintain, and encourage the use of IEEE/ANSI and equivalent ISO standards primarily within layers 1 and 2 of the ISO Reference Model. The committee conducts a plenary meeting three times a year and currently has 13 major working groups, each of which may have several meetings per year at locations throughout the world.

802 Committees

Table 2.1 lists the IEEE 802 committees involved in local and metropolitan area networks. In examining the lists of committees in Table 2.1, it is apparent that the IEEE early on noted that a number of different systems would be required to satisfy the requirements of a diverse end-user population. Accordingly, the IEEE adopted the CSMA/CD, Token-Bus, and Token-Ring as standards 802.3, 802.4, and 802.5, respectively.

The IEEE Committee 802 published draft standards for CSMA/CD and Token-Bus local area networks in 1982. Standard 802.3, which describes a baseband CSMA/CD network similar to Ethernet, was published in 1983. Since then, several addenda to the 802.3 standard have been adopted to govern the operation of CSMA/CD on different types of media. Those addenda include 10BASE-2, which defines a 10-Mbps baseband network operating on thin coaxial cable; 1BASE-5, which defines a 1-Mbps baseband network operating on twisted-pair; 10BASE-T, which defines a 10-Mbps baseband network operating on twisted-pair; and 10BROAD-36, which defines a broadband 10-Mbps network that operates on thick coaxial cable.

TABLE 2.1 IEEE Series 802 Committees/Standards

802	Overview — Architecture
802.1	Bridging — Management
802.2	Logical Link Control
802.3	CSMA/CD Access Method
802.4	Token-Passing Bus Access Method
802.5	Token-Passing Ring Access Method
802.6	Metropolitan Area Networks (DQDB Access Method)
802.7	Broadband LAN
802.8	Fiber Optic Technical Advisory Group
802.9	Integrated Voice and Data Networks
802.10	Network Security
802.11	Wireless LANs
802.12	Demand Priority Access

The IEEE 802.3 committee includes a large number of projects that resulted in the refinement and expansion of the CSMA/CD protocol. Some of those projects were completed several years ago, while others are currently ongoing. Table 2.2 lists nine examples of IEEE 802.3 CSMA/CD projects. A Fast Ethernet, which is denoted as 802.3μ in Table 2.2, is an addendum to the 802.3 standard, which was finalized in 1995. 802.3z represents the 802 committee project that was responsible for developing the Gigabit Ethernet standard.

The next major standard published by the IEEE was 802.4, which describes a token-passing bus–oriented network for both baseband and broadband transmission. This standard is similar to the Manufacturing Automation Protocol (MAP) standard developed by General Motors.

The third major LAN standard published by the IEEE was based on IBM's specifications for its Token-Ring network. Known as the 802.5 standard, it defines the operation of token-ring networks on shielded twisted-pair cable at data rates of 1 and 4 Mbps. That standard was later modified to acknowledge three IBM enhancements to Token-Ring network operations. These enhancements include the 16-Mbps operating rate, the ability to release a token early on a 16-Mbps network, and a bridge routing protocol known as *source routing*.

TABLE 2.2   IEEE 802.3 CSMA/CD Projects

803.2aa	Maintenance Revision #5 (100Base-T)
802.3ab	1000Base-T
802.3ad	Link Aggregation
802.3c	vLAN tag
802.3ae	10 Gbps Ethernet
802.3ag	Maintenance Revision #6
802.3i	Ethernet (10BASE-T)
802.3μ	Fast Ethernet
802.3x	Full Duplex
802.3z	Gigabit Ethernet

Two Ethernet standards that represent initial follow-on to the initial standard are 802.3μ and 802.12, both of which have their foundation in IEEE efforts that occurred during 1992. In that year the IEEE requested proposals for "Fast Ethernet," designed to raise the Ethernet operating rate from 10 Mbps to 100 Mbps. This request resulted in two initial proposals. One proposal, now referred to as a series of 100BASE proposals, was developed by a consortium that included Synoptics Communications, Inc., 3Com Corporation, and Ungermann-Bass, Inc. This proposal retained the CSMA/CD access proposal, which formed the basis for the operation of earlier versions of Ethernet. Now included in 802.3μ are 100BASE-TX, 100BASE-FX, and 100BASE-T4.

100BASE-TX defines the specifications for 100-Mbps CSMA/CD over two pairs of category 5 unshielded twisted-pair (UTP) cable. 100BASE-FX specifies 100-Mbps Ethernet over two pairs of optical fiber cable, while 100BASE-T4 defines the operation of 100-Mbps Ethernet over four pairs of category 3, 4, and 5 UTP or shielded twisted-pair (STP) cable.

The second 100-Mbps proposal, which is now referred to as 100VG-AnyLAN, was initially developed by AT&T Microelectronics and Hewlett-Packard Company. This proposal replaced the CSMA/CD access protocol by a demand-priority scheme that enables the support of Ethernet, Token-Ring, FDDI, and other types of local area networks. Since this proposal described operations on voice grade (VG) twisted pair, it received the mnemonic 100VG-AnyLAN. Because the operation of 100VG-AnyLAN is based upon the passing of a token that is used to prioritize access to a network, the actual name of the 802.12 committee is Demand Priority Access.

During 1994, the IEEE 802.9 working group completed a document that creates a 16.384-Mbps physical layer for operation on UTP category 3 or higher cable. Referred to as isoENET, the document is technically referred to as 802.9a. While both 100VG-AnyLAN and isoENET received a considerable level of interest when they were proposed, they never achieved any significant degree of commercial acceptance. Due to this, our coverage in this book of those versions of Ethernet will be limited to a brief overview of each technology.

The CSMA/CD protocol requires stations to listen for activity before transmitting data. This means that a four-wire connection with separate pairs for transmit and receive cannot be operated simultaneously to transmit and receive data, precluding true full-duplex operations from occurring. However, when an Ethernet station is connected to a port on a LAN switch, the two wire pairs between the station enable the switch port and workstation to simultaneously transmit and receive data without the possibility of a collision occurring. This method of full duplex CSMA/CD transmission was standardized by the IEEE as the 802.3x standard during 1996.

While the IEEE 802.3z standard for the operation of Gigabit Ethernet transmission was completed during 1998, that standard was limited to defining transmission at 1 Gbps over different types of optical fiber. It was not until 1999 that the 802.3ab standard was issued, which provided the physical layer specification for 1 Gbps transmission over metallic twisted-pair standardized as 1000BASE-T. Although it remained to be finalized, 10 Gbps Ethernet's physical layer specification over optical fiber was being worked on by the IEEE 802.3ae project.

Data Link Subdivision

One of the more interesting facets of IEEE 802 standards was the initial subdivision of the ISO Open System Interconnection Model's data link layer into two sublayers: logical link control (LLC) and medium access control (MAC). Figure 2.5 illustrates the relationship between IEEE 802 local area network standards and the first three layers of the OSI Reference Model.

The separation of the data link layer into two entities provides a mechanism for regulating access to the medium that is independent of the method for establishing, maintaining, and terminating the logical link between workstations. The method of regulating access to the medium is defined by the MAC portion of each LAN standard. This enables the LLC standard to be applicable to each type of network.

Figure 2.5 Relationship between IEEE standards and the OSI Reference Model.

Medium Access Control

The MAC sublayer is responsible for controlling access to the network. To accomplish this, it must ensure that two or more stations do not attempt to transmit data onto the network simultaneously. For Ethernet networks, this is accomplished through the use of the CSMA/CD access protocol.

In addition to network access control, the MAC sublayer is responsible for the orderly movement of data onto and off of the network. To accomplish this, the MAC sublayer is responsible for MAC addressing, frame type recognition, frame control, frame copying, and similar frame-related functions.

The MAC address represents the physical address of each station connected to the network. That address can belong to a single station, can represent a predefined group of stations (group address), or can represent all stations on the network (broadcast address). Through MAC addresses, the physical source and destination of frames are identified.

Frame type recognition enables the type and format of a frame to be recognized. To ensure that frames can be processed accurately, frame control prefixes each frame with a preamble, which consists of a predefined sequence of bits. In addition, a frame check sequence (FCS) is computed by applying an algorithm to the contents of the frame; the results of the operation are placed into the frame. This enables a receiving station to perform a similar operation. Then, if the locally computed FCS matches the FCS carried in the frame, the frame is considered to have arrived without error.

Once a frame arrives at a station that has the same address as the destination address in the frame, that station must copy the frame. The copying operation moves the contents of the frame into a buffer area in an Ethernet adapter card. The adapter card removes certain fields from the frame, such as the preamble and start of frame delimiter, and passes the information field into a predefined memory area in the station into which the adapter card is inserted.

Refer to Chapter 4 for detailed information concerning Ethernet frame formats, as well as information concerning how the MAC layer controls the transmission and reception of data on an Ethernet local area network.

Logical Link Control

Logical link control frames are used to provide a link between network layer protocols and media access control. This linkage is accomplished through the use of service access points (SAPs), which operate in much the same way as a mailbox. That is, both network layer protocols and logical link control have access to SAPs and can leave messages for each other in them.

Like a mailbox in a post office, each SAP has a distinct address. For the logical link control, a SAP represents the location of a network layer process, such as the location of an application within a workstation as viewed from the network. From the network layer perspective, a SAP represents the place to leave messages concerning the network services requested by an application.

LLC frames contain two special address fields, known as the destination services access point and the source services access point. The destination services access point (DSAP) is one byte in length and specifies the receiving network layer process. The source services access point (SSAP) is also one byte in length. The SSAP specifies the sending network layer process. Both DSAP and SSAP addresses are assigned by the IEEE. Refer to Chapter 4 for detailed information concerning LLC frame formats and data flow.

Additional Sublayering

As previously mentioned, the standardization of high-speed Ethernet resulted in an additional sublayer at the data link layer, and the subdivision of the physical layer. Figure 2.6 illustrates the relationship between the first two layers of the ISO Reference Model and the IEEE 802.3μ Fast Ethernet sublayers.

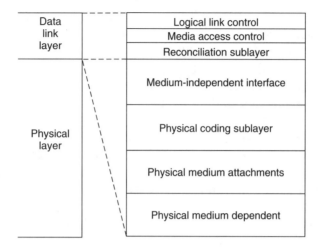

Figure 2.6   IEEE 802.3μ sublayering.

The additional sublayering illustrated in Figure 2.6 became necessary, as it was desired to support different media with one standard. To accomplish this required the physical layer to be independent from the data link layer, because there can be different coding schemes used to support transmission on different types of media.

To retain the CSMA/CD access protocol while supporting the use of different media required the use of different connectors, resulting in the introduction of a physical medium-dependent (PMD) sublayer. Because different data coding schemes are required to support 100 Mbps on different types of media, a physical coding sublayer was introduced. This sublayer defines the coding method used for transmission on different types of media. To map messages from the physical coding sublayer onto the transmission media resulted in those functions being performed by the physical medium attachment sublayer. Thus, the physical layer was subdivided into three sublayers.

Although not shown on Figure 2.6, it should be noted that an Auto-Negotiation function resides under the PMD. The Auto-Negotiation function was added to provide an ease of migration from 10 Mbps Ethernet to 100 Mbps Ethernet and results in the Media-Independent Interface (MII) supporting both 10 and 100 Mbps data transfer. To accomplish this the MII clock is capable of operating at 2.5 MHz and 25 MHz.

At the data link layer an additional sublayer, known as the *reconciliation sublayer*, was introduced. This sublayer is responsible for reconciling the MII from the physical layer, with the MAC signal.

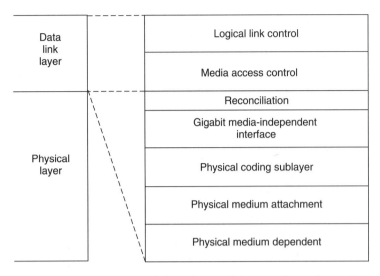

Figure 2.7   Subdivision of the physical layer of Gigabit Ethernet.

Recognizing that Gigabit Ethernet would operate on different types of media also resulted in the subdivision of its physical layer. That subdivision is illustrated in Figure 2.7.

The reconciliation sublayer represents a transparent interface between the MAC sublayer and the physical layer which decouples the MAC layer from the physical layer. The Gigabit Media Independent Interface (GMII) includes transmit and receive data paths that are 8 bits in width, which, when coupled with a clock that now operates at 125 MHz, results in a data transfer capability of 1 Gbps.

From a comparison of Figure 2.6 and Figure 2.7, you will note that the sublayering of Gigabit Ethernet is similar to that of Fast Ethernet. However, the sublayers perform different functions. For example, under Fast Ethernet coding is based on the FDDI specification. In comparison, under Gigabit Ethernet reliance is shifted to the physical sublayers previously specified for the Fiber channel, as the latter operates at approximately Gigabit data rates and was selected for use by the 802.38 project members.

2.4 Internet Standards

The Internet as we know it dates to 1967 when the Advanced Research Projects Agency (ARPA), operating as a part of the United States Office of the

Secretary of Defense, issued a Request for Proposal (RFP) for the creation of a packet switching network. The result of the RFP was a contract issued to Bolt, Beranek and Newmann (BBN), a then small company based in Cambridge, MA, whose efforts resulted in a network that enabled scientists and educators to share information. That network was known as ARPAnet.

RFC Evolution

In an effort to share information about the operation of ARPAnet, Steve Crocker, a then graduate student at UCLA, published the first Request for Comment (RFC) in April, 1969, which was titled "Host Software." The term RFC was used, as Mr Crocker wanted others to comment on the information he provided. As ARPAnet expanded and evolved into the Internet, various organizations came into being. The Internet Activities Board (IAB) became responsible for Internet design and planning. Two task forces reside under the IAB — the Internet Engineering Task Force (IETF) and the Internet Research Task Force (IRTF). The responsibility of the IETF involves the coordination of various technical aspects of the Internet to include the development and modification of protocols that may be necessary to obtain a desired level of functionality.

The IAB is currently responsible for defining protocols and operational procedures that require both dissemination to the Internet community and archiving. To accomplish this, the IAB primarily issues documents known as Requests for Comments (RFCs), the majority of which begin as working memorandums issued by the IETF.

Types and Submission

There are several types of RFCs. Types of RFCs can include a Draft Standard RFC, a Proposed Standard RFC, a Full Standard RFC, an Experimental RFC, a Best Current Practice RFC and a "For Your Information" RFC. While RFCs are not referred publications, they are technically reviewed by either individual technical experts, the RFC editor, or members of a task force. Anyone can submit a document for publication as an RFC. Once submitted to the RFC editor the document may be edited to comply with certain format rules, which are currently specified in RFC 2223, issued in October, 1997, which obsoleted RFC 1543.

An initial RFC submission is usually treated as a Preliminary Draft and is electronically distributed for comment. On its way to becoming a Full Standard, and it should be noted that many RFCs are not intended to be standards, the Preliminary Draft may first become a Proposed Standard.

Figure 2.8 Internet standards time track.

Figure 2.8 illustrates the typical track time for the development of an Internet standard. Once a Preliminary Draft is submitted it can take approximately six months for the receipt of comments concerning the draft and to allow the draft to be moved forward to be published as a Proposed Standard, and either dropped or promoted to a Draft Standard. After a review period of at least four months, a Draft Standard can be recommended for adoption as a Standard by the Internet Engineering Steering Group (IESC). The IESC consist of the chairperson of the IETF and other members of that group, and it performs an oversight and coordinating function for the IETF. Although the IESG is responsible for recommending the adoption of an RFC as a Standard, the IAB is responsible for the final decision concerning its adoption.

Obtaining RFCs

There are many Web sites where you can locate RFCs. The RFC Editor maintains the official repository of all RFCs and indexes to them. The RFC Editor web location is:

http://www.rfc-editor.org

In addition to the RFC Editor web site there are many locations that mirror RFC information. One popular web site is maintained by the Computer and Information Science Department of Ohio State University. The address of that web site is:

http://www.cis.ohio-state.edu/services/rfc

At this site you can review a complete index of all RFCs, view specific RFCs, and obtain the capability to perform a keyboard search of a comprehensive database of RFCs.

2.5 Cabling Standards

Any discussion of Ethernet networks requires knowledge of both existing and pending cabling standards. In this section we will focus our attention upon the EIA/TIA-568 standard, first examining existing standards and then turning our attention to developing cabling standards that may be in place by the time you read this book.

EIA/TIA-568

The Electronics Industry Association/Telecommunications Industries Association "Commercial Building Telecommunications Standard," commonly referred to as EIA/TIA-568, was ratified in 1992. This standard specifies a variety of building cabling parameters, ranging from backbone cabling used to connect a building's telecommunication closets to an equipment room, to horizontal cabling used to cable individual users to the equipment closet. The standard defines the performance characteristics of both backbone and horizontal cables as well as different types of connectors used with different types of cable.

Backbone Cabling

Four types of media are recognized by the EIA/TIA-568 standard for backbone cabling. Table 2.3 lists the media options supported by the EIA/TIA-568 standard for backbone cabling.

Horizontal Cabling

As previously indicated, horizontal cabling under the EIA/TIA-568 standard consists of cable that connects equipment in a telecommunications closet to a user's work area. The media options supported for horizontal cabling are

TABLE 2.3   EIA/TIA-568 Backbone Cabling Media Options

Media Type	Maximum Cable Distance
100-ohm UTP	800 meters (2624 feet)
150-ohm STP	700 meters (2296 feet)
50-ohm thick coaxial cable	500 meters (1640 feet)
62.5/125-μ multimode optical fiber	2000 meters (6560 feet)

the same as specified for backbone cabling, with the exception of coaxial cable for which 50-ohm thin cable is specified; however, cabling distances are restricted to 90 meters in length from equipment in the telecommunications closet to a telecommunications outlet. This permits a patch cord or drop cable up to 10 meters in length to be used to connect a user workstation to a telecommunications outlet, resulting in the total length of horizontal cabling not exceeding the 100-meter restriction associated with many LAN technologies that use UTP cabling.

UTP Categories

One of the more interesting aspects of the EIA/TIA-568 standard is its recognition that different signaling rates require different cable characteristics. This resulted in the EIA/TIA-568 standard initially classifying UTP cable into five categories. Those categories and their suitability for different types of voice and data applications are indicated in Table 2.4.

In examining the entries in Table 2.4, note that categories 3 through 5 support transmission with respect to indicated signaling rates. This means that the ability of those categories of UTP to support different types of LAN transmission will depend upon the signaling method used by different LANs. For example, consider a LAN encoding technique that results in 6 bits encoded into 4 signaling elements that have a 100-MHz signaling rate. Through the use of category 5 cable, a data transmission rate of 150 Mbps ((6/4) × 100) could be supported.

Category 3 cable is typically used for Ethernet and 4 Mbps Token-Ring LANs. Category 4 is normally used for 16-Mbps Token-Ring LANs, while category 5 cable supports 100-Mbps Ethernet LANs, such as 100VG-AnyLAN

TABLE 2.4   EIA/TIA-568 UTP Cable Categories

Category 1	Voice or low-speed data up to 56 Kbps; not useful for LANs.
Category 2	Data rates up to 1 Mbps.
Category 3	Supports transmission up to 16 MHz.
Category 4	Supports transmission up to 20 MHz.
Category 5	Supports transmission up to 100 MHz.

and 100BASE-T, and will support ATM to the desktop at a 155-Mbps operating rate. Two additional metallic cable categories being considered for standardization are category 5 extended (cat 5e) and category 6. Category 5e represents more stringent existing specifications as well as specifications for existing parameters that we will shortly review. Although cat 5e is only specified for operations up to 100 MHz, it is used to support 1000BASE-T. However, the proposed cat 6 standard that will support signaling up to 200 MHz should eventually become the preferred cable for supporting Gigabit Ethernet over copper media.

Cable Specifications

There are two basic metrics that define the capability of EIA/TIA-568 cable with respect to the signaling rate they support, which in turn defines the cable category. Those metrics are attenuation and near-end crosstalk (NEXT).

Attenuation

Attenuation represents the loss of signal power as a signal propagates from a transmitter at one end of a cable toward a receiving device located at the distant end of the cable. Attenuation is measured in decibels (dB) as indicated:

$$\text{Attenuation} = 20 \log_{10} \frac{\text{(transmit voltage)}}{\text{receive voltage}}$$

For those of us a little rusty with logarithms, let's examine a few examples of attenuation computations. First, let's assume the transmit voltage was 100, while the receive voltage was 1. Then,

$$\text{Attenuation} = 20 \log_{10} \frac{(100)}{1} = 20 \log_{10} 100$$

The value of $\log_{10} 100$ can be obtained by determining the power to which 10 should be raised to equal 100. Because the answer is 2 ($10^2 = 100$), $\log_{10} 100$ has a value of 2, and $20 \log_{10} 100$ then has a value of 40.

Now let's assume the transmit voltage was 10 while the receiver voltage was 1. Then,

$$\text{Attenuation} = 20 \log_{10} \frac{(10)}{1} = 20 \log_{10} 10$$

Because the value of $\log_{10} 10$ is 1 ($10^1 = 10$), then $20 \log_{10} 10$ has a value of 20. From the preceding, note that a lower level of signal power loss results in a lower level of attenuation.

NEXT

Crosstalk represents the electromagnetic interference caused by a signal on one wire pair being emitted onto another wire pair, resulting in the generation of noise. Because transmit and receive pairs are twisted and the transmit signal is strongest at its source, the maximum level of interference occurs at the cable connector and decreases as the transmit signal traverses the cable. Recognizing this fact of physics, crosstalk is measured at the near end, hence the term near-end crosstalk (NEXT).

NEXT denotes the induced or coupled signal flowing from the transmit pair to the receive pair even though the two pairs are not interconnected. Mathematically, NEXT is defined in decibels (dB) as follows:

$$\text{NEXT} = 20 \log_{10} \frac{\text{(transmitted voltage)}}{\text{coupled voltage}}$$

In the preceding equation the transmit voltage represents the power placed on the transmit pair, while the coupled signal is measured on the receive pair at the location where the transmit voltage was generated. Note that a larger dB NEXT measurement is better as it indicates a lower level of crosstalk and is the opposite of attenuation, because a lower attenuation reading indicates less signal loss and is better than a higher reading for that parameter. Table 2.5 indicates the EIA/TIA-568 specification limits for categories 3, 4, and 5 UTP cable. In examining Table 2.5, note that both attenuation and NEXT must be measured over a range of frequencies. That range is based upon the cable category. For example, because category 3 cable is designed to support signaling rates up to 16 MHz, attenuation and NEXT should be measured up to and including the highest signaling rate supported by that type of cable, which is 16 MHz.

Other Metrics

When the EIA/TIA considered the development of additional cabling specifications, it recognized the need to include additional parameters in the specifications it developed. Three of those additional specifications concern power sum NEXT (PS NEXT), Equal Level Far End Crosstalk (EL FEXT) and the power sum attenuation to crosstalk ratio (PS ACR).

PS NEXT

Power sum NEXT actually represents a computation and not an individual measurement. PS NEXT is obtained by computing the algebraic summation of

TABLE 2.5   EIA/TIA-568 Attenuation and NEXT Limits in dB

Frequency (MHz)	Category 3		Category 4		Category 5	
	Attenuation	NEXT	Attenuation	NEXT	Attenuation	NEXT
1.0	4.2	39.1	2.6	53.3	2.5	60.3
4.0	7.3	29.3	4.8	43.3	4.5	50.6
8.0	10.2	24.3	6.7	38.2	6.3	45.6
10.0	11.5	22.7	7.5	36.6	7.0	44.0
16.0	14.9	19.3	9.9	33.1	9.2	40.6
20.0	—	—	11.0	31.4	10.3	39.0
25.0	—	—	—	—	11.4	37.4
31.2	—	—	—	—	12.8	35.7
62.5	—	—	—	—	18.5	30.6
100.0	—	—	—	—	24.0	27.1

the individual NEXT effects on each pair by the other pairs in a cable. Because 1000BASE-T uses four pairs, PS NEXT represents an important measurement for qualifying cabling required to support Gigabit Ethernet over copper media.

PS NEXT represents a measure of difference in signal strength between disturbing pairs and a disturbed pair. This means that a larger number, which represents less crosstalk, is more desirable than a small number that represents more crosstalk.

EL FEXT

Equal Level Far End Crosstalk (EL FEXT) also represents a calculated specification and not a single measurement. EL FEXT is computed by subtracting the attenuation of the disturbing pair from the Far End Crosstalk that the pair introduces in adjacent pairs.

To illustrate the computation of EL FEXT, assume FEXT was measured to be -47 dB while attenuation was determined to be -12 dB. Then, EL FEXT becomes $-47 - (-12)$ or -35 dB. Note that EL FEXT provides a normalized computation based upon the length of a cable since attenuation varies by length.

TABLE 2.6   Recent and Emerging EIA/TIA Cable Specifications

Specification	Category 5	Category 5e	Category 6 (Proposed)
Frequency Range	1–100 MHz	1–100 MHz	1–200 MHz
Attenuation	24 dB	24 dB	21.7 dB
NEXT	27.1 dB	30.1 dB	39.9 dB
Power sum NEXT	N/A	27.1 dB	37.1 dB
ACR	3.1 dB	6.1 dB	18.2 dB
Power sum ACR	N/A	3.1 dB	15.4 dB
EL FEXT	17 dB	17.4 dB	23.2 dB
Power sum EL FEXT	14.4 dB	14.4 dB	20.2 dB
Return Loss	8 dB	10 dB	12.0 dB
Propagation Delay	548 ns	548 ns	548 ns
Delay Skew	50 ns	50 ns	50 ns

PS ACR

Similar to PS NEXT and EL FEXT, the power sum attenuation to crosstalk ratio (PS ACR) represents a computation and not an individual measurement. PS ACR is determined by computing an algebraic summation of individual ACR effects, with four results at each end of a link being tested.

Because ACR represents a measure of attenuation to crosstalk as a ratio, PS ACR also represents a summed ratio. Thus, a larger number that represents more signal and less noise is more desirable than a smaller number, which represents more noise and less signal.

Cat 5e and Cat 6

When this new edition was prepared, category 5e had been standardized while category 6 was being proposed as a new specification. To provide a frame of reference between the newly specified category 5e and proposed category 6 cabling, Table 2.6 provides a comparison of those specifications to category 5 cable. In examining Table 2.6 note that several category 5 specifications are not actually specified by that cabling specification and are only listed for comparison purposes.

chapter three

Ethernet Networks

From the title of this chapter, it is apparent that there is more than one type of Ethernet network. From a network access perspective, there is actually only one Ethernet network. However, the CSMA/CD access protocol used by Ethernet, as well as its general frame format and most of its operating characteristics, were used by the IEEE to develop a series of Ethernet-type networks under the IEEE 802.3 umbrella. Thus, this chapter will first focus on the different types of Ethernet networks by closely examining the components and operating characteristics of Ethernet and then comparing its major features with the different networks defined by the IEEE 802.3 standard. Once this is accomplished, we will focus our attention on the wiring, topology, and hardware components associated with each type of IEEE 802.3 Ethernet network. This will enable us to examine the construction of several types of 802.3 networks using a variety of hardware devices and then illustrate how those networks can be connected to one another—a process referred to as *internetworking*.

Although significant advances in Ethernet technology have occurred over the past decade, many features and constraints associated with newer technology are based upon the original technology. Due to this we will begin at the beginning in this chapter and examine the characteristics of each Ethernet Network in the order in which they were developed.

3.1 Ethernet

One of the key concepts behind Ethernet—that of allocating the use of a shared channel—can be traced to the pioneering efforts of Dr. Norman Abramson and his colleagues at the University of Hawaii during the early 1970s. Using a ground-based radio broadcasting system to connect different locations through the use of a shared channel, Abramson and his colleagues developed the concept of listening to the channel before transmission, transmitting a frame of information, listening to the channel output to determine whether a collision occurred, and, if it did, waiting a random period of time before retransmission. The resulting University of Hawaii ground-based radio broadcasting system, called ALOHA, formed the basis for the development of numerous channel contention systems, including Ethernet. In addition, the subdivision of transmission into frames of data was the pioneering work in the development of packet-switching networks. Thus, Norman Abramson and his colleagues can be considered the forefathers of two of the most important communications technologies, contention networks and packet-switching networks.

Evolution

The actual development of Ethernet occurred at the Xerox Palo Alto Research Center (PARC) in Palo Alto, California. A development team headed by Dr. Robert Metcalfe had to connect over 100 computers on a 1-km cable. The resulting system, which operated at 2.94 Mbps using the CSMA/CD access protocol, was referred to as "Ethernet" in a memorandum authored by Metcalfe. He named it after the luminiferous ether through which electromagnetic radiation was once thought to propagate.

During its progression from a research-based network into a manufactured product, Ethernet suffered several identity crises. During the 1970s, it endured such temporary names as the "Alto Aloha Network" and the "Xerox Wire." After reverting to the original name, Xerox decided, quite wisely, that the establishment of Ethernet as an industry standard for local area networks would be expedited by an alliance with other vendors. A resulting alliance with Digital Equipment Corporation and Intel Corporation, which was known as the DIX Consortium, resulted in the development of a 10-Mbps Ethernet network. It also provided Ethernet with a significant advantage over Datapoint's ARCNet and Wang Laboratories' Wangnet, proprietary local area networks that were the main competitors to Ethernet during the 1970s.

The alliance between Digital Equipment, Intel, and Xerox resulted in the publication of a "Blue Book Standard" for Ethernet Version 1. An enhancement to that standard occurred in 1982 and is referred to as Ethernet Version 2 or Ethernet II in many technical publications. Although the DIX Consortium submitted its Ethernet specification to the IEEE in 1980, it wasn't until 1982 that the IEEE 802.3 CSMA/CD standard was promulgated. Because the IEEE used Ethernet Version 2 as the basis for the 802.3 CSMA/CD standard, and Ethernet Version 1 has been obsolete for over approximately two decades, we will refer to Ethernet Version 2 as Ethernet in the remainder of this book.

Network Components

The 10-Mbps Ethernet network standard originally developed by Xerox, Digital Equipment Corporation, and Intel was based on the use of five hardware components. Those components include a coaxial cable, a cable tap, a transceiver, a transceiver cable, and an interface board (also known as an Ethernet controller). Figure 3.1 illustrates the relationships among Ethernet components.

Coaxial Cable

One of the problems faced by the designers of Ethernet was the selection of an appropriate medium. Although twisted-pair wire is relatively inexpensive and easy to use, the short distances between twists serve as an antenna for receiving electromagnetic and radio frequency interference in the form of noise. Thus, the use of twisted-pair cable restricts the network to relatively short distances. Coaxial cable, however, has a dielectric shielding the conductor. As long as the ends of the cable are terminated, coaxial cable can transmit over greater distances than twisted-pair cable. Because the original development of Ethernet was oriented toward interconnecting computers located in different

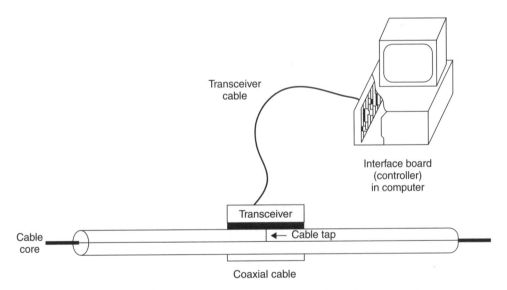

Figure 3.1   Ethernet hardware components. When thick coaxial cable is used for the bus, an Ethernet cable connection is made with a transceiver cable and a transceiver tapped into the cable.

buildings, the use of coaxial cable was well suited for this requirement. Thus, the initial selection for Ethernet transmission medium was coaxial cable.

There are two types of coaxial cable that can be used to form the main Ethernet bus. The first type of coaxial cable specified for Ethernet was a relatively thick 50-ohm cable, which is normally colored yellow and is commonly referred to as "thick" Ethernet. This cable has a marking every 2.5 meters to indicate where a tap should occur, if one is required to connect a station to the main cable at a particular location. These markings represent the minimum distance one tap must be separated from another on an Ethernet network. The outer insulation or jacket of the yellow-colored cable is constructed using PVC. A second popular type of 50-ohm cable has a Teflon jacket and is colored orange-brown. The Teflon jacket coax is used for plenum-required installations in air-handling spaces, referred to as plenums, to satisfy fire regulations. When installing a thick coaxial segment the cable should be rolled from a common cable spool or cable spools manufactured at the same time, referred to as a similar cable lot, to minimize irregularities between cables. Under the Ethernet specifications when the use of cable from different lots cannot be avoided, cable sections should be used that are either 23.4 m, 70.2 m, or 117 m in length. Those cable lengths minimize the possibility of excessive signal reflections occurring due to variances in the minor differences in cable produced by different vendors or from different cable lots from the same vendor.

A second type of coaxial cable used with Ethernet is smaller and more flexible; however, it is capable of providing a transmission distance only one-third of that obtainable on thick cable. This lighter and more flexible cable is referred to as "thin" Ethernet and also has an impedance of 50 ohms. When the IEEE standardized Ethernet, the thick coaxial cable–based network was assigned the designation 10BASE-5, while the network that uses the thinner cable was assigned the designator 10BASE-2. Later in this chapter we will examine IEEE 802.3 networks under which 10BASE-5, 10BASE-2, and other Ethernet network designators are defined.

Two of the major advantages of thin Ethernet over thick cable are its cost and its use of BNC connectors. Thin Ethernet is significantly less expensive than thick Ethernet. Thick Ethernet requires connections via taps, whereas the use of thin Ethernet permits connections to the bus via industry standard BNC connectors that form T-junctions.

Transceiver and Transceiver Cable

Transceiver is a shortened form of *transmitter-receiver*. This device contains electronics to transmit and receive signals carried by the coaxial cable.

The transceiver contains a tap that, when pushed against the coaxial cable, penetrates the cable and makes contact with the core of the cable. Ethernet transceivers are used for broadband transmission on a coaxial cable and usually include a removable tap assembly. The latter enables vendors to manufacture transceivers that can operate on thick and thin coaxial cable, enabling network installers to change only the tap instead of the entire device and eliminating the necessity to purchase multiple types of transceivers to accommodate different media requirements. In books and technical literature the transceiver, its tap, and its housing are often referred to as the *medium attachment unit (MAU)*.

The transceiver is responsible for carrier detection and collision detection. When a collision is detected during a transmission, the transceiver places a special signal, known as a *jam*, on the cable. This signal, described in Chapter 4, is of sufficient duration to propagate down the network bus and inform all of the other transceivers attached to the bus node that a collision has occurred.

The cable that connects the interface board to the transceiver is known as the *transceiver cable*. This cable can be up to 50 meters (165 feet) in length and contains five individually shielded twisted pairs. Two pairs are used for data in and data out, and two pairs are used for control signals in and out. The remaining pair, which is not always used, permits the power from the computer in which the interface board is inserted to power the transceiver.

Because collision detection is a critical part of the CSMA/CD access protocol, the original version of Ethernet was modified to inform the interface board that the transceiver collision circuitry is operational. This modification resulted in each transceiver's sending a signal to the attached interface board after every transmission, informing the board that the transceiver's collision circuitry is operational. This signal is sent by the transceiver over the collision pair of the transceiver cable and must start within 0.6 microseconds after each frame is transmitted. The duration of the signal can vary between 0.5 and 1.5 microseconds. Known as the *signal quality error* and also referred to as the *SQE* or *heartbeat*, this signal is supported by Ethernet Version 2.0, published as a standard in 1982, and by the IEEE 802.3 standard. Although the heartbeat (SQE) is between the transceiver and the system to which it is attached, under the IEEE 802.3 standard transceivers attached to a repeater must have their heartbeat disabled.

The SQE signal is simply a delayed response by a few bit times to the transmission of each frame, informing the interface card that everything is working normally. Because the SQE signal only flows from the transceiver back to the interface card, it does not delay packet transmission nor does it flow onto the network. Today most transceivers have a switch or jumper that enables the SQE signal, commonly labeled SQE Test, to be disabled. Because repeaters must monitor signals in real time and cannot use the Ethernet time gap of 9.6 ms between frames (which we will discuss later in this book), this means that they are not capable of recognizing a heartbeat signal. It should be noted that a twisted-pair 10BASE-T Ethernet hub is also a repeater. If you fail to disable the SQE Test signal, the repeater electronics to include hub ports will misinterpret the signal as a collision. This will result in the transmission of a jam signal on all hub ports other than the port receiving the SQE Test signal, significantly degrading network performance.

Interface Board

The *interface board*, or *network interface card (NIC)*, is inserted into an expansion slot within a computer and is responsible for transmitting frames to and receiving frames from the transceiver. This board contains several special chips, including a controller chip that assembles data into an Ethernet frame and computes the cyclic redundancy check used for error detection. Thus, this board is also referred to as an *Ethernet controller*.

Most Ethernet interface boards contain a DB-15 connector for connecting the board to the transceiver. Once thin Ethernet cabling became popular, many manufacturers made their interface boards with both DB-15 and BNC connectors. The latter was used to permit the interface board to be connected to a thin Ethernet cable through the use of a T-connector. Figure 3.2 illustrates the rear panel of a network interface card containing both DB-15 and BNC connectors. With the development of twisted-pair-based Ethernet, such as 10BASE-T, modern Ethernet interface boards, which are commonly referred to as network interface cards (NICs), also include an RJ-45 connector to accommodate a connection to twisted-wire-based networks.

Cabling Restrictions

Under the Ethernet standard developed by Xerox, Digital Equipment Corporation, and Intel Corporation, a thick coaxial cable is permitted a maximum length of 500 meters (1640 feet). Multiple cable segments can be joined together through the use of repeaters; however, the maximum cable distance between two transceivers is limited to 2.5 km (8200 feet), and no more than four repeaters can be traversed on any path between transceivers.

Each thick trunk cable segment must be terminated with what is known as an *N-series connector* on each end of the cable. The terminator "terminates"

Figure 3.2 Ethernet interface board connectors. The first generation Ethernet interface boards (network interface cards) contain both DB-15 and BNC connectors to support the use of either thick or thin coaxial cable. A second generation of interface cards included an RJ-45 connector to Accommodate a connection to twisted-wire-based networks.

the network and blocks electrical interference from flowing onto what would otherwise be exposed cable. One N-series connector also serves as a ground, when used with an attached grounding wire that can be connected to the middle screw of a dual AC electrical power outlet.

Figure 3.3 illustrates a thick Ethernet cable segment after an installer fastened N-series plugs to each cable end. This is normally accomplished after the desired length of coaxial cable is routed to form the required network bus. Next, an N-series terminator connector is fastened onto one N-series plug, while an N-series terminator with ground wire is fastened onto the N-series plug at the opposite end of the cable segment.

In addition, as previously mentioned, attachments to the common bus must be separated by multiples of 2.5 meters. The latter cabling restriction prevents reflections caused by taps in the main cable from adding up in phase and being mistaken by one transceiver for another's transmission. For the total network, up to 1024 attachments are allowed, including all cable sections connected through the use of repeaters; however, no more than 100 transceivers can be on any one cable segment.

Repeaters

A *repeater* is a device that can be used to connect two network segments together to form a larger local area network topology. The repeater receives,

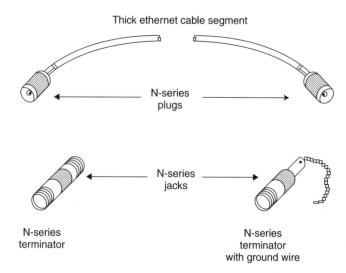

Figure 3.3 Each Ethernet thick coaxial cable segment has N-series plugs on each end. They are terminated through the use of N-series terminators, one of which contains a ground wire or ground wire connection.

amplifies, and retransmits signals, restoring the symmetry and position of each signal. Signal amplification results in the restoration of the original amplitude characteristics of the data signal. The restoration of signal symmetry results in each output signal pulse matching the shape of the originally transmitted signal. The last function performed by a repeater is the restoration of the signal position. More formally referred to as *retiming*, this repeater function results in the data signal output in its correct position by time, removing any prior shift or displacement in the placement of the received signal. That shift or displacement is known as *jitter*, while a very small shift or displacement of a transmitted signal is referred to as a *wander*.

Because a repeater operates at the physical layer, it is transparent to data and simply regenerates signals. Figure 3.4 illustrates the use of a repeater to connect two Ethernet cable segments. As indicated, a transceiver is taped to each cable segment to be connected, and the repeater is cabled to the transceiver. When used to connect cable segments, a repeater counts as one station on each connected segment. Thus, a segment capable of supporting up to 100 stations can support only 99 additional stations when a repeater is used to connect cable segments. Although not shown, each cable segment is terminated at each end with an N-series terminator and grounded at one end of one segment.

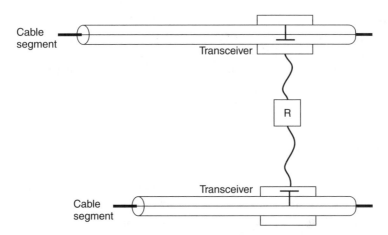

Figure 3.4 Using a repeater. Cable segments can be joined together by a repeater to expand the network. The repeater counts as a station on each cable segment.

In examining Figure 3.4, note that any data traffic carried on the top cable segment will be repeated onto the lower cable segment. Similarly, any cable traffic transported on the lower cable segment will be repeated onto the upper cable segment. Thus, the use of a repeater simply provides a mechanism to extend transmission between cable segments and should not be confused with the use of a bridge that normally isolates traffic to different segments unless data is destined to a station on a different segment.

The 5-4-3 Rule

When Ethernet was developed it was recognized that the use of repeaters to connect segments to form a larger network would result in pulse regeneration delays that could adversely affect the probability of collisions. Thus, a limit was required on the number of repeaters that could be used to connect segments together. This limit in turn limited the number of segments that could be interconnected. A further limitation involved the number of populated segments that could be joined together, because stations on populated segments generate traffic that can cause collisions, whereas nonpopulated segments are more suitable for extending the length of a network of interconnected segments. A result of the preceding was the "5-4-3 rule." That rule specifies that a maximum of five Ethernet segments can be joined through the use of a maximum of four repeaters. In actuality, this part of the Ethernet rule really means that no two communicating Ethernet nodes can be more than two repeaters away from one another. Finally, the "three" in the rule denotes the maximum number of Ethernet segments that can be populated. Figure 3.5 illustrates an example of the 5-4-3 rule for the original bus-based Ethernet. Note that this rule is also applicable to hub-based Ethernet LANs, such as 10BASE-T, which we will examine later in this chapter.

3.2 IEEE 802.3 Networks

The IEEE 802.3 standard is based on Ethernet. However, it has several significant differences, particularly its support of multiple physical layer options, which include 50- and 75-ohm coaxial cable, unshielded twisted-pair wire, and the use of optical fiber. Other differences between various types of IEEE 802.3 networks and Ethernet include the data rates supported by some 802.3 networks, their methods of signaling, the maximum cable segment lengths permitted before the use of repeaters, and their network topologies.

Network Names

The standards that define IEEE 802.3 networks have been given names that generally follow the form "s type l." Here, s refers to the speed of the network in Mbps, *type* is BASE for baseband and BROAD for broadband, and *l* refers to the maximum segment length in 100-meter multiples. Thus, 10BASE-5 refers to an IEEE 802.3 baseband network that operates at 10 Mbps and has a maximum segment length of 500 meters. One exception to this general form

Figure 3.5 The 5-4-3 rule. Under the 5-4-3 Ethernet rule a maximum of five segments can be connected through the use of four repeaters, with a maximum of three segments populated with nodes.

is 10BASE-T, which is the name for an IEEE 802.3 network that operates at 10 Mbps using UTP wire.

Although recently introduced high-speed Ethernet networks do not exactly follow the preceding form, they continue to resemble prior naming conventions. For example, 100BASE-TX, 100BASE-T4, and 100BASE-FX represent three physical layer versions of the Fast Ethernet standard. Each version operates at 100 Mbps and uses baseband signaling; however, the suffix now represents different types of media instead of a maximum segment length in 100-meter multiples.

Table 3.1 compares the operating characteristics of five IEEE 802.3 networks with Ethernet. Note that the comparisons indicated in Table 3.1 do not consider differences in the composition of Ethernet and IEEE 802.3 frames. Those differences preclude compatibility between Ethernet and IEEE 802.3 networks, and are discussed in detail in Chapter 4.

Also note that Table 3.1 does not include IEEE 802.3μ (Fast Ethernet) and IEEE 802.12 (100VG-AnyLAN) Ethernet networks nor any of the emerging Gigabit Ethernet networks specified under the IEEE 802.z standard. The first standard actually represents three standards for 100-Mbps CSMA/CD operations. The second standard supports 100-Mbps operations using a demand-priority scheme in place of the CSMA/CD access protocol. Fast Ethernet, 100VG-AnyLAN, and Gigabit Ethernet networks are covered at the end of this chapter when we turn our attention to high-speed Ethernet networks. Thus, the networks compared in Table 3.1 are limited to a 10-Mbps operating rate.

10BASE-5

As indicated in Table 3.1, the IEEE 10BASE-5 standard resembles the original Ethernet more closely than the other 802.3 standards. In fact, an examination of the operating characteristics of Ethernet and 10BASE-5 indicates that these networks are exactly the same. Similarities between Ethernet and 10BASE-5 include the use of DB-15 connectors on interface boards and transceivers (MAUs) and the termination of 10BASE-5 cable segments with N-series terminators.

However, there are differences in the frame format used by each network, and these differences preclude compatibility between Ethernet and all IEEE 802.3 standards. In addition, under the IEEE 802.3 specification, several network components have different names.

Figure 3.6 illustrates the major terminology changes between Ethernet and the IEEE 802.3 10BASE-5 network. These changes are in the media interface:

TABLE 3.1 Ethernet and IEEE 802.3 1-Mbps and 10-Mbps Network Characteristics

Operational Characteristics	Ethernet	10BASE-5	10BASE-2	1BASE-5	10BASE-T	10BROAD-36
Operating rate (Mbps)	10	10	10	1	10	10
Access protocol	CSMA/CD	CSMA/CD	CSMA/CD	CSMA/CD	CSMA/CD	CSMA/CD
Type of signaling	Baseband	Baseband	Baseband	Baseband	Baseband	Broadband
Data encoding	Manchester	Manchester	Manchester	Manchester	Manchester	Manchester
Maximum segment length (meters)	500	500	185	250	100	1,800
Stations/segment	100	100	30	12/hub	12/hub	100
Medium	50-ohm coaxial (thick)	50-ohm coaxial (thick)	50-ohm coaxial (thin)	Unshielded twisted pair	Unshielded twisted pair	75-ohm coaxial
Topology	Bus	Bus	Bus	Star	Star	Bus

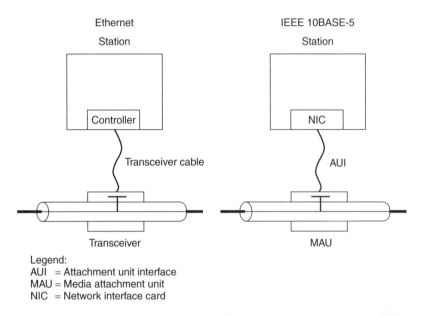

Figure 3.6 Ethernet and 10BASE-5 media interface differences. Terminology changes under the IEEE 10BASE-5 standard resulted in the transceiver being called the *media attachment unit*, while the transceiver cable is known as the *attachment unit interface.*

the transceiver cable is referred to as the *attachment unit interface (AUI)*, and the transceiver, including its tap and housing, is referred to as the *medium attachment unit (MAU)*. The Ethernet controller, also known as an interface board, is now known as the *network interface card (NIC)*. Other similarities between Ethernet and 10BASE-5 include the use of DB-15 connectors on network interface cards and MAUs and the termination of 10BASE-5 cable segments with the use of N-series 50-ohm terminators at each cable segment end. In addition, the 802.3 standard requires one end of the thick coax segment to be grounded for electrical safety. All other metal portions on the coax should be insulated and fastened in place using plastic or other nonmetallic cable ties to avoid accidentally connecting to the electrical ground.

The actual connection between the NIC and the MAU is limited to a maximum of 50 meters (164 feet). The 15-pin AUI connector is a socket (female) receptacle while the connector on the MAU is a 15-pin AUI connector with a pin (male) receptacle. The AUI cable consists of four pairs of shielded twisted wires, three of which transport data signals while one pair carries 12-volt DC power from the Ethernet interface to the MAU. The three data signal wire pairs include transmit data that go from the Ethernet interface to the network, receive data that carry data from the network to the interface, and a collision indicator signal wire pair that transports collision indications to the interface.

Although a standard AUI cable is approximately 0.4 inches in diameter and has a limited degree of flexibility, many cable manufacturers market thinner and more flexible cable. However, the trade-off when using such cable is a lower allowable cabling length from the interface to the MAU, because thinner cable has a higher amount of signal attenuation.

Both the original Ethernet and the IEEE 802.3 10BASE-5 standards support a data rate of 10 Mbps and a maximum cable segment length of 500 meters. 10BASE-5, like Ethernet, requires a minimum spacing of 2.5 meters between MAUs and supports a maximum of five segments in any end-to-end path through the traversal of up to four repeaters in any path. Within any path, no more than three cable segments can be *populated*—have stations attached to the cable—and the maximum number of attachments per segment is limited to 100. As previously discussed in our coverage of Ethernet, these restrictions are sometimes referred to as the 5-4-3 rule, referencing a maximum of five segments linked through four repeaters, with no more than three segments populated.

Advantages and Disadvantages

Similar to any technology there are various advantages and disadvantages associated with the use of a 10BASE-5 network. Major advantages associated with the use of 10BASE-5 include the span distance of 500 m (1650 feet), which makes it extremely useful for connecting multiple locations within a building without the use of repeaters, its ability to span up to 2.5 km (8200 feet) by connecting multiple segments together to form an extended backbone, and its heavily shielded media, making it suitable for use in electrically noisy environments.

The thick coax required by 10BASE-5 makes it a very inflexible network where the movement of a node can be difficult, if not impossible, to accomplish without a major restructuring of the network. In addition, the failure of any part of the cable or any node can cause the entire network to fail, resulting in 10BASE-T being fault-intolerant. This makes troubleshooting a failure, difficult and time-consuming, because each node and its connection has to be checked until the point of failure is located. A fourth disadvantage is the fact that power from different sources results in a difference in voltage between points on the network. This voltage differential causes current to flow through the shields of the cable, which can cause noise to be introduced into the center conductor, a situation referred to as creating a ground loop. 10BASE-5 networks are very susceptible to ground loops, which represent a weakness of the technology. Although common during the early 1980s, most new network requirements only consider 10BASE-5 as a backbone to connect multiple 10BASE-T hubs to create one large network as illustrated in Figure 3.7.

10BASE-2

10BASE-2 is a smaller and less expensive version of 10BASE-5. This standard uses a thinner RG-58 coaxial cable, more commonly referred to as RG-58 A/U or RG-58 C/U, thus earning the names of *cheapnet* and *thinnet*, as well as *thin Ethernet*. Although 10BASE-2 cable is both less expensive and easier to use than 10BASE-5 cable, it cannot carry signals as far as 10BASE-5 cable.

The coaxial cable used by 10BASE-2 is approximately 0.5 cm or 3/16 inch in diameter. This cable must have a 50-ohm impedance rating and a stranded center conductor. Although those specifications are met by RG-58 A/U and RG-58 C/U cable, it is important to note that vendors sometimes use those nomenclatures for cables with impedance ratings different from 50 ohms. Thus, it is important to verify both the nomenclature and impedance rating of the coaxial cable.

Figure 3.7 Using 10BASE-5 as a backbone. The use of 10BASE-5 as a backbone enables 10BASE-T hubs to be located further from one another than if they were wired together using unshielded twisted-pair cable.

Under the 10BASE-2 standard, the maximum cable segment length is reduced to 185 meters (607 feet), with a maximum of 30 stations per segment. This length limitation is often confused by persons that assume the *2* in the network nomenclature allows a 200-meter cable length. Perhaps the IEEE should have used the designator 10BASE-1.85, but it used 10BASE-2 even though the cable length limit is 185 meters.

Unlike 10BASE-5 that has spacing rules for MAUs, there are none for 10BASE-2. However, because the minimum length of coaxial cable required for a 10BASE-2 segment cannot be shorter than 0.5 meters (1.64 feet), this indirectly provides a minimum spacing between MAU connections of 0.5 meters.

Another difference between 10BASE-5 and 10BASE-2 concerns the integration of transceiver electronics into the network interface card under the 10BASE-2 standard. This permits the NIC to be directly cabled to the main trunk cable. In fact, under 10BASE-2 the Thin Ethernet cable is routed directly to each workstation location and routed through a BNC T-connector, one end of which is pressed into the BNC connector built into the rear of the network interface card.

The term BNC is considered by many persons as a mnemonic for "Bayonet Nut Connector," as you must push and turn one connector to mate with another. The mating side of BNC connectors always has the same dimensions; however, the side that connects to the cable can have different diameters based upon the type of coaxial cable that the connector is designed to support and the jacket (PVC, Teflon, etc.) of the cable.

Figure 3.8 illustrates the cabling of a one-segment 10BASE-2 network, which can support a maximum of 30 nodes or stations. BNC barrel connectors can be used to join two lengths of thin 10BASE-2 cable to form a cable segment, as long as the joined cable does not exceed 185 meters in length. A BNC terminator must be attached to each end of each 10BASE-2 cable segment. One of the two terminators on each segment contains a ground wire that should be connected to a ground source, such as the screw on an electrical outlet.

Station 1   Station 2   Station 3   Station 30

Figure 3.8 Cabling a 10BASE-2 network. A 10BASE-2 cable segment cannot exceed 185 meters and is limited to supporting up to 30 nodes or stations.

The Thinnet Tap

The coaxial cable that forms the network bus must be routed directly into each T-connector, which in turn is mated to a node or station. This means it is not possible to locate a node away from the BNC T-connector by connecting a single coaxial stub or drop cable between the T-connector and the node, limiting the flexibility of this network unless you employ a thinnet tap. Otherwise, the use of a single coaxial drop cable can result in the occurrence of signal reflections that can generate transmission errors.

A thinnet tap was developed by vendors to enable individual nodes to be located at a distance from the main 10BASE-2 network cable. This tap consists of a tap assembly that connects to the main coaxial 10BASE-2 cable and a drop cable with two coaxial cables and the equivalent of a BNC T-adapter. When the drop cable is connected to a tap assembly it triggers a switch in the tap, which electrically connects each side of the tap to one of the cables in the drop cable. This action loops the signal from the top of the node and back to the other side of the tap, resulting in an unbroken network, which from an electrical perspective, is the same as connecting the node via a conventional BNC T-connector. Figure 3.9 illustrates a schematic diagram of a tap assembly.

Multifunction Transceivers

Because of the similarities between 10BASE-5 and 10BASE-2, several vendors introduced transceivers that support both thick and thin coaxial cable. Figure 3.10 illustrates the Universal Ethernet Transceiver manufactured by

Figure 3.9 A 10BASE-2 tap assembly. Through the use of a 10BASE-2 tap assembly, it becomes possible to locate nodes at a distance from the backbone network.

Figure 3.10 Universal Ethernet Transceiver. The Universal Ethernet Transceiver manufactured by Transition Engineering of Edina, Minnesota, supports both 10BASE-2 and 10BASE-5 coaxial cable connections. (Photograph courtesy of Transition Engineering, Inc.)

Transition Engineering of Edina, Minnesota. The transceiver illustrated in the upper left corner of Figure 3.10 is a 10BASE-2 transceiver. It can be converted into a 10BASE-5 transceiver with an adapter that converts the BNC on the thinnet transceiver into a *vampire* tap–type connector, as illustrated in the lower right corner of Figure 3.10.

Grounding

Depending upon the type of coaxial-based Ethernet installed, you may require the cable to be grounded. The 10BASE-5 specification indicates that the coaxial cable should be grounded at one, and only one, point. In comparison, the 10BASE-2 specification indicates that thin coaxial cable may be grounded at one, and only one, point.

Regardless of the type of coaxial cable–based network you are using, it is normally a good idea to ground the cable at one location. Doing so alleviates the potential for static electricity to build up. In addition, many local electrical codes require network cabling to be grounded at one location. When grounding a coaxial-based network, it is also important to ensure you do so at only one location. Otherwise, multiple grounds on an Ethernet segment can result in a risk to equipment, shock to people, and network errors.

You can ground a network segment through the use of a coaxial cable terminator with ground wire, similar to the terminator illustrated in the lower right portion of Figure 3.3. If you install a repeater on one end of a segment, it is important to note that most repeaters can be set up to ground or *not* ground. Thus, you may be able to use a repeater to ground a segment. It's important to note that a 10BASE-2 network will have a 50 ohm terminator at each end. Only one of the terminators should be grounded. If you ground both, although the network will not completely fail, this will result in an increased error rate as well as slow data transfer on the network.

Expanding a 10BASE-2 Network

You can increase the number of stations that can be attached to a 10BASE-2 network, the total network distance, or both through the use of repeaters. As with a 10BASE-5 network, between any two nodes there can be up to five cable segments connected through four repeaters. Like a 10BASE-5 segment, each end of every 10BASE-2 segment must be terminated with a 50-ohm terminator, with one end of each segment grounded.

Figure 3.11 illustrates an expanded 10BASE-2 network consisting of three populated cable segments; two segments are used to extend the network span by simply connecting two repeaters. The latter segments are also commonly referred to as *interrepeater cable segments* (IRCS). Each cable segment shown in Figure 3.11 requires one MAU connection to a repeater. Because there are a maximum of 30 stations or MAU connections per segment, this means that segments connected by a repeater are limited to actually supporting 29 workstations.

Two-Tier Cabling   You can further expand a 10BASE-2 network by establishing a two-tier method of cabling. Under this cabling concept, the upper tier can consist of up to 30 repeaters, connected to one another through the use of interrepeater cable segments. These form a backbone network without direct station attachments, so populated segments on the backbone have to be connected on each segment end to a repeater. The lower tier then consists of repeaters connected to populated cable segments, with the lower-tier repeater cabled to the upper-tier repeater to obtain a connection to the backbone. Figure 3.12 illustrates the use of a two-tier cabling hierarchy that can be used to extend a 10BASE-2 network. As in Figure 3.11, between any pair of workstations there can be a maximum of five cable segments and four

Figure 3.11 Expanding a 10BASE-2 network. Up to five cable segments connected through the use of four repeaters can be used to expand a 10BASE-2 network.

repeaters. Of the five cable segments, up to three can be populated, and each populated segment is limited to a maximum of 30 connections, of which one or two will be repeater connections depending upon where the cable segment resides with respect to the interconnected network. In addition, the maximum distance between any two stations is limited to 100 meters (328 feet), while the minimum distance between BNC T-connectors is 0.5 meters (1.6 feet).

Advantages and Disadvantages

Similar to a 10BASE-5 network, the use of coaxial cable for a 10BASE-2 network makes it suitable for use in locations that require a high degree of immunity from electrical noise. Two additional advantages associated with 10BASE-2 include the fact that it is easy to establish because devices are daisy-chained together, and it is relatively inexpensive. Disadvantages of 10BASE-2 are also similar to the disadvantages associated with 10BASE-5. That is, a 10BASE-2 network is difficult to reconfigure; a single device failure or cable

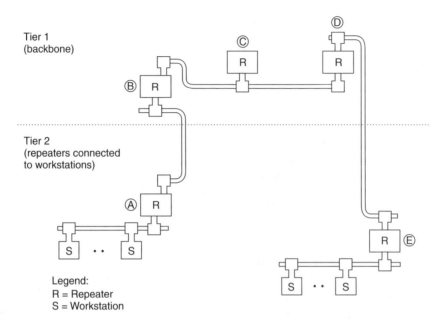

Tier 1
(backbone)

Tier 2
(repeaters connected
to workstations)

Legend:
R = Repeater
S = Workstation

Figure 3.12 Two-tier thin Ethernet 10BASE-2 network. A two-tier network permits expansion of a 10BASE-2 network by adding another level of repeaters to the backbone. The segment between repeaters B, C, and D is considered to be populated, because repeater C is counted as one connection on the segment.

break can bring down the entire network, making it fault-intolerant, and the isolation of a failure can be very time-consuming due to the need to check every device and cable section.

Normally 10BASE-2 is well-suited for small networks that are relatively static with respect to node relocations. Similar to 10BASE-5, the use of a 10BASE-2 network is often used as a backbone technology for interconnecting 10BASE-T hubs that must be located at cable distances beyond the range of that twisted-pair network. Although a 10BASE-2 backbone length is considerably less than that of a 10BASE-5 backbone, thinnet cable is cheaper and easier to install, making it popular for backbones that must span distances up to 185 meters per segment.

Combining 10BASE-5 and 10BASE-2 Networks

There are many situations in which a combination of thick and thin coaxial cable can better satisfy your cabling requirements than the exclusive use of one type of cable. For example, you may have several clusters of terminals located in different geographically separated areas within a large office complex. Instead of connecting the two clusters through the use of several thin 10BASE-2 cable segments and multiple repeaters, it may be easier to install one or more thick 10BASE-5 cable segments to serve as a backbone network for attachment to two 10BASE-2 cable segments. Thus, the ability of thick coaxial cable to support a longer transmission distance can eliminate or reduce the number of repeaters required in a combined network. In addition, a network built using thin 10BASE-2 cable, which was originally designed for a network span under 925 meters, cannot cover greater distances without mixing network media. Thus, the use of thick coaxial cable may provide the span of coverage not obtainable from the exclusive use of thin coaxial cable.

When thick and thin coaxial cable are combined to form a single cable segment, you must consider the length of each type of cable you anticipate using to develop a combined media cable segment. If the segment is entirely made up of thin cable, its maximum length is 607 feet, while a cable segment made up of thick cable has a maximum length of 1640 feet. Thus, a combined thin and thick cable segment should vary in length between 607 and 1640 feet. If L represents the length of a combined media cable you wish to construct, you can use the following equation to determine the maximum length of thin cable:

$$\text{thin cable} = \frac{1640 - L \text{ feet}}{3.28}$$

For example, suppose you want to construct a cable segment 1400 feet long. Then, the maximum length of thin 10BASE-2 cable you can use becomes:

$$\frac{1640 - 1400}{3.28} = 73 \text{ feet}$$

Thus, you could use 73 feet of 10BASE-2 cable and route that cable through T-connectors, which are fastened to the BNC connectors on the rear of network interface cards. Then, you could use thick cable for the remaining 1327 feet of cable required in the cable segment.

Figure 3.13 shows an example of a combined 10BASE-5 and 10BASE-2 cable segment that connects two groups of stations located at opposite ends of a building without using repeaters. At one end of the building, 10BASE-2 cable is used with BNC T-connectors to connect a large number of stations clustered together. At the other end of the building, we will assume there are only a few stations. Thus, we would use 10BASE-5 cable and connect each station to the thick cable through the use of an MAU (transceiver) and an AUI (transceiver cable).

Figure 3.13   Combined 10BASE-5 and 10BASE-2 cable segment. A combined thick and thin coaxial segment can be used to economically connect a group of stations clustered in one area of a building to a few stations located a relatively long distance away from the cluster.

In examining Figure 3.13, note that the end of the thin cable is terminated with a BNC terminator. The connection of thick and thin cable is accomplished through the use of an N-series jack to BNC jack, while the thick cable is terminated with an N-series terminator that has a ground wire.

10BROAD-36

10BROAD-36 is the only broadband network based on the CSMA/CD access protocol standardized by the IEEE. Unlike a baseband network, in which Manchester-encoded signals are placed directly onto the cable, the 10BROAD-36 standard requires the use of radio frequency (RF) modems. Those modems modulate nonreturn to zero (NRZ)–encoded signals for transmission on one channel at a specified frequency, and they demodulate received signals by listening for tones on another channel at a different frequency.

Cable

A 10BROAD-36 network is constructed with a 75-ohm coaxial cable, similar to the cable used in modern cable television (CATV) systems. Under the IEEE 802.3 broadband standard, either single or dual cables can be used to construct a network. If a single cable is used, the end of the cable (referred to as the *headend*) must be terminated with a frequency translator. That translator converts the signals received on one channel to the frequency assigned to the other channel, retransmitting the signal at the new frequency. Because the frequency band for a transmitted signal is below the frequency band 10BROAD-36 receivers scan, we say the frequency translator *upconverts* a transmitted signal and retransmits it for reception by other stations on the network. If two cables are used, the headend simply functions as a relay point, transferring the signal received on one cable onto the second cable.

Advantages

A broadband transmission system has several advantages over a baseband system. Two of the primary advantages of broadband are its ability to support multiple transmissions occurring on independent frequency bands simultaneously, and its ability to support a tree structure topology carrying multiple simultaneous transmissions. Using independent frequency bands, you can establish several independent networks. In fact, each network can be used to carry voice, data, and video over a common cable. As for topology, broadband permits the use of a tree structure network, such as the structure shown in Figure 3.14. In this example, the top of the tree would be the headend; it would contain a frequency translator, which would regenerate signals received at one frequency back onto the cable at another predefined frequency.

Disadvantages

Like the 10BASE-5 network, the 10BROAD-36 system uses an MAU. However, this MAU is more intelligent than a 10BASE-5 MAU, as it is responsible for modifying the 802.3 frame slightly for broadband transmission via a modulator. These frame modifications include the scrambling of the preamble, so that the modulation of the preamble does not result in a loss of clocking, and the addition of a postamble to each frame. The latter assists in the detection of the end-of-frame. Although a 10BASE-5 AUI cable can be connected to a 10BROAD-36 MAU, a 10BROAD-36 MAU obviously cannot be used with a 10BASE-5 network. However, the design specifications of the 10BROAD-36 network enable this network to support the connection of CSMA/CD

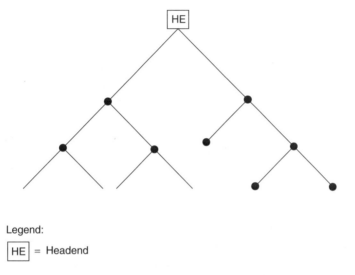

Legend:

| HE | = Headend

Figure 3.14 Broadband tree topology support. The headend receives transmissions at one frequency and regenerates the received signals back onto the network at another predefined frequency.

baseband equipment, and also provide a large degree of compatibility and interoperability with baseband systems.

The higher noise immunity of 75-ohm coaxial cable permits a 10BROAD-36 network to span 3600 meters, making this medium ideal for linking buildings on a campus. In addition, the ability of 10BROAD-36 to share channel space on a 75-ohm coaxial cable permits organizations that have an existing CATV system, such as one used for video security, to use that cable for part or all of their broadband CSMA/CD network. Although these advantages can be significant, the cost associated with more intelligent MAUs and RF modems has limited the use of broadband primarily to campus environments that require an expanded network span. In addition, the rapid development and acceptance of 10BASE-T and later twisted-pair-based Fast Ethernet and the decline in the cost of fiber cable to extend the span of 10BASE-T networks have severely limited what many people once anticipated as a promising future for 10BROAD-36 networks.

1BASE-5

The 1BASE-5 standard was based on AT&T's low-cost CSMA/CD network, known as StarLan. Thus, 1BASE-5 is commonly referred to as StarLan, although AT&T uses that term to refer to CSMA/CD networks operating at both 1 and 10 Mbps using unshielded twisted-pair cable. The latter is considered the predecessor to 10BASE-T.

The 1BASE-5 standard differs significantly from Ethernet and 10BASE-5 standards in its use of media and topology, and in its operating rate. The 1BASE-5 standard operates at 1 Mbps and uses UTP wiring in a star topology; all stations are wired to a hub, which is known as a *multiple-access unit* (MAU). To avoid confusion with the term *media access unit*, which also has the same abbreviation, we will refer to this wiring concentrator as a *hub*.

Topology

Each station in a 1BASE-5 network contains an NIC, cabled via UTP on a point-to-point basis to a hub port. The hub is responsible for repeating signals and detecting collisions. As we will shortly note, this cabling configuration represents a topology supported by two succeeding versions of Ethernet, 10BASE-T and 100BASE-T networks.

The maximum cabling distance from a station to a hub is 250 meters; up to five hubs can be cascaded together to produce a maximum network span of 2500 meters. The highest-level hub is known as the *header hub*, and it is responsible for broadcasting news of collisions to all other hubs in the network. These hubs, which are known as *intermediate hubs*, are responsible for reporting all collisions to the header hub.

Usage

AT&T's 1-Mbps StarLan network, along with other 1BASE-5 systems, initially received a degree of acceptance for use in small organizations. However, the introduction of 10BASE-T, which provided an operating rate ten times that obtainable under 1BASE-5, severely limited the further acceptance of 1BASE-5 networks.

The growth in the acceptance of 10BASE-T resulted in economies of scale in the manufacture of 10BASE-T hubs and network interface cards. This, in turn, enabled vendors to match or exceed price cuts of other vendors. One key result of this situation was the ability of end users to obtain a low-cost, high-performance local area networking capability through the use of 10BASE-T equipment. Needless to say, 10BASE-T became the preferred network technology of both small and large organizations during the early 1990s, and it essentially replaced the use of 1BASE-5.

10BASE-T

In the late 1980s, a committee of the IEEE recognized the requirement of organizations for transmitting Ethernet at a 10-Mbps operating rate over low-cost and readily available unshielded twisted-pair cable. Although several vendors had already introduced equipment that permitted Ethernet signaling via UTP cabling, such equipment was based on proprietary designs and was not interoperable. Thus, a new task of the IEEE was to develop a standard for 802.3 networks operating at 10 Mbps using UTP cable. The resulting standard was approved by the IEEE as 802.3i in September 1990, and is more commonly known as 10BASE-T, with the *T* referencing the use of twisted-pair wire.

UTP Use

The 10BASE-T standard supports an operating rate of 10 Mbps at a distance of up to 100 meters (328 feet) over 100 ohm Unshielded Twisted-Pair (UTP) cable without the use of a repeater. The UTP cable requires two pairs of twisted wire. One pair is used for transmitting, while the other pair is used for receiving. Each pair of wires is twisted together, and each twist is 180 degrees. Any electromagnetic interference (EMI) or radio frequency interference (RFI) is therefore received 180 degrees out of phase; this theoretically cancels out EMI and RFI noise while leaving the network signal. In reality, the wire between twists acts as an antenna and receives noise. This noise reception resulted in a 100-meter cable limit, until repeaters were used to regenerate the signal.

Because UTP cable previously installed in commercial buildings contains either three or four wire pairs, the RJ-45 jack used with 10BASE-T has eight-pin connectors. However, 10BASE-T uses two pairs of wires, and thus only four pins are actually used. Table 3.2 compares the 10BASE-T pin numbers with the RJ-45 jack numbers and indicates the signal names of the pins used with 10BASE-T UTP cable.

Although 10BASE-T was designed to support transmission distances of up to 100 meters under the Electronic Industry Association/Telecommunications Industry Association (EIA/TIA) cabling standard (previously described in Chapter 2), the cabling distance consists of three segments. The first segment, which can be up to 90 meters in length, runs from a patch panel in a wiring closet to a wall plate in an office. The second and third segments, which can be up to a total of 10 meters in length, allow patch cables at each end of the link while restricting signal loss on the total of three interconnected segments. The actual cable standard defined by the EIA/TIA for 10BASE-T is based upon the signaling rate of the network and not the type of network. Under EIA/TIA

TABLE 3.2 10BASE-T Wiring Sequence

10BASE-T Pin #	RJ-45 Jack #	10BASE-T Signal Name
1	1	Transmit Data +
2	2	Transmit Data −
3	3	Receive Data +
—	4	Not used
—	5	Not used
6	6	Receive Data −
—	7	Not used
—	8	Not used

cable standards, which were described in Chapter 2, category 3 cable, which provides support for a signaling rate up to 16 MHz, must be used in a 10BASE-T network. However, it is quite common for most organizations installing 10BASE-T today to use category 5 cabling, which supports transmission up to 100 MHz. This allows an organization to upgrade to a higher-speed LAN without having to replace their cabling infrastructure.

Link Integrity Test

Each version of Ethernet continuously monitors the received data path as a mechanism for determining if the link is operating correctly. To ensure the other station has a signal to receive even when there is no frame to receive, a link integrity test signal is transmitted during periods where there is no actual network traffic. Through the transmission of link test pulses a sufficient level of activity will occur on the receive data path to provide the receiver with the ability to check the integrity of the link.

Network Components

A 10BASE-T network can be constructed with network interface cards, UTP cable, and one or more hubs. Each NIC is installed in the expansion slot of a computer and wired on a point-to-point basis to a hub port. One exception to the preceding is built-in Ethernet chipsets now commonly added to laptop and notebook motherboards. When using such computers you only need to wire them to a hub port to become a participant on a network. When all of the ports on a hub are used, one hub can be connected to another to expand the network, resulting in a physical star, logical bus network structure.

The design of a 10BASE-T hub centric–based network provides a wiring scheme that can tolerate wiring failures much better than a bus-based coaxial cable network. For example, if a coaxial cable is broken at any point, the entire network segment fails. In comparison, the star-wiring topology of a 10BASE-T hub-based network eliminates the single point of failure of a common cable. This is because the failure of a cable between a hub port and a workstation will not affect other workstations. Although the hub is a central point of failure, it is normally a very reliable device, and you can probably expect numerous cable failures from everyday office activity to occur before a hub failure occurring.

Network Interface Cards   Most 10BASE-T network interface cards contain multiple connectors, which enable the card to be used with different types of 802.3 networks. For example, the NIC illustrated in Figure 3.15 includes an RJ-45 jack as well as BNC and DB-15 connectors. The RJ-45 jack supports the direct attachment of the NIC to a 10BASE-T network, while the BNC connector permits the NIC to be mated to a 10BASE-2 T-connector. The DB-15 connector enables the NIC to be cabled to a transceiver, and is more commonly referred to as the NIC's attachment unit interface (AUI) port.

Depending on the type of connectors built into your NIC, you may have several options to consider for connecting the NIC to a specific type of IEEE 802.3 network. For example, assume that your NIC is limited to supporting a thick or thin coaxial cable connection. In that case, you can still use the NIC to connect to a 10BASE-T network, using a transceiver similar to the one illustrated in Figure 3.16.

Figure 3.16 illustrates a 10BASE-T Ethernet transceiver manufactured by Transition Engineering, Inc. This transceiver allows you to connect an existing thick or thin 10BASE-5 or 10BASE-2 NIC's DB-15 AUI port to a 10BASE-T network. To do this, you would cable the NIC's DB-15 AUI port to the DB-15 connector at the left of the transceiver. Then, you would cable the transceiver to a hub port using UTP.

Hub   The wiring hub in a 10BASE-T network functions as a multiport repeater: it receives, retimes, and regenerates signals received from any attached station. The hub also functions as a filter: it discards severely distorted frames.

All hubs that conform to IEEE 10BASE-T specifications perform a core set of tasks in addition to receiving and regenerating signals. 10BASE-T hubs test

Figure 3.15 Multiple-media network interface card. Some multiple-media network interface cards, such as the one illustrated, support the direct attachment to UTP and thin coaxial cable, while the DB-15 connector permits the card to be cabled to an MAU connected to thick coaxial cable.

Figure 3.16 Transition Engineering 10BASE-T transceiver. With a 10BASE-T transceiver, you can connect existing thick or thin 10BASE-5 or 10BASE-2 NICs to a 10BASE-T network. (Photograph courtesy of Transition Engineering, Inc.)

each port connection, detect and handle excessive collisions, and ignore data that exceeds the maximum 802.3 frame size.

A 10BASE-T hub tests the integrity of the link from each hub port to a connected station by transmitting a special signal to the station. If the device doesn't respond, the hub will automatically shut down the port and may illuminate a status light-emitting diode (LED) to indicate the status of each port.

Hubs monitor, record, and count consecutive collisions that occur on each individual station link. Because an excessive number of consecutive collisions will prevent data transfer on all of the attached links, hubs are required to cut off or partition any link on which too many collisions have occurred. This partitioning enables the remainder of the network to operate in situations where a faulty NIC transmits continuously. Although the IEEE 802.3 standard does not specify a maximum number of consecutive collisions, the standard does specify that partitioning can be initiated only after 30 or more consecutive collisions occur. Thus, some hub vendors initiate partitioning when 31 consecutive collisions occur, while other manufacturers use a higher value.

Another operating function of 10BASE-T hubs is to ignore continuous data transmissions in which the frame length exceeds the maximum length of 1518 bytes. That length does not include the 8 byte preamble, which results in the maximum length of an Ethernet frame being 1518 bytes when inside an adapter and 1528 bytes when flowing on the wire. Such excessive length frames usually result from collisions and are referred to as *jabbering*. Most hubs also partition a jabbering port, and some hubs include a jabber indicator LED in addition to a partition status LED on each port.

Although a wiring hub is commonly referred to as a *concentrator*, this term is not technically correct. A 10BASE-T wiring hub is a self-contained unit that typically includes 8, 10, or 12 RJ-45 ports for direct connection to stations, and a BNC and/or DB-15 AUI port for expanding the hub to other network equipment. The BNC and AUI ports enable the 10BASE-T hub to be connected to 10BASE-2 and 10BASE-5 networks, respectively. For the latter, the AUI port is cabled to a 10BASE-5 MAU (transceiver), which is tapped into thick 10BASE-5 coaxial cable. One 10BASE-T hub can be connected to another with a UTP link between RJ-45 ports on each hub.

Figure 3.17 illustrates the connectors on a typical 10BASE-T hub. On some hubs, one RJ-45 jack is labeled uplink/downlink for use in cascading hubs, while other vendors permit any RJ-45 port to be used for connecting hubs.

Figure 3.17 10BASE-T hub connectors. In addition to 8, 10, or 12 RJ-45 modular jacks for terminal connections, most 10BASE-T hubs contain a BNC and DB-15 port to permit attachment to thin and thick backbone networks.

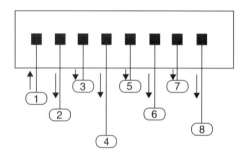

Figure 3.18 A 10BASE-T single hub–based network. A hub functions as a multiport repeater, regenerating data received on one port to all other ports.

Figure 3.18 illustrates the use of a 10BASE-T hub to form a single 10BASE-T network segment. Note that the twisted-pair connections allow workstations to be connected from different locations with respect to the hub, providing more cabling flexibility than bus-based Ethernet networks.

In examining Figure 3.18 note that station 1 is shown transmitting data to the hub. As previously mentioned, the hub functions as a repeater. Thus, it is shown retransmitting data received on one port back to all stations connected to other ports on the hub.

Wiring Requirements   There are two types of wiring used with 10BASE-T networks—straight-through and crossover. Each type of wiring is used to support a different type of equipment connection, thus it is important to understand where each type of wiring is used.

Straight-through Wiring   The wiring used with UTP cable for connecting a 10BASE-T hub to the network interface card consists of straight-through wiring. That is, each RJ-45 pin used by 10BASE-T would be routed directly from the connector at one end of the cable to the RJ-45 connector at the opposite end of the cable. Figure 3.19 indicates the 10BASE-T hub to NIC wiring requirements.

Crossover Wiring When one hub is connected to another, a special cable must be used. In that cable, the transmit and receive wire pairs have to be crossed over; that is, the receive pair at one end (pins 1 and 2) must be connected to the transmit pair (pins 3 and 6) at the other end of the cable and vice versa. Figure 3.20 illustrates the routing of crossover wiring used to connect two UTP hub ports to one another.

The only exception to using a crossover cable is when a special hub port containing the crossover function is provided. On some hubs this type of port is labeled *crossover*, and it enables a straight-through cable to be used to cascade one hub to another. On other hubs an *X* is placed on the crossover, functioning port as a label to indicate pin reversals.

Unlike a hub, a concentrator consists of a main housing into which modular cards are inserted. Although some modular cards may appear to represent hubs, and do indeed function as 10BASE-T hubs, the addition of other modules permits the network to be easily expanded from one location and allows additional features to be supported. For example, the insertion of a fiber-optic interrepeater module permits concentrators to be interconnected over relatively long distances of approximately 3 km.

Figure 3.19 10BASE-T hub to NIC wiring.

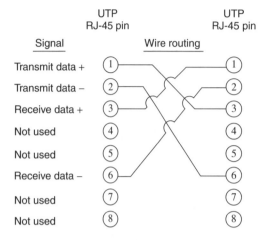

Figure 3.20   A crossover cable is required to connect hubs together.

Wiring Considerations

Because 10BASE-T uses RJ-45 jacks and telephone wire is commonly available, we may be tempted to use a silver satin color patch cable to connect a workstation to a hub port. Don't! The reason you should stay away from silver satin wire used to connect telephones to jacks is because they do not have twisted pairs inside. The lack of twisted pair means that the cable becomes a long antenna and can result in excessive crosstalk as transmit and receive signals interface with one another. In addition, excessive crosstalk signals can appear as simultaneous traffic, which can result in the false triggering of collision detection circuitry. The result of this triggering will be "late collisions," a term used to indicate collisions that are detected too late in the transmission of a frame to permit near immediate retransmission of the frame. Instead, the loss of the frame will be detected by application software and the resulting retransmission will be considerably slower. You can eliminate a major cause of the previously described problems by restricting your use of cable to twisted-pair rated for use for an applicable version of Ethernet. That is, use cat 3 cable for 10BASE-T and cat 5 for 100BASE-T, while cat 5e or cat 6 should be used for Gigabit Ethernet.

Expanding a 10BASE-T Network

A 10BASE-T network can be expanded with additional hubs once the number of stations serviced uses up the hub's available terminal ports. In expanding a 10BASE-T network, the wiring that joins each hub together is considered to represent a cable segment, while each hub is considered as a repeater. Thus, under the 802.3 specification, no two stations can be separated by more than four hubs connected together by five cable segments. In addition, two of the five segments cannot be populated, which results in 10BASE-T adhering to the previously described 5-4-3 rule.

Figure 3.21 illustrates the expansion of a 10BASE-T network through the use of five hubs. Note that the connection between station A and station B traverses five segments and four hubs, and does not violate IEEE 802.3 connection rules. Because the maximum span of a 10BASE-T network is 100 meters per segment times five segments, or 500 meters, it is quite common for 10BASE-T networks to use a 10BASE-5 or even a 10BASE-2 cable backbone. As in Figure 3.12, in which a 10BASE-5 cable provided a backbone for a 10BASE-2 network, either 10BASE-2 or 10BASE-5 cable can be used to support an extension of a 10BASE-T network. In such situations, the AUI port of a 10BASE-T hub is connected to a MAU (transceiver) connected to the 10BASE-5 (thick coaxial) cable, or the BNC connector is mated to a thin coaxial cable's T-connector. Another reason for using a thin or thick coaxial cable for a backbone is that you can thereby avoid the four-hub cascading limit of 10BASE-T. For example, if you cabled ten hubs to a 10BASE-5 coaxial

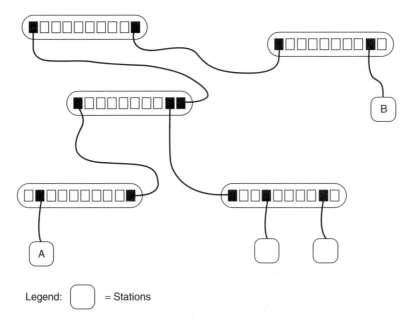

Legend: = Stations

Figure 3.21 Expanding a 10BASE-T network. No two stations can be separated by more than four hubs in a 10BASE-T network.

cable backbone, each station would traverse at most two hubs, and would thus comply with the IEEE rules. In comparison, you could not connect more than five hubs together in a conventional 10BASE-T network because of IEEE 802.3 rules.

Full-Duplex Operations

Because 10BASE-T wiring has separate transmission and receive signal paths it can instantly detect a collision as data is transmitted. However, if no collisions are possible, the ability to have simultaneously active signal paths is wasted. Because the direct connection of stations to a switch port precludes the possibility of a collision, 10BASE-T full duplex became possible in a switch environment, a network topology that will be covered later in this book.

3.3 Use of Fiber-Optic Technology

An addition to Ethernet, which allows transmission via pulses of light instead of electrical current, is known as FOIRL, an acronym that stands for *fiber-optic repeater link*. Although FOIRL is not an Ethernet network, this specification governs the transmission of Ethernet across dual-fiber cable — one fiber is used for the transmission of data in the form of light pulses, while the second fiber is used for the reception of data in the form of light pulses.

The fiber-optic repeater link (FOIRL) represents one of two fiber-optic specifications developed to support different types of Ethernet networks operating at 10 Mbps. The second standard, referred to as 10BASE-F, is designed to interoperate with older FOIRL-based equipment and provides backward compatibility with the older specification. Both standards provide immunity from electrical hazards to include electromechanically generated noise and lightning, enabling networks to be extended through gasoline refineries and other areas where metallic media would be banned.

The use of fiber permits you to support multiple Ethernet segments at distances up to 2000 meters (6600 feet) from one another. At a remote location connected through the use of fiber-optic technology, you can connect a single station directly using a fiber transceiver, or you can connect a 10BASE-T or fiber hub and support multiple stations. You would use the AUI port of the hub to provide a connection via a standard transceiver to different types of Ethernet networks, while you would use an optical transceiver to provide a connection to the dual-fiber cable.

FOIRL

The older IEEE 802.3 FOIRL standard enables a fiber link segment to be up to 1000 meters between two repeaters while the more recent 10BASE-F standard doubles the distance to 2000 meters. The greater distance is, however, only obtainable when 10BASE-F repeaters are used at both ends. When 10BASE-F is mixed with FOIRL, the maximum length of the segment is reduced to 1000 meters.

Other differences between FOIRL and 10BASE-F include the names associated with different fiber-optic components associated with each network technology and the optical transmit power levels, receive sensitivity, and power loss associated with each optical technology. In our examination of the use of 10-Mbps fiber-optic media, we will first turn our attention to the use of FOIRL components and, when appropriate, discuss its similarities and differences with respect to the more modern 10BASE-F standard. Once we complete our examination of FOIRL, we will then turn our attention to 10BASE-F.

Optical Transceiver

The optical transceiver is common to both FOIRL and 10BASE-F, with only the optical power transmit and receive levels differing between the two specifications. An optical transceiver consists of a pulse-generating LED, a photodetector, and associated transmit and receive circuitry. Transmit circuitry turns the LED on and off to convert electrical voltages representing data into a series of light pulses for transmission over the fiber. The photodetector recognizes received light pulses, while the receive circuitry generates electrical voltages and shapes pulses to correspond to the received light pulses.

Today, you can purchase a fiber network access unit (NAU), an optical transceiver mounted on an adapter card for installation in the system unit of a personal computer, for less than $150. A second type of optical transceiver used on Ethernet networks is built into fiber hubs, the use of which will be covered next in this section. This type of optical transmitter may be designed to share the use of a common power source and circuitry, resulting in a per-port hub cost usually less than the cost of a fiber adapter.

Fiber Hubs

Under the original FOIRL specification the use of a fiber-optic segment was only applicable between repeaters. This meant that you could not actually connect a distant station directly to a port on a hub. While industry waited for the development of 10BASE-F standards several vendors, including AT&T, incorporated FOIRL capability into hubs to provide network customers with additional capabilities while awaiting the ability to manufacture 10BASE-F products once appropriate standards were promulgated. Thus, when we discuss the operation of FOIRL ports in hubs, you should note that this actually references proprietary equipment, because that standard only governed transmission on fiber between repeaters.

A fiber hub is a special type of hub that contains a number of FOIRL ports, one AUI port, and usually one or more 10BASE-T ports. For example, AT&T's original StarLan fiber hub contained six FOIRL ports, one 10BASE-T port, and one AUI port. In comparison, Transition Engineering's Model 1050 fiber-optic hub contains 12 FOIRL ports and one AUI interface port.

In effect, a fiber hub is a grouping of fiber NAUs and one or more 10BASE-T and/or AUI ports. Thus, you can use a fiber hub to support several extended-distance Ethernet connections, and then link those connections directly to a 10BASE-T network with a 10BASE-T port built into the fiber hub, or indirectly to any type of Ethernet network with an AUI port built into the fiber hub. A more modern 10BASE-F hub consists of a series of fiber link (10BASE-FL) ports, with the key difference between 10BASE-F and FOIRL hubs being the optical transmit power and optical receiver sensitivity supported by each port on each hub.

Fiber Adapter

A third type of hardware product used with FOIRL is a fiber adapter. The fiber adapter is a media conversion device that converts between twisted-pair and fiber-optic cable. This device extends the transmission distance between a wire hub and an attached workstation—or another 10BASE-T wire hub—from 100 meters (328 feet) to 1000 meters. If a 10BASE-F fiber adapter is used with a 10BASE-F-compliant hub port, the transmission distance is extended to 2000 meters. For both FOIRL and 10BASE-F, unless the fiber adapter is connected directly to a fiber hub, an adapter is required at each end of an extended fiber link.

Wire and Fiber Distance Limits

Figure 3.22 illustrates the transmission distance limits associated with the use of 10BASE-T and FOIRL-compliant fiber hubs and fiber adapters. Note that a fiber network access unit installed in the system unit of a PC can communicate

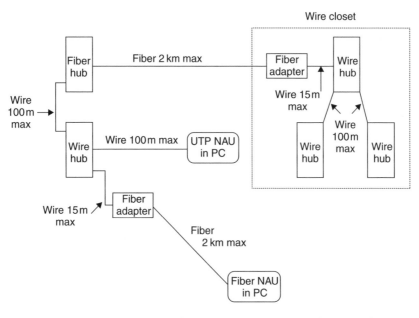

Figure 3.22 10BASE-T and FOIRL transmission distance limits.

up to 1000 meters via fiber-optic cable, either directly into a fiber hub or to a fiber adapter connected to a wire hub. Also note that in the upper right corner of Figure 3.22, it was assumed that three 10BASE-T wire hubs were installed in a wire closet. If that wire closet is located on a low floor in a building and your organization leases another floor hundreds of feet above the wire closet floor, the use of fiber-optic cable provides a mechanism to link two network segments together. Similarly, the wire closet shown in the illustration could be in one building on a university campus, with fiber used to connect that building to another building. This use of fiber-optic cable not only extends the transmission distance of the network, but also eliminates the possibility of electromagnetic interference (EMI), because fiber cable is immune to EMI.

The distance limitation associated with the use of FOIRL has nothing to do with the transmission constraints associated with optical signals. Instead, the FOIRL distance limitation is related to the timing constraints in the IEEE 802.3 standard.

Because the FOIRL standard is limited to point-to-point connections, when used to interconnect two 10BASE-2 networks you must consider the cable length of each segment. For example, assume you have two 10BASE-2 networks located in different areas on a large factory floor, as illustrated

Legend:

◯ = Workstation

OR = Optical repeater

Figure 3.23 Connecting 10BASE-2 networks using a fiber-optic interrepeater link.

in Figure 3.23. If segment A has a cable length of 300 meters and segment B has a cable length of 500 meters, what is the maximum FOIRL cable length? Because the maximum cabling distance of a 10BASE-2 network is 2500 meters, subtracting the sum of the cable lengths from that cable constraint (2500 − (300 + 500)) results in a maximum fiber-optic link of 1700 meters.

Another constraint you must consider is the Ethernet repeater limitation. Ethernet limits any interconnected network to a maximum of four repeaters between any two nodes. Thus, when considering the use of fiber-optic repeaters, you must take into consideration the maximum network length as well as the number of repeaters that can be placed between nodes. As we will shortly note, under 10BASE-F a mechanism exists that allows the 5-4-3 rule to be exceeded.

10BASE-F

The development and promulgation of the IEEE 10BASE-F standard officially provided network users with the ability to use fiber-optic hubs. As previously noted in the section covering the FOIRL specification, vendors integrated FOIRL capability into hubs; however, the actual standard that officially provided this capability was the 10BASE-F standard.

Under the 10BASE-F standard, which actually represents a set of fiber-optic media standards, three types of segments for optical transmission were defined. Those segments include 10BASE-FL, 10BASE-FB, and 10BASE-FP, each of which we will now examine.

10BASE-FL

The 10BASE-FL standard provides a fiber-optic link segment that can be up to 2000 meters in length, providing that only 10BASE-FL equipment is used at both ends of the segment. Otherwise, the mixing of 10BASE-FL and FOIRL equipment reduces the maximum length of the optical segment to 1000 meters.

The development of the 10BASE-FL standard was intended as a replacement for the older FOIRL specification. Unlike FOIRL that was restricted to providing an optical connection between repeaters, 10BASE-FL enables an optical segment to be routed between two workstations, two repeaters, or between a workstation and a repeater port.

The actual connection of a copper-based network node to a 10BASE-FL segment can be accomplished in one of two ways. First, a stand-alone fiber-optic MAU (FOMAU) can be connected via the 15-pin AUI connector on a network adapter to provide an electrical-to-optical conversion capability. A second method is to use a 10BASE-T/FL converter. The latter is used when only a 10BASE-T port is available on a NIC. Both the 10BASE-FL FOMAU and the 10BASE-T/FL converter include two fiber-optic connectors, one for transmitting and one for receiving data. Some 10BASE-T/FL converters include two RJ-45 connectors that provide a high degree of cabling flexibility. One RJ-45 connector functions as a crossover cable and allows hub-to-hub communications via optical media, while the second connector is for workstations that use a straight-through connection.

The top portion of Figure 3.24 illustrates the connection of a workstation to a 10BASE-FL FOMAU via a 15-pin AUI connector. The lower portion of that illustration shows the use of a 10BASE-T/FL converter. Both devices provide you with the ability to transmit up to 2000 meters via a fiber link when a 10BASE-F-compliant optical device is at the other end of the optical link.

In addition to the use of a 10BASE-FL FOMAU and 10BASE-T/FL converter, other types of converters have been developed to extend a fiber-optic transmission capability to other types of Ethernet networks. For example, a 10BASE-2/FL converter enables you to extend the transmission distance of a 10BASE-2 network via a fiber-optic connection.

The creation of a 10BASE-F optical hub is accomplished by the inclusion of two or more FOMAUs in the hub. This results in the hub becoming an optical repeater, which retransmits data received on one port onto all other ports. Under the 10BASE-F standard you can use multiple 10BASE-FL connections to connect several individual workstations at distances up to 2000 meters to a common hub equipped with FOMAU ports.

Network Media

When examining the potential use of a converter or a FOMAU, it is important to verify the type of optical media supported. Multimode fiber (MMF) is

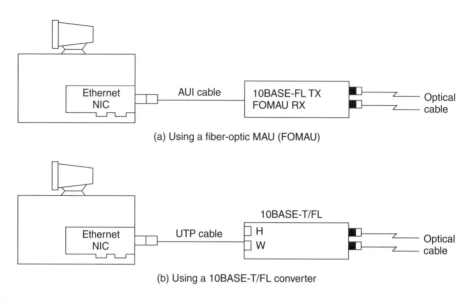

(a) Using a fiber-optic MAU (FOMAU)

(b) Using a 10BASE-T/FL converter

Figure 3.24 Options for connection of a workstation to a 10BASE-FL segment.

commonly used, with the most popular type of fiber having a 62.5-micron (μ) fiber-optic core and a 125-μ outer cladding. This type of multimode fiber is referenced by the numerics 62.5/125 μ. The wavelength of light used on a 62.5/125-μ MMF fiber link is 850 nanometers (nm), and the *optical loss budget*, a term used to reference the amount of optical power lost through attenuation, should not exceed the range 9.7 to 19.0 dB, with the exact amount dependent upon the type of fiber used. Table 3.3 provides a comparison of the optical attenuation for 10BASE-FL and FOIRL for six types of multimode fiber. In examining the entries in Table 3.3, you will note that 10BASE-FL has a higher loss budget than FOIRL for each type of multimode fiber. This explains why the transmission distance of 10BASE-FL optical repeaters exceeds the distance obtainable using FOIRL repeaters.

The connectors used on the previously described multimode fiber are referred to as ST connectors. The ST connector represents a spring-loaded bayonet connector whose outer ring locks onto the connection similar to the manner by which BNC connector's junction on 10BASE-2 segments. To facilitate the connection process, an ST connector has a key on the inner sleeve and an outer bayonet ring. To make a connection you would line up the key on the inner sleeve of the ST plug with a slot on an ST receptacle, push the connector inward and then twist the outer bayonet ring to lock the

TABLE 3.3 Comparing the Loss Budget (Optical Attenuation) of 10BASE-FL and FOIRL

Multimode, graded index fiber size (µm)	50/125	50/125	50/125	62.5/125	83/125	100/140
Numerical aperture	.20	.21	.22	.275	.26	.30
10BASE-FL Loss budget (dB)	9.7	9.2	9.6	13.5	15.7	19.0
FOIRL Loss budget (dB)	7.2	6.7	7.1	11.0	13.2	16.5

connection in place. This action not only results in a tight connection but, in addition, provides a precise alignment between the two portions of fiber-optic cable being joined.

It is important to note that the optical loss depends upon several factors. First, the length of the fiber governs optical loss, with a typical fiber illuminated at 850 nm having a loss between 4 dB and 5 dB per 1000 meters. Second, these of more connectors results in a higher optical loss. Third and perhaps most important to note since this is easy to rectify, if your connectors or fiber splices are poorly made or if dirt, finger oil or dust resides on connector ends, you will obtain a higher level of optical loss than necessary.

10BASE-FB

A second 10BASE-F specification is 10BASE-FB, with the B used to denote a synchronous signaling backbone segment. The 10BASE-FB specification enables the limit on the number of repeaters previously described in the 5-4-3 rule section to be exceeded. A 10BASE-FB signaling repeater is commonly used to connect repeater hubs together into a repeated backbone network infrastructure that can span multiple 2000-m links.

10BASE-FP

A third 10BASE-F specification was developed to support the connection of multiple stations via a common segment that can be up to 500 meters in length. Referred to as 10BASE-FP, the P references the fact that the end segment is a fiber-passive system. Under the 10BASE-FP specification a single fiber-optic passive-star coupler can be used to connect up to 33 stations. Those stations can be located up to 500 meters from a hub via the use of a shared fiber segment.

Although 10BASE-FP provides a clustering capability that might represent a practical networking solution to the requirements of some organizations, as well as reduce the cost associated with the use of multiple individual optical cables, most organizations prefer to link hubs together. Doing so also allows the use of a single pair of optical cables; however, the transmission distance to the cluster is then extended to 2000 meters.

3.4 High-Speed Ethernet

To differentiate Gigabit and 10 Gbps Ethernet from other versions of Ethernet whose operating rates exceed 10 Mbps but have a maximum operating rate one-tenth that of Gigabit, those versions of Ethernet that operate at or below 100 Mbps were classified as high-speed Ethernet and are covered in this section. This enables Gigabit and 10 Gbps Ethernet to be covered as a separate entity in Section 3.5.

There are three broad categories into which high-speed Ethernet networks fall. The first two types of high-speed Ethernet networks are represented by de jure standards for operations at 100 Mbps, while the third standard represents an extension to 10BASE-T that operates at 16 Mbps. As discussed in Chapter 2, the IEEE standardized two general types of 100-Mbps Ethernet networks, with the 802.3μ standard defining three types of 100-Mbps CSMA/CD networks, while the 802.12 standard defines a demand-priority operation that replaces the CSMA/CD access protocol. The third high-speed Ethernet network is considered as a high-speed network only when compared with the operating rate of Ethernet networks developed before 1992. This type of network, referred to as *isochronous Ethernet* (isoENET), operates at 16 Mbps. This section will focus upon obtaining a overview of the operation and use of each of these three types of Ethernet networks.

Isochronous Ethernet

Isochronous Ethernet, or isoENET, represents an extension to 10BASE-T technology. Isochronous Ethernet adds time-sensitive multimedia support through an addition of 6.144 Mbps of isochronous bandwidth to existing 10-Mbps 10BASE-T Ethernet. Here, the term *isochronous* references a series of repetitive time slots used for the transmission of constant bit-rate services at the physical bit-transmission level.

Although isoENET received a considerable degree of publicity during the early 1990s, it never received any significant degree of commercial acceptance. This was probably due to the development of Fast Ethernet, which provided over six times the transmission capacity of isoENET. However, because isoENET provided time slots for the transmission of time-sensitive information, its design in effect provided a Quality of Service (QoS) capability that is worth examining.

Isochronous Ethernet dates to 1992, when National Semiconductor and IBM, with support from Apple Computer, submitted the basics of isoENET to the IEEE 802.9 Integrated Services Local Area Networks working group. Better known by its trade names isoEthernet and isoENET, this technique was standardized by the IEEE as standard 802.9a, with the official designation Integrated Service Local Area Network (ISLAN16-T). Here, the *T* in the abbreviation denotes its capability to operate over twisted-pair wiring, while the *16* references its operating rate. In comparison with other Ethernet LANs that are asynchronous, isoENET was developed to support the 8-KHz sampling clock used as a worldwide standard for voice transmission. This synchronization capability was layered on top of the 10-Mbps 10BASE-T operating rate, enabling isoENET to support real-time communications in addition to conventional 10BASE-T asynchronous LAN transmission.

Isochronous Ethernet represented a hybrid type of Ethernet network, combining standard 10-Mbps 802.3 10BASE-T with a 6.144-Mbps isochronous networking capability. The 6.144 Mbps of additional bandwidth was designed to accommodate 96 integrated services digital network (ISDN) B-channels, either individually or in multiple combinations of $N \times 64$ Kbps. For example, a videoconference requiring 128 Kbps of bandwidth would be assigned two 64-Kbps channels, while digitized voice that requires 64 Kbps when pulse code modulation (PCM) is used for digitization would be assigned one channel.

Besides being designed to support 96 ISDN B-channels, the isochronous bandwidth supported one 64-Kbps ISDN D-channel for signaling and one 96-Kbps ISDN M-channel used to support ISDN maintenance functions. Figure 3.25 illustrates the allocation of isoENET bandwidth.

IsoENET replaced the Manchester encoding used by 10BASE-T with a 4B/5B encoding scheme, which represents the data encoding method used by the ANSI X3T9.5 FDDI standard. Under 4B/5B coding, each octet of data is split into two four-bit nibbles (4B). Each nibble is then coded using five bits (5B), resulting in an 80-percent level of utilization of the 20-MHz IEEE 802.3 clock signal. In comparison, Manchester encoding provides a 50-percent utilization of the 20-MHz clock. The change in the method of data coding provided an additional 6.144-Mbps bandwidth on existing 10BASE-T wiring, connector, and hub facilities. However, the use of the additional bandwidth required the installation of an isoENET hub and isoENET adapter cards for each local area network node that requires an isochronous communications capability.

Figure 3.25 Allocation of isoENET bandwidth.

Users who did not require an isochronous communications capability could use their existing 10BASE-T adapter cards, and 802.3 traffic would not notice any change to the operation of a 10BASE-T network. Figure 3.26 illustrates how an isoENET hub could support conventional 10BASE-T and isoENET network nodes.

Although at one time about a dozen vendors manufactured isoENET products and its use provides a mechanism to extend multimedia to the desktop, other Ethernet technologies dulled the demand for its 16-Mbps communications capability. The introduction of 100BASE-T and Gigabit Ethernet appears to resolve the bandwidth crunch experienced by many networks that added Internet connections and graphics-intensive applications. Because it appears that greater bandwidth was more important than obtaining a videoconferencing capability to the desktop, a majority of vendor and customer interest became focused upon faster Ethernet solutions than that provided by isoENET.

Figure 3.26 isoENET supports the addition of 6.155 Mbps to nodes equipped with isoENET adapter cards.

Fast Ethernet

Fast Ethernet is not actually a local area network, but a term commonly used to reference a series of three 100-Mbps physical-layer LAN specifications in the IEEE 802.3μ addendum. Those specifications include 100BASE-TX, 100BASE-FX, and 100BASE-T4. Each specification maintains the use of the MAC protocol used by earlier Ethernet/IEEE 802.3 standards, CSMA/CD.

100BASE-T specifies 100-Mbps operations using the CSMA/CD protocol over two pairs of category 5 UTP cable. 100BASE-FX changes the LAN transport media to two pairs of fiber, while 100BASE-T4 supports four pairs of category 3, 4, and 5 UTP or STP cable. Table 3.4 provides a summary of the three types of Fast Ethernet with respect to their IEEE media specification designation, types of media supported, types of connectors supported, and the coding scheme used.

100BASE-T Overview

At the beginning of this section we noted that the IEEE standardized two types of 100 Mbps Ethernet networks. The 802.3μ standard defines three types of CSMA/CD operations and is referred to as Fast Ethernet or 100BASE-T.

A second 100 Mbps Ethernet network standard resulted in the development of a different access control mechanism, referred to as a demand priority mechanism. The IEEE standardized the 100 Mbps LAN using a demand priority mechanism as the 802.12 standard and its support of either Ethernet or Token-Ring resulted in the name 100VG-AnyLAN being used to reference the standard. Although both standards received a considerable degree of interest, actual implementation and commercial success is another story. Of

TABLE 3.4   Fast Ethernet Functionality

IEEE Media Specifications	Cable Support	Connector Support	Coding Scheme
100BASE-TX	Category 5 UTP (2-pair wire)	RJ-45	4B/5B
	100-ohm STP (2-pair wire)	DB-9	
100BASE-FX	62.5/125-micron fiber-optic cable (2 multimode fibers)	SC or ST	4B/5B
100BASE-T4	Category 3, 4, or 5 UTP (4-pair wire)	RJ-45	8B6T

Legend: UTP, unshielded twisted pair; STP, shielded twisted pair.

the two standards 100BASE-T is by far a commercial success while 100VG-AnyLAN is anything but. Thus, the primary focus of our attention in the remaining of this chapter will be upon 100BASE-T, although we will briefly conclude this section with an overview of the technology associated with 100VG-AnyLAN.

The standardization of 100BASE-T required an extension of previously developed IEEE 802.3 standards. In the definition process of standardization development, both the Ethernet media access control (MAC) and physical layer required adjustments to permit 100-Mbps operational support. For the MAC layer, scaling its speed to 100 Mbps from the 10BASE-T 10-Mbps operational rate required a minimal adjustment, because in theory the 10BASE-T MAC layer was developed independently of the data rate. For the physical layer, more than a minor adjustment was required, because Fast Ethernet was designed to support three types of media. Using work developed in the standardization process of FDDI in defining 125-Mbps full-duplex signaling to accommodate optical fiber, UTP, and STP through physical media-dependent (PMD) sublayers, Fast Ethernet borrowed this strategy. Because a mechanism was required to map the PMD's continuous signaling system to the start-stop *half-duplex* system used at the Ethernet MAC layer, the physical layer was subdivided. This subdivision is illustrated in Figure 3.27.

Note that the version of Fast Ethernet that operates using four pairs of telephone-grade twisted pair wire is known as 100BASE-T4, while 100BASE-TX operates over two pairs of data-grade twisted-pair. The third version of Fast Ethernet, which operates over fiber-optic media, is 100BASE-FX. The

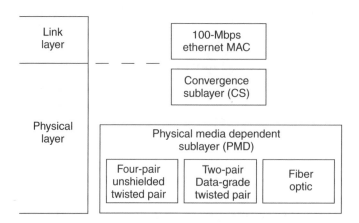

Figure 3.27   Fast Ethernet physical layering subdivision overview.

PMD sublayer supports the appropriate media to be used, while the convergence sublayer (CS), which was later renamed the physical coding sublayer, performs the mapping between the PMD and the Ethernet MAC layer.

Although Fast Ethernet represents a tenfold increase in the LAN operating rate from 10BASE-T to ensure proper collision detection, the 100BASE-T network span was reduced to 200 meters, with a maximum of 100 meters permitted between a network node and a hub. The smaller network diameter reduces potential propagation delay. When coupled with a tenfold operating rate increase and no change in network frame size, the ratio of frame duration to network propagation delay for a 100BASE-T network is the same as for a 10BASE-T network.

In addition to reducing the 100BASE-T network span to 200 meters, the Fast Ethernet specification recognized the need to provide an automatic capability for equipment to support older 10BASE-T equipment. This automatic support is in the form of an Auto-Negotiation mechanism referred to as Nway, which will be covered later in this section.

Physical Layer

The physical layer subdivision previously illustrated in Figure 3.27, as indicated in the title of the figure, presents an overview of the true layer subdivision. In actuality, a number of changes were required at the physical layer to obtain a 10-Mbps operating rate. Those changes include the use of three wire pairs for data (the fourth is used for collision detection), 8B6T ternary coding (for 100BASE-T4) instead of Manchester coding, and an increase in the clock signaling speed from 20 MHz to 25 MHz. As indicated in Table 3.5, in comparison to 10BASE-T the differences at the physical layer resulted in a tenfold increase in the 100BASE-T operating rate.

When the specifications for Fast Ethernet were being developed, it was recognized that the physical signaling layer would incorporate medium-dependent functions if support was extended to two-pair cable (100BASE-TX) operations.

TABLE 3.5 100BASE-T System Throughput Compared with 10BASE-T

Transmit on 3 pairs vs. 1 pair	×3.00
8B6T coding instead of Manchester	×2.65
20 to 25 MHz clock increase	×1.25
Total throughput increase	10.00

To separate medium-dependent interfaces to accommodate multiple physical layers, a common interface referred to as the medium-independent interface (MII) was inserted between the MAC layer and the physical encoding sublayer. The MII represents a common point of interoperability between the medium and the MAC layer. The MII can support two specific data rates, 10 Mbps and 100 Mbps, permitting older 10BASE-T nodes to be supported at Fast Ethernet hubs. To reconcile the MII signal with the MAC signal, a reconciliation sublayer was added under the MAC layer, resulting in the subdivision of the link layer into three parts — a logical link control layer, a media access control layer, and a reconciliation layer. The top portion of Figure 3.28 illustrates this subdivision.

That portion of Fast Ethernet below the MII, which is the new physical layer, is now subdivided into four sublayers. The lower portion of Figure 3.28 illustrates the physical sublayers for 100BASE-T4 and 100BASE-TX.

The physical coding sublayer performs the data encoding, transmit, receive, and carrier sense functions. Because the data coding method differs between 100BASE-T4 and 100BASE-TX, this difference requires distinct physical coding sublayers for each version of Fast Ethernet.

The physical medium attachment (PMA) sublayer maps messages from the physical coding sublayer (PCS) onto the twisted-pair transmission media, and vice versa.

The auto-negotiation block shown in Figure 3.28 is not actually a layer but a function built into 100BASE-T4 and 100BASE-TX. As noted earlier in this section, auto-negotiation provides 100BASE-T copper media ports and adapters with the ability to automatically adjust to 10 or 100 Mbps operations.

The medium-dependent interface (MDI) sublayer specifies the use of a standard RJ-45 connector. Although the same connector is used for 100BASE-TX, the use of two pairs of cable instead of four results in different pin assignments.

100BASE-T4

100BASE-T4 supports a 100-Mbps operating rate over four pairs of category 3, 4, or 5 UTP wiring that supports a segment upto 100 meters in length. Figure 3.29 illustrates the RJ-45 pin assignments of wire pairs used by 100BASE-T4. Note that wire pairs D1 and D2 are unidirectional. As indicated in Figure 3.29, three wire pairs are available for data transmission and reception in each direction, while the fourth pair is used for collision detection. Each wire pair is polarized, with one wire of the pair transporting a positive (+) signal while the other transports a negative (−) signal. Thus,

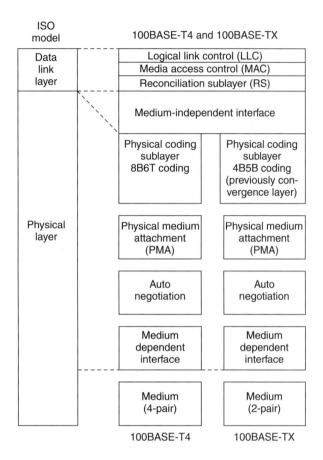

Figure 3.28   100BASE-T4 versus 100BASE-TX physical and link layers.

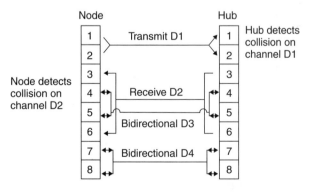

Figure 3.29   100BASE-T4 pin assignments.

another common mechanism used to denote the function of the pins in the 100BASE-T4 eight-pin connector is to denote their use (transmit TX, receive RX, or bi-directional BI), the data pair (D1, D2, D3 or D4) and type of signal (+ or −) transported. Based upon the preceding, Figure 3.30 illustrates the signals transported by the 100BASE-T4 eight-in connector.

In examining the signals based upon pin position shown in Figure 3.30, you can note that the interconnection of devices connected to a 100BASE-T4 segment would require a crossover of signals. Otherwise, for example, TX_D1+ would be cabled to TX_D1+ and the transmission at one end would not be placed onto the receive side at the other end. Thus, a signal crossover cable is normally required to interconnect a station to a hub port. An exception to this is when the hub has the crossover function built into the device, which is usually denoted by marketing on the port in the form of a tilted X. Figure 3.31 illustrates the crossover cable wiring for 100BASE-T4.

In examining the 100BASE-T4 crossover cable note that the TX pair at one end of a cable is connected or strapped to the RX pair at the other end of the cable. In addition, the BI_D3 pair at one end is connected to the BI_D4 pair at the other end. Each of the cross-connections occurs in each direction to provide a crossover cable. Because 100BASE-T4 can operate on category 3, which is used for 10BASE-T, this feature enables many organizations to migrate to a 100-Mbps network without changing their wiring infrastructure.

The 100BASE-T4 physical coding sublayer implements 8B6T block coding. Under this coding technique, each block of eight input bits is transformed into a unique code group of six ternary symbols. Figure 3.32 provides an overview of the 8B6T coding process used by 100BASE-T4.

Pin Number	Signal
1	TX_D1+
2	TX_D1−
3	RX_D2+
4	BI_D3+
5	BI_D3−
6	RX_D2−
7	BI_D4+
8	BI_D4−

Figure 3.30   Signals transported on the 100BASE-T4 eight-pin connector.

Pin number	Signal		Signal	Pin number
1	TX_D1+		TX_D1+	1
2	TX_D1−		TX_D1−	2
3	RX_D2+		RX_D2+	3
6	RX_D2−		RX_D2−	6
4	BI_D3+		BI_D3+	4
5	BI_D3−		BI_D3−	5
7	BI_D4+		BI_D4+	7
8	BI_D4−		BI_D4−	8

Figure 3.31 100BASE-T4 crossover wiring.

Figure 3.32 8B6T coding process.

The output code groups resulting from 8B6T coding flow out to three parallel channels that are placed on three twisted pairs. Thus, the effective data rate on each pair is 100 Mbps/3, or 33.33 Mbps. Because 6 bits are represented by 8 bit positions, the signaling rate or baud rate on each cable pair becomes 33 Mbps × 6/8, or 25 MHz, which is the clock rate used at the MII sublayer.

100BASE-TX

100BASE-TX represents the use of two pairs of category 5 UTP cabling with RJ-45 connectors or two pairs of category 5 STP cable terminated with the common DB-9 communications connector used on the serial port of many notebook computers.

Because UTP is relatively inexpensive and two pair is less costly than four pair, 100BASE-TX represents a more popular version of Fast Ethernet than 100BASE-T4. The UTP wire actually used must meet the EIA/TIA 568 category 5 wire specifications. A 100BASE-TX network requires a hub, and the maximum cable run is 100 meters from hub port to node, with a maximum network diameter of 200 meters.

Figure 3.33 illustrates the cabling of two pairs of UTP wires between a hub and node to support 100BASE-TX transmission. One pair of wires is used for

Figure 3.33 100BASE-TX cabling.

transmission, while the second pair is used for collision detection and reception of data. The use of a 125-MHz frequency requires the use of a *data grade* cable. Thus, 100BASE-TX is based upon the use of category 5 UTP and STP.

Similar to 100BASE-T4, 100BASE-TX uses an eight-pin connector when UTP is employed. Figure 3.34 illustrates the use of each of the eight pins. Note that the transmit and receive data signals on each pair transport positive (+) and negative (−) signals. Also note that 100BASE-TX transmission via UTP uses the same pin assignments as 10BASE-T hardware, enabling the same category 5 wiring system to be used without any change to wiring being required. This provides network administrators with a considerable degree of flexibility for upgrading from 10BASE-T to 100BASE-TX once category 5 cabling is installed.

Similar to our discussion concerning 100BASE-TX, when two stations are connected over a segment the transmit data pins on one side must be wired to the receive data pins on the distant end and vice versa. Thus, unless a hub has a port with a built-in crossover you need to use a 100BASE-TX crossover cable to connect a station to a hub. Figure 3.35 illustrates the connection of pins required for a 100BASE-TX crossover cable.

Similar to 10BASE-T, 100BASE-TX has separate transmit and receive signal paths. Because these paths can be simultaneously active 100BASE-TX can support full duplex transmission. If STP cabling is used the connector will be

Pin Number	Signal
1	TX+
2	TX−
3	RX+
4	Unused
5	Unused
6	RX−
7	Unused
8	Unused

Figure 3.34 100BASE-TX eight pin connector used with UTP.

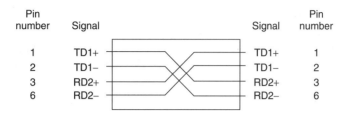

Pin number	Signal			Signal	Pin number
1	TD1+			TD1+	1
2	TD1−			TD1−	2
3	RD2+			RD2+	3
6	RD2−			RD2−	6

Figure 3.35 100BASE-TX crossover cable.

Pin Number	Signal
1	RX+
2	Unused
3	Unused
4	Unused
5	TX+
6	RX−
7	Unused
8	Unused
9	TX−

Figure 3.36 100BASE-TX nine-pin D-connector for STP use.

a nine-pin "D-type" connector similar to the ones used on the serial port of notebook computers. Figure 3.36 illustrates the use of the pins on the 9-pin D-connector.

Although the 100BASE-TX physical layer structure resembles the 100BASE-T4 layer, there are significant differences between the two to accommodate the differences in media used. At the physical coding sublayer, the 100-Mbps start-stop bit stream from the MII is first converted to a full-duplex 125-Mbps bit stream. This conversion is accomplished by the use of the FDDI PMD as the 100BASE-TX PMD. Next, the data stream is encoded using a 4B5B coding scheme. The 100BASE-TX PMD decodes symbols from the 125-Mbps continuous bit stream and converts the stream to 100-Mbps start-stop data bits when the data flow is reversed.

4B5B Coding

The use of a 4B5B coding scheme enables data and control information to be carried in each symbol represented by a 5-bit code group. In addition, an inter-Stream fill code (IDLE) is defined, as well as a symbol used to force signaling errors. Because 4 data bits are mapped into a 5-bit code, only 16 symbols are required to represent data. The remaining symbols not used for control or to denote an IDLE condition are not used by 100BASE-TX and are considered as invalid.

Table 3.6 lists the 4B5B 100BASE-TX code groups. Because an explanation of the use of the control codes and IDLE code requires an examination of the MAC frame, we will defer our discussion of those symbols until Chapter 4, as frame formats are discussed in that chapter.

100BASE-FX

100BASE-FX represents the third 100BASE-T wiring scheme, defining Fast Ethernet transmission over fiber-optic media. 100BASE-FX requires the use of two-strand 62.5/125-micron multimode fiber media and supports the 4B5B coding scheme, identical to the one used by 100BASE-TX.

100BASE-FX provides an extended network diameter of up to 400 meters. However, in a mixed 100BASE-T4 and 100BASE-FX environment, the collision domain should not exceed 231 meters, consisting of 100 meters for 100BASE-T4 and 131 meters for 100BASE-FX. Concerning connectors, 100BASE-FX supports both ST and SC fiber connectors, which were originally defined for FDDI.

Network Construction and Use

Similar to 10-Mbps Ethernet networks, you can use adapter cards, cable, and hubs to construct a variety of Fast Ethernet networks to satisfy different organizational network requirements. However, when doing so, it is important to understand the role of repeaters in a Fast Ethernet environment, as the standard defines two types, each having a different effect upon network construction.

Repeater Rules

When we examined Ethernet we discussed the 5-4-3 rule, which applied to a common type of repeater. When we discuss Fast Ethernet we must consider two types of repeaters, referred to as Class I and Class II repeaters.

TABLE 3.6   4B/5B Code Groups

PCS Code Group		MII (TXD/RXD)	
4 3 2 1 0	Name	3 2 1 0	Interpretation
DATA			
1 1 1 1 0	0	0 0 0 0	Data 0
0 1 0 0 1	1	0 0 0 1	Data 1
1 0 1 0 0	2	0 0 1 0	Data 2
1 0 1 0 1	3	0 0 1 1	Data 3
0 1 0 1 0	4	0 1 0 0	Data 4
0 1 0 1 1	5	0 1 0 1	Data 5
0 1 1 1 0	6	0 1 1 0	Data 6
0 1 1 1 1	7	0 1 1 1	Data 7
1 0 0 1 0	8	1 0 0 0	Data 8
1 0 0 1 1	9	1 0 0 1	Data 9
1 0 1 1 0	A	1 0 1 0	Data A
1 0 1 1 1	B	1 0 1 1	Data B
1 1 0 1 0	C	1 1 0 0	Data C
1 1 0 1 1	D	1 1 0 1	Data D
1 1 1 0 0	E	1 1 1 0	Data E
1 1 1 0 1	F	1 1 1 1	Data F
IDLE			
1 1 1 1 1	I		IDLE: Used as inter-Stream fill code
CONTROL			
1 1 0 0 0	J		Start-of-stream delimiter, part 1 of 2; always used in pairs with K.
1 0 0 0 1	K		Start-of-stream delimiter, part 2 of 2; always used in pairs with J.

(continued overleaf)

TABLE 3.6 (*Continued*)

PCS Code Group		MII (TXD/RXD)	
4 3 2 1 0	Name	3 2 1 0	Interpretation
0 1 1 0 1	T		End-of-stream delimiter, part 1 of 2; always used in pairs with R.
0 0 1 1 1	R		End-of-stream delimiter, part 2 of 2; always used in pairs with T.
INVALID			
0 0 1 0 0	H		Transmit error; used to force signaling errors.
0 0 0 0 0	V		Invalid code
0 0 0 0 1	V		Invalid code
0 0 0 1 0	V		Invalid code
0 0 0 1 1	V		Invalid code
0 0 1 0 1	V		Invalid code
0 0 1 1 0	V		Invalid code
0 1 0 0 0	V		Invalid code
0 1 1 0 0	V		Invalid code
1 0 0 0 0	V		Invalid code
1 1 0 0 1	V		Invalid code

A Class I repeater has a greater budget for timing delay, enabling it to be used to support dissimilar physical media segments that use dissimilar signaling such as 100BASE-T4 and 100BASE-TX. This support is possible because the greater timing budget of the Class I repeater enables it to translate the line signal received on one port to a different type of signal for transmission onto other ports. Only one Class I repeater can be installed in a segment. In comparison, a Class II repeater has a lower budget for timing delay, resulting in it being faster than a Class I repeater. This enables up to two Class II repeaters to be used in a segment; however, in doing so the interrepeater cable length is limited to 5 meters when data terminal equipment are 100 meters from repeaters. Because a Class II repeater immediately repeats an incoming signal onto all other ports other than the port data was received on without a translation process being possible, it can only be used to interconnect segment types that use the same signaling method, such as 100BASE-TX and 100BASE-FX.

The actual span distance obtainable through the use of repeaters depends upon the type of repeater used and the media cable. Figure 3.37 illustrates the cable restrictions associated with Fast Ethernet. In examining the entries in Figure 3.37, note that the repeater references a Fast Ethernet hub, because the hub receives information on one port and rebroadcasts the received data onto all other ports. To exceed the cable limits shown in Figure 3.37, you must connect the workstation or hub port to a switch, bridge, or router, which results in a new segment being established. Concerning those cable limits, although all vendors support the first two cabling distances shown in Figure 3.37a and 3.37b, there are minor differences in the construction of Class II–type repeaters between some vendors that may reduce the span distance from that shown in Figure 3.37c for a mixture of TX and FX or FX usage. In addition, the use of two Class II repeaters manufactured by different vendors can also result in a slight reduction from the span distances shown

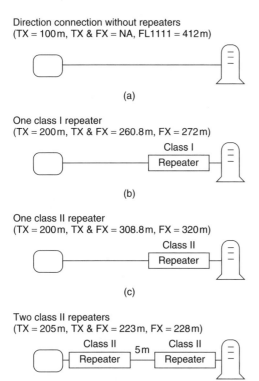

Direction connection without repeaters
(TX = 100 m, TX & FX = NA, FL1111 = 412 m)

(a)

One class I repeater
(TX = 200 m, TX & FX = 260.8 m, FX = 272 m)

Class I
Repeater

(b)

One class II repeater
(TX = 200 m, TX & FX = 308.8 m, FX = 320 m)

Class II
Repeater

(c)

Two class II repeaters
(TX = 205 m, TX & FX = 223 m, FX = 228 m)

Class II   Class II
Repeater   5m   Repeater

(d)

Figure 3.37 Fast Ethernet cable restrictions.

in Figure 3.37d for a mixture of TX and FX and FX repeater use. Thus, it is highly recommended to check vendor specification sheets concerning the network guidelines associated with a particular type of repeater.

Because 100BASE-T4 and 100BASE-TX preserve the 10BASE-T MAC layer, both standards are capable of interoperability with existing 10BASE-T networks as well as with other low-speed Ethernet technology. Through the use of NWay autosensing logic, Fast Ethernet adapters, hub, and switch ports can determine if attached equipment can transmit at 10 or 100 Mbps and adjust to the operating rate of the distant device.

Autonegotiation

Auto-negotiation represents an optical feature which was added to the metallic copper versions of Fast Ethernet and which is now incorporated into most types of such hardware. The basis for auto-negotiation can be traced to a technology referred to as NWay. NWay represents a cable and transmission autosensing scheme proposed by National Semiconductor to the IEEE 802.3 standards group in May 1994. NWay incorporated an autosensing scheme to permit Ethernet circuits to detect both the cable type and speed of incoming Ethernet data, as well as enabled Ethernet repeaters to configure themselves for correct network operations. Because NWay can detect 10-Mbps versus 100-Mbps operations, as well as half- and full-duplex transmission, it formed the basis for autonegotiation which permits Ethernet circuits to be developed to automatically adjust to the operating rate and cabling scheme used. This in turn simplifies the efforts of network managers and administrators, because products incorporating autonegotiation are self-configurable and do not require the setting of DIP switches or software parameters.

Auto-negotiation relies upon a modification to the link integrity test used by 10BASE-T, replacing the link test pulse with a burst of pulses referred to as fast link pulses (FLPs). Each FLP consists of a series of clock and data pulses, with the data pulses used to form a 16-bit link code work (LCW).

Figure 3.38 illustrates the composition of the LCW. Note that the five-bit selector field makes it possible for auto-negotiation to be supported by Token-Ring (802.5) networks. In comparison, the eight-bit Technology Ability field defines the technology supported. The Pause bit in the Technology Ability Field was added to support full-duplex operations and when set indicates if the device supports a Pause Mechanism. If so, the other device can transmit a Pause Frame that will inform the receiving device to delay its transmission. This form of flow control becomes necessary when a 100-Mbps device communicates with a lower-speed device and the latter could be overwhelmed with data. Thus, the 100-Mbps device will need to inform other

Figure 3.38   The format of the link code word.

devices to delay their transmission. In Chapter 4 when we examine the format of different types of Ethernet frames we will also examine the Pause Frame.

Returning our attention to Figure 3.38, the Remote Fault indicates the presence of a fault detected by the station at the opposite end of the link. When this bit (RF) is set, it indicates that the distant device is in its link-failed state, a condition typically resulting from a malfunctioning receiver or broken cable. The next to last bit in the LCW is the ACK bit. This bit is used to indicate the successful receipt of the previously transmitted LCW. The last bit is the next page bit. When set this bit indicates that additional proprietary information follows.

The link code word is transmitted on power-up or when requested by either device on a link. The composition of fast link pulses appears similar to a link integrity test, enabling a 10BASE-T device to respond. However, if the remote station is a 100 Mbps device, its receive clock will be sufficient to interpret the individual pulses that form the LCM, enabling the determination of operations at 10 Mbps or 100 Mbps.

When two devices that support auto-negotiation have multiple capabilities, they need to determine their highest performance mode of operation. In doing so, they consult a priority table. Table 3.7 lists the priorities for auto-negotiation from highest to lowest. Note that full duplex has a higher priority than half duplex since the former has a higher throughput capability than the latter.

Autonegotiation can operate on an individual end basis or with autonegotiation-compliant devices at both ends of a twisted-pair link. An example of this autonegotiation capability is shown in Figure 3.39 in which

TABLE 3.7   Auto-negotiation Priority Table

Priority	Technology	Cable
1	100BASE-TX Full Duplex	2 pair, category 5
2	100BASE-T4	4 pair, category 3
3	100BASE-TX	2 pair, category 5
4	10BASE-T Full Duplex	2 pair, category 3
5	10BASE-T	2 pair, category 3

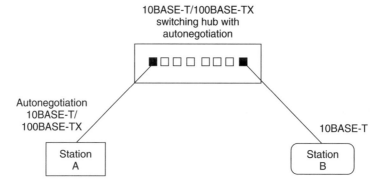

Figure 3.39   Autonegotiation. Through the use of autonegotiation, the 10BASE-T/100BASE-TX switching hub will operate at 100 Mbps with station A and at 10 Mbps with station B.

station A has a NIC with autonegotiation capability that is cabled to a 10BASE-T/100BASE-TX switching hub whose port has an autonegotiation capability, while station B has a conventional 10BASE-T NIC. In this example, the hub port connected to station A would operate at 100 Mbps as 100BASE-TX devices. In comparison, the hub port connection to station B would recognize the 10BASE-T signals from station B and switch to 10BASE-T operations.

Operation

There are several network configurations you can consider for Fast Ethernet operations. First, you can construct a 100BASE-TX network similar to a 10BASE-T network, using an appropriate hub and workstations that support the specific network type. This type of network, commonly referred to as a *shared-media hub-based* network, should be considered when most, if not all, network users access one or a limited number of servers to perform graphic-intensive or similar bandwidth-intensive operations, and the sharing of the 100-Mbps transmission capability provides an acceptable average bandwidth per network node. Figure 3.40a illustrates a Fast Ethernet shared-media hub network configuration.

In examining Figure 3.40a note that the single CSMA/CD network represents a collision domain. Here the term collision domain references a network structure in which a collision will occur if two computers attached to the network transmit at the same time. If one hub is wired to another or two segments are joined together by a repeater the resulting network structure continues to function as a single collision domain.

Another common use for Fast Ethernet is in its incorporation into one or more ports in an Ethernet switch. An Ethernet switch can be viewed as

All connections operate at 100 Mbps.

(a) Shared-media hub.

Some connections operate at 100 Mbps and some at 10 Mbps.

(b) 10/100 Mbps ethernet switch.

Legend:

◯ = Workstation

━ = Fat pipe

Figure 3.40   Fast Ethernet network applications.

a sophisticated hub that can be programmed to transmit packets arriving on one input port to a predefined output port. This is accomplished by the switch reading the destination address in the frame and comparing that address to a table of preconfigured address-port relationships. Readers are referred to Chapter 5 for specific information concerning the operation and use of Ethernet switches. In the interim, in examining the use of Fast Ethernet switches, note that some older switches contain one or two 100-Mbps operating ports, while the other ports are conventional 10BASE-T ports. Due to economies of scale, most Fast Ethernet switches manufactured since the beginning of the new millennium support 10/100-Mbps port operations on all switch ports. The only major exception to the support of dual-speed auto-negotiation ports is when the switch includes one or more Gigabit Ethernet ports, with the latter restricted to operating at 1 Gbps. Typically you would connect servers that have a heavy workload to 100-Mbps Fast Ethernet ports, such as an image/video server and a database server. Figure 3.40 illustrates the use of a 10/100-Mbps Ethernet switch. In examining Figure 3.40a and b, note that the heavily shaded connections to all workstations in Figure 3.40a and to the servers in Figure 3.40b represent 100-Mbps Fast Ethernet ports requiring Fast Ethernet adapter cards to be installed in each server or workstation connected to a 100-Mbps port. A common term used to reference the 100-Mbps connection is *fat pipe*.

Because a Fast Ethernet port provides downward compatibility with 10BASE-T, you can interconnect conventional 10BASE-T hubs to a Fast Ethernet shared-media hub or Fast Ethernet switch. Similar to having the ability to interconnect two hubs to extend a Fast Ethernet network, you can interconnect two switches. However, unlike the connection of hubs, which extends the collision domain, each switch port will not forward collision signals received, enabling attached segments to operate independently of one another. This means you can use LAN switches to construct larger networks by interconnecting shared media segments via one or more switches.

Configuration Guidelines

To facilitate the creation of a Fast Ethernet network you need to consider the maximum collision domain based upon the type of repeater used and the media supported. In addition to the previously mentioned Class I and Class II repeaters, you need to remember that a connection from a station to a hub port represents a repeater on a single segment. With this in mind, Table 3.8 indicates the maximum collision domain based upon the class of repeater, and the type of media used.

TABLE 3.8 Fast Ethernet Maximum Collision Domain (Meters)

| | Type of Media | | | |
Type of Repeater	Copper	Fiber	Copper and Fiber (T4 and FX)	Copper and Fiber (TX and FX)
Single Segment	100	412	N/A	N/A
One Class I	200	272	231*	260*
One Class II	200	320	N/A†	308*
Two Class II	205	228	N/A†	216‡

Notes:
*Assumes 100 meters of copper and one fiber link.
†Not applicable as T4 and FX cannot be interconnected using a Class II repeater.
‡Assumes 105 meters of copper and one fiber link.

In examining the entries in Table 3.8 note that the first entry represents a station-to-station connection with no intermediate repeaters. As indicated, the maximum amount of cabling is 100 meters when copper is used and 412 meters when fiber-optic cable is employed. Figure 3.41 illustrates an example of the structure of a Fast Ethernet network consisting of three shared media hubs and a switch.

An examination of Figure 3.41 should be performed in conjunction with the entries in Table 3.8 for the figure to be meaningful. For example, from Table 3.8, the maximum collision domain for a class II repeater is 205 meters. If you focus your attention upon collision domain 1 in Figure 3.41, you will note that the inter-repeater segment is shown as 5 meters to keep the maximum collision diameter equal or below 205 meters. You can increase the inter-repeater segment length; however, you would then need to reduce the other segments to ensure that the maximum collision diameter in the domain does not exceed 205 meters.

Computer Bus Considerations

In addition to having to consider the type or types of NIC connectors, it is also extremely important to consider the bus they are designed to work with along with driver support for different operating systems. Some NICs are limited to one type of connector, requiring the purchase of a separate converter if you decide to use a different media other than the media the NIC was manufactured to directly support.

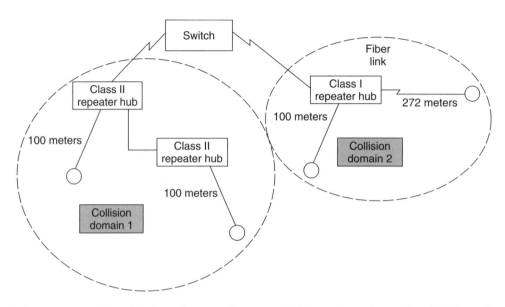

Figure 3.41 Considering the maximum collision domain and cable length when configuring a Fast Ethernet network.

Concerning computer bus support, in the DOS/Windows world you can select NICs that work with the original IBM PC 8- and 16-bit industry-standard architecture (ISA) bus, the 32-bit extended industry-standard architecture (EISA) bus, IBM's proprietary and essentially now obsolete microchannel architecture (MCA) 16- and 32-bit buses, and the 32- and 64-bit peripheral-component interconnect (PCI) bus. The key difference between adapters supporting different computer buses is in their ability to transmit and receive sustained bursts of traffic such as file transfers. The ISA bus has a throughput between 4 Mbytes/sec and 5 Mbytes/sec, while the first-generation EISA bus has a throughput of 16 Mbytes/sec, later modified to support burst speeds up to 33 Mbytes/sec. IBM's 16-bit MCA bus can reach 20 Mbytes/sec, with its 32-bit bus slightly exceeding 36 Mbytes/sec. While all of the preceding buses can normally support small bursts of traffic onto a network operating at 10 Mbps, when used for sustained transfers onto a 100-Mbps network those buses cannot keep up with the network, resulting in a suboptimal level of performance. However, the use of a PCI-based NIC can resolve such problems. This is because the 32-bit PCI bus can support data bursts up to 132 Mbytes/sec while a 64-bit PCI bus can reach 264 Mbytes/sec, sufficient for operations at 100 Mbps.

Figure 3.42 The 3Com Corporation Fast Etherlink TX NIC supports the use of the ISA bus. (Photograph courtesy of 3Com Corporation.)

Figures 3.42 through 3.44 illustrate three 3Com Corporation Fast Ethernet NICs manufactured to support different computer buses. Figure 3.42 shows the 3Com 3C515-TX NIC, which supports the ISA bus. Figure 3.43 shows the 3Com Corporation's Fast Etherlink PT adapter, which supports the EISA bus. The third 3Com NIC shown in Figure 3.44 is the Fast Etherlink XL, designed to support the PCI bus.

A third NIC-related item that warrants careful consideration when selecting an appropriate NIC is the drivers available for use with the adapter. Today, in addition to different versions of NetWare and Windows, there are other operating systems ranging from LINUX to different versions of UNIX you may need to support. Although support for many NICs and protocols is built into many operating systems, such support is not all-inclusive. This means you may have to obtain one or more files from the NIC manufacturer to be able to use the NIC with a particular operating system. Figure 3.45 illustrates how under Windows NT Version 4.0 you would select the "Have Disk" option if your NIC wasn't directly supported, resulting in the display of the "Insert Disk" dialog box to enable NT to recognize your adapter.

One of the more interesting aspects concerning the use of NIC drivers, obtained from firsthand experience, is to ensure you have the appropriate

Figure 3.43 The 3Com Corporation Fast Etherlink PT NIC supports the use of the EISA bus. (Photograph courtesy of 3Com Corporation.)

Figure 3.44 The 3Com Corporation Fast Etherlink XL NIC supports the use of the PCI bus. (Photograph courtesy of 3Com Corporation.)

Figure 3.45 When using Windows NT you can specify a "Have Disk" option to use a NIC adapter not directly supported by that operating system.

driver. On occasion, it was found that the diskette packaged with the NIC manual and shipped with a newly purchased computer did not contain the appropriate driver for the computer. Although the operating system would use the driver, the computer would freeze about once a month, a situation corrected when it was determined that the computer manufacturer had a Web site with updated drivers for the NIC shipped with their computer.

100VG-AnyLAN

100VG-AnyLAN was originally proposed by AT&T Microelectronics and Hewlett-Packard Company as a mechanism to support evolving LAN-based multimedia applications. To accomplish this, the proposal, which became the IEEE 802.12 standard, replaced the CSMA/CD access protocol by a demand-priority scheme. This scheme enables the transmission of time-sensitive video and voice associated with multimedia applications in preference to conventional data that is relatively time-insensitive. In addition, the use of a demand-priority scheme extends 100VG-AnyLAN beyond Ethernet, enabling this network to support Token-Ring, FDDI, and other types of local area networks.

Although 100VG-AnyLAN included many interesting technical characteristics, it never achieved widespread adoption. The significant commercial success of 100BASE-T, as well as the rapid reduction in the cost of Gigabit Ethernet hardware, more than likely affected its adoption. In late 2000, Hewlett-Packard, which was the major proponent of 100VG-AnyLAN, announced plans to discontinue the sale and future development of interface cards, software license and documentation for its e3000 business servers.

Architecture

While recognizing that the market for VG-AnyLAN is minimal, in order to provide readers with information about different types of Ethernet networks, in concluding this section we will briefly examine the architecture and basic operation associated with the technology.

100VG-AnyLAN was designed as a hub-centric network architecture. A central hub, known as a level-1 or *root* hub, functions as an inverted tree base in establishing a 100VG-AnyLAN network. From this hub other hubs and/or nodes form a star topology, fanning out underneath the root hub, as illustrated in Figure 3.46. All hubs located in the same network segment must be configured to support the same frame format — IEEE 802.3 Ethernet or IEEE 802.5 Token-Ring. Through the attachment of a bridge or router to a hub port you can extend the 100VG-AnyLAN network to interconnect with other Ethernet or Token-Ring networks, FDDI- and ATM-based networks, or a wide area network transmission facility.

Each hub in a 100VG-AnyLAN network has one up-link port, labeled *up* in Figure 3.46; and *n* down-link ports, labeled 1 through *N*. The up-link port on each hub is reserved for connecting lower-level hubs to an upper-level hub, while the down-link ports are used to connect an upper-level hub to workstations, bridges, routers, and other network devices to include lower-level hubs. Up to three levels of cascading can be used on a 100VG-AnyLAN network.

Hub Operation

Each hub port can be configured to operate in one of two modes — normal or monitor. Ports configured to operate in their normal mode are forwarded only those packets specifically addressed to the attached node. In comparison, ports configured to operate in the monitor mode are forwarded every packet received by the hub.

Level-1 *Root* hub

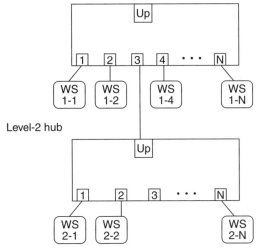

Level-2 hub

Legend: WS 1-p = workstation hub level-port

Figure 3.46   100VG-AnyLAN topology.

Devices connected to nodes gain access to a 100VG-AnyLAN network through the use of a centrally controlled access method, referred to as demand-priority. Under the demand-priority access method a node issues a request, referred to as a demand, to the hub it is connected to, to transmit a packet onto the 100VG-AnyLAN network. Each request includes a priority label assigned by the upper-layer application. The priority label is either normal, for normal data packets, or high, for packets carrying time-critical multimedia information. As you might expect, high-priority requests are granted access to the network before normal-priority requests are granted.

The level 1 or root hub continuously scans its ports using a round-robin sequence for requests. Lower-level hubs connected as nodes also perform a round-robin scanning process and forward node requests to the root hub. The root hub determines which nodes are requesting permission to transmit a packet as well as the priority level associated with the packet. Each hub maintains a separate list for both normal- and high-priority requests.

Normal-priority requests are serviced in their port order until a higher-priority request is received. Upon receipt of a higher-priority request the hub will complete any packet transmission in progress and then service the high-priority packet before returning to service the normal-priority list.

To prevent a long sequence of high-priority requests from abnormally delaying low-priority requests from being serviced, the hub also monitors node request-to-send response times. If the delay exceeds a predefined time, the hub automatically raises the normal-priority level to a high-priority level.

Round-Robin Scanning

Figure 3.47 illustrates an example of the 100VG-AnyLAN hub round-robin scanning process. Assume all ports initially have normal-priority requests pending. Then, the round-robin sequence at the root or level 1 hub results in the packet service order commencing at the level 1 hub's first port (1-1). Next, the level 1 hub's second port is serviced (1-2). When the third port is examined, it inserts the round-robin sequence generated by the level 2 hub. That is, it inserts the packet order sequence 2-1, 2-2, 2-3, ..., 2-N. This sequence is then followed by adding the remaining level 1 hub ports. Thus, the inserted packet order sequence is followed by the sequence 1-4, ..., 1-N. Now let's assume at time t = 0 nodes 2-1 and 1-4 generate high-priority requests. Then, the packet service order at the level 1 hub would be revised, becoming 2-1, 1-4, 1-1, 1-2, 2-2, ..., 2-N, 1-5, ..., 1-N.

Level-1 Root hub

Level-2 hub

If all ports have normal-priority requests pending, then:
Level-1 scan 1-1, 1-2, 1-3, 1-4, ..., 1-N

Level-2 scan 2-1, 2-2, 2-3, ..., 2-N

Level-1 resulting packet order sequence
1-1, 1-2, 2-1, 2-2, 2-3, ..., 2-N, 1-4, ..., 1-N

Figure 3.47 100VG-AnyLAN hub round-robin scanning.

Cabling Requirements

100VG-AnyLAN products provide a 100-Mbps data rate using 4-pair category 3, 4, or 5 unshielded twisted-pair cable. 100VG-AnyLAN also supports 2-pair UTP, 2-pair STP, and fiber-optic cabling. The cabling medium required for 4-pair 100VG-AnyLAN is 4-pair UTP that meets the specifications of the EIA/TIA-568 standard for 100-ohm category 3, 4, or 5 cable. Such cable connects to RJ-45 wall jacks and can go through punch-down blocks or patch panels in a wiring closet.

Figure 3.48 indicates the RJ-45 modular plug pin assignments for 4-UTP 100VG-AnyLAN. In addition, this illustration indicates for comparison purposes the pairs used by 10BASE-T and Token-Ring cable.

Comparing Technologies

Both 100BASE-T and 100VG-AnyLAN provide users with a tenfold increase in network operating rates with respect to 10BASE-T. However, the 100-Mbps

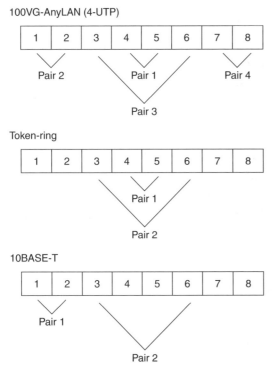

Figure 3.48   RJ-45 modular plug pin assignments.

operating rate represents one of the few common operating characteristics between the two technologies.

100BASE-T was designed as a mechanism to provide a growth path from 100BASE-T while enabling organizations to retain the invested base of 10BASE-T adapter cards and cabling for workstations that do not require a 100-Mbps operational capability. In doing so, no provision was made to prioritize traffic. Thus, while a lightly or medium loaded 100BASE-T network can transport multimedia data, this may not be true as the network load increases.

The replacement of the CSMA/CD access protocol by a demand-priority protocol results in 100VG-AnyLAN being more suitable for multimedia applications. Unfortunately, there is a cost associated with the additional technology incorporated into 100VG-AnyLAN, which resulted in network adapters initially costing 50 percent more than 100BASE-T adapters and precluded its widespread adoption. Table 3.9 provides a comparison of the operating characteristics of 100BASE-T and 100VG-AnyLAN.

A comparison of 100VG-AnyLAN to 100BASE-T is probably similar to a comparison of Beta to VHS. While Beta was a superior technology, the VHS extended record and playback time better satisfied consumer requirements. If we turn our focus back to LANs, 100BASE-T better interoperates with 10BASE-T through an auto-negotiation capability. This makes it easier to construct interoperable networks. Based upon the preceding, 100BASE-T products dominate the high-speed Ethernet marketplace.

3.5 Gigabit Ethernet

Gigabit Ethernet represents an extension to the 10-Mbps and 100-Mbps IEEE 802.3 Ethernet standards. Providing a data transmission capability of 1000 Mbps, Gigabit Ethernet supports the CMSA/CD access protocol, which makes various types of Ethernet networks scalable from 10 Mbps to 1 Gbps, with the pending standardization of 10-Gigabit Ethernet providing additional scalability to 10 Gbps.

Components

Similar to 10BASE-T and Fast Ethernet, Gigabit Ethernet can be used as a shared network through the attachment of network devices to a 1-Gbps repeater hub providing shared use of the 1-Gbps operating rate or as a switch,

TABLE 3.9 Operating Characteristics Comparison

Data rate	100BASE-T	100VG-AnyLAN
	100 Mbps	100 Mbps
Access protocol	CSMA/CD	Demand-priority
Frame support	802.3 Ethernet	802.3 Ethernet
	802.5 Token-Ring	
Physical topology	Star	Star
Cable support		
2-pair Category 5 UTP	100BASE-TX	Not planned
4-pair Category 3, 4, or 5 UTP	100BASE-T4	Yes
2-pair STP	100BASE-TX	Yes
Fiber	100BASE-FX	Yes
Maximum UTP drive distance	100 meters on Category 5 UTP	100 meters Category 3, 4, UTP
Maximum repeaters allowed	2	4
Maximum UTP network diameter	200 meters	4,000 meters
Other cabling	2-pair Type 1 STP; optical fiber; 4-pair Category 3, 4, 5 UTP	2-pair Type 1 STP; optical fiber; 2-pair Category 5 UTP
Full duplex support	Yes	Yes

the latter providing 1-Gbps ports to accommodate high-speed access to servers while lower operating rate ports provide access to 10-Mbps and 100-Mbps workstations and hubs. Although few organizations can be expected to require the use of a 1-Gbps shared media network as illustrated in Figure 3.49a, the use of Gigabit switches can be expected to play an important role in providing a high-speed backbone linking 100-Mbps network users to large databases, mainframes, and other types of resources that can tax lower-speed networks. In addition to hubs and switches, Gigabit Ethernet operations require workstations, bridges, and routers to use a network interface card to connect to a 1-Gbps network. Gigabit Ethernet NICs introduced when this book was written were designed for PCI bus operations and use an SC fiber connector to support 62.5/125 and 50/125 micron fiber. Such adapters provide 1 Gbps of bandwidth for shared media operations and 2 Gbps aggregate bandwidth when used for a full-duplex connection to a switch port. In Chapter 5, when

In a shared media environment the 1-Gbps bandwidth provided by
Gigabit Ethernet is shared among all users.

(a) Shared media hub use

In a switch environment each 1-Gbps port can provide a full–duplex
2-Gbps data transfer capability.

Legend: ◯ = workstations

(b) Switching hub use

Figure 3.49 Using Gigabit Ethernet.

we review switching, we will examine in more detail how Gigabit switches
can be used to provide a backbone network capability.

Sublayer Architecture

Similar to Fast Ethernet, it was recognized that Gigabit Ethernet would operate
over different types of media, resulting in the need to develop an architecture
that included sublayers well suited to support the coding necessary for the
different media. Figure 3.50 illustrates the sublayer architecture of Gigabit
Ethernet and the relationship of the sublayers to the lower two layers of the
ISO's Open System Interconnection (OSI) Reference Model.

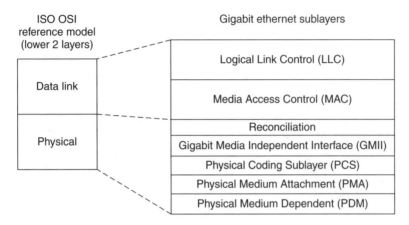

Figure 3.50 Gigabit Ethernet Sublayer Architecture.

In examining the Gigabit Ethernet sublayer architecture shown in Figure 3.50 you will note its resemblance to Fast Ethernet. The reconciliation sub-layer represents a transparent interface between the MAC sublayer and the physical layer, decoupling the above sublayer from the physical sublayer. The function of the reconciliation layer is to collect 8-bit bytes from the MAC layer for transfer onto the Gigabit Media Independent Interface (GMII). The GMII contains 8-bit transmit and receive data paths and a 125-MHz clock, resulting in a data transfer rate to and from the MAC layer of 1 Gbps.

Under the GMII the same basic sublayers are used as under Fast Ethernet. However, instead of using FDDI coding and signaling, Gigabit Ethernet relies on the physical sublayers of the Fiber Channel standard.

Media Support

There are five types of media supported by Gigabit Ethernet — single-mode fiber, multimode fiber, short runs of coaxial cable or shielded twisted pair, and longer runs of unshielded twisted pair. Figure 3.51 illustrates the relationship of Gigabit Ethernet's MAC and physical layers to include the drive distances supported for each type of media. Table 3.10 summarizes the flavors of Gigabit Ethernet indicating the IEEE designator used to reference Gigabit operations on a specific type of media and the maximum transmission distance associated with the use of each type of media.

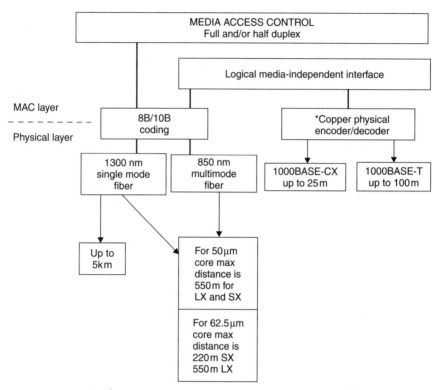

Figure 3.51 Gigabit Ethernet media support. Encoding method for 1000BASE-T to be defined by the IEEE 802.3ab Task Force, probably during late 1998.

TABLE 3.10 The Flavors of Gigabit Ethernet

Media Designator	Media Type	Transmission Distance
1000BASE-LX	SMF 8/125 μ	5 km
1000BASE-LH	SMF 8/125 μ	70 km
1000BASE-LX	MMF, 50/125 μ	550 m
1000BASE-LX	MMF, 62.5/125 μ	550 m
1000BASE-SX	MMF, 50/125 μ	550 m
1000BASE-SX	MMF, 62.5/125 μ	220 m
1000BASE-CX	Shielded balanced copper(coaxor STP)	25 m
1000BASE-T	UTP,Category 5	100 m

SMF, single-mode fiber; MMF, multimode fiber; UTP, unshielded twisted pair; STP, shielded twisted pair.

Single-Mode Fiber

The specification that governs the use of single-mode fiber is referred to as 1000BASE-LX, where *L* represents recognition of the use of long-wave light pulses. The maximum distance obtainable for Gigabit Ethernet when transmission occurs using a 1330-nanometer (nm) frequency on single-mode fiber is 5 km. The 1000BASE-LX cabling standard is based upon the use of a 1300 nm laser, which is also used in FDDI. This provides a transmission distance up to 5 km when the laser is used with single-mode fiber. When a 1300 nm laser is used with multi-mode fiber the maximum transmission distance is reduced to 550 m.

1000BASE-LH

Although not part of the original Gigabit Ethernet specification the use of a 1550 nm laser with single-mode fiber has received considerable attention and is referred to as 1000BASE-LH. When a 1550 nm laser is used with 8/125μ single-mode fiber, a transmission range up to 70 km becomes possible, which expands the potential use of Gigabit Ethernet to wide area networking.

In examining Figure 3.51, note that the 8B/10B coding scheme used for both single-mode and multimode fiber represents the coding scheme used by the Fibre Channel. Due to the importance of Fibre Channel technology incorporated into Gigabit Ethernet, a short digression to discuss that technology is warranted.

The Fibre Channel The Fibre Channel actually represents a rather old technology, dating back to 1988 when the American National Standards Institute charted a working group to develop a high-speed data transfer capability for supporting data transfers between computers and peripheral devices. Initially, the Fibre Channel was developed to support fiber-optic cabling. When support for copper media was added, an ISO task force renamed the spelling of fiber to reduce the association of fiber optics while maintaining the name recognition of the technology. Today both optical and electrical copper-based media are supported by the Fibre Channel, with operating rates ranging from 133 Mbps to 1.062 Gbps provided by most equipment. In 1995 ANSI approved 2.134- and 4.25-Gbps speed rates as enhancements to the previously developed Fibre Channel specifications.

The Fibre Channel supports point-to-point, shared media, and switch network topologies, with Fibre Channel hubs, switches, loop access controllers, and NICs installed on computers used to provide different network structures. The Fibre Channel supports a five-layer protocol stack from FC-0 through

FC-4. The three lower layers form the Fibre Channel physical standard, while the two upper layers provide the interface to network protocols and applications. The FC-0 layer defines the physical characteristics of the media, transmitters, receivers, and connectors available for use, transmission rates supported, electrical and optical characteristics, and other physical layer standards. The second layer, FC-1, defines the 8B/10B encoding and decoding method used, a serial physical transport, timing recovery, and serial line balance. The 8B/10B encoding and decoding scheme was patented by IBM and is the same technique used in that vendor's 200-Mbps ESCON channel technology. Under 8B/10B coding eight data bits are transmitted as a 10-bit group. The two extra bits are used for error detection and correction.

To enable 1-Gbps operations the transmission rate of the Fibre Channel was raised to 1.25 Gbps. Then, the use of an 8B/10B coding technique permits data transfer at 80 percent of the operating rate or $1.256 * 80$, resulting in the modified Fibre Channel technology being capable of supporting the 1-Gbps data transfer of Gigabit Ethernet.

The third layer, FC-2, functions as the transport mechanism. This layer defines the framing rules of data transmitted between devices and how data flow is regulated. Although Ethernet frames are encapsulated within Fibre Channel frames for transmission between devices, the encapsulation is transparent to the Ethernet frame. Thus, the use of a modified Fibre Channel technology enabled the IEEE to use a proven technology as a transport mechanism for connecting Gigabit Ethernet devices while enabling the CSMA/CD protocol and Ethernet frame to be retained.

Multimode Fiber

The support of multimode fiber is applicable to both long-wave (LX) and short-wave (SX) versions of Gigabit Ethernet. When transmission occurs on multimode fiber the short-wave version of Gigabit Ethernet, which is referred to as 1000BASE-SX, uses an 850-nm frequency, providing a 220-meter maximum distance when transmission occurs over a 62.5-micron (μm) core. Note that in some trade publications and books the maximum transmission distance may be indicated as either 260 or 300 meters; however, in September 1997, the IEEE task force working on the development of Gigabit Ethernet standards lowered the maximum distance to 260 meters from 300 meters and, due to problems encountered from using an extremely high-frequency light source over multi-mode fiber referred to as differential mode delay, had again to lower the maximum transmission distance. That distance is now 220 meters when 62.5/125μ multi-mode fiber is used. When 50/125μ multi-mode fiber is used the maximum transmission distance is 550 meters. When a 1300-nm frequency is used on a 62.5-μm core, which represents 1000BASE-LX, a maximum transmission distance of 550 meters becomes possible. This distance was formerly 500 meters and was reduced by the IEEE Gigabit Ethernet task force and then revised back above its original valve. When a 50-micron core fiber is used, the maximum distance is 550 meters for both LX and SX specifications.

Copper Media

Gigabit Ethernet supports three types of copper media—category 5 STP, coaxial cable, and UTP. The use of the first two types of copper media are defined by the 1000BASE-CX standard, which governs the use of patch cords and jumpers that provide a maximum cabling distance of 25 meters. This standard also uses the Fibre Channel–based 8B/10B coding method at a serial line operating rate of 125 Gbps, and runs over a 150-ohm balanced, shielded, cable assembly, referred to as twinax cable as well as on STP. The 25-meter maximum cabling distance makes 1000BASE-CX suitable for use in a wiring closet or a computer room as a short jumper interconnection cable. In comparison, the 1000BASE-T standard defines the use of four-pair HTP cable, with each wire carrying a 125-MHz signal in each direction.

The transmission of data at 1 Gbps over copper represented a daunting challenge. Not only was the data rate on a per-wire-pair basis extremely high at 250 Mbps, but, in addition, developers needed to consider the dual-duplex transmission method by which signals could flow in both directions simultaneously on all four wire pairs. This challenge resulted in the need to charter a separate working group referred to as the IEEE 802.3ab task force to develop specifications for the transmission of Gigabit over VTP. The task force examined three encoding schemes referred to as QAM (quadrature amplitude modulation), PAM (pulse amplitude modulation), and CAP (carrierless amplitude phase modulation). Each coding scheme uses a different procedure and operates between 75 and 125 MHz in frequency. Both the selection of an encoding scheme and the method for manufacturers of NICs to block frequencies above 30 MHz under FCC regulations were required to be addressed.

As a result of the efforts of the IEEE 802.3ab task force a five-level version of PAM was selected as the coding method, with each level representing a symbol that transports two bits of information. Under five-level PAM each transmitted symbol represents one of five different levels (-2, -1, 0, $+1$, $+2$). For example, a signal level of -2 could be used to represent the dibit pair 00 while the signal level -1 could represent the dibit pair 01. To support bi-directional transmission over each wire pair digital signal processors (DSPs) are used. The DSPs operate similar to DSPs used in modem transmission that support full-duplex operations over a wire pair. That is, the DSPs support echo cancellation in which the transported signal is then suppressed.

Gigabit Repeater

To extend the transmission distance of Gigabit Ethernet the IEEE defined two types of repeaters. Those repeaters are known as Transmission System Model 1 and Transmission System Model 2. The use of either type of repeater is governed by the round-trip propagation delay characteristics associated with different network devices to include data terminal equipment (DTE) adapter card delays and repeater delays.

Under the Transmission System Model 1 rules are defined for DTE to DTE direct connections as well as for the use of a single repeater used to inter-connect media using different signaling methods. The use of a Transmission System Model 1 repeater connects segments into a single collision domain. Table 3.11 lists the maximum transmission distances associated with the use of a transmission system 1 repeater.

The second type of repeater specified for Gigabit Ethernet is referred to as a Transmission System Model 2 repeater. Similar to a model 1 system, a model 2 system is used to interconnect DTEs. The constraints concerning the use of a Model 2 repeater include use of only one such repeater and the round trip propagation delay between two interconnected DTEs should not exceed 4096 bit times. While the use of a Model 2 repeater provides more flexibility

TABLE 3.11 Maximum Transmission Distance Using a Transmission System Model 1 Repeater

Media (DTE to DTE)	Maximum Distance (Meters)
Category 5 UTP	200
Twin-axial	50
1000BASE-LX or 1000BASE-SX	220
Category 5 UTP and 1000BASE-LX or 1000BASE-SX	210*
Twin-axial and 1000BASE-LX or 1000BASE-SX	220[†]

Notes:
*Assumes 1000 meters of category 5 UTP.
[†]Assumes 25 meters of twin-axial.

than the use of a Model 1 repeater, the user becomes responsible for ensuring that the round trip propagation delay constraint is not violated.

When computing the round-trip propagation delay you need to consider the media delays, DTE delays, repeater delay and a safety margin, with the last specified as 32 bit times. Table 3.12 indicates the maximum round-trip delays associated with different Gigabit Ethernet network components.

To illustrate the use of the delay times listed in Table 3.12, let's assume we want to interconnect two DTEs through the use of 100 meters of UTP and 110 meters of 1000BASE-LX. When using a Transmission System Model 2 repeater our computations would be as in Table 3.13. Note that the total of 4095 bit times is less than the 4096 maximum permitted bit time, which means that the use of the repeater is just within tolerance.

TABLE 3.12   Gigabit Ethernet Component Delay Time

Component	Round Trip Delay (Bit Times)
Safety Margin	32
Each DTE	432
Repeater	976
Category 5 UTP	11.12 bit times/meter
Twin-axial	10.10 bit times/meter
1000BAE-LX or SX	10.10 bit times/meter

TABLE 3.13   Computations for a Transmission Model 2 Repeater

Component	Bit Time
DTE1	432
100 meters UTP	1112
Repeater	976
100 meters 1000BASE-LX	1111
DTE2	432
Safety Margin	32
Total bit time	4095

Duplex Capability

Gigabit Ethernet supports a full-duplex operating mode for switch-to-switch and switch-to-end station connections, while a half-duplex operating mode is used for shared connections using repeaters. Although not supported in the 802.3z standard, several vendors announced full-duplex, multiport, hublike devices to be used to interconnect two or more 802.3 links operating at 1 Gbps. Referred to as a buffered distributor, this device functions as a repeater, forwarding all incoming data received on one port onto all ports other than the original port. However, unlike conventional repeaters, the buffered distributor has the ability to buffer one or more inbound frames on each port before forwarding them.

In addition to having memory, the buffered distributor supports the IEEE 802.3z flow control standard. These two features enable each port on a buffered distributor to provide transmission support at a rate that matches the maximum rate of the 1-Gbps shared bus used to broadcast frames received on one port to all other ports. Because the buffered distributor supports 802.3z full-duplex flow control, the situation where an offered load exceeds the bandwidth of the shared bus is easily handled. This is accomplished by a port transmitting a flow control frame to the transmitting system, indicating that the port cannot accommodate additional data. The 802.3z-compliant transmitting device will then cease transmission until the port forwards a frame indicating it can accept additional data.

To illustrate the operation of a buffered distributor, consider Figure 3.52, which illustrates the use of a four-port buffered distributor. Let's assume that at a certain point in time devices connected to ports 1 and 3 are transmitting

Legend : ⟶ = Enable/Disable flow control frames

Figure 3.52 A buffered distributor uses IEEE 802.3z flow control whenever the offered traffic exceeds the bandwidth of its shared bus.

data to the buffered distributor at 700 Mbps and 400 Mbps, respectively. It should be noted that those data rates represent traffic carried and not the operating rate of those devices which would be 1 Gbps. Because the aggregate rate exceeds 1 Gbps, a normal repeater would not be able to support this traffic load. However, a buffered repeater includes a memory buffer area into which the excessive 100-Mbps transmission (1100 − 1000) rapidly fills. To insure that its buffers do not overflow, the buffered repeater will issue a flow control signal telling the transmitters to reduce their transmission rate. This flow control signal will occur once the occupancy of the buffer reaches a predefined level of occupancy, as indicated in the right portion of Figure 3.52. Once data from the buffer is serviced to the point where occupancy is at a predefined low level, the buffered distributor will use flow control to enable transmission to the distributor by disabling flow control.

To provide an equitable method for sharing the 1-Gbps bus, the buffered distributor uses a round-robin algorithm to determine which port can transmit onto the bus. This round-robin method occurs one frame at a time, with port 1 serviced, followed by port 2, and so on. Through the use of a buffered distributor, it becomes possible to support applications that require a many-to-one transmission capability, such as a LAN with a local server used for graphic database queries, e-mail, and similar applications. Instead of migrating the LAN to a switch environment, a buffered distributor may represent another possible network solution to network bottlenecks for power users.

3.6 10 Gigabit Ethernet

The focus of this section is upon the next generation Ethernet standard, which increases the CSMA/CD operating rate to 10 Gbps. In this section we will examine the rationale for 10 Gbps Ethernet, its architecture and expected operating rates.

Rationale

For many organizations it is hard to imagine the need for transporting data at 1 Gbps. For other organizations Gigabit Ethernet represents a needed but insufficient transport capability to satisfy existing or evolving communications requirements. As we noted in the prior section in this chapter, the use of 1000BASE-LH provides a transmission distance of 70 km and extends Gigabit Ethernet into the wide area network. This makes Gigabit Ethernet a viable transport for use by communications carriers. However, because such carriers transport information from numerous organizations over the WAN, Gigabit

Ethernet may not provide sufficient capacity. Similarly, when used by an Internet Service Provider (ISP) in a LAN environment, the growth in the use of the Internet has placed a considerable load on Gigabit networks. As a result of the preceding as well as other networking examples, the IEEE formed a High Speed Study Group (HSSG) during 1999 to develop a standard for 10 Gbps Ethernet. The primary objectives of the study group included maintaining the Ethernet frame format while increasing the operating rate of Gigabit Ethernet by an order of magnitude at a cost between two to three times the cost of Gigabit Ethernet.

At the time this book revision occurred the evolving 10 Gbps Ethernet standard was being developed for use over multi-mode and single-mode optical fiber since the data rate was too high to be transported over copper media. Initially developed specifications are for full-duplex operation using an architecture similar to that developed for Gigabit Ethernet.

Architecture

The architecture of 10 Gigabit Ethernet is similar to that used for Gigabit Ethernet. Figure 3.53 illustrates the sublayers of 10 Gigabit Ethernet compared to the lower two layers of the ISO OSI Reference Model. In comparing Gigabit and 10 Gigabit Ethernet you will note the primary difference is the use of

Figure 3.53 10 Gigabit Ethernet architecture.

a 10 Gigabit Ethernet Media Independent Interface (10 GMII) for 10 Gigabit Ethernet. Similar to the GMII used by Gigabit Ethernet, the 10 GMII provides an interface between the MAC and the physical layer, isolating each from one another.

A key difference between the 10 GMII and the GMII is the width of the data path between the MAC sublayer and the physical layer. Under Gigabit Ethernet the GMII data bus is 8 bits in width. Under 10 GMII a 32-bit data path is used. Figure 3.54 illustrates the structure of the 10 GMII used for 10 Gigabit Ethernet. Note that the actual signal interface is 72 bits in width. That signal interface includes 32-bit data paths for transmit and receive and four control bits to govern transmission and reception. In addition to the signal interface the 10 GMII includes two clocking lines and a TX_word_hold lines.

The TX_word_hold line is used to support word-oriented pacing. The 32-bit data paths provide transmit and receive functions that employ four control bits, with one control bit used for each 8-bit data byte. A control bit is set to 1 for denoting delimiters and special characters and to a binary 0 for data. Examples of delimiter and special characters include:

- IDLE used during inter-packet gap and when there is no data to transmit.
- SOP used to indicate the start of each packet.
- EOP used to indicate the end of each packet.
- ERROR used to indicate the detection of an error in the received signal or when an error condition needs to be transmitted.

Returning our attention to the architecture of 10 Gigabit Ethernet, the physical coding sublayer (PCS) is responsible for coding and decoding data streams flowing to and from the MAC layer. The PCS layer uses 8B/10B coding

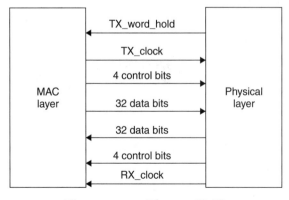

Figure 3.54 The 10 GMII.

employed by Gigabit Ethernet, which was originally developed by IBM. In comparison, the Physical Medium Attachment (PMA) sublayer is responsible for taking parallel data and serializing code groups into a bit stream suitable for serial bit-oriented communications as well as performing the reverse operation. In doing so the PMA is also responsible for providing applicable synchronization. Below the PMA is the Physical Medium Dependent (PMD) sublayer. The PMD is responsible for signal transmission to include amplification, modulation and wave shaping. Optical transceivers can be considered to represent devices that operate at the PMD sublayer. Different PMD sublayers can be expected to be employed to support different types of media. In fact, at the time this book revision was prepared the IEEE 802.3ae Task Force had developed a draft standard that requires the support of four distinct link distances over different types of optical fiber. To meet the Task Force distance objectives required four PMDs, as indicated in Table 3.14. In examining the entries in Table 3.14 you will note the Task Force selected two versions of wide wavelength division multiplexing. A 1310 nanometer (nm) version was selected for use over single-mode fiber to provide a transmission distance of 10 km, while a 1310 nm PMD was selected to provide a drive distance of 300 meters over multimode fiber. The latter PMD recognizes the fact that many organizations have existing multimode fiber and its replacement would represent an expenditure of time and material, so the ability to run 10 Gigabit Ethernet over existing multimode fiber became an objective of the IEEE Task Force.

The use of 850 nm laser over multimode fiber also provides organizations with an upgrade path without having to change their cabling infrastructure. The selection of a 1550 nm laser to provide a link transmission of 40 km provides a mechanism to use 10 Gigabit Ethernet in metropolitan as well as private long-distance applications.

TABLE 3.14 10 Gigabit PMD Support

Optical Transceiver	Type of Fiber Supported	Target Transmission Distance
850 nm serial	Multi-mode	65 m
1310 nm WWDM	Multi-mode	300 m
1310 nm WWDM	Single mode	10 km
1310 nm serial	Single mode	10 km
1550 nm serial	Single mode	40 km

Returning our attention to the 10 Gigabit Ethernet architecture shown in Figure 3.53, the Media Dependent Interface (MDI) provides the connector to a particular media.

Operating Rates

While it would appear that the specifications of a data rate for 10 Gbps Ethernet would be simple task, in actuality it wasn't. While proponents of the use of 10 Gbps Ethernet in a LAN environment want the data rate to be ten times the 1 Gbps Ethernet rate, proponents of the use of 10 Gbps Ethernet in the WAN prefer the optical carrier (OC)-192 data payload rate of approximately 9.29 Gbps. Due to the diligent requirements of LAN and WAN proponents of 10 Gigabit Ethernet, it appears that both operating rates will be supported by the evolving standard.

chapter four

Frame Operations

In this chapter, we will first focus our attention on the composition of different types of Ethernet frames. In reality, there is only one physical Ethernet frame. However, the composition of the frame was altered by the IEEE when the CSMA/CD original Ethernet frame format was standardized by that organization as the 802.3 frame. In addition, the logical composition of the data field within the 802.3 frame can vary based upon the protocol transported.

Once we obtain an understanding of the composition of Ethernet and IEEE 802.3 frames, we will examine the function of fields within each frame, as well as the manner in which the placement of frames on the media is controlled — a process known as *media access control*. After this is accomplished, we will turn our attention to the manner by which protocol information is carried within an IEEE 802.3 frame to include logical link control (LLC), NetWare, TCP/IP, and other protocols.

Although the composition of the IEEE 802.3 frame remains the same from 10-Mbps through 10-Gbps operations, there are certain restrictions on the framing of frames and the minimum size of the information field at different network operating rates. Thus, in the last two sections in this chapter, we will examine certain modifications and restrictions on frames transported on Fast Ethernet and Gigabit and 10 Gigabit Ethernet networks.

4.1 Frame Composition

Figure 4.1 illustrates the general frame composition of Ethernet and IEEE 802.3 frames. You will note that they differ slightly. An Ethernet frame contains an eight-byte preamble, while the IEEE 802.3 frame contains a seven-byte preamble followed by a one-byte start-of-frame delimiter field. A second difference between the composition of Ethernet and IEEE 802.3 frames concerns

Ethernet

Preamble	Destination address	Source address	Type	Data	Frame check sequence
8 bytes	6 bytes	6 bytes	2 bytes	46–1500 bytes	4 bytes

IEEE 802.3

Preamble	Start of frame delimiter	Destination address	Source address	Length	Data	Frame check sequence
7 bytes	1 byte	2/6 bytes	2/6 bytes	2 bytes	46–1500 bytes	4 bytes

Figure 4.1 Ethernet and IEEE 802.3 frame formats.

the two-byte Ethernet type field. That field is used by Ethernet to specify the protocol carried in the frame, enabling several protocols to be carried independently of one another. Under the IEEE 802.3 frame format, the type field was replaced by a two-byte length field, which specifies the number of bytes that follow that field as data.

The differences between Ethernet and IEEE 802.3 frames, while minor, make the two incompatible with one another. This means that your network must contain either all Ethernet-compatible NICs or all IEEE 802.3–compatible NICs. Fortunately, the fact that the IEEE 802.3 frame format represents a standard means that almost all vendors now market 802.3-compliant hardware and software. Although a few vendors continue to manufacture Ethernet or dual functioning Ethernet/IEEE 802.3 hardware, such products are primarily used to provide organizations with the ability to expand previously developed networks without requiring the wholesale replacement of NICs. Although the IEEE 802.3 frame does not directly support a type field within the frame, as we will note in Section 4 in this chapter, the IEEE defined a special type of frame to obtain compatibility with Ethernet LANs. That frame is referred to as an Ethernet Subnetwork Access Protocol (Ethernet-SNAP) frame, which enables a type subfield to be included in the data field. While the IEEE 802.3 standard has essentially replaced Ethernet, because of their similarities and the fact that 802.3 was based upon Ethernet, we will consider both to be Ethernet.

Now that we have an overview of the structure of Ethernet and 802.3 frames, let's probe more deeply and examine the composition of each frame field. We will take advantage of the similarity between Ethernet and IEEE 802.3 frames to examine the fields of each frame on a composite basis, noting the differences between the two when appropriate.

Preamble Field

The preamble field consists of eight (Ethernet) or seven (IEEE 802.3) bytes of alternating 1 and 0 bits. The purpose of this field is to announce the frame and to enable all receivers on the network to synchronize themselves to the incoming frame.

Start-of-Frame Delimiter Field

This field is applicable only to the IEEE 802.3 standard and can be viewed as a continuation of the preamble. In fact, the composition of this field continues in the same manner as the format of the preamble, with alternating 1 and 0 bits used for the first six bit positions of this one-byte field. The last two bit positions of this field are 11 — this breaks the synchronization pattern and alerts the receiver that frame data follows.

Both the preamble field and the start-of-frame delimiter field are removed by the controller when it places a received frame in its buffer. Similarly, when a controller transmits a frame, it prefixes the frame with those two fields (if it is transmitting an IEEE 802.3 frame) or a preamble field (if it is transmitting a true Ethernet frame).

Destination Address Field

The destination address identifies the recipient of the frame. Although this may appear to be a simple field, in reality its length can vary between IEEE 802.3 and Ethernet frames. In addition, each field can consist of two or more subfields, whose settings govern such network operations as the type of addressing used on the LAN, and whether the frame is addressed to a specific station or more than one station. To obtain an appreciation for the use of this field, let's examine how this field is used under the IEEE 802.3 standard as one of the two field formats applicable to Ethernet.

Figure 4.2 illustrates the composition of the source and destination address fields. As indicated, the two-byte source and destination address fields are applicable only to IEEE 802.3 networks, while the six-byte source and destination address fields are applicable to both Ethernet and IEEE 802.3 networks. A user can select either a two- or six-byte destination address field; however, with IEEE 802.3 equipment, all stations on the LAN must use the same addressing structure. Today, almost all 802.3 networks use six-byte addressing, because the inclusion of a two-byte field option was designed primarily to accommodate early LANs that use 16-bit address fields.

(a) 2 byte field (IEEE 802.3)

(b) 6 byte field (ethernet and IEEE 802.3)

I/G bit subfield '0' = individual address '1' = group address
U/L bit subfield '0' = universally administrated addressing
'1' = locally administrated addressing

* Set to '0' in source address field

Figure 4.2   Source and destination address field formats.

Both destination and source addresses are normally displayed by network monitors in hexadecimal, with the first three bytes separated from the last three by a colon (:) when six-byte addressing is used. For example, the source address 02608C876543 would be displayed as 02608C:876543. As we will shortly note, the first three bytes identify the manufacturer of the adapter card, while the following three bytes identify a specific adapter manufactured by the vendor identified by the first three bytes or six hex digits.

I/G Subfield

The one-bit I/G subfield is set to a 0 to indicate that the frame is destined to an individual station, or 1 to indicate that the frame is addressed to more than one station—a *group address*. One special example of a group address is the assignment of all 1s to the address field. Hex "FFFFFFFFFFFF" is recognized as a broadcast address, and each station on the network will receive and accept frames with that destination address.

An example of the use of a broadcast destination address is the service advertising packet (SAP) transmitted every 60 seconds by NetWare servers. The SAP is used to inform other servers and workstations on the network of the presence of that server. Because the SAP uses a destination address of FF-FF-FF-FF-FF-FF, it is recognized by every node on the network.

When a destination address specifies a single station, the address is referred to as a *unicast address*. A group address that defines multiple stations is known as a *multicast address*, while a group address that specifies all stations on the network is, as previously mentioned, referred to as a *broadcast address*.

U/L Subfield

The U/L subfield is applicable only to the six-byte destination address field. The setting of this field's bit position indicates whether the destination address is an address that was assigned by the IEEE (universally administered) or assigned by the organization via software (locally administered).

Universal versus Locally Administered Addressing

Each Ethernet NIC contains a unique address burned into its read-only memory (ROM) at the time of manufacture. To ensure that this universally administered address is not duplicated, the IEEE assigns blocks of addresses to each manufacturer. These addresses normally include a three-byte prefix, which identifies the manufacturer and is assigned by the IEEE, and a three-byte suffix, which is assigned by the adapter manufacturer to its NIC. For example, the prefix 02608C identifies an NIC manufactured by 3Com, while a prefix of hex 08002 identifies an NIC manufactured by Digital Equipment Company, which was acquired by compaq computer.

Although the use of universally administered addressing eliminates the potential for duplicate network addresses, it does not provide the flexibility obtainable from locally administered addressing. For example, under locally administered addressing, you can configure mainframe software to work with a predefined group of addresses via a gateway PC. Then, as you add new stations to your LAN, you simply use your installation program to assign a locally administered address to the NIC instead of using its universally administered address. As long as your mainframe computer has a pool of locally administered addresses that includes your recent assignment, you do not have to modify your mainframe communications software configuration. Because the modification of mainframe communications software typically requires recompiling and reloading, the attached network must become inoperative for a short period of time. Because a large mainframe may service hundreds to thousands of users, such changes are normally performed late in the evening or on a weekend. Thus, the changes required for locally administered addressing are more responsive to users accessing certain types of mainframe computers than those required for universally administered addressing.

Source Address Field

The source address field identifies the station that transmitted the frame. Like the destination address field, the source address can be either two or six bytes in length.

The two-byte source address is supported only under the IEEE 802.3 standard and requires the use of a two-byte destination address; all stations on the network must use two-byte addressing fields. The six-byte source address field is supported by both Ethernet and the IEEE 802.3 standard. When a six-byte address is used, the first three bytes represent the address assigned by the IEEE to the manufacturer for incorporation into each NIC's ROM. The vendor then normally assigns the last three bytes for each of its NICs.

Table 4.1 lists the NIC identifiers for 85 Ethernet card manufacturers. Note that many organizations including Cisco Systems, 3Com, IBM, MIPS, Ungermann-Bass, and Data General were assigned two or more blocks of addresses by the IEEE. Also note that organizations listed in Table 4.1 range in scope from well-known communications and computer manufacturers to universities and even a commercial firm probably best known for its watch commercials. The entries in Table 4.1 represent a portion of three-byte identifiers assigned by the IEEE over the past decade and do not include identifiers currently assigned to all vendors. For a comprehensive list of currently assigned three-byte identifiers, readers should contact the IEEE. You can contact the IEEE at:

IEEE Standards Department

445 Hoes Lane

P.O. Box 1331

Piscataway, NJ 08855

Telephone: +1 (732) 562-3813

Fax: +1 (732) 562-1571

Many software- and hardware-based network analyzers include the capability to identify each station on a LAN, count the number of frames transmitted by the station and destined to the station, as well as identify the manufacturer of the NIC used in the station. Concerning the latter capability, this is accomplished by the network analyzer containing a table of three-byte identifiers assigned by the IEEE to each NIC manufacturer, along with the name of the manufacturer. Then the analyzer compares the three-byte identifier read from frames flowing on the network and compares each identifier with the

TABLE 4.1   Representative Ethernet NIC Manufacturer IDs

NIC Manufacturer	Three-Byte Identifier
Cisco	00-00-0C
Fujitsu	00-00-0E
Cabletron	00-00-1D
NeXT	00-00-0F
TRW	00-00-2A
Hughes LAN Systems (formerly Sytek)	00-00-10
Tektronix	00-00-11
Datapoint Corporation	00-00-15
Olicom	00-00-24
AT&T	00-00-3D
NEC	00-00-4C
Network General	00-00-65
MIPS	00-00-6B
Madge Networks	00-00-6F
MIPS	00-00-77
Proteon	00-00-93
Cross Com Communications (now part of Olicom)	00-00-98
Wellfleet (now Bay Networks)	00-00-A2
Xerox	00-00-AA
RND (RAD Network Devices)	00-00-B0
Western Digital	00-00-C0
Emulex	00-00-C9
Develcon Electronics, Ltd.	00-00-D0
Adaptec, Inc.	00-00-D1
Gandalf Data Ltd.	00-00-F3
Allied Telesis, Inc.	00-00-F4

TABLE 4.1 (*Continued*)

NIC Manufacturer	Three-Byte Identifier
Racal Datacom	00-07-01
XYlan	00-20-DA
Crescendo (now owned by Cisco)	00-40-OB
Ascom	00-40-15
AST Research	00-40-1C
Netcomm	00-40-28
Nokia Data Communications	00-40-43
Cable and Wireless	00-40-74
AMP Incorporated	00-40-76
DigiBoard	00-40-9D
Cray Research, Inc.	00-40-A6
Mocom Communications Corp.	00-40-C5
PlainTree Systems, Inc.	00-40-EA
3Com	00-60-08
Cisco Systems, Inc.	00-60-09
Cisco Systems, Inc.	00-60-2F
Cisco Systems, Inc.	00-60-3E
Cisco Systems, Inc.	00-60-5C
Cisco Systems, Inc.	00-60-70
Cisco Systems, Inc.	00-60-83
3Com	00-60-8C
3Com	00-60-97
Hewlett-Packard	00-60-BO
Thomas Conrad Corporation	00-80-13
Bell Atlantic	00-80-1A
Newbridge Networks Corporation	00-80-21
Kalpana (acquired by Cisco)	00-80-24

TABLE 4.1   (*Continued*)

NIC Manufacturer	Three-Byte Identifier
University of Toronto	00-80-46
Compaq Computer Corporation	00-80-5F
Nippon Steel Corporation	00-80-6E
Xircom, Inc.	00-80-C7
Shiva	00-80-D3
Zenith Communications Products	00-80-F7
Azure Technologies, Inc.	00-80-FE
Bay Networks	00-A0-00
National Semiconductor	00-A0-D1
Allied Telesyn	00-A0-D2
Intel	00-AA-00
Ungermann-Bass	00-DD-00
Ungermann-Bass	00-DD-01
Racal Interlan	02-07-01
3Com	02-60-8C
BBN	08-00-08
Hewlett Packard	08-00-09
Unisys	08-00-0B
Tektronix	08-00-11
Data General	08-00-A
Data General	08-00-1B
Sun	08-00-20
DEC	08-00-2B
Bull	08-00-38
Sony	08-00-46
Sequent	08-00-47
Stanford University	08-00-56

TABLE 4.1 (*Continued*)

NIC Manufacturer	Three-Byte Identifier
IBM	08-00-5A
Silicon Graphics	08-00-69
Silicon Graphics	08-00-79
Seiko	08-00-83
Excelan	08-00-6E
Danish Data Elektronix	08-00-75
AT&T	80-00-10

identifiers stored in its identifier table. By providing information concerning network statistics, network errors, and the vendor identifier for the NIC in each station, you may be able to isolate problems faster or better consider future decisions concerning the acquisition of additional NICs.

An example of the use of NIC manufacturer IDs can be obtained by examining two monitoring screen displays of the Triticom EtherVision network monitoring and analysis program. Figure 4.3 illustrates the monitoring screen during the program's autodiscovery process. During this process the program reads the source address of each frame transmitted on the segment that the computer executing the program is connected to. Although obscured by the highlighted bar, the first three bytes of the adapter address first discovered is 00-60-8C, which represents a block of addresses assigned by the IEEE to 3 Com Corporation. If you glance at the first column in Figure 4.3, you will note that the second row, fourth row, ninth row, and a few additional rows also have NIC addresses that commence with hex 00-60-8C. By pressing the F2 key the program will display the manufacturer of each NIC encountered and for which statistics are being accumulated. This is indicated in Figure 4.4, which shows the first three bytes of each address replaced by the vendor assigned to the appropriate manufacturer ID. Thus, rows 1, 4, 9, and a few other rows commence with ''3Com'' to indicate the manufacturer of the NIC.

Organizations can request the assignment of a vendor code by contacting the IEEE Registration Authority at the previously listed address for the IEEE provided in this section. A full list of assigned vendor codes is obtainable by FTP at ftp.ieee.org as the file ieee/info/info.stds.oui. Readers should note that the list is limited to those companies that agreed to make their vendor code assignment(s) public.

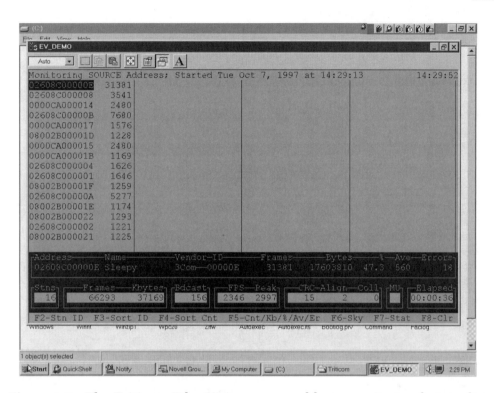

Figure 4.3 The Triticom EtherVision source address monitoring feature discovers the hardware address of each NIC. At the time this screen was captured 16 stations were identified.

Type Field

The two-byte type field is applicable only to the Ethernet frame. This field identifies the higher-level protocol contained in the data field. Thus, this field tells the receiving device how to interpret the data field.

Under Ethernet, multiple protocols can exist on the LAN at the same time. Xerox served as the custodian of Ethernet address ranges licensed to NIC manufacturers and defined the protocols supported by the assignment of type field values.

Table 4.2 lists 31 of the more common Ethernet type field assignments. To illustrate the ability of Ethernet to transport multiple protocols, assume a common LAN was used to connect stations to both UNIX and NetWare servers. Frames with the hex value 0800 in the type field would identify the IP protocol, while frames with the hex value 8137 in the type field would

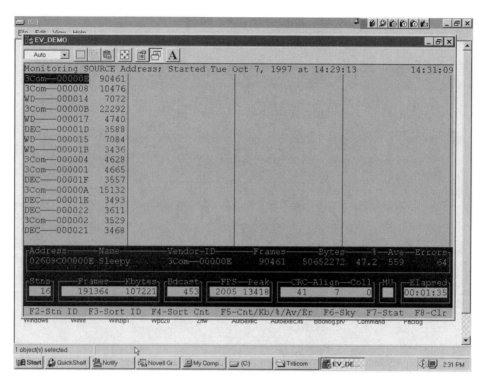

Figure 4.4 By pressing the F2 key, EtherVision will convert the three-byte hex NIC manufacturer ID to the vendor name or an appropriate mnemonic.

identify the transport of IPX and SPX protocols. Thus, the placement of an appropriate hex value in the Ethernet type field provides a mechanism to support the transport of multiple protocols on the local area network.

Under the IEEE 802.3 standard, the type field was replaced by a length field, which precludes compatibility between pure Ethernet and 802.3 frames.

Length Field

The two-byte length field, applicable to the IEEE 802.3 standard, defines the number of bytes contained in the data field. Under both Ethernet and IEEE 802.3 standards, the minimum size frame must be 64 bytes in length from preamble through FCS fields. This minimum size frame ensures that there is sufficient transmission time to enable Ethernet NICs to detect collisions accurately, based on the maximum Ethernet cable length specified for a network and the time required for a frame to propagate the length of the cable.

TABLE 4.2   Representative Ethernet Type Field Assignments

Protocol	Hex Value Assigned
Experimental	0101-DIFF
Xerox XNS	0600
IP	0800
X.75 Internet	0801
NBS Internet	0802
ECMA Internet	0803
CHAOSmet	0804
X.25 Level 3	0805
Address Resolution Protocol	0806
XNS Compatibility	0807
Banyan Systems	0BAD
BBN Simnet	5208
DEC MOP Dump/Load	6001
DEC MOP Remote Console	6002
DEC DECNET Phase IV Route	6003
DEC LAT	6004
DEC Diagnostic Protocol	6005
3Com Corporation	6010–6014
Proteon	7030
AT&T	8008
Excelan	8010
Tymshare	802E
DEC LANBridge	8038
DEC Ethernet Encryption	803D
AT&T	8046–8047
AppleTalk	809B
IBM SNA Service on Ethernet	80D5
AppleTalk ARP	80F3
Wellfleet	80FF–8103
NetWare IPX/SPX	8137–8138
SNMP	814C

Based on the minimum frame length of 64 bytes and the possibility of using two-byte addressing fields, this means that each data field must be a minimum of 46 bytes in length. The only exception to the preceding involves Gigabit Ethernet. At a 1000-Mbps operating rate the original 802.3 standard would not provide a frame duration long enough to permit a 100-meter cable run over copper media. This is because at a 1000-Mbps data rate there is a high probability that a station could be in the middle of transmitting a frame before it becomes aware of any collision that might have occurred at the other end of the segment. Recognizing this problem resulted in the development of a carrier extension, which extends the minimum Ethernet frame to 512 bytes. The carrier extension is discussed in detail in Section 4.6 when we turn our attention to the Gigabit Ethernet carrier extension.

For all versions of Ethernet except Gigabit Ethernet, if data being transported is less than 46 bytes, the data field is padded to obtain 46 bytes. However, the number of PAD characters is not included in the length field value. NICs that support both Ethernet and IEEE 802.3 frame formats use the value in this field to distinguish between the two frames. That is, because the maximum length of the data field is 1,500 bytes, a value that exceeds hex 05DC indicates that instead of a length field (IEEE 802.3), the field is a type field (Ethernet).

Data Field

As previously discussed, the data field must be a minimum of 46 bytes in length to ensure that the frame is at least 64 bytes in length. This means that the transmission of 1 byte of information must be carried within a 46-byte data field; if the information to be placed in the field is less than 46 bytes, the remainder of the field must be padded. Although some publications subdivide the data field to include a PAD subfield, the latter actually represents optional fill characters that are added to the information in the data field to ensure a length of 46 bytes. The maximum length of the data field is 1500 bytes.

Frame Check Sequence Field

The frame check sequence field, applicable to both Ethernet and the IEEE 802.3 standard, provides a mechanism for error detection. Each transmitter computes a cyclic redundancy check (CRC) that covers both address fields, the type/length field, and the data field. The transmitter then places the computed CRC in the four-byte FCS field.

The CRC treats the previously mentioned fields as one long binary number. The n bits to be covered by the CRC are considered to represent the coefficients of a polynomial M(X) of degree n − 1. Here, the first bit in the destination address field corresponds to the X^{n-1} term, while the last bit in the data field corresponds to the X^0 term. Next, M(X) is multiplied by X^{32}, and the result of that multiplication process is divided by the following polynomial:

$$G(X) = X^{32} + X^{26} + X^{23} + X^{22} + X^{16} + X^{12} + X^{11} + X^{10} + X^8 + X^7 + X^5 + X^4 + X^2 + X + 1$$

Note that the term X^n represents the setting of a bit to a 1 in position n. Thus, part of the generating polynomial $X^5 + X^4 + X^2 + X^1$ represents the binary value 11011.

This division produces a quotient and remainder. The quotient is discarded, and the remainder becomes the CRC value placed in the four-byte FCS field. This 32-bit CRC reduces the probability of an undetected error to 1 bit in every 4.3 billion, or approximately 1 bit in $2^{32} − 1$ bits.

Once a frame reaches its destination, the receiver uses the same polynomial to perform the same operation upon the received data. If the CRC computed by the receiver matches the CRC in the FCS field, the frame is accepted. Otherwise, the receiver discards the received frame, as it is considered to have one or more bits in error. The receiver will also consider a received frame to be invalid and discard it under two additional conditions. Those conditions occur when the frame does not contain an integral number of bytes, or when the length of the data field does not match the value contained in the length field. The latter condition obviously is only applicable to the 802.3 standard, because an Ethernet frame uses a type field instead of a length field.

Interframe Gap

Under the 10-Mbps versions of the CSMA/CD protocol a 9.6 microsecond (μs) quiet time occurs between transmitted frames. This quiet time, which is referred to as an interframe gap, permits clocking circuitry used within repeaters and workstations and hub ports to be resynchronized to the known local clock. Under Fast Ethernet the interframe gap is 0.96 ms, while under Gigabit Ethernet the gap is reduced to 0.096 ms.

4.2 Media Access Control

In the first section in this chapter, we examined the frame format by which data is transported on an Ethernet network. Under the IEEE 802 series of 10-Mbps operating standards, the data link layer of the OSI Reference Model is subdivided into two sublayers—logical link control (LLC) and medium access control (MAC). The frame formats examined in Section 4.1 represent the manner in which LLC information is transported. Directly under the LLC sublayer is the MAC sublayer. The MAC sublayer, which is the focus of this section, is responsible for checking the channel and transmitting data if the channel is idle, checking for the occurrence of a collision, and taking a series of predefined steps if a collision is detected. Thus, this layer provides the required logic to control the network.

Figure 4.5 illustrates the relationship between the physical and LLC layers with respect to the MAC layer. The MAC layer is an interface between user data and the physical placement and retrieval of data on the network. To better understand the functions performed by the MAC layer, let us examine the four major functions performed by that layer—transmitting data operations, transmitting medium access management, receiving data operations, and receiving medium access management. Each of those four functions can be viewed as a functional area, because a group of activities is associated with

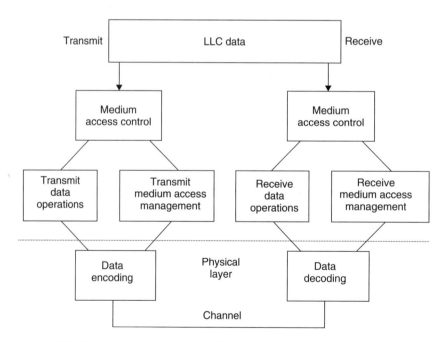

Figure 4.5 Medium access control. The medium access control (MAC) layer can be considered an interface between user data and the physical placement and retrieval of data on the network.

TABLE 4.3   MAC Functional Areas

Transmit data operations	♦ Accept data from the LLC sublayer and construct a frame by appending preamble and start-of-frame delimiter; insert destination and source address, length count; if frame is less than 64 bytes, insert sufficient PAD characters in the data field.
	♦ Calculate the CRC and place in the FCS field.
Transmit media access management	♦ Defer transmission if the medium is busy.
	♦ Delay transmission for a specified interframe gap period.
	♦ Present a serial bit stream to the physical layer for transmission.
	♦ Halt transmission when a collision is detected.
	♦ Transmit a jam signal to ensure that news of a collision propagates throughout the network.
	♦ Reschedule retransmissions after a collision until successful, or until a specified retry limit is reached.
Receive data operations	♦ Discard all frames not addressed to the receiving station.
	♦ Recognize all broadcast frames and frames specifically addressed to station.
	♦ Perform a CRC check.
	♦ Remove preamble, start-of-frame delimiter, destination and source addresses, length count, and FCS; if necessary, remove PAD fill characters.
	♦ Pass data to LLC sublayer.
Receive media access management	♦ Receive a serial bit stream from the physical layer.
	♦ Verify byte boundary and length of frame.
	♦ Discard frames not an even eight bits in length or less than the minimum frame length.

each area. Table 4.3 lists the four MAC functional areas and the activities associated with each area. Although the transmission and reception of data operations activities are self-explanatory, the transmission and reception of media access management require some elaboration. Therefore, let's focus our attention on the activities associated with each of those functional areas.

Transmit Media Access Management

CSMA/CD can be described as a *listen-before-acting* access method. Thus, the first function associated with transmit media access management is to find out whether any data is already being transmitted on the network and, if so, to defer transmission. During the listening process, each station attempts to sense the carrier signal of another station, hence the prefix *carrier sense* (CS) for this access method. Although broadband networks use RF modems that generate a carrier signal, a baseband network has no carrier signal in the conventional sense of a carrier as a periodic waveform altered to convey information. Thus, a logical question you may have is how the MAC sublayer on a baseband network can sense a carrier signal if there is no carrier. The answer to this question lies in the use of a digital signaling method, known as *Manchester encoding* on 10-Mbps Ethernet LANs, that a station can monitor to note whether another station is transmitting. Although NRZI encoding is used on broadband networks, the actual data is modulated after it is encoded. Thus, the presence or absence of a carrier is directly indicated by the presence or absence of a carrier signal on a broadband network.

Collision Detection

As discussed in Chapter 3, under Manchester encoding, a transition occurs at the middle of each bit period. This transition serves as both a clocking mechanism, enabling a receiver to clock itself to incoming data, and as a mechanism to represent data. Under Manchester coding, a binary 1 is represented by a high-to-low transition, while a binary 0 is represented by a low-to-high voltage transition. Thus, an examination of the voltage on the medium of a baseband network enables a station to determine whether a carrier signal is present.

If a carrier signal is found, the station with data to transmit will continue to monitor the channel. When the current transmission ends, the station will then transmit its data, while checking the channel for collisions. Because Ethernet and IEEE 802.3 Manchester-encoded signals have a 1-volt average DC voltage level, a collision results at an average DC level of 2 volts. Thus, a transceiver or network interface card can detect collisions by monitoring the voltage level of the Manchester line signal.

Jam Pattern

If a collision is detected during transmission, the transmitting station will cease transmission of data and initiate transmission of a jam pattern. The jam pattern consists of 32 to 48 bits. These bits can have any value other than the CRC value that corresponds to the partial frame transmitted before the jam. The transmission of the jam pattern ensures that the collision lasts long enough to be detected by all stations on the network.

When a repeater is used to connect multiple segments, it must recognize a collision occurring on one port and place a jam signal on all other ports. Doing so results in the occurrence of a collision with signals from stations that may have been in the process of beginning to transmit on one segment when the collision occurred on the other segment. In addition, the jam signal serves as a mechanism to cause nontransmitting stations to wait until the jam signal ends before attempting to transmit, alleviating additional potential collisions from occurring.

Wait Time

Once a collision is detected, the transmitting station waits a random number of slot times before attempting to retransmit. The term *slot* represents 512 bits on a 10-Mbps network, or a minimum frame length of 64 bytes. The actual number of slot times the station waits is selected by a randomization process, formally known as a *truncated binary exponential backoff*. Under this randomization process, a randomly selected integer r defines the number of slot times the station waits before listening to determine whether the channel is clear. If it is, the station begins to retransmit the frame, while listening for another collision.

If the station transmits the complete frame successfully and has additional data to transmit, it will again listen to the channel as it prepares another frame for transmission. If a collision occurs on a retransmission attempt, a slightly different procedure is followed. After a jam signal is transmitted, the station simply doubles the previously generated random number and then waits the prescribed number of slot intervals before attempting a retransmission. Up to 16 retransmission attempts can occur before the station aborts the transmission and declares the occurrence of a multiple collision error condition.

Figure 4.6 illustrates the collision detection process by which a station can determine that a frame was not successfully transmitted. At time t_0 both stations A and B are listening and fail to detect the occurrence of a collision, and at time t_1 station A commences the transmission of a frame. As station A's frame begins to propagate down the bus in both directions, station B begins the transmission of a frame, since at time t_2 it appears to station B that there is no activity on the network.

Shortly after time t_2 the frames transmitted by stations A and B collide, resulting in a doubling of the Manchester encoded signal level for a very short

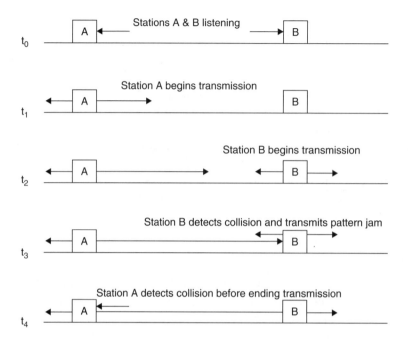

Figure 4.6 Collision detection.

period of time. This doubling of the Manchester encoded signal's voltage level is detected by station B at time t_3, since station B is closer to the collision than station A. Station B then generates a jam pattern that is detected by station A.

Late Collisions

A late collision is a term used to reference the detection of a collision only after a station places a complete frame on the network. A late collision is normally caused by an excessive network segment cable length, resulting in the time for a signal to propagate from one end of a segment to another part of the segment being longer than the time required to place a full frame on the network. This results in two devices communicating at the same time never seeing the other's transmission until their signals collide.

A late collision is detected by a transmitter after the first slot time of 64 bytes and is applicable only for frames whose lengths exceed 65 bytes. The detection of a late collision occurs in exactly the same manner as a normal collision; however, it happens later than normal. Although the primary cause of late collisions is excessive segment cable lengths, an excessive number of repeaters, faulty connectors, and defective Ethernet transceivers or controllers can also result in late collisions. Many network analyzers provide information on late collisions, which can be used as a guide to check the previously mentioned items when late collisions occur.

Service Primitives

As previously mentioned, the MAC sublayer isolates the physical layer from the LLC sublayer. Thus, one of the functions of the MAC sublayer is to provide services to the LLC. To accomplish this task, a series of service primitives was defined to govern the exchange of LLC data between a local MAC sublayer and its peer LLC sublayer.

The basic MAC service primitives used in all IEEE MAC standards include the medium access data request (MA_DATA.request), medium access data confirm (MA_DATA.confirm), medium access data indicate (MA_DATA.indicate), and medium access data response (MA_DATA.response).

MA_DATA.request

The medium access data request is generated whenever the LLC sublayer has data to be transmitted. This primitive is passed from layer n to layer $n - 1$ to request the initiation of service, and results in the MAC sublayer formatting the request in a MAC frame and passing it to the physical layer for transmission.

MA_DATA.confirm

The medium access data confirm primitive is generated by the MAC sublayer in response to an MA_DATA.request generated by the local LLC sublayer. The confirm primitive is passed from layer $n - 1$ to layer n, and includes a status parameter that indicates the outcome of the request primitive.

MA_DATA.indicate

The medium access data indicate primitive is passed from layer $n - 1$ to layer n to indicate that a valid frame has arrived at the local MAC sublayer. Thus, this service primitive denotes that the frame was received without CRC, length, or frame-alignment error.

MA_DATA.response

The medium access data response primitive is passed from layer n to layer $n - 1$. This primitive acknowledges the MA_DATA.indicate service primitive.

Primitive Operations

To illustrate the use of MAC service primitives, let us assume that station A on a network wants to communicate with station B. As illustrated in Figure 4.7, the LLC sublayer of station A requests transmission of a frame to the MAC sublayer service interface via the issuance of an MA_DATA.request service primitive. In response to the MA_DATA.request, a frame is transmitted to station B. Upon receipt of that frame, the MAC sublayer at that station generates an MA_DATA.indicate to inform the LLC sublayer of the arrival of the frame. The LLC sublayer accepts the frame and generates an MA_DATA.response to inform the MAC sublayer that it has the frame. That response flows across the network to station A, where the MAC sublayer generates an MA_DATA.confirm to inform the LLC sublayer that the frame was received without error.

Half- versus Full-duplex Operation

Ethernet was originally designed as a half-duplex LAN transmission method. The CSMA/CD algorithm required the receive pair in the two pair wiring used for 10BASE-T to be used both to receive data and to detect collisions. In fact, if the transmit and receive wire pairs became simultaneously activated, the MAC

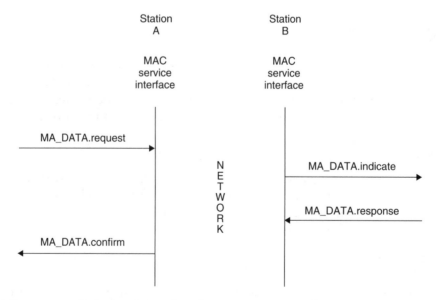

Figure 4.7 Relationship of medium access control service primitives.

layer would cause the ongoing transmission to terminate and would initiate the previously described truncated binary exponential backoff algorithm.

With the development of Ethernet switches during the mid-1980s, it became possible to cable a station to a switch port directly. When this operation occurred it eliminated the possibility of a collision. Recognizing the fact that the CSMA/CD algorithm was not efficient for use in a switch environment, the IEEE assigned a task force to examine modifying the MAC layer for switch operations. In 1987 the IEEE 802.3x standard was approved; this introduced a modified MAC layer that added support for full duplex operations in a switch environment. A related standard, referred to as the IEEE 802.3y specification, defines a flow control mechanism, which is important when devices with dissimilar operating rates communicate with one another through a switch, such as a server operating at 100 Mbps communicating with a workstation operating at 10 Mbps. Although the Ethernet switch will include buffer memory, to preclude such memory from being filled and subsequent data transmitted by the server being lost, the switch will initiate flow control to the server to temporarily stop its transmission. Once sufficient buffer memory is available in the switch, flow control will be disabled. Later in this book we will examine flow control in more detail.

4.3 Logical Link Control

As discussed in Chapter 2, the LLC sublayer was defined under the IEEE 802.2 standard to make the method of link control independent of a specific access method. Thus, the 802.2 method of link control spans Ethernet (IEEE 802.3), Token Bus (IEEE 802.4), and Token-Ring (IEEE 802.5) local area networks. Functions performed by the LLC include generating and interpreting commands to control the flow of data, including recovery operations for when a transmission error is detected.

Link control information is carried within the data field of an IEEE 802.3 frame as an LLC protocol data unit (PDU). Figure 4.8 illustrates the relationship between the IEEE 802.3 frame and the LLC PDU.

As discussed in Chapter 2, service access points (SAPs) function much like a mailbox. Because the LLC layer is bounded below the MAC sublayer and bounded above by the network layer, SAPs provide a mechanism for exchanging information between the LLC layer and the MAC and network layers. For example, from the network layer perspective, a SAP represents the place to leave messages about the services requested by an application. There are two broad categories of SAPs, IEEE-administered and manufacturer-implemented.

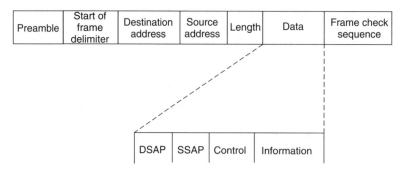

Figure 4.8 Formation of LLC protocol data unit. Control information is carried within a MAC frame.

TABLE 4.4 Representative Examples of SAP Addresses

Address (Hex)	Assignment
IEEE-administered	
00	Null SAP
02	Individual LLC sublayer management functions
06	ARPANET Internet Protocol (IP)
42	IEEE 802.1 Bridge-Spanning Tree Protocol
AA	Sub-Network Access Protocol (SNAP)
FE	ISO Network Layer Protocol
Manufacturer-implemented	
80	Xerox Network Systems
BC	Banyan VINES
EO	Novell NetWare
FO	IBM NetBIOS
F8	IBM Remote Program Load (RPL)
FA	Ungermann-Bass

Table 4.4 provides six examples of each type of SAP. In examining the entries in Table 4.4, the hex value AA represents one of the more commonly used SAPs today. When that value is encoded in both DSAP and SSAP fields, it indicates a special type of Ethernet frame referred to as an Ethernet

SNAP frame. The SNAP frame, as we will shortly note when we cover it in Section 4.4, unlike the Ethernet 802.3 frame, enables several different protocols to be transported.

The destination services access point (DSAP) is one byte in length and is used to specify the receiving network layer process. Because an IEEE 802.3 frame does not include a type field, the DSAP field is used to denote the destination upper-layer protocol carried within the frame. For example, the DSAP hex value E0 indicates that the data field contains NetWare data.

The source service access point (SSAP) is also one byte in length. The SSAP specifies the sending network layer process. Because the destination and source protocols must be the same, the value of the SSAP field will always match the value of the DSAP field. Both DSAP and SSAP addresses are assigned by the IEEE. For example, hex address "FF" represents a DSAP broadcast address.

The control field contains information concerning the type and class of service being used for transporting LLC data. For example, a hex value of 03 when NetWare is being transported indicates that the frame is using an unnumbered format for connectionless services.

Types and Classes of Service

Under the 802.2 standard, there are three types of service available for sending and receiving LLC data. These types are discussed in the next three paragraphs. Figure 4.9 provides a visual summary of the operation of each LLC service type.

Type 1

Type 1 is an unacknowledged connectionless service. The term *connectionless* refers to the fact that transmission does not occur between two devices as if a logical connection were established. Instead, transmission flows on the channel to all stations; however, only the destination address acts upon the data. As the name of this service implies, there is no provision for the acknowledgment of frames. Neither are there provisions for flow control or for error recovery. Therefore, this is an unreliable service.

Despite those shortcomings, Type 1 is the most commonly used service, because most protocol suites use a reliable transport mechanism at the transport layer, thus eliminating the need for reliability at the link layer. In addition, by eliminating the time needed to establish a virtual link and the overhead of acknowledgments, a Type 1 service can provide a greater throughput than other LLC types of services.

Figure 4.9   Local link control service types.

Type 2

The Type 2 connection-oriented service requires that a logical link be estab-lished between the sender and the receiver before information transfer. Once the logical connection is established, data will flow between the sender and receiver until either party terminates the connection. During data transfer, a Type 2 LLC service provides all of the functions lacking in a Type 1 service, using a sliding window for flow control. When IBM's SNA data is transported on a LAN, it uses connection-oriented services. Type 2 LLC is also commonly referred to as LLC 2.

Type 3

The Type 3 acknowledged connectionless service contains provision for the setup and disconnection of transmission; it acknowledges individual frames using the stop-and-wait flow control method. Type 3 service is primarily used in an automated factory process-control environment, where one central computer communicates with many remote devices that typically have a limited storage capacity.

Classes of Service

All logical link control stations support Type 1 operations. This level of support is known as Class I service. The classes of service supported by

LLC indicate the combinations of the three LLC service types supported by a station. Class I supports Type 1 service, Class II supports both Type 1 and Type 2, Class III supports Type 1 and Type 3 service, and Class IV supports all three service types. Because service Type 1 is supported by all classes, it can be considered a least common denominator, enabling all stations to communicate using a common form of service.

Service Primitives

The LLC sublayer uses service primitives similar to those that govern the exchange of data between the MAC sublayer and its peer LLC sublayer. In doing so, the LLC sublayer supports the Request, Confirm, Indicate, and Response primitives described in Section 4.2 of this chapter. The major difference between the LLC and MAC service primitives is that the LLC sublayer supports three types of services. As previously discussed, the available LLC services are unacknowledged connectionless, connection-oriented, and acknowledged connectionless. Thus, the use of LLC service primitives varies in conjunction with the type of LLC service initiated. For example, a connection-oriented service uses service primitives in the same manner as that illustrated in Figure 4.7. If the service is unacknowledged connectionless, the only service primitives used are the Request and Indicate, because there is no Response nor Confirmation.

4.4 Other Ethernet Frame Types

Three additional frame types that warrant discussion are Ethernet-802.3, Ethernet-SNAP, and the IEEE 802.1Q tagged frame. In actuality, the first two types of frames represent a logical variation of the IEEE 802.3 frame, in which the composition of the data field varies from the composition of the LLC protocol data unit previously illustrated in Figure 4.8. The third type of frame provides the ability to form virtual LANs (vLANs) as well as to assign a priority level to a frame.

Ethernet-802.3

The Ethernet-802.3 frame represents a proprietary subdivision of the IEEE 802.3 data field to transport NetWare. Ethernet-802.3 is one of several types of frames that can be used to transport NetWare. The actual frame type used is defined at system setup by binding NetWare to a specific type of frame.

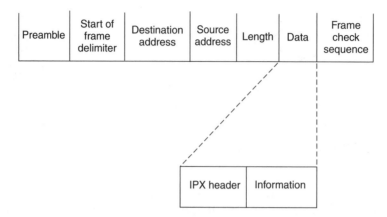

Figure 4.10   Novell's NetWare Ethernet-802.3 frame. An Ethernet-802.3 frame subdivides the data field into an IPX header field and an information field.

Figure 4.10 illustrates the format of the Ethernet-802.3 frame. Due to the absence of LLC fields, this frame is often referred to as *raw 802.3*.

For those using or thinking of using NetWare, a word of caution is in order concerning frame types. Novell uses the term Ethernet-802.2 to refer to the IEEE 802.3 frame. Thus, if you set up NetWare for Ethernet-802.2 frames, in effect, your network is IEEE 802.3–compliant.

Ethernet-SNAP

The Ethernet-SNAP frame, unlike the Ethernet-802.3 frame, can be used to transport several protocols. AppleTalk Phase II, NetWare, and TCP/IP protocols can be transported due to the inclusion of an Ethernet type field in the Ethernet-SNAP frame. Thus, SNAP can be considered as an extension that permits vendors to create their own Ethernet protocol transports. Ethernet-SNAP was defined by the IEEE 802.1 committee to facilitate interoperability between IEEE 802.3 LANs and Ethernet LANs. This was accomplished, as we will soon note, by the inclusion of a type field in the Ethernet-SNAP frame.

Figure 4.11 illustrates the format of an Ethernet-SNAP frame. Although the format of this frame is based upon the IEEE 802.3 frame format, it does not use DSAP and SSAP mailbox facilities and the control field. Instead, it places specific values in those fields to indicate that the frame is a SNAP frame.

The value hex AA is placed into the DSAP and SSAP fields, while hex 03 is placed into the control field to indicate that a SNAP frame is being transported.

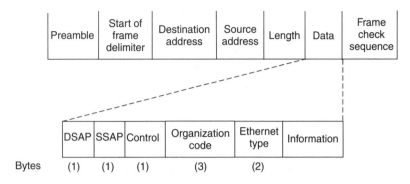

Figure 4.11   Ethernet-SNAP frame format.

The hex 03 value in the control field defines the use of an unnumbered format, which is the only format supported by a SNAP frame.

The three-byte organization code field references the organizational body that assigned the value placed in the following field, the Ethernet type field. A hex value of 00-00-00 in the organization code field indicates that Xerox assigned the value in the Ethernet type field. In comparison, a hex value of 08-00-07 would indicate Apple computer as the organizational body that assigned the valve in the following field. Concerning that following field, the SNAP frame uses two bytes to identify the protocol being transported, which significantly extends the number of protocols that can be transported. Although shown as the Ethernet Type field in Figure 4.11, the formal name for this field is Protocol Identifier (PID). Through the use of the Ethernet-SNAP frame, you obtain the ability to transport multiple protocols in a manner similar to the original Ethernet frame that used the type field for this purpose. Here the hex value of 00-00-00 in the organization code field enables the values previously listed in Table 4.2 to represent different protocols carried by the SNAP frame.

IEEE 802.1Q Frame

With the development of LAN switches it became possible to group workstations together based upon such criteria as their MAC address, their switch port connection or even the higher layer network address assigned to the workstation. The grouping of workstations resulted in the formation of a virtual LAN.

Recognizing the importance of a standardized method for informing devices of the association of frames with a particular vLAN, the IEEE formed a task force to work on the standardization effort, resulting in the development of a "tag" for identifying vLAN frames. At the same time as this effort commenced, a separate task force was working on the prioritization of frames. The work of the vLAN task force resulted in the specifications for what is referred to as the 802.1Q frame header. That header incorporates a three-bit priority field that is used to convey priorities specified by the task force that standardized frame priority, which is the 802.1p standard. Thus, the 802.1Q frame header can transport 802.1p priority information. Now that we know the IEEE Ps and Qs, let's examine the format associated with the 802.1Q frame header.

Figure 4.12 illustrates the format of an IEEE 802.1Q tagged frame. Note that the tag is inserted after the source address field and consists of four fields. The first field is the tag protocol identifier (TPI) and is two bytes in length. The valve of the TPI field is set to 8100 to identify the frame as an 802.1Q tagged frame. The second field is a three-bit priority field that can be used to specify one of eight levels of priority (binary 000 to 111). The Priority field is followed by a one-bit canonical format identifier (CFI). When set, this field indicates that a Token-Ring frame is encapsulated within the tagged Ethernet frame. The fourth field is the vLAN identification field (VID), which is 12 bits in length. The value in this field uniquely identifies the vLAN to which the frame belongs. Later in this book, when we examine LAN switches, we will also examine the operation and utilization of vLANs.

Frame Determination

Through software, a receiving station can determine the type of frame and correctly interpret the data carried in the frame. To accomplish this, the value

Figure 4.12   The format of the IEEE 802.1Q tagged frame.

of the two bytes that follow the source address is first examined. If the value is greater than 1500, this indicates the occurrence of an Ethernet frame. As previously noted, if the value is 8100, then the frame is an IEEE 802.1Q tagged frame and software would look further into the tag to determine the vLAN identification and other information. If the value is less than or equal to 1500, the frame can be either a pure IEEE 802.3 frame or a variation of that frame. Thus, more bytes must be examined.

If the next two bytes have the hex value FF:FF, the frame is a NetWare Ethernet-802.3 frame. This is because the IPX header has the value hex FF:FF in the checksum field contained in the first two bytes in the IPX header. If the two bytes contain the hex value AA:AA, this indicates that it is an Ethernet-SNAP frame. Any other value determined to reside in those two bytes then indicates that the frame must be an Ethernet-802.3 frame.

4.5 Fast Ethernet

The frame composition associated with each of the three Fast Ethernet standards is illustrated in Figure 4.13. In comparing the composition of the Fast Ethernet frame with Ethernet and IEEE 802.3 frame formats previously illustrated in Figure 4.1, you will note that other than the addition of starting and ending stream delimiters, the Fast Ethernet frame duplicates the older frames. A third difference between the two is not shown, as it is not actually observable from a comparison of frames, because this difference is associated with the time between frames. Ethernet and IEEE 802.3 frames are Manchester encoded and have an interframe gap of 9.6 μsec between frames. In

SSD 1 byte	Preamble 7 bytes	SFD 1 byte	Destination address 6 bytes	Source address 6 bytes	L/T 2 bytes	Data 46 to 1500 bytes	FCS 1 byte	ESD 1 byte

Legend:
SSD = Start of stream delimiter
SFD = Start of frame delimiter
L/T = Length (IEEE 802.3)/type (ethernet)
ESD = End of stream delimiter

Figure 4.13   Fast Ethernet frame. The 100BASE-TX frame differs from the IEEE 802.3 MAC frame through the addition of a byte at each end to mark the beginning and end of the stream delimiter.

comparison, the Fast Ethernet 100BASE-TX frame is transmitted using 4B5B encoding, and IDLE codes (refer to Table 3.6) representing sequences of I (binary 11111) symbols are used to mark a 0.96-μs interpacket gap. Now that we have an overview of the differences between Ethernet/IEEE 802.3 and Fast Ethernet frames, let's focus upon the new fields associated with the Fast Ethernet frame format.

Start-of-Stream Delimiter

The start-of-stream delimiter (SSD) is used to align a received frame for subsequent decoding. The SSD field consists of a sequence of J and K symbols, which defines the unique code 11000 10001. This field replaces the first octet of the preamble in Ethernet and IEEE 802.3 frames whose composition is 10101010.

End-of-Stream Delimiter

The end-of-stream delimiter (ESD) is used as an indicator that data transmission terminated normally, and a properly formed stream was transmitted. This one-byte field is created by the use of T and R codes (see Table 3.6) whose bit composition is 01101 00111. The ESD field lies outside of the Ethernet/IEEE 802.3 frame and for comparison purposes can be considered to fall within the interframe gap of those frames.

4.6 Gigabit Ethernet

Earlier in this chapter it was briefly mentioned that the Ethernet frame was extended for operations at 1 Gbps. In actuality the Gigabit Ethernet standard resulted in two modifications to conventional CSMA/CD operations. The first modification, which is referred to as carrier extension, is only applicable for half-duplex links and was required to maintain an approximate 200-meter topology at Gigabit speeds. Instead of actually extending the fame, as we will shortly note, the time the frame is on the wire is extended. A second modification, referred to as packet burst, enables Gigabit-compatible network devices to transmit bursts of relatively short packets without having to relinquish control of the network. Both carrier extension and packet bursting represent modifications to the CSMA/CD protocol to extend the collision domain and enhance the efficiency of copper-media Gigabit Ethernet, respectively. Both topics are covered in detail in this section.

Carrier Extension

In an Ethernet network, the attachment of workstations to a hub creates a segment. That segment or multiple segments interconnected via the use of one or more repeaters forms a collision domain. The latter term is formally defined as a single CSMA/CD network in which a collision will occur if two devices attached to the network transmit at or approximately the same time. The reason we can say approximately the same time is due to the fact that there is a propagation delay time associated with the transmission of signals on a conductor. Thus, if one station is relatively close to another the propagation delay time is relatively short, requiring both stations to transmit data at nearly the same time for a collision to occur. If two stations are at opposite ends of the network the propagation delay for a signal placed on the network by one station to reach the other station is much greater. This means that one station could initiate transmission and actually transmit a portion of a frame while the second station might listen to the network, hear no activity, and begin to transmit, resulting in a collision.

Figure 4.14 illustrates the relationship between a single collision domain and two collision windows. Note that as stations are closer to one another the collision window, which represents the propagation delay time during which one station could transmit and another would assume there is no network activity decreases.

Ethernet requires that a station should be able to hear any resulting collision for the frame it is transmitting before it completes the transmission of the entire frame. This means that the transmission of the next-to-last bit of a frame

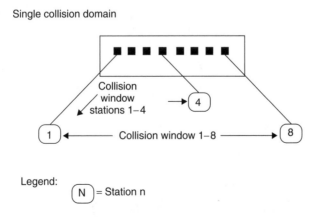

Figure 4.14   Relationship between a collision domain and collision windows.

that results in a collision should allow the transmitting station to hear the collision voltage increase before it transmits the last bit. Thus, the maximum allowable cabling distance is limited by the bit duration associated with the network operating rate and the speed of electrons on the wire.

When Ethernet operates at 1 Gbps, the allowable cabling distance would be reduced to approximately 10 meters or 33 feet. Clearly, this would be a major restriction on the ability of Gigabit Ethernet to be effectively used in a shared media half-duplex environment. To overcome this transmission distance limitation, Sun Microsystems, Inc., suggested the carrier extension scheme, which became part of the Gigabit Ethernet standard for half-duplex operations.

Under the carrier extension scheme, the original Ethernet frame is extended by increasing the time the frame is on the wire. The timing extension occurs after the end of the standard CSMA/CD frame as illustrated in Figure 4.15. The carrier extension extends the frame timing to guarantee at least a 512-byte slot time for half-duplex Ethernet. Note that Ethernet's slot time is considered as the time from the first bit of the destination address field reaching the wire through the last bit of the frame check sequence field. The increase in the minimum length frame does not change the frame size and only alters the time the frame is on the wire. Due to this compatibility it is maintained between the original Ethernet frame and the Gigabit Ethernet frame.

Although the carrier extension scheme enables the cable length of a half-duplex Gigabit network to be extended to a 200-meter diameter, that extension is not without a price. That price is one of overhead, because extension symbols attached to a short frame waste bandwidth. For example, a frame with a 64-byte data field would have 448 bytes of wasted carrier extension

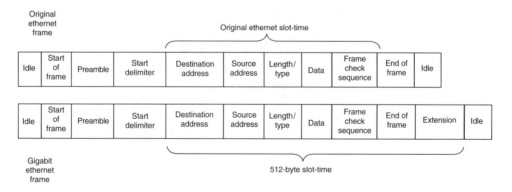

Figure 4.15 Half-duplex Gigabit Ethernet uses a carrier extension scheme to extend timing so that the slot time consists of at least 512 bytes.

symbols attached to it. To further complicate bandwidth utilization, when the data field is less than 46 bytes in length, nulls are added to produce a 64-byte minimum-length data field. Thus, a simple query to be transported by Ethernet, such as "Enter your age" consisting of 44 data characters, would be padded with 32 null characters when transported by Ethernet to ensure a minimum 72-byte length frame. Under Gigabit Ethernet, the minimum 512-byte time slot would require the use of 448 carrier extension symbols to ensure that the time slot from destination address through any required extension is at least 512 bytes in length.

In examining Figure 4.15, it is important to note that the carrier extension scheme does not extend the Ethernet frame beyond a 512-byte time slot. Thus, Ethernet frames with a time slot equal to or exceeding 512 bytes have no carrier extension. Another important item to note concerning the carrier extension scheme is that it has no relationship to a Jumbo Frames feature that is proprietary to a specific vendor. That feature is supported by a switch manufactured by Alteon Networks and is used to enhance data transfers between servers, permitting a maximum frame size of up to 9 Kbytes to be supported. Because Jumbo Frames are not part of the Gigabit Ethernet standard, you must disable that feature to obtain interoperability between that vendor's 1-Gbps switch and other vendors' Gigabit Ethernet products.

Frame Bursting

Frame bursting represents a scheme added to Gigabit Ethernet to counteract the overhead associated with transmitting relatively short frames. This scheme was proposed by NBase Communications and is included in the Gigabit Ethernet standard as an addition to carrier extension.

Under frame bursting, each time the first frame in a sequence of short frames successfully passes the 512-byte collision window using the carrier extension scheme previously described, subsequent frames are transmitted without including the carrier extension. The effect of frame bursting is to average the wasted time represented by the use of carrier extension symbols over a series of short frames. The limit on the number of frames that can be bursted is a total of 1500 bytes for the series of frames, which represents the longest data field supported by Ethernet. To inhibit other stations from initiating transmission during a burst carrier extension, signals are inserted between frames in the burst. Figure 4.16 illustrates an example of Gigabit Ethernet frame bursting. Note that the interframe gaps are filled with extension bits.

In addition to enhancing network use and minimizing bandwidth overhead, frame bursting also reduces the probability of collisions occurring. This is

Figure 4.16 Frame bursting.

because the burst of frames are only susceptible to a collision during the first frame in the sequence. Thereafter, carrier extension symbols between frames followed by additional short frames are recognized by all other stations on the segment, and inhibit those stations from initiating a transmission that would result in the occurrence of a collision.

4.7 10 Gigabit Ethernet

As noted earlier in this book, 10 Gigabit Ethernet is restricted to operating over optical fiber. In being restricted to operating over optical fiber, 10 Gigabit Ethernet represents a full-duplex technology. This means that it does not need the CSMA/CD protocol that is employed by slower, half-duplex versions of Ethernet. This also means that in an effort to retain scalability to 10-Gbps operations the frame formats used by other versions of Ethernet are continued to be supported. Thus, you can encounter NetWare, true 802.3 or 802.3Q tagged frames in a 10 Gigabit Ethernet environment.

chapter five

Networking Hardware and Software

Until this chapter, our primary hardware focus was on generic products designed to construct Ethernet-type networks at a single location. Although we discussed the use of electrical fiber-optic repeaters, that discussion was limited to a few network expansion examples. In addition, until now we have essentially avoided discussing the use of bridges, routers, and gateways to extend Ethernet connectivity beyond a single network, and the role of network software and how it relates to your personal computer's operating system. In this chapter, we will focus our attention on those two areas.

First, we will focus our attention on the basic operation of several hardware components that are the building blocks essential to extending the connectivity capability of an Ethernet local area network: repeaters, bridges, routers, brouters, gateways, servers, and wiring hubs. Because Ethernet networks are no longer restricted to a wired environment, in this chapter we will also describe and discuss the role of wireless Ethernet LAN adapters, access points and routers that include a built-in access point. Next, we will discuss the role and operation of three major types of software required for local area network operations: computer operating systems, LAN operating systems, and application programs. This will be followed by a discussion of the software used to route data from one LAN to another using different internet hardware and software products. By examining hardware and software, we will obtain an appreciation for the methods used to link LANs both directly and through wide area networks.

In this chapter and throughout this book, we will use the terms *local area network* and *network* synonymously. We will use the term *internetwork* or just *internet* to refer to the joining of two or more local area networks. Note that we will use the latter term to refer to the combining of networks and not to the specific network called the Internet, whose first letter is capitalized. In Chapter 7 we will examine the connection of Ethernet-based networks to that network, focusing our attention upon the configuration of workstations, servers, and routers to enable an Ethernet network to be connected to the Internet.

5.1 Wired Network Hardware Components

In this section we will examine hardware products essential to the construction and interconnection of local area networks that transmit information over wired media, such as coaxial cable, twisted pair of optical fiber. These products provide us with the ability to extend the distance of local area network coverage, connect local networks to distant ones, and obtain access to centralized computational facilities.

Repeaters

A repeater is the simplest type of hardware component in terms of design, operation, and functionality. This device operates at the physical layer of the ISO Open Systems Interconnection Reference Model, regenerating a signal received on one cable segment and then retransmitting the signal onto another cable segment. Figure 5.1 illustrates the operation of a repeater with respect to the ISO OSI Reference Model.

Types

There are two basic types of repeaters. An *electrical repeater* simply receives an electrical signal and then regenerates the signal. During the signal regeneration process, a new signal is formed that matches the original characteristics of the received signal. This process is illustrated in the lower portion of Figure 5.1. By transmitting a new signal, the repeater removes any previous distortion and attenuation, enabling an extension in the permissible transmission distance. Although several network segments can be connected by the use of repeaters to extend the coverage of a network, there are constraints that govern the maximum permissible length of a LAN. For example, a 50-ohm coaxial bus-based Ethernet supports a maximum cabling distance of 2.3 km, and that distance cannot be extended through the use of repeaters.

The second type of repeater commonly used is an *electrical-optical device*, such as the FOIRL repeater, the use and general operation of which were discussed in Chapter 3. This type of repeater converts an electrical signal into an optical signal for transmission and performs a reverse function when receiving

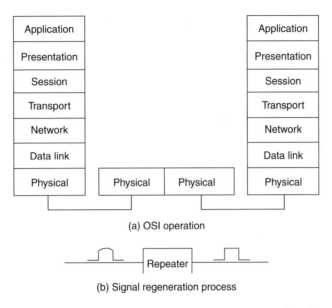

(a) OSI operation

(b) Signal regeneration process

Figure 5.1   Repeater operation. A repeater connects two local area networks or network segments at the OSI physical layer (cable) by regenerating the signal received on one LAN or LAN segment onto the other network or network segment.

a light signal. Similar to an electrical repeater, the electrical-optical repeater extends the distance that a signal can be carried on a local area network.

Because a repeater is restricted to operating at the OSI physical layer, it is transparent to data flow. This restricts the use of a repeater to linking identical networks or network segments. For example, you could use repeaters to connect two Ethernet or two Token-Ring network segments, but not to connect an Ethernet network to a Token-Ring network.

Utilization

Figure 5.2 illustrates the use of a repeater to connect two Ethernet bus-based LANs, one serving the accounting department, and the other network serving the data processing department. In this situation, all messages on one local area network are passed to the other, regardless of their intended recipient. The use of repeaters in this manner increases the sum of the traffic on each LAN. If this system is implemented without knowledge of the traffic flow and utilization levels on each network, performance problems may result when separate networks are interconnected through the use of repeaters.

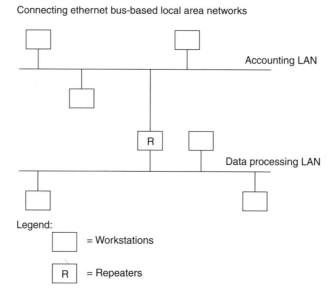

Connecting ethernet bus-based local area networks

Accounting LAN

R

Data processing LAN

Legend:

= Workstations

R = Repeaters

Figure 5.2 Using a repeater to link separate network segments. When a repeater is used to connect separate network segments, traffic on each segment is regenerated onto the other segment.

One special type of electrical repeater is a twisted-pair-based hub, such as a 10BASE-T hub. As previously discussed in this book, a hub receives data on one port and regenerates such data bit by bit onto all other ports. Another special type of repeater is a buffered distributor. A buffered distributor represents a relatively new type of IEEE 802.3 hub, which is designed to connect two or more 802.3 links, each operating at 1 Gbps. Similar to other 802.3 repeaters, the buffer distributor is a nonaddressable device, forwarding all inbound frames received on one port onto all other ports. Unlike other repeaters, the buffered distributor, as its name implies, contains an internal memory area that allows one or more incoming frames to be buffered before forwarding those frames. Through the buffering of frames and the ability to use the IEEE 802.3x flow control scheme to manage its internal buffer level of occupancy, the buffered distributor is not subject to the Ethernet collision-domain constraint nor other topology limitations.

Constraints

There are several constraints associated with the use of repeaters. Those constraints include the previously discussed 5-4-3 rule, disabling of the

SQE test signal to repeaters to include hub ports, and topology restrictions associated with the use of different types of repeaters. Concerning topology, when a metallic repeater receives a signal, it uses the received signal to recover clocking. If you recall our prior discussion of the composition of Ethernet frames, we noted that a 64-bit preamble prefixes frame data for synchronization. As a repeater samples the preamble, it may lose a few bits as it recovers clocking. This bit loss shrinks the gap between frames that should normally be 9.6 μs at 10 Mbps. In fact, according to the IEEE 802.3 specifications, the interframe gap (IFG) can be as low as 6.8 μs. However, due to the gap shrinking the Ethernet specification does not permit more than two repeaters to be located between any two communicating devices located in the same collision domain. Note that this specification treats both a shared media hub and a stand-alone repeater as repeaters. Thus, while you could use one stand-alone repeater to extend the transmission distance from a station to a hub, you could not perform a similar extension for a second workstation connected to the hub. This is because the hub functions as a repeater, which would result in the flow of data through three repeaters, violating the two-repeater limit within a collision domain.

You can use the information presented in this book as well as vendor specification sheets to determine the specific constraints associated with different types of repeaters. Concerning vendor specification sheets, their use is highly recommended, as the constraints associated with the use of different types of repeaters can vary from one manufacturer to another.

Bridges

Unlike repeaters, which lack intelligence and are restricted to linking similar LANs and LAN segments, bridges are intelligent devices that can connect similar and dissimilar local area networks. To obtain an appreciation for the functions performed by bridges, let us examine the use of this type of networking product.

Operation

Figure 5.3 illustrates the operation of a bridge with respect to the OSI Reference Model, as well as its use to connect two separate Ethernet local area networks. Although the use of the bridge in the lower portion of Figure 5.3 looks similar to the use of a repeater previously shown in Figure 5.2, the operation of each device includes a number of key differences.

When a bridge begins to operate, it examines each frame transmitted on connected local area networks at the data link layer—a process beyond

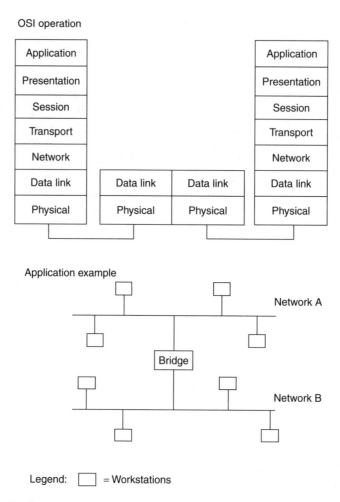

OSI operation

Application example

Legend: ☐ = Workstations

Figure 5.3 Bridge operation. A bridge connects two local area networks or network segments at the data link layer.

the capability of a repeater, which operates transparent to data. By reading the source address included in each frame, the bridge assembles a table of local addresses for each network. In addition to reading each source address, the bridge also reads the destination address contained in the frame. If the destination address is not contained in the local address table that the bridge constructs, this fact indicates that the frame's destination is not on the current network or network segment. In this situation, the bridge transmits the frame onto the other network or network segment. If the destination address is contained in the local address table, this indicates that the frame should remain on the local network. In this situation, the bridge simply repeats the frame without altering its routing.

We can summarize the operation of the bridge illustrated in the lower portion of Figure 5.3 as follows:

- Bridge reads all frames transmitted on network A.
- Frames with destination address on network A are discarded by the bridge.
- Frames with destination address on network B are retransmitted onto network B.
- The above process is reversed for traffic on network B.

To illustrate the method by which bridges operate, let's assume a three-port bridge is used to connect three Ethernet segments together, as illustrated in the top portion of Figure 5.4. In this example, for simplicity, each port address is denoted by a letter of the alphabet while each station address is denoted by a numeric. It should be noted that each bridge port has a MAC address as it is a participant on a LAN. Although the MAC address of bridge ports and stations have the same format and are six hex digits in length, we will use one alphabetic character for each bridge port and one numeric character for each station for simplicity of illustration.

The table in the lower portion of Figure 5.4 provides examples of the three operations a bridge performs — flooding frames, forwarding frames, and discarding frames. In the first entry, station 1 is presumed to transmit data to station 2. Since we will assume the bridge was just powered on and has no entries in its address-port table, it does not know which port station 2 is connected to. Thus, it transmits the frame onto all other ports other than the port it was received on, a technique referred to as flooding. Because station 2 is on the same segment as station 1, the transmission of frames onto the other segments only interferes with traffic on those segments but will not be recognized by a station, because no station connected to port B or C has address 2.

In addition to flooding packets when the location of the destination address is not known, there are two other situations where bridge flooding can occur. Those situations include the receipt of a multicast or broadcast frame at one port on a bridge, which results in such frames being transmitted onto all ports other than the port they are received on. Returning to the example shown in Figure 5.4, when the frame from station 1 is flooded by the bridge, it enters the source address and port that the frame was received on into its address-port table. Hence the entry "1, A." When the frame reaches station 2, we will

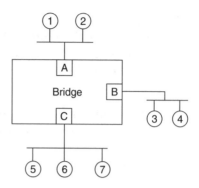

Data Transfer Requirement	Bridge Operation	Address-Port Table
1 Transmits to 2	Frame flooded	1,A
2 Transmits to 1	Frame discarded	1,A 2,A
5 Transmits to 1	Frame forwarded	1,A 2,A 5,C
6 Transmits to 3	Frame flooded	1,A 2,A 5,C 6,C
3 Transmits to 6	Frame forwarded	1,A 2,A 3,B 5,C 6,C

Figure 5.4 Bridges are self-learning networking devices that automatically construct address-port table entries used to route data between network segments.

assume 2 transmits a response to 1. As the frame propagates down the segment and is read by bridge port A, it notes that address 1 is on port A. Thus, there is no need for the bridge to forward the frame and it simply discards it. However, the bridge notes address 2 is on port A and updates its address-port table.

For the third example, it was assumed that station 5 transmits to station 1. Because the address-port table holds the relationship of address 1 with port A, the bridge forwards the frame onto port A and updates its address-port table. Next, when station 6 transmits to station 3 and the bridge checks its address-port table, it finds no entry for address 3, resulting in the bridge flooding the frame onto ports B and C. Then the bridge notes that station 6 is not in its address-port table and updates that table. In the last example, station 3 transmits a response to station 6. Because an entry for station 6 was just made in the address-port table, the bridge forwards the frame onto port C.

In addition to associating addresses with ports, a bridge also time stamps each entry and updates the time stamp when an address is referenced. As storage is used up and the bridge needs to purge old entries to make room for new entries, it will purge the oldest entries based upon the use of the time stamp.

The previously described method of bridging operation is referred to as *transparent bridging*. Refer to Chapter 6 for detailed information concerning different methods of bridge operations.

Filtering and Forwarding The process of examining each frame is known as *filtering*. The *filtering rate* of a bridge is directly related to its level of performance. That is, the higher the filtering rate of a bridge, the lower the probability it will become a bottleneck to network performance. A second performance measurement associated with bridges is their *forwarding rate*. The forwarding rate is expressed in frames per second and denotes the maximum capability of a bridge to transmit traffic from one network to another. In Chapter 6, we will expand our examination of bridges to determine their maximum filtering and forwarding rates when used on Ethernet networks.

Types

There are two general types of bridges: transparent and translating. Each type of bridge can be obtained as a local or remote device; a remote device includes a wide area network interface and the ability to convert frames into a WAN transmission protocol.

Transparent Bridge A transparent bridge provides a connection between two local area networks that employ the same data link protocol. Thus, the bridge shown in the lower portion of Figure 5.3 and the bridge shown in the upper portion of Figure 5.4 are both examples of transparent bridges. At the physical layer, some transparent bridges have multiple ports that support different media. Thus, a transparent bridge does not have to be transparent at the physical level, although the majority of such bridges are.

Although a transparent bridge provides a high level of performance for a small number of network interconnections, its level of performance decreases as the number of interconnected networks increases. The rationale for this loss in performance is based on the method used by transparent bridges to develop a route between LANs. Refer to Chapter 6 for specific information concerning bridge routing and performance issues.

Translating Bridge   A translating bridge provides a connection capability between two local area networks that employ different protocols at the data link layer. Because networks using different data link layer protocols normally use different media, a translating bridge also provides support for different physical layer connections.

Figure 5.5 illustrates the use of a translating bridge to interconnect a Token-Ring and an Ethernet local area network. In this example, the bridge functions as an Ethernet node on the Ethernet and as a Token-Ring node on the Token-Ring. When a frame from one network has a destination on the other network, the bridge will perform a series of operations, including frame and transmission rate conversion. For example, consider an Ethernet frame destined to the Token-Ring network. The bridge will strip the frame's preamble and FCS, then it will convert the frame into a Token-Ring frame format. Once the bridge receives a free token, the new frame will be transmitted onto the Token-Ring; however, the transmission rate will be at the Token-Ring network rate and not at the Ethernet rate. For frames going from the Token-Ring to the Ethernet, the process is reversed.

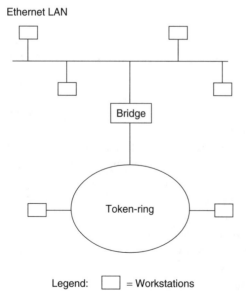

Figure 5.5   Translating bridge operation. A translating bridge connects local area networks that employ different protocols at the data link layer. In this example, the translating bridge is used to connect an Ethernet local area network to a Token-Ring network.

One of the problems associated with the use of a translating bridge is the conversion of frames from their format on one network to the format required for use on another network. As indicated in Chapter 2, the information field of an Ethernet frame can vary from 64 to 1500 bytes. In comparison, a Token-Ring can have a maximum information field size of 4500 bytes when the ring operates at 4 Mbps, or 18,000 bytes when the ring operates at 16 Mbps. If a station on a Token-Ring network has a frame with an information field that exceeds 1500 bytes in length, the bridging of that frame onto an Ethernet network cannot occur. This is because there is no provision within either layer 2 protocol to inform a station that a frame flowing from one network to another was fragmented and requires reassembly. Using a bridge effectively in this situation requires that software on each workstation on each network be configured to use the smallest maximum frame size of any interconnected network. In this example, Token-Ring workstations would not be allowed to transmit information fields greater than 1500 bytes.

Features

The functionality of a bridge is based on the features incorporated into this device. Following is a list of the 11 major bridge features that define both the functionality and the performance level of a bridge.

- Filtering and forwarding rate
- Selective forwarding capability
- Multiple port support
- Wide area network interface support
- Local area network interface support
- Transparent operation at the data link layer
- Translating operation to link dissimilar networks
- Encapsulation operation to support wide area network use
- Stand-alone and adapter-based fabrication
- Self-learning (transparent) routing
- Source routing

Filtering and Forwarding   The filtering and forwarding rates indicate the ability of the bridge to accept, examine, and regenerate frames on the same network (filtering) and transfer frames onto a different network (forwarding). Higher filtering and forwarding rates indicate better bridge performance.

Selective Forwarding   Some bridges have a selective forwarding capability. Bridges with this feature can be configured to forward frames selectively, based on predefined source and destination addresses. With a selective forwarding capability, you can develop predefined routes for frames to take when flowing between networks, and enable or inhibit the transfer of information between predefined workstations.

Figure 5.6 illustrates the use of the selective forwarding capability of two bridges to provide two independent routes for data transfer between an Ethernet and a Token-Ring network. In this example, you might enable all workstations with source address 1 or 2 to have data destined to the Token-Ring flow over bridge 1, while workstations with a source address of 3 or 4 are configured to use bridge 2. Although the bridges illustrated in Figure 5.5 appear to form a closed loop, in effect the previously described method of selective forwarding results in a single logical path for each station on the Ethernet. This ensures there are no closed loops—a condition that would violate the spanning tree bridging algorithm supported by Ethernet bridges. The operation of that algorithm is described in Chapter 6.

Multiple Port Support The multiple port support capability of a bridge is related to its local and wide area network media interface support. Some

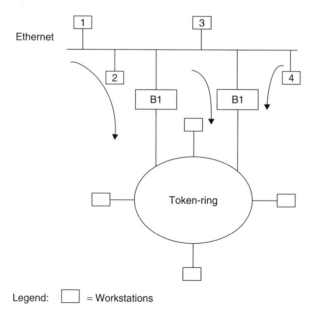

Figure 5.6 Using bridge selective forwarding capability. Using the selective forwarding capability of bridges enables the data flow between networks to be distributed based upon source or destination addresses.

bridges support additional ports beyond the two that make up a basic bridge. Doing so enables a bridge to provide connectivity between three or more local area networks.

Figure 5.7 illustrates one potential use of a multiple port bridge to link an Ethernet network to two Token-Ring networks.

Local and Wide Area Interface Support Local area media interfaces supported by bridges can include thin and thick Ethernet coaxial cable, shielded and unshielded twisted-pair metallic, cable, and different types of fiber optic cable. Wide area network interfaces are incorporated into remote bridges that are designed to provide an internetworking capability between two or more geographically dispersed LANs linked by a WAN. Common WAN media interfaces can include RS-232 for data rates at or below 19.2 Kbps, ITU X.21 for packet network access at data rates up to 128 Kbps, ITU V.35 for data rates up to approximately 6 Mbps, and a T1/E1 interface for operations at 1.544 Mbps and 2.048 Mbps, respectively.

Transparent Operation Although bridges are thought of as transparent to data, this is not always true. For interconnecting different networks located in

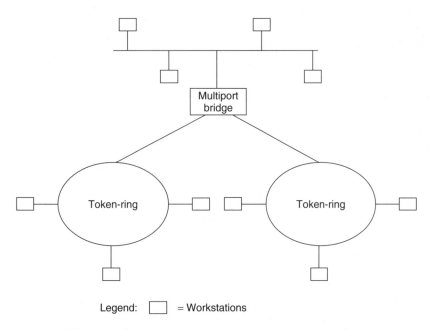

Figure 5.7 Using a multiport bridge. With a multiport bridge, you can interconnect three or more local area networks.

the same geographical area, bridges are normally transparent to data. However, some remote bridges use data compression algorithms to reduce the quantity of data transmitted between bridges connected via a wide area network. Such compression performing bridges are not transparent to data, although they restore data to its original form.

Frame Translation For interconnecting different types of local area networks, bridges must perform a translation of frames. For example, an Ethernet frame must be changed into a Token-Ring frame when the frame is routed from an Ethernet to a Token-Ring network. As previously mentioned, because frames cannot be fragmented at the data link layer, you must set the workstations on the Token-Ring network to the smallest maximum information field of an Ethernet frame, 1500 bytes.

When data is transferred between colocated local area networks, the frame format on one network is suitable for transfer onto the other network; it is modified for transfer when the media access control layers differ. When a bridge is used to connect two local area networks via a wide area network facility, a WAN protocol is employed to control data transfer. The wide area network protocol is better suited for transmission over the WAN, as it is standardized to incorporate error detection and correction, enable a large number of unacknowledged WAN frames to exist to speed information transfer, and support full-duplex data transfers. Examples of such wide area network protocols include IBM's SDLC, and the ITU's HDLC and X.25.

Frame Encapsulation Figure 5.8 illustrates the operation of a pair of remote bridges connecting two local area networks via a wide area network. For transmission from network A to network B, user data from a network A station is first converted into logical link control and media access control frames. The bridge then encapsulates one or more LAN frames into the bridging protocol frame used for communications over the wide area network. Because the local area network frame is wrapped in another protocol, we say the LAN frame is *tunneled* within the WAN protocol. At the opposite end of the wide area network, the distant remote bridge performs a reverse operation, removing the WAN protocol header and trailer from each frame.

Fabrication Some bridges are manufactured as stand-alone products. Such devices are called *plug and play*, because you simply connect the bridge ports to the media and turn them on. Other bridges are manufactured as adapter cards for insertion into the system unit of a personal computer, workstation, or reduced instruction set computer (RISC). Through the use of software

Figure 5.8 Remote bridge operation. A remote bridge wraps the logical link control (LLC) and media access control (MAC) frames in another protocol for transmission over a wide area network.

developed in conjunction with hardware, you may obtain more flexibility with this type of bridge than with a stand-alone device whose software is fixed in ROM.

Routing Method   The routing capability of a bridge governs its capability to interconnect local area networks and its level of performance. As previously examined through the use of Figure 5.4, a transparent bridge automatically develops routing tables. Thus, this device is known as a *self-learning bridge* and represents the most elementary type of bridge routing. In the IBM Token-Ring frame, there is an optional routing field that can be used to develop routing information for frames routed through a series of bridges — a technique referred to as *source routing*. Refer to Chapter 6 for an in-depth discussion of bridge routing methods, as well as translating operations that enable a bridge to connect IEEE 802.3 and 802.5 networks.

Routers

A router is a device that operates at the network layer of the ISO OSI Reference Model, as illustrated in Figure 5.9. What this means is that a router examines network addresses and makes decisions about whether data on a local area network should remain on the network or should be transmitted

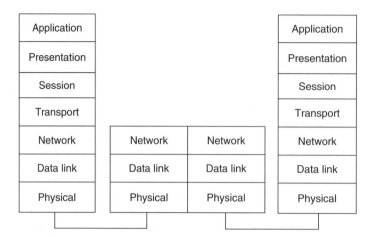

Figure 5.9 Router operation. A router operates at the network layer of the ISO OSI Reference Model. This enables a router to provide network layer services, such as flow control and frame fragmentation.

to a different network. Although this level of operation may appear to be insignificant compared with that of a bridge operating at the data link layer, there is actually a considerable difference in the routing capability of bridges and routers.

Operation

A bridge uses 48-bit MAC addresses it associates with ports as a mechanism to determine whether a frame received on one port is ignored, forwarded onto another port, or flooded onto all ports other than the port it was received on. At the data link layer there is no mechanism to distinguish one network from another. Thus, the delivery of frames between networks requires bridges to learn MAC addresses and base their forwarding decisions on such addresses. Although this is an acceptable technique for linking a few networks together, as the number of networks increase and the number of workstations on interconnected networks increase, bridges would spend a considerable amount of time purging old entries and flooding frames, causing unacceptable performance problems. This resulted in the development of routers that prevent the flooding of frames between networks and operate by using network addresses.

To understand the concept behind routing, consider Figure 5.10, which illustrates two networks connected by a pair of routers. In this example, assume addresses A, B, C, and D represent MAC addresses of workstations, and E and F represent the MAC address of each router connected to each

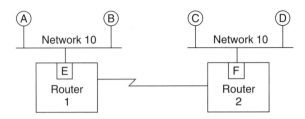

Figure 5.10   Routing between two networks. When a workstation on one network transmits data to a device on another network, an application program provides the destination network address, which is used by routers as a basis for their routing decisions.

network. Assuming workstation A has data to transmit to workstation C, an application program executing on workstation A assigns network 20 as the destination network address in a packet it prepares at the network layer. That packet is transported via one or more MAC frames to MAC address E, which is the data link address of the network adapter card installed in router 1.

In actuality, each device on a network can have a unique network address, with a portion of the address denoting the network and the remainder of the address denoting each host or router interface. This enables the application program on workstation A to transmit a packet destined to workstation C to router 1, with the data link layer passing the packet to MAC address E as a frame or sequence of frames. The router receives the frame or sequence of frames explicitly addressed to it and notes that the packet has the destination address for network 20. The router then searches its routing tables and determines that it should relay the packet to router 2. When the packet is received at router 2, it recognizes the fact that network 20 is connected to the router via its connection to the LAN by an adapter card using MAC address F. Thus, the router will transport the packet to its destination using one or more frames at the data link layer with a MAC source address of F.

The preceding description represents a simplified description of the routing process. A more detailed description will be presented later in this book after we investigate the TCP/IP protocol suite. We will examine the TCP/IP protocol suite in the second section in this chapter when we turn our attention to net-working software and focus our attention upon router operations in Chapter 7.

The ability to operate at the network layer enables a router to extend networking across multiple data links in an orderly and predefined manner. This means that a router can determine the best path through a series of data links from a source network to a destination network. To accomplish this, the router operates under a network protocol, such as the Internet Protocol (IP), Digital Equipment Corporation's DECnet Phase V, or Novell's IPX. This networking protocol must operate on both the source and destination network when protocol-dependent routers are used. If you use protocol-independent routers, you can interconnect networks using different protocols. The protocol-independent router can be considered a sophisticated transparent bridge. Its operation and utilization are described in detail in Chapter 7.

In comparison, because a bridge operates at the data link layer, it can always be used to transfer information between networks operating under different network protocols. This makes a bridge more efficient for linking networks that only have one or a few paths, while a router is more efficient for interconnecting multiple network links via multiple paths.

Network Address Utilization   Unlike a bridge, which must monitor all frames at the media access control layer, a router is specifically addressed at the network layer. This means that a router has to examine only frames explicitly addressed to that device. In communications terminology, the monitoring of all frames is referred to as a *promiscuous* mode of operation, while the selective examination of frames is referred to as a *nonpromiscuous* mode of operation.

Another difference between the operation of bridges and routers is the structure of the addresses on which they operate. Bridges operate at the data link layer, which means that they typically examine physical addresses that are contained in ROM on adapter cards and used in the generation of frames. In comparison, routers operate at the network layer, where addresses are normally assigned by a network administrator to a group of stations having a common characteristic, such as being connected on an Ethernet in one area of a building. This type of address is known as a *logical address*, and can be assigned and modified by the network administrator.

Table Operation   Like bridges, routers make forwarding decisions using tables. However, unlike a bridge, which may employ a simple table look-up procedure to determine if a destination address is on a particular network, a router may employ much more sophisticated forwarding decision criteria. For example, a router may be configured to analyze several paths using an algorithm and dynamically select a path based upon the results of the algorithm. Routing algorithms and protocols are discussed in Chapter 7.

Advantages of Use   The use of routers provides a number of significant advantages over the use of bridges. To illustrate these advantages, we will

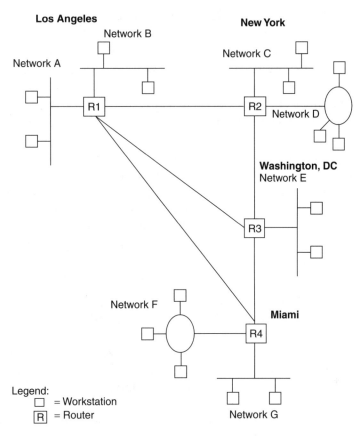

Figure 5.11 Building an internet using routers. Routers can be used to establish complex networks in which traffic is varied over network facilities. This variation is based on the operational status and utilization of different network paths.

examine the use of routers in Figure 5.11, in which four corporate offices containing seven local area networks are interconnected through the use of four routers. In this example, networks A and B are located in a building in Los Angeles, networks C and D are located in New York, network E is located in Washington, DC, and networks F and G are located in Miami.

Multiple Path Transmission and Routing Control Suppose a station on network A in Los Angeles requires transmission to a station on network G in Miami. Initially, router R1 might use the path R1-R4 to transmit data between networks. If the path should fail, or if an excessive amount of traffic flows between Los Angeles and Miami using that path, router R1 can seek to establish other paths, such as R1-R3-R4 or even R1-R2-R3-R4. In fact, many routers will consider each packet as a separate entity, routing the packet to its destination over the best available path at the time of transmission. Although this could conceivably result in packets arriving at R4 out of sequence, routers have the capability to resequence packets into their original order before passing data onto the destination network.

Flow Control   As data flows through multiple paths toward its destination, a link can become congested. For example, data from stations on network C and network E routed to network G might build up to the point where the path R3-R4 becomes congested. To eliminate the possibility of packet loss, routers will use flow control. That is, they will inhibit transmission onto a link and notify other routers to inhibit data flow until there is an available level of bandwidth for traffic.

Frame Fragmentation   As previously mentioned, bridges cannot break a frame into a series of frames when transmission occurs between networks with different frame sizes. This situation requires workstations to be configured to use the smallest maximum frame size of any of the networks to be connected together. In comparison, most network protocols supported by routers include a provision for fragmentation and reassembly of packets.

The higher level of functionality of routers over bridges is not without a price. That price is in terms of packet processing, software complexity, and cost. Since routers provide a more complex series of functions than bridges, their ability to process packets is typically one-half to two-thirds of the processing capability of bridges. In addition, the development time required to program a more complex series of functions adds to the cost of routers. Thus, routers are generally more expensive than bridges. Table 5.1 summarizes the major differences between bridges and routers in terms of their operation, functionality, complexity, and cost.

Brouters

A brouter is a hybrid device, representing a combination of bridging and routing capabilities. Although brouters are no longer marketed using this term, their functionality lives on in modern routers that include a bridging capability.

TABLE 5.1   Bridge/Router Comparison

Characteristic	Bridge	Router
Routing based upon an algorithm or protocol	Normally no	Yes
Protocol transparency	Yes	Only protocol-independent router
Uses network addresses	No	Yes
Promiscuous mode of operation	Yes	No
Forwarding decision	Elementary	Can be complex
Multiple path transmission	Limited	High
Routing control	Limited	High
Flow control	No	Yes
Frame fragmentation	No	Yes
Packet processing rate	High	Moderate
Cost	Less expensive	More expensive

Operation

When a brouter receives a frame, it examines that frame to determine whether it is destined for another local area network. If it is, the brouter then checks the protocol of the frame to determine whether it is supported at the network layer supported by the router function. If the frame's protocol is supported, the brouter will route the frame as if it were a router. However, if the brouter does not support the protocol, it will instead bridge the frame using layer 2 information.

In comparison to routers, brouters provide an additional level of connectivity between networks, although that connectivity takes place at a lower level in the OSI Reference Model hierarchy. This is because a router would simply ignore a frame for which it does not support the network protocol, while a brouter would bridge the frame.

Utilization

The key advantage of using a brouter is the ability of this device to both bridge and route data. Its ability to perform this dual function enables a brouter to replace the use of separate bridges and routers in some networking applications. For example, consider the use of a separate bridge and router in the top portion of Figure 5.12. In this example, the bridge provides an interconnection capability between two neighboring networks, while the router provides an interconnection capability to distant networks. By replacing the separate bridge and router with a brouter, you can obtain the same level of functionality, as illustrated in the lower portion of Figure 5.12. Of course, you want to ensure that the filtering and forwarding rates of the brouter are sufficient to be used in the manner illustrated. Otherwise, the replacement of separate bridges and routers by brouters may introduce delays that affect network performance. As previously noted, many modern routers include a built-in bridging capability and, as such, can be considered to represent a brouter. Refer to Chapters 6 and 7 for information concerning the processing requirements of bridges and routers.

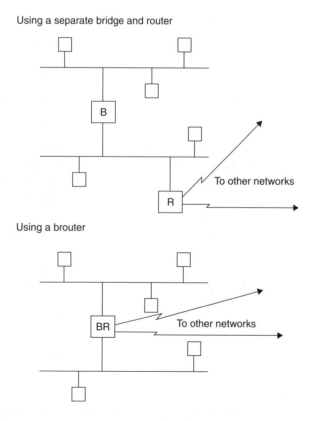

Figure 5.12   Replacing a separate bridge and router with a brouter.

Gateway

The well-known phrase "one person's passion is another's poison" can, in many ways, apply to gateways. The term *gateway* was originally coined to refer to a device providing a communications path between two local area networks, or between a LAN and a mainframe computer, from the physical layer through the application layer. When applied to a device interconnecting networks, the term gateway was originally used and is still commonly used to reference a router. In fact, many programs used to configure workstation and server network operations request the entry of the gateway network address, even though it is more appropriate today to use the term *router*.

Figure 5.13 illustrates the operation of a gateway with respect to the ISO OSI Reference Model. Unfortunately, the term *gateway* has been used loosely to describe a range of products, ranging from bridges and routers that interconnect two or more local area networks to protocol converters that provide asynchronous dial-up access into an IBM SNA network. Thus, a definition of the term is warranted.

Definition

In this book, we will use the term *gateway*, unless otherwise noted, to describe a product that performs protocol conversion through all seven layers of the ISO OSI Reference Model. As such, a gateway performs all of the functions of a router, as well as any protocol conversions required through the application layer.

Application	Application	Application	Application
Presentation	Presentation	Presentation	Presentation
Session	Session	Session	Session
Transport	Transport	Transport	Transport
Network	Network	Network	Network
Data link	Data link	Data link	Data link
Physical	Physical	Physical	Physical

Figure 5.13 Gateway operation. A gateway operates at all seven layers of the ISO OSI Reference Model.

One of the most common types of gateways is an electronic mail (e-mail) gateway, which converts documents from one e-mail format to another. For example, an internal corporate network might be operating Lotus Development Corporation's CC:MAIL. If they require connectivity with the Internet, the gateway must convert internal CC:MAIL documents so that they can be transported via the Simple Mail Transport Protocol (SMTP), which is a TCP/IP electronic mail application. Similarly, SMTP mail delivered via the Internet to the organization's gateway must be converted by the gateway into the format used by CC:MAIL. A second type of popular gateway enables workstations on a network to communicate with a mainframe as if the workstation was a specific type of terminal device. This type of gateway also operates at all seven layers of the ISO Reference Model.

Operation

Gateways are protocol-specific in function, typically used to provide access to a mainframe computer. Some vendors manufacture multiprotocol gateways. Such products are normally manufactured as adapter cards, containing separate processors that are installed in the system unit of a personal computer or in a specially designed vendor hardware platform. When used in conjunction with appropriate vendor software, this type of gateway is actually an N-in-1 gateway, where N is the number of protocol conversions and separate connections the gateway can perform.

Figure 5.14 shows a multiprotocol gateway used to link LAN stations to an IBM mainframe via an SDLC link and an X.25 connection to a packet switching network. Once connected to the packet switching network, LAN traffic may be further converted by gateway facilities built into that network, or traffic may be routed to a packet network node and transmitted from that node to its final destination in its X.25 packet format.

Gateways are primarily designed and used for LAN-WAN connections and not for inter-LAN communications. Because they perform more sophisticated functions than routers, they are slower in providing network throughput. In addition, because the configuration of a gateway requires the consideration of a large number of protocol options, a gateway installation is considerably more difficult than the setup of a router. Refer to Chapter 8 for specific information concerning the operation and utilization of gateways.

File Servers

The file server is the central repository of information upon which a local area network is normally constructed. The file server is normally a personal

Figure 5.14 Multiprotocol gateway operation. A multiprotocol gateway can be used to provide local area network stations access to different computational facilities, either directly or through the use of a packet network.

computer or workstation that has a very powerful microprocessor, such as an Intel Pentium, Digital Alpha, or a RISC chip, and a large amount of fast-access on-line storage. The on-line storage is used to hold the local area network operating system and the application programs that other stations on the network may use. Several software vendors have split application programs, enabling portions of a program to be run on a network station, while other portions, such as the updating of a database, occur on the server. This technique is known as *client–server processing*.

In comparison, the general term *client/server operations* references the access of one computer by another on a network. The computer being accessed, while normally considered to represent a file server, can also be a mainframe or minicomputer. For either situation, the client uses a network to access one or more features of the server. Those features can range in scope from a spreadsheet program stored on a file server to a database query program on a mainframe that provides access to billions of records.

Connectivity Functions

As the heart of a local area network, the server supports every network application. It is therefore in an ideal position to perform connectivity functions. Some servers are designed to function as asynchronous gateways, providing access to one or more modems that individual network stations can access for communications via the switched telephone network. Here, software on the server considers the group of modems as a pool for access purposes. Hence, the term *modem pooling* is used to refer to a server used to provide this service.

Other servers contain software and hardware to provide access to mainframe computers via a specific protocol, such as SDLC, X.25, or TCP/IP. Depending on the capabilities of the network operating system used on the server, the server may support server-to-server communications on an intra- and inter-LAN basis. When supporting intra-LAN server-to-server communications, you can assign network users to a specific default server for an initial network log-on, distributing the use of servers so that no one server becomes overused. Then, the network operating system would support the transfer of information between servers, such as an electronic mail message created by a network user assigned to one server, who addresses the message to another employee assigned to a different server. If your network operating system supports inter-LAN server-to-server communications, the server in effect functions as a remote bridge.

Types of Servers

The first type of server developed for use with local area networks primarily supported file and printer sharing. Thus, although referred to as a file server, the server also permitted a few printers to be connected to the computer as network-accessible devices. As the concept of local area networking gained acceptance, servers were developed to perform specific functions. Today, popular types of servers include application servers, communications servers, print servers, and remote access servers (RASs). Figure 5.15 illustrates an Ethernet network that contains four distinct types of servers.

The RAS can be considered to represent a hybrid device that consists of a modem pool and router. This type of server permits the support of serial communications in the form of analog modems, digital ISDN calls, and the connection of a T1 circuit that contains 24 individual connections grouped together on a common circuit. Incoming communications are prompted for access validation, typically in the form of a user ID and password, to gain access from the RAS onto the network. Once connected to the network, they then obtain access privileges commensurate with the network account they have.

Although a communications server also provides connectivity between a network and a serial communications facility, there are some distinct differences between this server and an RAS. First, a communications server is

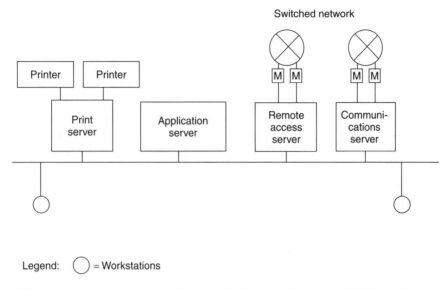

Figure 5.15 Servers can be acquired to perform specific functions.

primarily used for outbound traffic from network users, although if should be Noted that it supports full-duplex communications. Thus, it may not support inbound traffic, and if it does, it probably just places the traffic onto the network without checking the validity of the user. Secondly, most communications servers function as replacements for users having individual modems. Thus, another popular name for a limited capability communications server is a modem pooler.

Location Considerations

Figure 5.16 illustrates a file server used both in its traditional role as a repository for application programs and for modem pooling and gateway operations. The transmission of information between workstations and servers far exceeds transmission between workstations. The location of file servers on an Ethernet local area network is therefore critical for ensuring that network performance remains at an acceptable level. In the example shown in Figure 5.16, the server is located at a point on an Ethernet bus-based local area network in which the transmission distance between each workstation and the server is maximized. This location results in the greatest propagation delay for the transmission of data between each workstation and the server.

Legend:
□ = Workstation

Figure 5.16 Server placement. The location of a server on a network is critical for ensuring network performance. In this example, because each workstation requires access to the server, its location requires the greatest transmission distance between individual workstations and the server. This, therefore, is probably a poor server location.

This is probably a poor location with respect to network performance if each workstation requires a similar level of access to the server.

The reason for this representing a poor placement is the fact that the longer the distance between two network devices on a CSMA/CD access protocol network, the greater the probability that one station will listen to the network and not hear a signal while another has just began transmitting. This, in turn, results in an increased number of collisions that adversely affects network performance. Because collisions result in the occurrence of a random back-off time interval during which no data can be transferred on the network, the proper location of a server can increase network transmission efficiency.

Wire Hubs

As mentioned in Chapter 3, 10BASE-T, 100BASE-T, and the half-duplex version of Gigabit Ethernet use wiring concentrators, or *hubs*. Hubs are typically located in telephone wiring closets, with stations cabled to the hub in the form of a star. Hubs are then connected to one another to form a bus. Only if the closest workstations to the server require a disproportionate level of server access, in comparison to other workstations, is the server location shown in Figure 5.16 correct. If each workstation has an equal level of server access, the server should be relocated to the middle of the network. This move would minimize propagation delays between the workstations and the server — which, in turn, would minimize the probability of collisions.

Advantages

Ethernet hubs employ standard wiring between stations and the hub in the form of twisted-pair cable. Because workstations are connected to a single point, administration of a hub-based network is normally simple and economical, because a central point allows network configuration and reconfiguration, monitoring, and management. Due to the value of hubs in local area networking, several vendors introduced products commonly referred to as *intelligent hubs*. This product provides users with the ability to build local area networks, ranging in scope from a single LAN with a small number of nodes to mixed-protocol LANs with several thousand nodes that can be monitored, modified, and analyzed from a single point.

Intelligent Hubs

An intelligent hub represents an advance in functionality and capability over conventional wire hubs. The intelligent hub includes its own microprocessor and memory, which not only provide a network management capability, but, in addition, may provide the ability to interconnect separate networks through integrated bridges and routers.

Most intelligent hubs include a multibus backplane, which enables bridges and routers to access and route data originating over multiple types of media. When operating in this manner, the intelligent hub can be viewed as a PBX, providing connectivity between any station on any network connected through the hub, while providing a centralized management and control capability.

Through the use of an intelligent hub, the administrator can enable or disable network ports from a network management workstation, segment a network to balance traffic better and improve performance, and facilitate troubleshooting and maintenance operations. As networks became more sophisticated, intelligent hubs evolved to facilitate their operation and management. With the ability of some intelligent hubs to bring together various media flavors of different local area networks, this device also provides a mechanism for the integration of prior piece-by-piece planning, or for the correction of a plan gone astray. Thus, the use of an intelligent hub may provide you with an umbrella mechanism to bring together separate networks and media previously installed in a building.

Switching Hubs

Improvements in the design of intelligent hubs to include faster backplanes, port memory buffers, and one or more mechanisms to control the flow of information resulted in the development of a series of Ethernet hardware products. Collectively referred to as *switching hubs* or LAN switches, products in this broad category of equipment examine the destination address of each frame as a decision criteria for invoking a switching operation.

A switching hub can be considered to represent a sophisticated bridge that has the ability to support multiple bridging operations at the same time. This is illustrated in Figure 5.17, which shows a 6-port switch with workstations connected to ports 3 and 4 having frames transported to servers connected to ports 5 and 6. If each port operates at 10 Mbps then the two cross-connections provide 20 Mbps of bandwidth. In comparison, a conventional shared media 10BASE-T network only permits one frame at a time to be on the network, limiting bandwidth to 10 Mbps.

Some switching hubs are limited to working with individual workstations connected to each port, while other switching hubs are designed to switch frames from all workstations on a segment connected to the hub. The first type of switching is referred to as port switching, while the second type of switching is referred to as segment-based switching. The development of 100-Mbps high-speed Ethernet technology resulted in several vendors introducing multiple-speed switching hubs during 1994 and 1995, which could be used to significantly improve the performance of many types of networks. This improvement primarily resulted from the connection of 100-Mbps ports to file servers, while 10-Mbps ports are connected to 10BASE-T workstations and conventional hubs. Similarly, the first series of Gigabit Ethernet switches, which reached the market during 1997, have 100-Mbps and 1-Gbps ports, with the 100-Mbps ports used to support Fast Ethernet connections. Continuing the switching evolution, during 2001 several switches

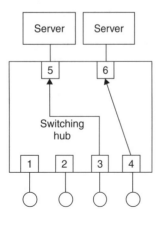

Legend: ◯ = Workstations

Figure 5.17 A switching hub supports multiple simultaneous cross-connection operations, which enhance available network bandwidth.

were introduced that included one or two 10 Gigabit Ethernet ports, while the remainder of the switch was limited to supporting Gigabit transmission. Another technology incorporated into switching hubs is a full-duplex operating capability, permitting the simultaneous transmission and reception of data on a connection. Although many switching hub manufacturers denote this capability for a 10BASE-T connection; for example, as a 20-Mbps Ethernet port, in reality you obtain a 20-Mbps transmission rate only when a device is simultaneously transmitting and receiving information. Because file servers benefit more than workstations from a full-duplex transmission capability, most network designers connect their file servers to the full-duplex port on a switching hub that supports this capability, and use the conventional ports for connections to workstations. Readers are referred to Chapter 6 for an in-depth examination of the operation and utilization of switching hubs.

5.2 Wireless Network Hardware Components

Because this chapter is focused upon network hardware and software, this author would be remiss if he did not review wireless Ethernet LAN components. However, prior to doing so, a brief description of the two types of networking infrastructure supported via wireless LANs is in order.

Network Topologies

The ability to communicate via the use of the air requires computers to have a wireless LAN network adapter card. That network adapter card functions similarly to a wired LAN adapter card, taking application data and forming frames. However, those frames are created to flow over the air and the physical layer of the wireless LAN adapter card supports radio frequency communications instead of communications over a metallic or fiber-optic media.

There are two types of network topologies supported by wireless LANs. Those topologies are referred to as ad hoc or simultaneous and infrastructure. An ad hoc network is formed when two clients with wireless LAN network adapters come into close proximity with one another. The second type of wireless LAN topology is referred to as an infrastructure. Under this networking topology, wireless LAN clients communicate with one another, as well as with their wired relatives, through an access point. Thus, in order to obtain an appreciation of the infrastructure topology, the reader requires an understanding of the manner by which an access point operates.

Access Point

An access point can be considered to represent a two-port bridge. However, instead of each port being connected to a wired LAN, one port is connected to an antenna.

Figure 5.18 illustrates the use of an access point to provide a wireless infrastructure communications topology. Note that in this example two wireless clients with wireless LAN adapter cards first access the access point in order to obtain access to the wired LAN. Because the access point functions as a bridge it constructs a port-address table in a manner similar to that of a conventional bridge. However, the addresses for the second port represent those destination addresses associated with wireless clients whose addresses it learns as the clients access the access point while the latter devices note their source address.

In addition to wireless LAN network adapter cards and access points, there are two additional wireless devices that warrant attention. Those devices include a wireless router and a wireless bridge. Thus, in concluding our examination of the devices used to create a wireless LAN infrastructure let's focus our attention upon each of these.

Wireless Router

A wireless router represents a router with a built-in access point. This device may also be constructed with two or more built-in Ethernet switch ports.

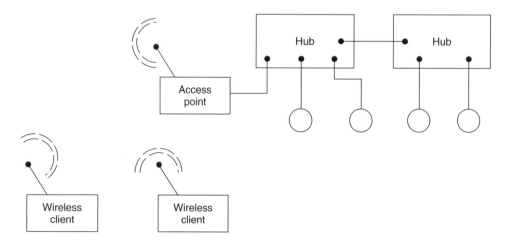

Figure 5.18 Using an access point enables wireless LAN clients to gain access to a wired LAN.

The most common use of the wireless router is in the home or small-office environment. In this environment a cable or DSL modem is connected to an Ethernet port built into the router. Because the router includes a network address translation capability, it can be used to enable many wireless clients to simultaneously access the Internet even though the Internet Service Provider may only allocate a single IP address to the cable modem or DSL modem connection. The Ethernet switch ports provide connectivity to other workstations or a wired LAN. Figure 5.19 illustrates the potential use of a wireless router to create an infrastructure where both wired and wireless clients can share access to the Internet.

Wireless Bridge

We previously noted that an access point represents a bridge that provides connectivity between a wired and an over-the-air interface. Thus, you may now be a bit curious as to what a wireless bridge represents, so let's discuss its operation.

A wireless bridge represents an access point and an antenna that are physically separated from one another. The access point is connected to a wired LAN while the antenna is commonly mounted on the top or side of a building. The access point is then cabled to the antenna. Through the use of

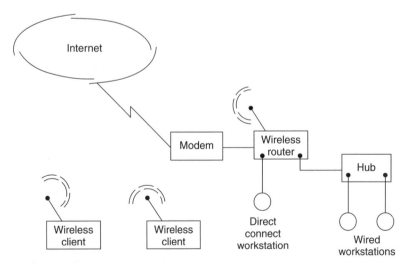

Figure 5.19 Using a wireless router to provide wireless and wired clients with shared access to each other and the Internet.

very sensitive highly directional antennas it becomes possible to interconnect a pair of wired LANs via a pair of wireless LAN bridges at distances up to approximately ten miles. However, to achieve this range the antennas used for each bridge must be within a line of sight of each other. Readers are referred to Chapter 8 for detailed information concerning wireless Ethernet LAN operations.

5.3 Networking Software

The installation of a local area network requires a variety of hardware and software products. At minimum, each workstation on the network normally requires the installation of an interface card into its system unit. This interface card contains a number of ROM modules and specialized circuitry, as well as a microprocessor that implements the access method used to communicate on the common cable.

In some local area networks, one personal computer must be reserved to process the network commands and functions. Because it services these commands and functions, it is normally called the *network server*, although the term *file server* is also commonly used to reference this computer. A combination of specialized software that overlays the operating system on each workstation and software placed on the server governs the operation of the network; this relationship provides a *client–server processing* capability. In comparison, the flow of data from one workstation to another without the use of a server is known as *peer-to-peer processing*. Because the vast majority of Ethernet LANs use servers, we will focus our attention in this section on the software required to support client/server operations. To understand the role of the network server and the functions of LAN software, let us first review how a personal computer operates under a conventional version of the disk operating system (DOS) used in the IBM PC personal computer environment.

DOS

DOS is a single-user operating system designed to provide access to peripherals attached to the system and control of those peripherals, interpretation of commands to perform various functions on the system, and management of disk storage and memory. Under DOS, your keyboard is the standard input device and your display is the standard output device, and control of the personal computer is limited to one user. When you turn on your PC, one of the functions performed by DOS is to load a command processor into a predefined area of your computer's memory. The command processor contains coding that examines your keyboard entries, and coding that performs predefined functions when certain commands are recognized from your keyboard entries. The commands for which the command processor immediately executes code are known as *internal commands*. When other commands are recognized, the command processor loads a predefined file into memory and then executes its contents. These commands are known as *external commands*, because the code used to perform the functions associated with these commands resides on a file external to the command processor's code in memory.

Network Software Components

As soon as a networked personal computer is initialized, its network software routines are added to DOS, permitting the computer to interact with the rest of the network. Before the introduction of DOS Version 3.1, this software was normally an overlay to DOS that served to filter commands, and that translated those commands requiring network access into code to transmit data via the LAN adapter card. Unfortunately, each network operating system vendor developed code to interface the adapter card in a proprietary manner, and software developed to work with one manufacturer's adapter card may not necessarily work with another manufacturer's adapter card.

When a command is issued on the PC, the software overlay permits the command to pass directly to DOS for execution. If a command is issued that refers to the network, the software overlay intercepts or filters the command from reaching DOS and, in conjunction with the adapter board, transmits the command onto the network. If the network is server-based, the nonlocal commands must be sent to a server for additional processing. The left-hand portion of Figure 5.20 illustrates the hardware and software components required when LAN software was originally designed as an overlay to DOS.

Before the introduction of DOS 3.1, most LAN operating system vendors developed proprietary methods to access the LAN adapter card, and either developed proprietary methods to lock files and records or ignored incorporating such features. In effect, this limited their networks to simple file-swapping and printer-sharing applications. Because there was no Network Basic Input/Output System (NetBIOS), a proprietary network BIOS was developed and accessed via the vendor's LAN overlay software to send and receive data from the LAN adapter card. Here, NetBIOS is the lowest level of software on a local area network, translating commands to send and receive data via the adapter card into the instructions that actually perform the requested functions.

Figure 5.20 Original PC LAN hardware and software relationships in an IBM PC environment.

With the introduction of IBM's first local area network, referred to as the PC Network, in August 1984, IBM released all three components required to implement an IBM local area network using IBM equipment: the IBM PC Network Program, PC DOS 3.1, and the IBM PC Network Adapter. The IBM PC Network Program was actually a tailored version of Microsoft Corporation's Microsoft Networks (MS-NET) software, which is essentially a program that overlays DOS and permits workstations on a network to share their disks and peripheral devices. DOS 3.1, also developed by Microsoft, added file- and record-locking capabilities to DOS, permitting multiple users to access and modify data. Without file- and record-locking capabilities in DOS, custom software was required to obtain these functions—without them, the last person saving data onto a file would overwrite changes made to the file by other persons. Thus, DOS 3.1 provided networking and application programmers with a set of standards they could use in developing network software.

Included on the IBM PC Network Adapter card in ROM is an extensive number of programming instructions, known as NetBIOS. The middle portion of Figure 5.18 illustrates the hardware and software components of an IBM PC LAN network.

When the IBM Token-Ring Network was introduced, NetBIOS was removed from the adapter card and incorporated as a separate software program, activated from DOS. The right-hand column of Figure 5.18 illustrates this new relationship between hardware and software. At first, NetBIOS was designed to operate with Token-Ring adapter cards. Later, IBM extended NetBIOS to work with CSMA/CD Ethernet adapter cards.

Due to the standardization of file-and-record locking under DOS 3.1, any multiuser software program written for DOS Version 3.1 or later will run on any LAN that supports this version of DOS. Although DOS 3.1 supports many networking functions, it was not a networking operating system. In fact, a variety of networking operating systems support DOS 3.1 and later versions of DOS, including MS-NET, IBM's PC Network Program, IBM's Token-Ring Program, Microsoft's Windows NT, and Novell's NetWare. You can therefore select a third-party network operating system to use with IBM or non-IBM network hardware, or you can consider obtaining both third-party hardware and software to construct your local area network.

Network Operating Systems

A modern network operating system operates as an overlay to the personal computer's operating system, providing the connectivity that enables personal computers to communicate with one another and share such network resources as hard disks, CD-ROM jukebox drives, and printers, and even obtain access to mainframes and minicomputers. Four of the more popular LAN operating systems are Microsoft Corporation's Windows NT, its successors, Windows 2000 and Windows XP, and Novell Corporation's NetWare.

Both versions of Windows and NetWare are file server–based network operating systems. This means that most network modules reside on the file server. A shell program loaded into each workstation works in conjunction with the server modules. The shell program workstation filters commands, directing user-entered commands to DOS or to the network modules residing on the server. Communications between the shell and the server modules occur at the OSI Reference Model's Network Layer. Microsoft's Windows uses NetBIOS Extended User Interface, commonly referred to as NetBEUI, which is automatically installed when the operating system is installed, while Novell's NetWare uses its Internetwork Packet Exchange (IPX) protocol as the language in which the workstation communicates with the file server. Both Windows and NetWare support the concurrent use of multiple protocols. For example, Windows includes built-in support for TCP/IP, NWLink, and Data Link control. Until the mid-1980s, it was difficult to support more than one protocol at a time due to the manner by which network software residing on a workstation or server communicated with one or more software modules known as the protocol stack. Once we examine the manner by which a client gains access to a server and obtain an overview of NetWare and Windows, we will then turn our attention to the method by which multiple stacks can be employed to support multiple protocols.

Services

The process by which the shell enables a workstation to communicate with a set of services residing on a server is known as a *client/server relationship*. Services provided by network modules on the server can range in scope from file access and transfer, shared printer utilization, and printer queuing to electronic mail. Other features available in most network operating systems include the ability to partition disk storage and allocate such storage to different network users, and the assignment of various types of security levels to individual network users, groups of users, directories, files, and printers. Some network operating systems include a disk mirroring feature and a remote console dial-in capability.

Because file information in the form of updated accounting, payroll, and engineering data can be critical to the health of a company, it is often very important to have duplicate copies of information in case a hard disk should fail. Disk mirroring is a feature that duplicates network information on two or more disks simultaneously. Thus, if one disk fails, network operations can continue.

A remote console dial-in capability enables a network user to gain access to the network from a remote location. This feature can be particularly advantageous for people who travel and wish to transmit and receive messages with people back at the office or obtain access to information residing on the network. Because the administration of a network can be a complex process, a remote dial-in feature may also make life less taxing for a network administrator. Working at home or at another location, the administrator can reassign privileges and perform other network functions that may not be possible in an eight-hour day.

Looking at NetWare

Because the best way to obtain information concerning the relationship of a network operating system to network hardware is to examine the software, we will do so. We will discuss Novell Corporation's NetWare and Microsoft's Windows, as those network operating systems (NOS) are by far the most popular of all network operating systems used.

Architecture

The architecture or structure of NetWare can be mapped to the OSI Reference Model. It provides an indication of the method by which this network operating system provides support for different types of hardware, and includes the

Figure 5.21   NetWare and the OSI Reference Model.

capability for the routing of packets between networks. Figure 5.21 illustrates the general relationship between NetWare and the OSI Reference Model.

In examining Figure 5.21, note that NetWare supports numerous types of local area networks. This means that you can use NetWare as the network operating system on Ethernet, Token-Ring, ARCnet, and other types of networks. In fact, NetWare also supports different types of personal computer operating systems, such as DOS, OS/2, different versions of Windows, UNIX, and Macintosh. This means that NetWare is capable of supporting different types of local area networks as well as workstations that use different operating systems.

Using NetWare on a PC requires the loading of two Novell files whenever you turn on your computer or perform a system reset. Those files are IPX and NETx, where x indicates a specific version of the NET file used with a specific version of DOS, such as NET3 used with DOS 3.

The use of IPX and NETx are required through NetWare Release 3.11. In Release 3.12 and in NetWare Version 4.X and later versions of this network operating system, NETx was replaced by the use of a virtual loadable module (VLM). Later in this section, we will discuss the use of NetWare's VLM.EXE program.

Both IPX and NET are workstation shell programs that interpret and filter commands entered from the keyboard and provide a mechanism for communications between the workstation and the server. Before NetWare Version 2.1, the shell was known as ANET3.COM, and was combined with IPX and NETx into one file. Later versions of NetWare separated IPX from NETx.

To automate the loading of NetWare on your workstation to establish a network connection, you would normally insert appropriate commands into your computer's AUTO-EXEC.BAT file. Those commands would include:

```
IPX
NETx
F:
LOGIN <servername/username>
```

IPX The command IPX would cause Novell's IPX.COM file to be loaded and executed. This file is a driver that establishes communications with the network interface board, and it is responsible for providing communications with servers and other stations on the network using a network protocol known as IPX. At the network layer, Novell's IPX protocol performs addressing and internet routing functions. To accomplish this, an IPX packet contains both the source and destination network addresses. Those addresses are assigned by a network administrator, and they provide the mechanism for the routing of data between networks by routers which examine the network layer.

IPX is a connectionless network layer protocol that does not guarantee the delivery of data. To provide a reliable delivery mechanism, Novell developed its Sequenced Packet eXchange (SPX)—a transport level interface that provides a connection-oriented packet delivery service.

NCP At the session and presentation layers, NetWare uses a NetBIOS emulator, which provides an interface between application programs written in compliance with NetBIOS and NetWare. As previously mentioned, the NetWare shell operates on each workstation and communicates with a core set of modules that reside on servers. That core set of modules is known as the NetWare Core Protocol (NCP). NCP provides such functions as workstation and network naming management, file partitioning, access and locking capabilities, accounting, and security.

NET The command NETx loads NETx.COM, which is the true workstation shell, because it interprets and filters commands entered from the keyboard. In addition, NETx supports a large number of NetWare commands, which, when entered, are converted into IPX packets and transmitted to the server for processing. The NetWare Core Protocol decodes the command request, processes the request, and then transmits a response to the workstation using one or more IPX packets. The workstation's NET module then processes and displays the response. For example, typing the NetWare command CHKVOL at the workstation transmits a request to the server to obtain statistics concerning the logical driver (volume) assigned to the workstation user. The results of that request are transmitted back to the workstation and displayed on its screen the same way a DOS CHKDSK command is displayed.

When the shell (NETx) is loaded, it normally establishes a connection to a network server by sending a request to IPX to broadcast a Get Nearest Server command. The first server that responds to the request then establishes a connection to the workstation and displays the message "Attached to server <servername>" on your computer's console. You can also specify a preferred server by adding the PS = parameter to the NETx command; this provides you with the ability to distribute workstation server usage over a number of servers.

Once a connection to a NetWare server occurs, the command F: in the AUTOEXEC.BAT file moves the workstation user to the server's SYS:LOGIN directory. That directory is designated or mapped to drive F: on your DOS-operated workstation. Once this is accomplished, the command LOGIN initiates the LOGIN module on the server. If you include the servername and username, LOGIN will then request only your password to obtain access to the server.

Versions Several versions of NetWare have been marketed during the past ten years. NetWare 286, which was renamed NetWare 2.2, was designed to operate on Intel 286–based servers. This operating system supported up to 100 users. NetWare 386 (renamed NetWare 3.1), operated on Intel 386–based servers. This network operating system supported up to 250 users.

The introduction of NetWare 4.0 and the release of NetWare 4.1, followed by releases 5.0 and 6.0, extended Novell's NetWare support to local area networks consisting of up to several thousand workstations. As previously discussed, NetWare 3.12 as well as all versions of NetWare 4.X resulted in the replacement of NETx by the virtual loadable module VLM.EXE. By including the command VLM.EXE in your AUTOEXEC.BAT file, you would cause the executable virtual loadable module to be loaded. This executable file will automatically load a number of files with the .VLM extension, tailoring NetWare to your workstation.

A second change to NetWare is the fact that in November 1991 Novell ceased supporting its dedicated IPX driver. IPX was specific to the network interface card and version of NetWare being used on a workstation, and required you to create a new version each time you installed a new network card. A second problem associated with IPX is the fact that once used with an adapter card, you cannot use another protocol with that card. For example, if you want to communicate using TCP/IP to a UNIX server with the same card, you would have to change your AUTOEXEC.BAT file, remove or *comment out* via REM statements your invocation of IPX and NETx, add your TCP/IP commands, and reboot your computer. Obviously this was not a pleasant situation.

Recognizing the preceding problems, Novell released a new architecture known as the Open Data-Link Interface (ODI) in 1989. By 1991, ODI became the only IPX standard interface supported by Novell. Through the use of ODI, you can support multiple protocols through a common adapter without requiring the rearrangement of statements in your AUTOEXEC.BAT file and rebooting your computer. To do so, you must obtain the following special files—LSL, IPXODI, and an interface driver. LSL is a link support layer program that you must obtain from Novell. The interface driver is provided by the manufacturer of the adapter card, while IPXODI is furnished by both Novell and the adapter card manufacturer.

Figure 5.22 illustrates the relationship of the three previously mentioned programs when a multiprotocol or dual stack operation is desired. The interface driver provides low-level I/O operations to and from the adapter card, and passes information received from the LAN to the Link Support Program. That program examines incoming data to determine if it is NetWare (IPX) or IP (TCP/IP) in the example illustrated in Figure 5.22. LSL then passes received data to the appropriate stack. Thus, IPXODI represents a modification to IPX, which permits it to interface Novell's LSL program.

Although LSL resides on top of the interface driver, you must load it before loading that driver. Thus, your AUTOEXEC.BAT file would have the following generic entries to support ODI on your workstation:

```
LSL
HRDRIVER
IPXODI
```

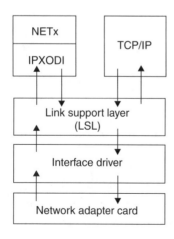

Figure 5.22 Multiprotocol support using Novell's ODI.

```
NETX
F:
LOGIN
```

In examining the preceding entries, note that *HRDRIVER* would be replaced by the actual name of your adapter card's interface driver. In addition, under NetWare 3.12 and 4.X and later versions of this operating system, you would replace NETx with VLM.

To add the TCP/IP protocol stack under DOS you would add the appropriate statements to your AUTOEXEC.BAT file. Those statements must follow the execution of LSL.COM but can either precede or succeed the statements used to invoke the NetWare protocol stack. For example, assume NetWare files are located in the NetWare directory and the appropriate packet driver is contained in the file ODIPKT and the TCP/IP program is contained in the file TCPIP, while both the ODIPKT and TCP/IP files are located in the directory TCP. Then, the AUTOEXEC.BAT file would contain the following statements with the REM(ark) statements optionally added for clarity.

```
REM *Install NetWare*
C:\NETWARE\LSL.COM
C:\NETWARE\LANDRIVER
C:\NETWARE\IPXODI.COM
C:\NETWARE\NETx.EXE
F:
LOGIN GHELD
REM *Install TCP/IP*
C:\TCP\ODIPKT
C:\TCP\TCPIP
```

NET.CFG One important file not shown in Figure 5.22 and until now not discussed is NET.CFG. This file describes the network adapter card configuration to the ODI driver and should be located in the same directory as the IPXODI and NETx files. However, through the use of an appropriate PATH statement you can actually locate NET.CFG anywhere you desire.

NET.CFG is an ASCII text file that can contain up to four main areas of information, which describe the environment of a workstation. Those areas include a link support area, protocol area, link driver area, and parameter area.

Link Support Area The link support area is used to define the number of communications buffers and memory set aside for those buffers. This area is required to be defined when running TCP/IP, however, because

IPX does not use buffers or memory pools maintained by LSL you can skip this section if you are only using a NetWare protocol stack. The following illustration represents an example of the coding of the link support area in the NET.CFG file to support TCP/IP. The actual coding you would enter depends upon the network adapter card to be used and you would obtain the appropriate information from the manual accompanying the adapter card.

```
LINK SUPPORT
BUFFERS 8 1144
MemPool 4096
MaxStacks 8
```

Protocol Area   The protocol area is used to bind one or more protocols to specific network adapter cards. By default, IPXODI binds to the network adapter in the lowest system expansion slot as it scans slots in their numeric order. If you have two or more network adapter cards in a workstation, you can use the protocol area to specify which protocols you want to bind to each card. You can also accomplish this at the link driver area by specifying *Slot n*, where *n* is the slot number of the network adapter card you are configuring. Assuming you wish to bind IPX to an adapter card whose address is h123, you would add the following statements to the NET.CFG file.

```
Protocol
     PROTOCOL IPX
     BIND h123
```

Because each computer using TCP/IP requires an IP address, the IP address information must be included in the NET.CFG file if you intend to use the TCP/IP protocol stack. For example, if the network administrator assigned your computer the IP address 133.49.108.05, the IP address information would be entered as follows:

```
PROTOCOL TCP/IP
ip_address 133.49.108.05
```

When using TCP/IP, each workstation on the network is assigned the address of a default router (commonly referred to as a gateway) by the network administrator. Thus, another statement commonly added to the NET.CFG file includes the address of the router that the workstation will use. For example, if the router's address is 133.49.108.17, then you would add the following statement to the NET.CFG file in its protocol area.

```
ip_router 133.49.108.17
```

The ip_address and ip_router statements can be avoided if the network administrator sets up a Reverse Address Resolution Protocol (RARP) server configured with IP and hardware addresses for workstations on the network. Then, when the workstation is powered on it will broadcast an RARP packet that will contain its hardware address. The RARP server will respond with the workstation's IP address associated with the hardware address.

Link Driver Area   The link driver area is used to set the hardware configuration of the network adapter card so it is recognized by LAN drivers. If you are only using Novell's IPX, the first line of your NET.CFG file is a LINK DRIVER statement which tells NETX the type of LAN card installed in the workstation, such as

```
Link Driver 3C5X9
```

The reason this statement becomes the first statement is because the link support area is omitted and, if you only have one adapter card, you do not require a protocol area.

If you're using an NE 2000 Ethernet card, your link driver area would appear as follows:

```
Link Driver NE2000
     INT 5
     PORT 300
     Frame Ethernet_802.3
     Frame Ethernet_II
     Protocol IPX 0 Ethernet_802.3
     Protocol IP 8137 Ethernet_II
```

In this example the frame statements define the types of frames that will be supported by the adapter cards. Although most adapter cards include software that automatically construct or modify the NET.CFG file, upon occasion you may have to customize the contents of that file. To do so you can use the manual accompanying the network adapter card, which will normally indicate the statements required to be placed in the file.

Virtual Loadable Modules The introduction of NetWare 4.0 resulted in the replacement of NETX by VLMs that sit behind DOS. In comparison, NETX sat in front of DOS and acted as a filter to identify and act upon network requests entered from the keyboard. VLMs are referred to as the NetWare DOS Requester as they use DOS redirection to satisfy file and print service requests. Because VLMs replace NETX.EXE, you would load VLM.EXE in the position previously used for NETX.EXE. That is, the sequence of commands placed in your AUTOEXEC.BAT file to initialize the NetWare protocol stack would appear as follows:

```
C:\NETWARE\LSL
C:\NETWARE\LANDRIVER
C:\NETWARE\IPXODI
C:\NETWARE\VLM.EXE
F:
LOGIN GHELD
```

To modify the AUTOEXEC.BAT file to support dual-stack operations you could add the appropriate commands either after invoking LSL or after the "Login" statement.

Looking at Windows

Windows, to include workstation and server versions of NT, 2000 and XP, represents both a computer operating system and network operating system that can function together or independently. The basic networking protocol used by each version of Windows is NetBEUI, which provides a network user interface for local workstations and servers.

NetBIOS The NetBIOS Extended User Interface (NetBEUI) represents an extension of PC BIOS to the network. NetBIOS was originally developed by IBM as a simple network protocol for interconnecting PCs on a common network. The naming structure of the protocol results in names assigned to devices being translated into network adapter card (that is, MAC) addresses. This results in NetBIOS operating at the data link layer. In addition, because the NetBIOS naming structure is nonhierarchical, there is no provision for specifying network addresses. Due to this, NetBIOS is considered to be nonroutable. Thus, the initial method used to join two or more NetBIOS networks together was restricted to bridging.

NetBEUI Recognizing the routability problem of NetBIOS, NetBEUI allows data to be transported by a transport protocol to obtain the ability to interconnect separate networks. In fact, NetBEUI can be transported by TCP/IP and even IPX/SPX. To accomplish this, NetBEUI maintains a table of NAMES that are associated with TCP/IP addresses when TCP/IP is used as a transport protocol, and a similar table matched to NetWare network addresses and station MAC addresses when NetBEUI is transported via IPX/SPX.

To illustrate the operation of a few of the capabilities of Windows networking, we will briefly use a Windows NT workstation and a Windows NT server to illustrate the installation of network software and adapter cards. In addition, we will use a Windows NT workstation to display the servers on a network where both NT and NetWare servers reside, transferring a file from an NT workstation to a Novell file server. Both NetWare and Windows NT can communicate on a common network, because NT supports the NWLink protocol that provides communications compatibility with NetWare's IPX/SPX protocol.

Adapter and Software Support Windows workstation and server products use common methods to add support for network software and adapter cards. Although the screen display for configuring network software and adapter cards varies between versions of Windows, the basic methods remain the same. Thus, although Figure 5.23 illustrates the network settings screen for Version 3.51 of NT, the basic methods we will describe are also applicable to other versions of NT, Windows 2000 and Windows XP.

In examining Figure 5.23, note that five network software modules are shown in the upper box labeled Installed Network Software, and one adapter card is shown as being installed in the lower box labeled Installed Adapter Card. Windows supports the binding of multiple protocols to a common adapter via the use of the network driver interface specification (NDIS), which will be described at the end of this section. You can add network software, such as TCP/IP, by clicking on the Add Software button shown in Figure 5.23. This action will result in the display of a list of networking software directly supported by Windows. Similarly, if you want to add another adapter you would click on the Add Adapter button. If the adapter you wish to add is not directly supported by Windows, you can select the option "Other—have disk" at the end of the list of supported adapters. This will allow you to add support for a wide range of NICs that are commonly shipped with Windows drivers, but which are not directly supported by the version of Windows you are using.

Network Operation Figure 5.24 illustrates the use of File Manager on a Windows NT workstation to view the names of devices on both a Windows

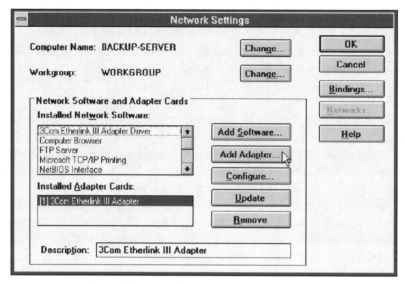

Figure 5.23 Using the Windows NT dialog box to review, add, or change network software and adapter card support.

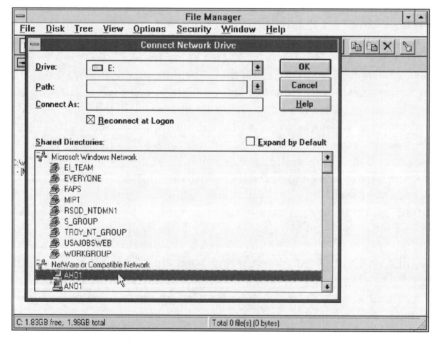

Figure 5.24 Viewing devices on both a Windows and a Novell network through the Windows NT File Manager.

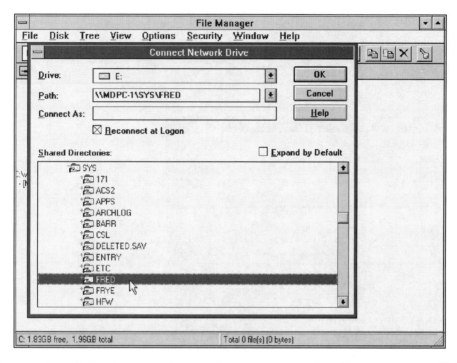

Figure 5.25 Selecting a path to a directory on a Novell server that will be mapped to drive E on a local workstation.

network and a NetWare network. Figure 5.25 illustrates the result obtained by first selecting an appropriate NetWare server and then selecting a directory on that server that we wish to access. This action will result in the mapping of drive E on the local workstation to the path shown in Figure 5.25. Once we enter the appropriate connection information, drive E on the local Windows NT workstation will be mapped to the directory FRED located under the directory SYS on the server MDPC-1.

After we correctly log onto the server, we can run network applications or transfer data to or from the server. Figure 5.26 illustrates how you could select "Move" from the File menu and enter the command c:\funds*.* to move all files under the subdirectory FUNDS on the local workstation to the network server.

NDIS Operation Considerations   Similar to the manner by which Novell developed an architecture for supporting multiple protocols via a common adapter, Microsoft developed a competing standard referred to as NDIS. In this

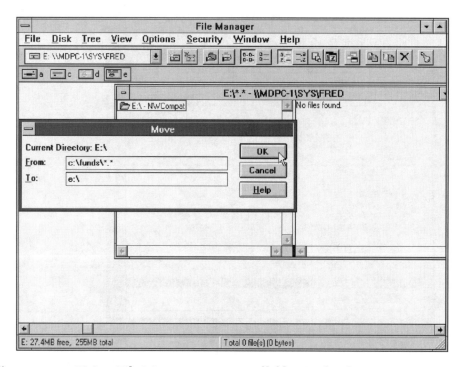

Figure 5.26 Using File Manager to move all files in the directory FUNDS on the local workstation to the directory FRED on the file server.

section we will focus our attention upon obtaining an overview of the structure of NDIS, even though it is well-hidden from view when you use a Windows operating environment. Although NDIS provides a dual-stack capability similar to that provided by ODI, its setup for operation varies considerably from the previously discussed dual-stack mechanism. Figure 5.27 illustrates the

Figure 5.27 NDIS architecture.

relationship between NDIS software modules, upper-layer protocol stacks, and the network adapter card.

CONFIG.SYS Usage   Unlike ODI, which represents a series of files loaded from an AUTOEXEC.BAT file, NDIS was designed as a series of device drivers that are loaded through the CONFIG.SYS file. In a DOS environment the first statement in the CONFIG.SYS file required for NDIS is:

```
DEVICE=drive:\path\PROTMAN.DOS
```

PROTMAN.DOS represents the NDIS Protocol Manager for each workstation operating DOS. The Protocol Manager reads the file PROTOCOL.INI, which contains initialization parameters and stores the contents of that file in memory for use by other NDIS drivers. Thus, a short discussion of PROTOCOL.INI file is in order.

PROTOCOL.INI Overview   The PROTOCOL.INI file can be considered to represent the NDIS equivalent of the NET.CFG file associated with ODI. Although most network products including various versions of Windows will automatically create or modify the PROTOCOL.INI file, some products require users to create or modify that file. In addition, you may be able to enhance network performance by modifying an existing parameter set by a network program that does not consider your total user environment.

Entries in PROTOCOL.INI occur in sections, with each section name surrounded in brackets ([]). Under each section name are one or more named configuration entries, which appear in the format "name = value". Although configuration entries can appear anywhere in a line under the section name, normal practice is to indent each entry three character positions to enhance readability.

Depending upon the version of Windows you are using, the first section in the PROTOCOL.INI file may have the heading [PROTMAN_MOD]. The first configuration entry for DOS is the device name PROTMAN$. Thus, the first section entry becomes:

```
[PROTMAN_MOD]
    DriverName = PROTMAN
```

Other versions of Windows may commence with an NDIS help section followed by the PROTMAN_MOD section.

Other entries in the [PROTMAN_MOD] section are optional and can include keywords Dynamic, Priority, and Bindstatus in assignment statements. The

Dynamic statement can be set to "YES" (Dynamic = YES) to support both static and dynamic binding or "NO" (Dynamic = NO) to set the Protocol Manager to operate only in static mode, which is its default. In static mode protocol drivers are loaded once at system initialization and remain in memory. In the dynamic mode drivers load at the point in time when they are bound by Protocol Manager. In addition, if the drivers support a dynamic unloading capability they can be unloaded if the software unbinds them when they are not needed, freeing memory.

The Priority keyword is used to specify the order of priority of protocol processing modules. Under NDIS an incoming LAN packet is first offered to the protocol with the highest priority. Other protocols will see the packet only if a higher protocol does not first recognize and process the packet. Protocols not specified in a priority list are the last to inspect incoming packets.

The Bindstatus keyword is used to specify whether Protocol Manager can optimize memory and can be set to "YES" or "NO". If the keyword is not used, a default of "NO" is assumed.

The second communications statement included in a CONFIG.SYS file for NDIS operations invokes the network adapter card driver. For example, if you were using the NE2000 adapter, you would include the following statement in the CONFIG.SYS file.

```
DEVICE=[drive:]\path\NE2000.DOS
```

NDIS Adapter Support   The adapter driver, which is compatible with the NDIS Protocol Manager, is referred to as an NDIS MAC driver. The NDIS MAC driver is normally contained on a diskette that is included in a box in which your NDIS-compatible network adapter is packaged. When using Windows NT the operating system includes built-in NDIS support for approximately 30 adapter cards. As previously explained, if the adapter you are using is not directly supported by Windows NT, you would select the Other option from the install adapter card entry from the network configuration display obtained from the Windows Control Panel. Then you would use the diskette that accompanies your adapter card to install the required driver.

Once you install your adapter card and appropriate communications protocols under Windows, the operating system will automatically connect the software layers as required to form appropriate protocol stacks. Microsoft refers to this as network bindings, and Figure 5.28 illustrates an example of the NT Network Bindings display after a large number of protocols were installed.

Figure 5.28 Viewing an example of the Windows NT Network Bindings display.

Application Software

The third major component of software required for productive work to occur on a local area network is application software. These application programs support electronic mail, multiple access to database records, or the use of spreadsheet programs; they operate at the top layer of the OSI Reference Model.

Until the mid-1980s, most application programs used on LANs were not tailored to operate correctly in a multiuser environment. A large part of their inability to work correctly was due to the absence of file- and record-locking capabilities on PC operating systems — a situation that was corrected with the introduction of DOS 3.1. A second problem associated with application programs occurred when the program was written to bypass the personal computer's BIOS. Although this action in many instances would speed up screen displays, disk access, and other operations, in this case it resulted in nonstandardized program actions. This made it difficult, if not impossible, for some network operating systems to support ill-defined programs, because an interrupt clash could bring the entire network to a rapid halt.

Today, most application programs use BIOS calls and are well defined. Such programs are easily supported by network operating systems. A few programs that bypass BIOS may also be supported, because the application program that caused operating system vendors to tailor their software to support such applications was so popular.

5.4 The TCP/IP Protocol Suite

No discussion of networking hardware and software related to Ethernet would be complete without covering the TCP/IP protocol suite. Although the development of TCP/IP occurred at the Advanced Research Projects Agency (ARPA), which was funded by the U.S. Department of Defense, while Ethernet traces its origin to the Xerox Palo Alto Research Center, within a short period of time the two were linked together. Ethernet frames provide the data link (layer 2) transportation mechanism for the delivery of network layer (layer 3) IP and transport layer (layer 4) TCP packets that transport such application data as file transfer, remote access, and Web server information on an intra-LAN basis. In comparison, TCP/IP provides the mechanism to route data between LANs and convert IP addresses used by the protocol suite to MAC addresses used by Ethernet so that TCP/IP packets can be delivered by Ethernet frames.

Overview

TCP/IP represents a collection of network protocols that provide services at the network and transport layers of the ISO's OSI Reference Model. Originally developed based upon work performed by the U.S. Department of Defense Advanced Research Projects Agency Network (ARPANET), TCP/IP is also commonly referred to as the DOD protocols or the Internet protocol suite.

Protocol Development

In actuality, a reference to the TCP/IP protocol suite includes applications that use the TCP/IP protocol stack as a transport mechanism. Such applications range in scope from a remote terminal access program known as Telnet to a file transfer program appropriately referred to as FTP, as well as the Web browser transport mechanism referred to as the HyperText Transport Protocol (HTTP).

The effort behind the development of the TCP/IP protocol suite has its roots in the establishment of ARPANET. The research performed by ARPANET resulted in the development of three specific protocols for the transmission of information — the Transmission Control Protocol (TCP), the Internet Protocol (IP), and the User Datagram Protocol (UDP). Both TCP and UDP represent transport layer protocols. Transmission Control Protocol provides end-to-end reliable transmission while UDP represents a connectionless layer 4 transport protocol. Thus, UDP operates on a best-effort basis and depends upon higher layers of the protocol stack for error detection and correction and other functions associated with end-to-end reliable transmission. Transmission Control Protocol includes such functions as flow control, error control, and the exchange of status information, and is based upon a connection being established between source and destination before the exchange of information occurs. Thus, TCP provides an orderly and error-free mechanism for the exchange of information.

At the network layer, the IP protocol was developed as a mechanism to route messages between networks. To accomplish this task, IP was developed as a connectionless mode network layer protocol and includes the capability to segment or fragment and reassemble messages that must be routed between networks that support different packet sizes than the size supported by the source and/or destination networks.

The TCP/IP Structure

TCP/IP represents one of the earliest developed layered communications protocols, grouping functions into defined network layers. Figure 5.29 illustrates

Legend:

ARP = Address Resolution Protocol
DNS = Domain Name Service
FDDI = Fiber Data Distributed Interface
FTP = File Transfer Protocol
NSF = Network File System
SMTP = Simple Mail Transfer Protocol
SNMP = Simple Network Management Protocol

Figure 5.29 TCP/IP protocols and services.

the relationship of the TCP/IP protocol suite and the services they provide with respect to the OSI Reference Model. In examining Figure 5.29 note that only seven of literally hundreds of TCP/IP application services are shown. Because TCP/IP preceded the development of the OSI Reference Model, its developers grouped what are now session, presentation, and application layers that correspond to layers 5 through 7 of the OSI Reference Model into one higher layer. Thus, TCP/IP applications, when compared with the OSI Reference Model, are normally illustrated as corresponding to the upper three layers of that model. Continuing our examination of Figure 5.29, you will note that the subdivision of the transport layer indicates which applications are carried via TCP and those that are transported by UDP.

As we will note later in this section, TCP represents a connection-oriented error-free transport protocol. This means that it is well suited for transporting applications that require the acknowledgement of the availability of a distant device prior to the actual transfer of data, such as a file transfer application. In comparison, UDP represents a best-effort, unreliable transport protocol. This means that UDP can immediately be used to transport data without requiring a prior handshaking operation to be successful. This also means that data is transmitted under UDP without error detection and correction, making the application responsible for deciding if this is needed.

Thus, FTP, Telnet, HTTP, and SMTP represent applications transported by TCP that require a connection to be established prior to data being transported and need an error detection and correction capability. Domain Name Service (DNS), Network File System (NFS), and Simple Network Management Protocol (SNMP) represent applications that do not require a prior connection and occur on a best effort basis. Thus, DNS, NFS and SNMP are transported via UDP.

While the prior examples of TCP and UDP usage are well defined, it should be noted that some applications, such as Internet Telephony, use both transport protocols. For example, call control information such as a dialed number must flow through the Internet error-free and are carried via TCP. In comparison, real-time digitized voice cannot be retransmitted when errors are detected since this would result in awkward delays at the receiver. Thus, the actual digitized voice portion of an Internet Telephony call is transported via UDP.

Although not officially layer 3 protocols, both the Address Resolution Protocol (ARP) and the Internet Control Message Protocol (ICMP) reside in a "gray" area and are commonly shown as residing at that location, so we will also do this. In addition, because ICMP, as we will shortly note, is transported with an IP header, it makes sense to consider it residing within layer 3 of the TCP/IP protocol stack.

Returning to our examination of Figure 5.29, note that TCP/IP can be transported at the data link layer by a number of popular LANs, to include Ethernet, Fast Ethernet, Gigabit Ethernet, Token-Ring, and FDDI frames. Due to the considerable effort expended in the development of LAN adapter cards to support the bus structures used in Apple MacIntosh, IBM PCs and compatible computers, DEC Alphas and SUN Microsystem's workstations, and even IBM mainframes, the development of software-based protocol stacks to facilitate the transmission of TCP/IP on LANs provides the capability to interconnect LAN-based computers to one another whether they are on the same network and only require the transmission of frames on a common cable, or if they are located on networks separated thousands of miles from one another. Thus, TCP/IP represents both a local and wide area network transmission capability.

Datagrams versus Virtual Circuits

In examining Figure 5.29 you will note that IP provides a common layer 3 transport for TCP and UDP. As briefly noted earlier in this section, TCP is a connection-oriented protocol that requires the acknowledgment of the existence of the connection and for packets transmitted once the connection is established. In comparison, UDP is a connectionless mode service that provides a parallel service to TCP. Here *datagram* represents a term used to identify the basic unit of information that represents a portion of a message and that is transported across a TCP/IP network.

A datagram can be transported either via an acknowledged connection-oriented service or via an unacknowledged, connectionless service, where each information element is addressed to its destination and its transmission is at the mercy of network nodes. IP represents an unacknowledged connectionless service; however, although it is an unreliable transmission method, you should view the term in the context that delivery is not guaranteed instead of having second thoughts concerning its use. As a nonguaranteed delivery mechanism IP is susceptible to queuing delays and other problems that can result in the loss of data. However, higher layers in the protocol suite, such as TCP, can provide error detection and correction, which results in the retransmission of IP datagrams.

Datagrams are routed via the best path available to the destination as the datagram is placed onto the network. An alternative to datagram transmission is the use of a virtual circuit, where network nodes establish a fixed path when a connection is initiated and subsequent data exchanges occur on that path. TCP implements transmission via the use of a virtual circuit, while IP provides a datagram-oriented gateway transmission service between networks.

The routing of datagrams through a network can occur over different paths, with some datagrams arriving out of sequence from the order in which they were transmitted. In addition, as datagrams flow between networks they encounter physical limitations imposed upon the amount of data that can be transported based upon the transport mechanism used to move data on the network. For example, the information field in an Ethernet frame is limited to 1500 bytes, while a 4-Mbps Token-Ring can transport 4500 bytes in its information field. Thus, as datagrams flow between networks, they may have to be fragmented into two or more datagrams to be transported through different networks to their ultimate destination. For example, consider the transfer of a 20,000-byte file from a file server connected to a Token-Ring network to a workstation connected to an Ethernet LAN via a pair of routers providing a connection between the two local area networks. The 4-Mbps Token-Ring network supports a maximum information field of 4500 bytes in each frame transmitted on that network, while the maximum size of the information field in an Ethernet frame is 1500 bytes. In addition, depending upon the protocol used on the wide area network connection between routers, the WAN protocol's information field could be limited to 512 or 1024 bytes. Thus, the IP protocol must break up the file transfer into a series of datagrams whose size is acceptable for transmission between networks. As an alternative, IP can transmit data using a small maximum datagram size, commonly 576 bytes, to prevent fragmentation. If fragmentation is necessary, the source host can transmit using the maximum datagram size available on its network. When the datagram arrives at the router, IP operating on that communications device will then fragment each datagram into a series of smaller datagrams. Upon receipt at the destination, each datagram must then be put back into its correct sequence so that the file can be correctly reformed, a responsibility of IP residing on the destination host.

Figure 5.30 illustrates the routing of two datagrams from workstation 1 on a Token-Ring network to server 2 connected to an Ethernet LAN. As the routing of datagrams is a connectionless service, no call setup is required, which enhances transmission efficiency. In comparison, when TCP is used, it provides a connection-oriented service regardless of the lower-layer delivery system (for example, IP).

TCP requires the establishment of a virtual circuit in which a temporary path is developed between source and destination. This path is fixed and the flow of datagrams is restricted to the established path. When UDP, a different layer 4 protocol in the TCP/IP protocol suite, is used in place of TCP, the flow of data at the transport layer continues to be connectionless and results in the

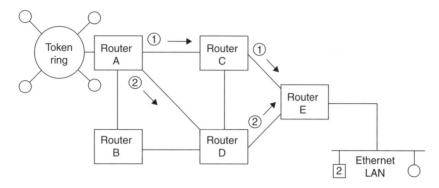

Figure 5.30   Routing of datagrams can occur over different paths.

transport of datagrams over available paths rather than a fixed path resulting from the establishment of a virtual circuit.

The actual division of a message into datagrams is the responsibility of the layer 4 protocol, either TCP or UDP, while fragmentation is the responsibility of IP. In addition, when the TCP protocol is used, that protocol is responsible for reassembling datagrams at their destination as well as for requesting the retransmission of lost datagrams. In comparison, IP is responsible for routing of individual datagrams from source to destination. When UDP is used as the layer 4 protocol, there is no provision for the retransmission of lost or garbled datagrams. As previously noted by our discussion of IP, this is not necessarily a bad situation, as applications that use UDP then become responsible for managing communications.

Figure 5.31 illustrates the relationship of an IP datagram, UDP datagram, and TCP segment to a LAN frame. The headers shown in Figure 5.31 represent a group of bytes added to the beginning of a datagram to allow a degree of control over the datagram. For example, the TCP header will contain information that allows this layer 4 protocol to track the sequence of the delivery of datagrams so they can be placed into their correct order if they arrive out of sequence. Before focusing our attention on TCP and IP, let's discuss the role of ICMP and ARP, two additional network layer protocols in the TCP/IP suite.

ICMP

The Internet Control Message Protocol (ICMP) provides a mechanism for communicating control message and error reports. Both gateways and hosts use ICMP to transmit problem reports about datagrams back to the datagram originator.

Figure 5.31 Forming a LAN frame.

An ICMP message is formed by prefixing an IP header to the ICMP message. Each ICMP message consists of four fields, of which only two are mandatory. Figure 5.32 illustrates the formation of an IPMP message to include the fields in the ICMP message.

In Figure 5.32 the Type field defines the type of ICMP message. The code field can optionally further define the reason for the ICMP message. For example, a type field value of 3 indicates a Destination Unreachable ICMP message, which is returned to the originator to inform them that their transmitted datagram cannot reach its destination. The code field value further defines why the destination was unreachable, with a value of 1 indicating the network was unreachable while a value of 2 indicates the host was unreachable,

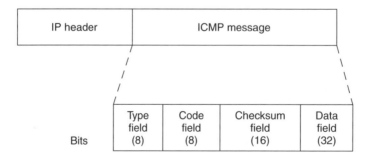

Figure 5.32 Formation and composition of an ICMP message.

and so on. Not all ICMP messages need further elaboration and as a result some messages do not have any code field values. The checksum field represents a 16-bit one's complement of the one's complement sum of the ICMP message commencing with the type field. The Data field may or may not be used depending upon the message. Table 5.2 provides a summary of ICMP messages to include their type and code values.

In examining the entries in Table 5.3 a few words are in order concerning their meaning and utilization. ICMP Type 0 and Type 8 messages form the basis for the application known as Ping. Ping results in the transmission of

TABLE 5.2 ICMP Message Type and Code Values

Type Value	Message/Code Values
0	Echo Reply
3	Destination Unreachable 0 = network unreachable 1 = host unreachable 2 = protocol unreachable 3 = port unreachable 4 = fragmentation needed 5 = source route failed
4	Source Quench
5	Redirect 0 = redirect datagrams for the network 1 = redirect datagrams for the host 2 = redirect datagrams for the type of service and the network 3 = redirect datagrams for the type of service and the host
8	Echo
11	Time Exceeded 0 = time to live exceeded in transit 1 = fragment reassembly time exceeded
12	Parameter Problem 0 = pointer in data field indicates the error
13	Timestamp
14	Timestamp Reply
15	Information Request
16	Information Reply

TABLE 5.3 Examples of TCP/IP Application Layer Protocol Use of Well-Known Ports

Name	Acronym	Description	Well-Known Port
Domain Name Protocol	DOMAIN	Defines the DNS	53
File Transfer Protocol	FTP	Supports file transfers between hosts	20,21
Finger Protocol	FINGER	Provides information about a specified user	79
HyperText Transmission Protocol	HTTP	Transmits information between a Web browser and a Web server	80
Post Office Protocol	POP	Enables host users to access mail from a mail server	110
Simple Mail Transfer Protocol	SMTP	Provides for the exchange of network management information	161,162
TELENET Protocol	Telnet	Provides remote terminal access to a host.	23

a sequence of Echo messages to a host address. If the host is operational it responds with a series of Echo Reply messages. Because the origination of the Echo messages sets a timer when each message is transmitted, the arrival of the response permits the round-trip delay to be computed. Thus, Ping tells us if a distant host is operational as well as the round-trip delay to that host. When installing a computer onto a TCP/IP network, it is quite common to use Ping to insure your computer can reach the outside world as well as be reached. Thus, Ping plays an important role as a diagnostic testing tool.

Figure 5.33 illustrates an example of Ping options in a Microsoft Windows environment as well as the use of the utility application. The top portion of Figure 5.33 shows the various command options for the program, while the lower portion illustrates the "pinging" of a Web server.

ARP

The Address Resolution Protocol (ARP) maps the high-level IP address configured via software to a low-level physical hardware address, typically the NIC's ROM address. The high-level IP address is 32 bits in length (IP version 4)

Figure 5.33 Using the Ping utility.

and is commonly represented by four decimal numbers, ranging from 0 to 255 per number, separated from one another by decimals. Thus, another term used to reference an IP address is the *dotted decimal address*. The physical hardware address represents the MAC address. Thus, ARP provides an IP to MAC address resolution, which enables an IP packet to be transported in a LAN frame to its appropriate MAC address. Later in this section we will examine IP addresses in detail.

To illustrate the operation of ARP, consider Figure 5.34, which shows the format of an Address Resolution Protocol (ARP) packet. The value of the Hardware field is set to 1 to denote Ethernet. The second field, Protocol, identifies the protocol address in use and is set to hex 0800 to identify the use of IP addresses.

The Hardware Length (HLEN) and Protocol Length (PLEN) fields define the length in bytes of the addresses to be used. In an IP-to-Ethernet environment the hardware address will be six bytes in length while the protocol will be four bytes in length. This corresponds to the four-byte IPv4 32-bit address and the 48-bit or six-byte Ethernet MAC address. The operation field indicates an ARP request (1) or ARP Reply (2).

When a layer 3 operating device, such as a router or gateway, receives an IP packet for LAN delivery it must form a LAN frame. Thus, it must determine the MAC address that corresponds to the IP destination address. To accomplish this address resolution, the router transmits an ARP Request message as a

0   15

| Hardware type |
| Protocol type |
| HLEN   PLEN |
| Operation |
| Sender hardware address |
| Sender protocol address |
| Target hardware address |

Figure 5.34   The Address Resolution Protocol (ARP) packet format. HLEN = Hardware Length; PLEN = Protocol Length.

broadcast to all station on the LAN. Since the hardware address field value is unknown, it is sent filled with zeros. The station that recognizes its IP address inserts its hardware address into the message, changes the operation field value to 2 and transmits the message using a destination frame address equal to the source address that transported the ARP. When the router receives the response, it places the hardware and IP addresses in memory, referred to as an ARP cache, to expedite future datagram deliveries. It then forms a frame with the appropriate hardware destination address to deliver the IP datagram.

TCP

The Transmission Control Protocol (TCP) represents a layer 4 connection-oriented reliable protocol. TCP provides a virtual circuit connection mode service for applications that require connection setup, error detection, and automatic retransmission. In addition, TCP is structured to support multiple application programs on one host to communicate concurrently with processes on other hosts, as well as for a host to demultiplex and service incoming traffic among different applications or processes running on the host.

Each unit of data carried by TCP is referred to as a segment. Segments are created by TCP subdividing the stream of data passed down by application layer protocols that use its services, with each segment identified by the use of a sequence number. This segment identification process enables a receiver, if required, to reassemble data segments into their correct order.

Figure 5.35 illustrates the format of the TCP protocol header. To obtain an appreciation for the functionality and capability of TCP, let's examine the fields in its header.

Source and Destination Port Fields

The source and destination ports are each 16 bits in length and identify a process or service at the host receiver. The source port field entry is optional and when not used is padded with zeros. Both source and destination port values are commonly referred to as "well-known ports," as they typically identify an application layer protocol or process. Table 5.3 lists the well-known port numbers associated with eight popular TCP/IP application layer protocols. In examining the entries in the previously referenced table, note that some protocols, such as FTP, use two port addresses or logical connections. In the case of FTP, one address (21) is used for the transmission of commands, responses, and functions as a control path. In comparison, the second port address (20) is used for the actual file transfer.

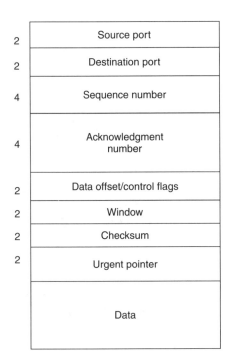

Figure 5.35 TCP protocol header.

Sequence Fields

The sequence number is used to identify the data segment transported. The acknowledgment number interpretation depends upon the setting of the ACK control flag which is not directly shown in Figure 5.35. If the ACK control flag bit position is set, the acknowledgment field will contain the next sequence number the sender expects to receive. Otherwise TCP the field is ignored.

Control Field Flags

There are six control field flags that are used to establish, maintain, and terminate connections. Those flags include URG (urgent), SYN, ACK, RST (reset), PSH (push), and FIN (finish).

Setting URG = 1 indicates to the receiver urgent data is arriving. The SYN flag is set to 1 as a connection request and thus serves to establish a connection. As previously discussed, the ACK flag, when set, indicates that the acknowledgment flag is relevant. The RST flag, when set, means the connection should be reset, while the PSH flag tells the receiver to immediately deliver the data in the segment. Finally, the setting of the FIN flag indicates the sender is done and the connection should be terminated.

The setting of the SYN bit in the TCP header is used to commence what is referred to as the beginning of a three-way handshake. When a TCP session commences the originator sets its SYN bit. The receiver will acknowledge the TCP segment by setting the SYN and ACK bits in the responding TCP header. The receiver will also set its Window field value, described next, to denote the quantity of data it can receive. The originator will then respond by setting the SYN bit in its header, completing the three-way handshake.

While the three-way handshake permits devices to negotiate the amount of data to be transferred per segment, it also represents a security vulnerability. That vulnerability occurs as a computer can only handle a certain amount of open connections. Thus, one hacker technique that has received a degree of trade press coverage is to flood a server with initial TCP SYN requests and not respond to the returned SYN/ACK responses. This action creates numerous open connections on the server and forms what is referred to as a denial of service (DOS) attack.

Window Field

The window field is used to convey the number of bytes the sender can accept and functions as a flow control mechanism. This 16-bit field indicates the number of octets, beginning with the one in the acknowledgment field, that the originator of the segment can control. Since TCP is a full-duplex protocol, each host can use the window field to control the quantity of data that can be sent to the computer. This enables the recipient to, in effect, control its destiny. For example, if a receiving host becomes overloaded with processing or another reason results in the inability of the device to receive large chunks of data, it can use the window field as a flow control mechanism to reduce the size of data chunks sent to it. At the end of our review of TCP header fields, we will examine a TCP transmission sequence to note the interrelated role of the sequence, acknowledgment, and window fields.

Checksum Field

The checksum provides error detection for the TCP header and data carried in the segment. Thus, this field provides the mechanism for the detection of errors in each segment.

Urgent Pointer Field

The urgent pointer field is used in conjunction with the URG flag as a mechanism to identify the position of urgent data within a TCP segment. When the URG flag is set the value in the urgent pointer field represents the last byte of urgent data.

   When an application uses TCP, TCP breaks the stream of data provided by the application into segments and adds an appropriate TCP header. Next, an IP header is prefixed to the TCP header to transport the segment via the network layer. As data arrives at its destination network, it's converted into a data link layer transport mechanism. For example, on an Ethernet network TCP data would be transported within Ethernet frames.

TCP Transmission Sequence Example

To illustrate the interrelationship between the sequence, acknowledgment, and window fields, let's examine the transmission of a sequence of TCP segments between two hosts. Figure 5.36 illustrates via the use of a time chart the transmission of a sequence of TCP segments.

   At the top of Figure 5.36 it was assumed that a window size of 16 segments is in use. Although TCP supports full-duplex transmission, for simplicity of illustration we will use a half-duplex model in the time chart.

   Assuming the host, whose address is ftp.fbi.gov, is transmitting a program or performing a similar lengthy file transfer operation, the first series of segments will have sequence numbers 64 through 79, assuming sequence number 63 was just acknowledged. The ACK value of 28 acknowledges that segments

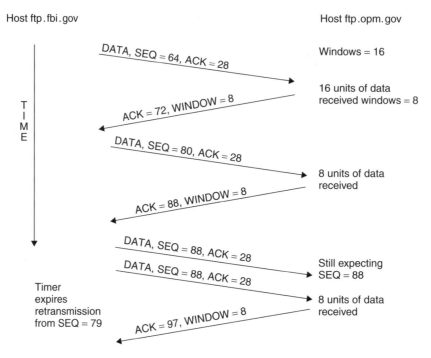

Host ftp.fbi.gov

Host ftp.opm.gov

TIME

DATA, SEQ = 64, ACK = 28

Windows = 16

16 units of data
received windows = 8

ACK = 72, WINDOW = 8

DATA, SEQ = 80, ACK = 28

8 units of data
received

ACK = 88, WINDOW = 8

DATA, SEQ = 88, ACK = 28

DATA, SEQ = 88, ACK = 28

Still expecting
SEQ = 88

Timer
expires
retransmission
from SEQ = 79

8 units of data
received

ACK = 97, WINDOW = 8

Figure 5.36 A TCP transmission sequence.

through number 27 were received by the host ftp.opm.gov and that it next expects to receive segment 28.

Assuming segments 64 through 79 arrive error-free, the host with the address ftp.opm.gov returns an ACK value of 80 to indicate the next segment it expects to receive. At this point in time, let's assume host ftp.opm.gov is running out of buffer space and halves the window size to 8. Thus, host ftp.opm.gov sets the window field value in the TCP header it transmits to host ftp.fbi.gov to 8. Upon receipt of the TCP segment, host ftp.fbi.gov reduces the number of segments it will transmit to 8 and uses an initial SEQ value of 80, increasing that value by 1 each time it transmits a new segment until 8 new segments are transmitted. Assuming all 8 segments were received error-free, host ftp.opm.gov then returns an ACK value of 88, which acknowledges the receipt of segments with sequence field numbers through 87.

Next, host ftp.fbi.gov transmits to host ftp.opm.gov another sequence of 8 segments using sequence field values of 88 to 95. However, let's assume a transmission impairment occurs that results in the segments being incorrectly received or perhaps not even received at all at their intended destination. If host ftp.opm.gov does not receive anything, it does not transmit anything back to host ftp.fbi.gov. Instead of waiting forever for a response, the TCP/IP protocol stack includes an internal timer that clicks down to zero while host ftp.fbi.gov waits for a response. When that value is reached, the timer expires and the transmitting station retransmits its sequence of 8 segments. On the second time around, the sequence of 8 segments are shown acknowledged at the bottom of Figure 5.36. If the impairment continued, the transmitting station would attempt a predefined number of retransmissions after which it would terminate the session if no response was received.

The altering of window field values provides a sliding window that can be used to control the flow of information. That is, by adjusting the value of the window field, a receiving host can inform a transmitting station whether or not an adjustment in the number of segments transmitted is required. In doing so there are two special window field values that can be used to further control the flow of information. A window field value of 0 means a host has shut down communications, while a window field value of 1 requires an acknowledgment for each unit of data transmitted, limiting transmission to a segment-by-segment basis.

UDP

The User Datagram Protocol (UDP) represents a second layer 4 transport service supported by the TCP/IP protocol suite. UDP is a connectionless service, which means that the higher-layer application is responsible for the reliable delivery of the transported message. Figure 5.37 illustrates the composition of the UDP header.

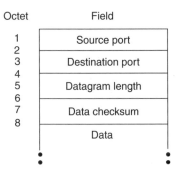

Figure 5.37 The UDP header.

Source and Destination Port Fields

The source and destination port fields are each 16 bits in length and, as previously described for TCP, identify the port number of the sending and receiving process, respectively. Here each port number process identifies an application running at the corresponding IP address in the IP header prefixed for the UDP header. The use of a port number provides a mechanism for identifying network services as they denote communications points where particular services can be accessed. For example, a value of 161 in a port field is used in UDP to identify SNMP.

Length Fields

The length field indicates the length of the UDP packets in octets to include the header and user data. The checksum, which is one's complement arithmetic sum, is computed over a pseudoheader and the entire UDP packet. The pseudoheader is created by the conceptual prefix of 12 octets to the header previously illustrated in Figure 5.37. The first 8 octets are used by source and destination IP addresses obtained from the IP packet. This is followed by a zero-filled octet and an octet that identifies the protocol. The last 2 octets in the pseudoheader denote the length of the UDP packet. By computing the UDP checksum over the pseudoheader and user data, a degree of additional data integrity is obtained.

IP

As previously mentioned, IP provides a datagram-oriented gateway service for transmission between subnetworks. This provides a mechanism for hosts to access other hosts on a best-effort basis but does not enhance reliability as it relies on upper-layer protocols for error detection and correction. As a layer 3 protocol, IP is responsible for the routing and delivery of datagrams. To accomplish this task IP performs a number of communications functions to include addressing, status information, management, fragmentation, and reassembly of datagrams when necessary.

IP Header Format

Figure 5.38 illustrates the IP header format while Table 5.4 provides a brief description of the fields in the IP header.

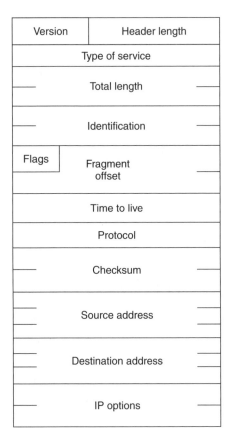

Figure 5.38   IP header format.

Version Field

The four-bit version field identifies the version of the IP protocol used to create the datagram. The current version of the IP protocol is 4 and is encoded as 0100 in binary. The next-generation IP protocol is version 6, which is encoded as 0110 in binary. In our discussion of IP we will focus on IPv4 in this section.

Header Length and Total Length Fields

The header length field follows the version field and is also 4 bits in length. This field indicates the length of the header in 32-bit words. In comparison, the total length field indicates the total length of the datagram to include its header and higher-layer information. The use of 16 bits for the total length field enables an IP datagram to be up to 2^{16} or 65,535 octets in length.

TABLE 5.4 IP Header Fields

Field	Description
Version	The version of the IP protocol used to create the datagram.
Header length	Header length in 32-bit words.
Type of service	Specifies how the datagram should be handled.

```
 0      1      2  3  4  5    6     7
┌─────────────┬──┬──┬──┬──────────┐
│ PRECEDENCE  │D │T │R │ UNUSED   │
└─────────────┴──┴──┴──┴──────────┘
```

PRECEDENCE indicates importance of the datagram
D   When set requests low delay
T   When set requests high throughput
R   When set requests high reliability

Field	Description
Total length	Specifies the total length to include header and data.
Identification	Used with source address to identify fragments belonging to specific datagrams.
Flags	Middle bit when set disables possible fragmentation. Low-order bit specifies whether the fragment contains data from the middle of the original datagram or the end.
Fragment offset	Specifies the offset in the original datagram of data being carried in a fragment.
Time to live	Specifies the time in seconds a datagram is allowed to remain in the internet.
Protocol	Specifies the higher-level protocol used to create the message carried in the data field.
Header checksum	Protects the integrity of the header.
Source IP address	The 32-bit IP address of the datagram's sender.
Destination IP address	The 32-bit IP address of the datagram's intended recipient.
IP options	Primarily used for network testing or debugging.

```
 0        1      2      3  4    5      6      7
┌────────┬──────────────┬────────────────────┐
│ COPY   │ OPTION CLASS │ OPTION NUMBER       │
└────────┴──────────────┴────────────────────┘
```

When copy bit set it tells gateways that the option should be copied into all fragments.

TABLE 5.4 (*Continued*)

Field	Description
	When set to 0 the option is copied into the first fragment.

Option Class	Meaning
0	Datagram or network control
1	Reserved for future use
2	Debugging
3	Reserved for future use

The option number defines a specific option within a class.

Type of Service Field

The type of service field identifies how the datagram is handled. Three of the eight bits in this field are used to denote the precedence or level of importance assigned by the originator. Thus, this field provides a priority mechanism for routing IP datagrams.

Identification and Fragment Offset Fields

To obtain an appreciation for the role of the fragment offset field a brief discussion of IP fragmentation is in order. When an IP protocol stack transmits a datagram, its size is limited by what is referred to as the Maximum Transmission Unit (MTU). The MTU is usually set when a device driver initializes an interface and the MTU represents the payload portion of a datagram (its length less header length).

Most TCP/IP protocol stacks support MTUs up to 64K − 1 bytes, or 65,535 bytes. The MTU supported by a protocol stack for an interface is also known as an interface MTU. Another MTU worth noting is a route MTU, which represents the MTU that can be used from source to destination without requiring fragmentation. The route MTU is usually maintained as a field value in a host's routing table and set either manually or via an MTU discovery process.

When a route MTU is smaller than the length of a datagram to be transferred, the routing entity will either fragment the datagram or drop it. All implementations of IP must support IP fragmentation based upon RFC 791. If the *DON'T_FRAGMENT* bit is set in the header, then fragmentation is not allowed and the datagram is dropped.

IP fragmentation places the burden of the effort on the receiving station and the routing entity. When a station receives an IP fragment it must fully reassemble the complete IP datagram prior to being able to extract the TCP segment, resulting in a requirement for additional buffer memory and CPU processing power at the receiver. In addition, if any fragments are dropped, the original datagram must be resent. Due to this, most vendors set the *DON'T_FRAGMENT* bit in the header.

Setting the *DON'T_FRAGMENT* bit causes an oversized IP datagram to be dropped, resulting in an *ICMP DESTINATION UNREACHABLE-FRAGMEN-TATION NEEDED* message to be sent to the sender. This will result in the MTU discover algorithm selecting a smaller MTU for the path and using that MTU for subsequent transmissions.

The identification field enables each datagram or fragmented datagram to be identified. If a datagram was previously fragmented, the fragment offset field specifies the offset in the original datagram of the data being carried. In effect, this field indicates where the fragment belongs in the complete message. The actual value in this field is an integer that corresponds to a unit of eight octets, providing an offset in 64-bit units.

Time to Live Field

The time to live (TTL) field specifies the maximum time that a datagram can live. Because an exact time is difficult to measure, almost all routers decrement this field by one as a datagram flows between networks, with the datagram being discarded when the field value reaches zero. Thus, this field more accurately represents a hop count field. You can consider this field to represent a fail-safe mechanism, as it prevents misaddressed datagrams from continuously flowing on the Internet.

The time-to-live (TTL) field is the key to the operation of a utility program included in the TCP/IP protocol suite that provides you with the ability to trace a route through an IP network. That utility program is traceroute, which in a Microsoft Windows environment is called *tracert*.

When you use traceroute the program sets a timer and then sets a TTL value of 1 in the IP datagram prior to transmitting it to the intended recipient. The first router in the path decrements the value of the TTL field by 1 and, since it is now 0, throws it into the great bit bucket in the sky and returns a destination unreachable ICMP message. This action provides the round-trip delay and address of the first router on the path to the destination. The program then increments the value of the TTL field to 2 and transmits another datagram to locate the second router in the path to the destination, and so on until the destination is reached.

Flags Field

The flags field contains two bits that indicate how fragmentation occurs while a third bit is currently unassigned. The setting of one bit can be viewed as a direct fragment control mechanism as a value of zero indicates the datagram can be fragmented, while a value of one denotes don't fragment. The second bit is set to zero to indicate that a fragment in a datagram is the last fragment and set to a value of one to indicate more fragments follow the current protocol.

Protocol Field

The protocol field specifies the higher-level protocol used to create the message carried in the datagram. For example, a value of decimal 6 would indicate TCP, while a value of decimal 17 would indicate UDP.

Source and Destination Address Fields

The source and destination address fields are both 32 bits in length. As previously discussed, each address represents both a network and a host computer on the network.

In examining the IP header a common network problem relates to the IP address carried in the source and destination address fields. Thus, a description of IP addressing is warranted as it forms the basis for network addressing as well as the domain name service translation of English-type mnemonics, representing computers or host names, into what is known as dotted decimal IP addresses.

IP Addressing

The IP addressing scheme uses a 32-bit address, which is divided into an assigned network number and a host number. The latter can be further segmented into a subnet number and a host number. Through subnetting you can construct multiple networks while localizing the traffic of hosts to specific subnets, a technique I will shortly illustrate.

IP addressing numbers are assigned by the InterNIC network information center and can fall into one of five unique network classes, referenced as Classes A through E. Figure 5.39 illustrates the IP address formats for Class A, B, and C networks. Class D addresses are reserved for multicast groups, while Class E addresses are reserved for future use and are considered as experimental.

In examining Figure 5.39, note that by examining the first bit in the IP address you can distinguish a Class A address from Class B and C addresses.

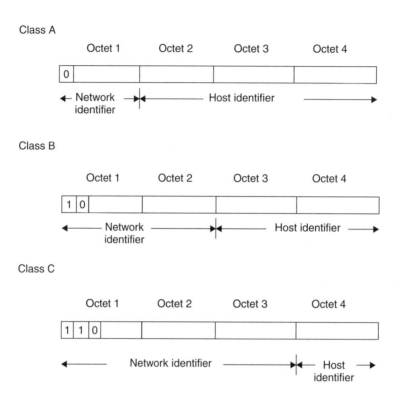

Figure 5.39 IP Classfull address formats.

Thereafter, examining the composition of the second bit position enables a Class B address to be distinguished from a Class C address.

An IP 32-bit address is expressed as four decimal numbers, with each number ranging in value from 0 to 255 and separated from another number by a dot (decimal point). This explains why an IP address is commonly referred to as a dotted decimal address.

To facilitate determining the decimal value of an eight-bit binary number you can use the following positional bit values for a byte:

128	64	32	16	8	4	2	1

Based upon the above, a byte with the bit composition 10000011 would have the decimal value $128 + 2 + 1$, or 131 decimal. Similarly, a byte with the bit composition 01010111 would have the decimal value $64 + 16 + 4 + 2 + 1$, or 87 decimal.

Class A In examining Figure 5.39, note that a Class A address has three bytes available for identifying hosts on one network or on subnets, which provide support for more hosts than other address classes. Thus, Class A addresses are only assigned to large organizations or countries. Since the first bit in a Class A address must be 0, the first byte ranges in value from 1 to 127 instead of to 255. Through the use of 7 bits for the network portion and 24 bits for the host portion of the address, 128 networks can be defined with approximately 16.78 million hosts capable of being addressed on each Class A network. In actuality, network 127.0.0.0 is not used. This is because any IP address commencing with 127 with a host value of 1 or greater represents a loopback address. Thus, you could ping 127.0.0.1 to test the operation of a TCP/IP protocol stack on your computer.

Class B A Class B address uses two bytes for the network identifier and two for the host or subnet identifier. This permits up to 65,636 hosts and/or subnets to be assigned; however, since the first 2 bits of the network portion of the address are used to identify a Class B address, the network portion is reduced to a width of 14 bits. Thus, up to 16,384 Class B networks can be assigned. Due to the manner by which Class B network addresses are subdivided into network and host portions, such addresses are normally assigned to relatively large organizations with tens of thousands of employees.

Class C In a Class C address three octets are used to identify the network, leaving one octet to identify hosts and/or subnets. The use of 21 bits for a network address enables approximately two million distinct networks to be supported by the Class C address class. Because one octet only permits 256 hosts or subnets to be identified, many small organizations with a requirement to provide more than 256 hosts with access to the Internet must obtain multiple Class C addresses.

Host Restrictions In actuality the host portion of an IP address has two restrictions, which reduces the number of hosts that can be assigned to a network. First, the host portion cannot be set to all-zero bits, as an all-zeros host number is used to identify a base network. Secondly, an all-ones host number represents the broadcast address for a network or subnetwork. Thus, the maximum number of hosts on a network must be reduced by two. For a Class C network, a maximum of 254 hosts can then be configured for operation.

Subnetting Through the use of subnetting you can use a single IP address as a mechanism for connecting multiple physical networks. This action extends the use of scarce IP network addresses as well as reduces the number of routing table entries required. To accomplish subnetting you logically divide the host portion of an IP address into a network address and a host address.

Figure 5.40 illustrates an example of the IP subnet addressing format for a Class B address. In this example, all traffic routed to the address XY, where X and Y represent the value of the first two Class B address octets, flows to a common location connected to the Internet, typically a router. The router in turn connects two or more Class B subnets, each with a distinct address formed by the third decimal digit, which represents the subnet identifier. Figure 5.41 illustrates a Class B network address location with two physical networks using subnet addressing.

Subnet Masks   The implementation of a subnet addressing scheme is accomplished by the partitioning of the host identifier portion of an IP address. To accomplish this a 32-bit subnet mask must be created for each network, with bits set to 1 in the subnet mask to indicate the network portion of the IP address, while bits are set to 0 to indicate the host identifier portion. Thus, the Class B subnet address format illustrated in the lower portion of Figure 5.40 would require the following 32-bit subnet mask if there were no subnets:

11111111 11111111 00000000 00000000

Class B address format

Class B subnet address format

Figure 5.40   Class B subnetting.

Figure 5.41 A Class B network address location with two physical networks using subnet addressing. IP datagrams with the destination address X.Y.Z.Z, where Z can be any decimal value representing a Class B network address that can consist of 256 subnets, with 256 hosts on each subnet.

The prior mask would then be entered as 255.255.0.0 in dotted decimal representation into a router configuration screen as well as in software configuration screens on TCP/IP program stacks operating on each subnet. Concerning the latter, you must then configure each station to indicate its subnet and host identifier so that each station obtains a full 4-digit dotted decimal address.

Because a Class B network address by default uses two bytes for the network address and two for the host the prior mask does not allow for any subnets. To allow for subnets we must internally (to our organization) extend the subnet mask into the host portion of the address. Each one-bit extension permits 2^n subnets to be defined. For example, consider the following subnet:

$$11111111\ 11111111\ 11100000\ 00000000$$

This subnet is 255.255.224 in dotted decimal and would support up to eight (2^3) subnets. Note that internally to our organization the number of bit positions for hosts on a subnet becomes $16 - 3$, or 13 positions. Thus, each subnet can have a maximum of $2^{13} - 2$ hosts as each subnet cannot be all 0's or all 1's, similar to regular network restrictions.

Domain Name Service

Addressing on a TCP/IP network occurs through the use of four decimal numbers ranging from 0 to 255, which are separated from one another by a dot.

This dotted decimal notation represents a 32-bit address, which consists of an assigned network number and a host number as previously described during our examination of IP addressing. Because numeric addresses are difficult to work with, TCP/IP also supports a naming convention based upon English words or mnemonics that are both easier to work with and remember. The translation of English words or mnemonics to 32-bit IP addresses is performed by a domain name server. Each network normally has at least one domain name server, and the communications established between such servers on TCP/IP networks connected to the Internet are referred to as a domain name service (DNS).

The DNS is the naming protocol used in the TCP/IP protocol suite, which enables IP routing to occur indirectly through the use of names instead of IP addresses. To accomplish this, DNS provides a domain name to IP address translation service.

A domain is a subdivision of a wide area network. When applied to the Internet where the capitalized *I* references the collection of networks interconnected to one another, there are six top-level and seven recently added domain names, which were specified by the Internet Corporation for Assigned Names and Numbers (ICANN) at the time this book was prepared. Those top-level domains are listed in Table 5.5.

Under each top-level domain the InterNIC will register subdomains, which are assigned an IP network address. An organization receiving an IP network address can further subdivide their domain into two or more subdomains. In addition, instead of using dotted decimal notation to describe the location of each host, they can assign names to hosts as long as they follow certain rules and install a name server that provides IP address translation between named hosts and their IP addresses.

To illustrate the operation of a name server, consider the network domain illustrated in Figure 5.42. In this example we will assume that a well-known government agency has a local area network with several computers that will be connected to the Internet. Each host address will contain the specific name of the host plus the names of all of the subdomains and domains to which it belongs. Thus, the computer *warrants* would have the official address:

telnet.warrants.fbi.gov

Similarly, the computer *cops* would have the address:

ftp.cops.fbi.gov

TABLE 5.5   Internet Top-Level Domain Names

Domain Name	Assignment
.COM	Commercial organization
.EDU	Educational organization
.GOV	Government agency
.MIL	Department of Defense
.NET	Networking organization
.ORG	Not-for-profit organization
Recently added	
.aevo	Air-transport industry
.biz	Businesses
.coop	Cooperatives
.info	Information/services (unrestricted use)
.museum	Museums
.name	For registration by individuals
.pro	Accountants, lawyers, physicians, and other professionals

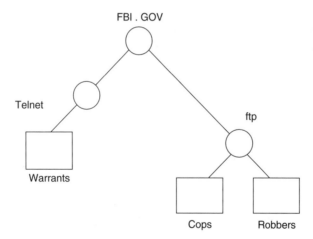

Figure 5.42   A domain-naming hierarchy.

In examining the domain-naming structure illustrated in Figure 5.39 note that computers were placed in subdomains using common Internet application names, such as telnet and ftp. This is a common technique that organizations use to make it easier for network users within and outside of the organization to remember mnemonics that represent specific hosts on their network.

Although domain names provide a mechanism for identifying objects connected to wide area networks, hosts in a domain require network addresses to transfer information. Thus, another host functioning as a name server is required to provide a name-to-address translation service.

Name Server

The name server plays an important role in TCP/IP networks. In addition to providing a name-to-IP address translation service, it must recognize that an address is outside its administrative zone of authority. For example, assume a host located on the domain illustrated in Figure 5.42 will use the address fred.microwear.com to transmit a message. The name server must recognize that that address does not reside in the current domain and must forward the address to another name server for translation into an appropriate IP address. Because most domains are connected to the Internet via an Internet service provider, the name server on the domain illustrated in Figure 5.42 would have a pointer to the name server of the Internet service provider (ISP) and forward the query to that name server. The ISP's name server will either have an entry in its table-in-cache memory or forward the query to another higher-level name server. Eventually, a name server will be reached that has administrative authority over the domain containing the host name to resolve and will return an IP address through a reversed hierarchy to provide the originating name server with a response to its query. Most name servers cache the results of previous name queries, which can considerably reduce off-domain or Internet DNS queries. In the event a response is not received, possibly due to an incorrect name or the entry of a name no longer used, the local name server will generate a "failure to resolve" message after a period of time that will be displayed on the requesting host's display.

TCP/IP Configuration

The configuration of a station on a TCP/IP network normally requires the specification of four IP addresses as well as the station's host and domain names. To illustrate the configuration of a TCP/IP station, Figures 5.43 through 5.45 show the screen settings on a Microsoft Windows NT server used to configure the station as a participant on a TCP/IP network.

Figure 5.44 illustrates the Windows NT Network Settings dialog box with the TCP/IP protocol selected in the installed network software box. Note that at the top of that box the entry NWLink IPX/SPX Compatible Transport is shown. Windows NT has the ability to operate multiple protocol stacks to

Figure 5.43 Using the Windows NT Network Settings dialog box to configure the use of the TCP/IP protocol.

Figure 5.44 The Windows NT TCP/IP configuration dialog box with entries for the IP address of the network interface, subnet mask, and default gateway.

Figure 5.45 Using the Windows NT DNS Configuration dialog box to specify the station's name and domain name as well as two name server addresses.

include NWLink, which is Microsoft's implementation of the Novell IPX and SPX protocols. Also note that we previously configured the server to use a 3 Com Etherlink III Adapter as indicated in the box labeled Installed Adapter Cards in the lower left portion of the screen display.

Clicking on the button labeled Configure in Figure 5.44 results in the display of another dialog box, this one labeled TCP/IP Configuration. Figure 5.45 illustrates the TCP/IP Configuration dialog box with three address entries shown. Those address entries indicate the IP address of the interface assigned to the selected adapter card, the subnet mask, and the IP address of the default gateway. Note that a computer can have multiple adapter cards, thus IP addresses are actually assigned to network interfaces. Also note that the term gateway dates to when such devices routed packets to other networks if their address was not on the local network. Thus, a more modern term for gateway is router.

After configuring the entries shown in Figure 5.44, you will require a few more entries. Those entries include the address of the name server used to translate near-English mnemonics into IP addresses as well as the name of your computer and domain. To configure the address of the name server, you would first click on the button labeled DNS in Figure 5.44. This action will result in the display of a dialog box labeled DNS Configuration, which is shown in Figure 5.45.

The Windows NT DNS Configuration dialog box enables you to specify your host computer name and your domain name. Those entries are optional; however, if you do not include those entries and your local DNS uses this configuration information, other TCP/IP users either on your network or a distant network will not be able to access your computer by entering your computer's near-English address name, which in Figure 5.45 would be www.xyz.com. Instead, users would have to know your numeric IP address.

The DNS entry area in Figure 5.45 allows you to specify up to three name servers in the order they should be searched. Many organizations operate two name servers, so the ability to enter three should suffice for most organizations.

Operating Multiple Stacks

In concluding this chapter we will use three Windows NT screens to expand upon illustrating the flexibility you can obtain from operating multiple

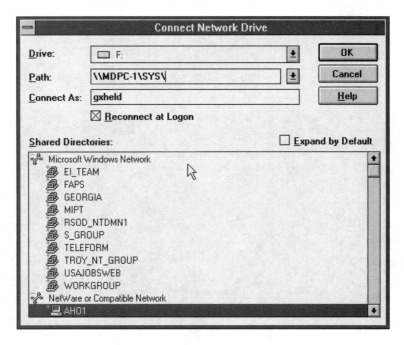

Figure 5.46 Using the Windows NT Connect Network Drive dialog box to view Windows and NetWare network devices.

protocol stacks. In the example we will shortly view, we will use Microsoft's Windows NT to show how to access both Windows NT and NetWare networks as well as operate a Netscape browser to run a TCP/IP application.

Figure 5.46 illustrates the use of the Windows NT Connect Network Drive dialog box to view both Microsoft Windows and Novell NetWare network devices that can operate on a common network or network infrastructure. By moving a highlight bar over a particular entry and clicking on the entry, you obtain the ability to log into NT or NetWare servers or access-shared directories on NT devices. For those readers from Missouri, Figure 5.47 illustrates the execution of a NetWare server program viewed on a Windows NT workstation. In this example, the NT workstation is running Microsoft's NWLink IPX/SPX compatible protocol, which enables it to communicate in a client/server environment as a participant on a NetWare LAN.

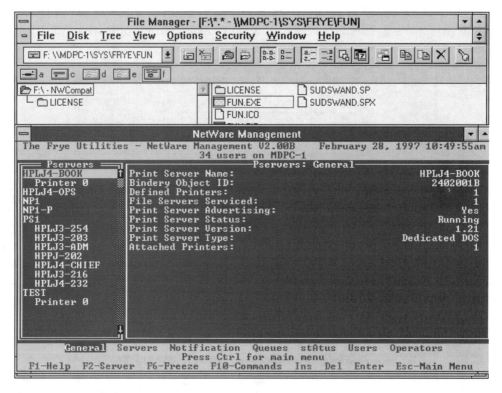

Figure 5.47 Viewing the execution of a NetWare server program on a Windows NT workstation.

Figure 5.48 Using the Microsoft Internet Explorer browser to access the home page of the author's publisher.

For our last stack example, since we previously configured TCP/IP we should be able to operate a TCP/IP application. Figure 5.48 illustrates the use of the Microsoft Internet Explorer browser to access the home page of this author's publisher. Thus, this short section illustrates the worth of operating multiple protocol stacks to access NT and NetWare servers as well as a Web server.

chapter six

Bridging and Switching Methods and Performance Issues

In Chapter 5, an overview of bridge operations was presented, along with information concerning the functionality of other local area network hardware and software components. That chapter deferred until now a detailed examination of bridging methods, to include their network use and performance issues. In this chapter, we will focus our attention on those issues, examining different methods that bridges use for routing frames, performance issues that govern their ability to examine and forward frames without introducing network bottlenecks, and their typical employment for interconnecting LANs. Because LAN switches represent a special type of multiport bridge, we will also focus our attention upon this topic later in this chapter. Thus, once we have an appreciation for the operation and utilization of bridges, we will turn our attention to LAN switches.

6.1 Bridging Methods

Bridges operate by examining MAC layer addresses, using the destination and source addresses within a frame as a decision criterion to make their forwarding decisions. Operating at the MAC layer, bridges are not addressed, and must therefore examine all frames that flow on a network. Because bridges operate at the MAC layer, they in effect terminate a collision domain. That is, if a collision is detected upon one port of a bridge, it is not propagated onto any output port. This means that, unlike a repeater, a bridge can be used to extend the span of a LAN.

Address Issues

Since bridges connect networks, it is important to ensure that duplicate MAC addresses do not occur on joined internal networks — a topology we will refer to as an *intranet*. While duplicate addresses will not occur when universally administered addressing is used, when locally administered addressing is used duplicate addresses become possible. Thus, the addresses assigned to stations on separate networks joined to form an intranet should be reviewed before using bridges to connect two or more separate networks.

Two primary routing methods are used by bridges for connecting wired local area networks: transparent or self-learning and source routing. Transparent bridges were originally developed to support the connection of Ethernet networks, as briefly described in Chapter 5.

Transparent Bridging

A transparent bridge examines MAC frames to learn the addresses of stations on the network, storing information in internal memory in the form of an address table. Thus, this type of bridge is also known as a *self-learning bridge*. To understand the operation of a transparent bridge in more detail and realize some of the limitations associated with the use of this device, consider the simple intranet illustrated in Figure 6.1. This intranet consists

Figure 6.1 Transparent bridge operation. A transparent or self-learning bridge examines the source and destination addresses to form port/address or routing tables in memory.

of three Ethernet local area network segments connected through the use of two self-learning bridges. For simplicity of illustration, only two workstations are shown and labeled on each local area network. Those labels represent the 48-bit MAC address of each station.

Port/Address Table Construction

As previously noted in Chapter 5, a bridge constructs its port/address table by using what can be referred to as the "three F's"—flooding, filtering, and forwarding. If a bridge encounters a frame with a destination address that is not in its port/address table, it transmits the frame onto all other ports except the port it was received on. If the destination address is in its port/address table and does not represent the port the frame was received on, the bridge forwards the frame onto the port corresponding to the entry in the table for the destination address. If the destination address is in the port/address table and represents the port the frame was received on, there is no need to forward the frame. Thus, the frame is filtered by the bridge.

In examining the construction of bridge port/address tables for the network shown in Figure 6.1, we will assume that each bridge operates as a transparent bridge. As frames flow on the Ethernet, bridge 1 examines the source address of each frame. Eventually, after both stations A and B have become active, the bridge associates their address as being on port 1 of that device. Any frames with a destination address other than stations A or B are considered to be on another network. Thus, bridge 1 would eventually associate addresses C, D, E, and F with port 2, once it receives frames with those addresses in their destination address fields. Similarly, bridge 2 constructs its own port/address table. Since frames from Ethernet 1 and 1 Ethernet 2 can have source addresses of A, B, C, or D, eventually the port/address table of bridge 2 associates those addresses with port 1 of that device. Since frames from Ethernet 1 or Ethernet 2 with a destination address of E or F are not on those local area networks, bridge 2 then associates those addresses with port 2 of that device.

The port/address tables previously shown in Figure 6.1 are normally stored in bridge memory sorted by MAC address. In addition, the time the entry occurred is also added to the table, resulting in a three-column table. The time of occurrence is used by bridges to periodically purge old entries. Entry purging is important because inactive entries both use finite memory and extend the search time associated with the reading of each frame received on a bridge port and its comparison to entries in the port/address table. This searching is required to determine if the frame is to be forwarded along with the port onto which the frame should be placed.

Advantages

One of the key advantages of a transparent bridge is that it operates independently of the contents of the information field and is protocol-independent. Because this type of bridge is self-learning, it requires no manual configuration and is essentially a "plug and play" device. Thus, this type of bridge is attractive for connecting a few local area networks together, and is usually sufficient for most small and medium-sized businesses. Unfortunately, its use limits the development of certain interconnection topologies, as we will soon see.

Disadvantages

To see the disadvantages associated with transparent bridges, consider Figure 6.2, in which the three Ethernet local area networks are interconnected through the use of three bridges. In this example, the interconnected networks form a *circular* or *loop topology*. Because a transparent bridge views stations as being connected to either port 1 or port 2, a circular or loop topology will create problems. Those problems can result in an unnecessary duplication of frames, which not only degrades the overall level of performance of the

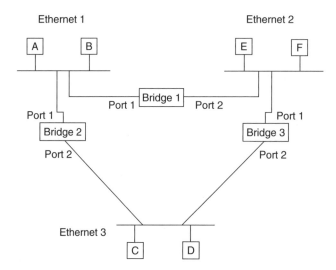

Figure 6.2 Transparent bridges do not support network loops. The construction of a circular or loop topology with transparent bridges can result in an unnecessary duplication of frames, and may confuse end stations. To avoid these problems, the Spanning Tree Protocol (STP) opens a loop by placing one bridge in a standby mode of operation.

interconnected networks, but will quite possibly confuse the end stations. For example, consider a frame whose source address is A and whose destination address is F. Both bridge 1 and bridge 2 will forward the frame. Although bridge 1 will forward the frame to its appropriate network using the most direct route, the frame will also be forwarded via bridge 2 and bridge 3 to Ethernet 2, resulting in a duplicate frame arriving at workstation F. At station F, a mechanism would be required to reject duplicate frames. Even if such a mechanism is available, the additional traffic flowing across multiple internet paths would result in an increase in network usage. This, in turn, would saturate some networks, while significantly reducing the level of performance of other networks. For these reasons, transparent bridging is prohibited from creating a loop or circular topology. However, transparent bridging supports concurrently active multiple bridges, using an algorithm known as the *spanning tree* to determine which bridges should forward and which bridges should only filter frames.

Spanning Tree Protocol

The problem of active loops was addressed by the IEEE Committee 802 in the 802.1D standard with an intelligent algorithm known as the Spanning Tree Protocol (STP). The STP, based on graph theory, converts a loop into a tree topology by disabling a link. This action ensures there is a unique path from any node in an intranet to every other node. Disabled nodes are then kept in a standby mode of operation until a network failure occurs. At that time, the STP will attempt to construct a new tree using any of the previously disabled links.

Operation

To illustrate the operation of the STP, we must first become familiar with the difference between the physical and active topology of bridged networks. In addition, there are a number of terms associated with the spanning tree algorithm, as defined by the protocol, that we should become familiar with. Thus, we will also review those terms before discussing the operation of the algorithm.

Physical versus Active Topology

In transparent bridging, a distinction is made between the physical and active topology resulting from bridged local area networks. This distinction enables the construction of a network topology in which inactive but physically constructed routes can be placed into operation if a primary route should fail, and in which the inactive and active routes would form an illegal circular path violating the spanning tree algorithm if both routes were active at the same time.

The top of Figure 6.3 illustrates one possible physical topology of bridged networks. The cost (C) assigned to each bridge will be discussed later in this chapter. The lower portion of Figure 6.3 illustrates a possible active topology for the physical configuration shown at the top of that illustration.

When a bridge is used to construct an active path, it will forward frames through those ports used to form active paths. The ports through which frames are forwarded are said to be in a *forwarding state of operation*. Ports that cannot forward frames because their operation forms a loop are said to be in a *blocking state of operation*.

Under the spanning tree algorithm, a port in a blocking state can be placed into a forwarding state to provide a path that becomes part of the active network topology. This new path usually occurs because of the failure of another path, bridge component, or the reconfiguration of interconnected networks, and must not form a closed loop.

Spanning Tree Algorithm

The basis for the spanning tree algorithm is a tree structure, since a tree forms a pattern of connections that has no loops. The term *spanning* is used because the branches of a tree structure span or connect subnetworks.

As a review for readers unfamiliar with graph theory, let's examine the concept behind spanning trees. To appropriately do so we need a point of reference, so let's begin with the graph structure shown at the top of Figure 6.4. A spanning tree of a graph is a subgraph that connects all nodes and represents a tree. The graph shown at the top of Figure 6.4 has eight distinct spanning trees. The lower portion of Figure 6.4 illustrates the spanning trees associated with the graph structure illustrated at the top of the previously referenced figure.

Minimum Spanning Tree

Suppose the links connecting each node are assigned a length or weight. Then, the weight of a tree represents the sum of its links or edges. If the weight or length of the links or tree edges differ, then different tree structures will have different weights. Thus, the identification of the minimum spanning tree requires us to examine each of the spanning trees supported by a graph and identify the structure that has the minimum length or weight.

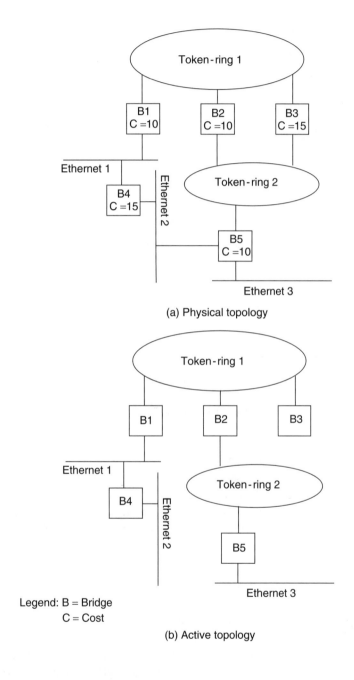

(a) Physical topology

(b) Active topology

Legend: B = Bridge
C = Cost

Figure 6.3 Physical versus active topology. When transparent bridges are used, the active topology cannot form a closed loop in the intranet.

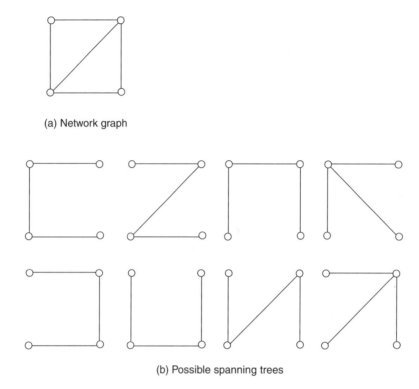

(a) Network graph

(b) Possible spanning trees

Figure 6.4   Forming spanning trees from a network graph.

The identification of the minimum spanning tree can be accomplished by listing all spanning trees and finding the minimum weight or length associated with the list. This is a brute force method that always works but is not exactly efficient, especially when a graph becomes complex and can contain a significant number of trees. A far better method is obtained by the use of an appropriate algorithm.

Kruskal's Algorithm

There are several popular algorithms developed for solving the minimum spanning tree of a graph. One of those algorithms is the Kruskal algorithm which is relatively easy to understand and will be used to illustrate the computation of a minimum spanning tree. Because we need weights or lengths assigned to each edge or link in a graph, let's revise the network graph previously shown in Figure 6.4 and add some weights. Figure 6.5 illustrates the weighted graph.

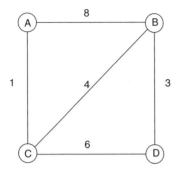

Figure 6.5 A weighted network graph.

Kruskal's algorithm can be expressed as follows:

1. Sort the edges of the graph (G) in their increasing order by weight or length.
2. Construct a subgraph (S) of G and initially set it to the empty state.
3. For each edge (e) in sorted order:
   If the endpoints of the edges (e) are disconnected in S, add them to S.

Using the graph shown in Figure 6.5, let's apply Kruskal's algorithm as follows:

1. The sorted edges of the graph in their increasing order by weight or length produces the following table:

Edge	Weight/Length
A-C	1
B-D	3
C-B	4
C-D	6
A-B	8

2. Set the subgraph of G to the empty state. Thus, S = null.
3. For each edge add to S as long as the endpoints are disconnected. Thus, the first operation produces:

The next operation produces:

S = (A,C) + (B,D)   or

The third operation produces:

S = (A,B) + (B,D) + (C,B)   or

Note that we cannot continue as the endpoints in S are now all connected. Thus, the minimum spanning tree consists of the edges or links $(A, B) + (B, D) + (C, B)$ and has the weight $1 + 4 + 3$, or 7. Now that we have an appreciation for the method by which a minimum spanning tree is formed, let's turn our attention to its applicability in transparent bridge-based networks.

Similar to the root of a tree, one bridge in a spanning tree network will be assigned to a unique position in the network. Known as the *root bridge*, this bridge is assigned as the top of the spanning tree, and because of this position, it has the potential to carry the largest amount of intranet traffic due to its position.

Because bridges and bridge ports can be active or inactive, a mechanism is required to identify bridges and bridge ports. Each bridge in a spanning tree network is assigned a unique bridge identifier. This identifier is the MAC address on the bridge's lowest port number and a two-byte bridge priority level. The priority level is defined when a bridge is installed and functions as a bridge number. Similar to the bridge priority level, each adapter on a bridge that functions as a port has a two-byte port identifier. Thus, the unique bridge identifier and port identifier enable each port on a bridge to be uniquely identified.

Path Cost

Under the spanning tree algorithm, the difference in physical routes between bridges is recognized, and a mechanism is provided to indicate the preference for one route over another. That mechanism is accomplished by the ability to assign a path cost to each path. Thus, you could assign a low cost to a preferred route and a high cost to a route you only want to be used in a backup situation.

Once path costs are assigned to each path in an intranet, each bridge will have one or more costs associated with different paths to the root bridge. One of those costs is lower than all other path costs. That cost is known as the bridge's *root path cost*, and the port used to provide the least path cost toward the root bridge is known as the *root port*.

Designated Bridge

As previously discussed, the spanning tree algorithm does not permit active loops in an interconnected network. To prevent this situation from occurring, only one bridge linking two networks can be in a forwarding state at any particular time. That bridge is known as the designated bridge, while all other bridges linking two networks will not forward frames and will be in a blocking state of operation.

Constructing the Spanning Tree

The spanning tree algorithm employs a three-step process to develop an active topology. First, the root bridge is identified. To accomplish this, each bridge in the intranet will initially assume it is the root bridge. To determine which bridge should actually act as the root bridge, each bridge will periodically transmit bridge protocol data unit (BPDU) frames that are described in the following section. BPDU frames under Ethernet version 2 are referred to as HELLO frames or messages and are transmitted on all bridge ports. Each BPDU frame includes the priority of the bridge defined at installation time. As the bridges in the intranet periodically transmit their BPDU frames, bridges receiving a BPDU with a lower priority value than its own cease transmitting their BPDUs; however, they forward BPDUs with a lower priority value. Thus, after a short period of time the bridge with the lowest priority value is recognized as the root bridge. In Figure 6.3b we will assume bridge 1 was selected as the root bridge. Next, the path cost from each bridge to the root bridge is determined, and the minimum cost from each bridge becomes the root path cost. The port in the direction of the least path cost to the root bridge, known as the root port, is then determined for each bridge. If the root path cost is the same for two or more bridges linking LANs, then the bridge with the highest priority will be selected to furnish the minimum path cost. Once the paths are selected, the designated ports are activated.

In examining Figure 6.3a, let us now use the cost entries assigned to each bridge. Let us assume that bridge 1 was selected as the root bridge, since we expect a large amount of traffic to flow between Token-Ring 1 and Ethernet 1 networks. Therefore, bridge 1 will become the designated bridge between Token-Ring 1 and Ethernet 1 networks. Here the term designated bridge references the bridge that has the bridge port with the lowest-cost path to the root bridge.

In examining the path costs to the root bridge, note that the path through bridge 2 was assigned a cost of 10, while the path through bridge 3 was assigned a cost of 15. Thus, the path from Token-Ring 2 via bridge 2 to Token-Ring 1 becomes the designated bridge between those two networks. Hence, Figure 6.3b shows bridge 3 inactive by the omission of a connection to the Token-Ring 2 network. Similarly, the path cost for connecting the Ethernet 3 network to the root bridge is lower by routing through the Token-Ring 2 and Token-Ring 1 networks. Thus, bridge 5 becomes the designated bridge for the Ethernet 3 and Token-Ring 2 networks.

Bridge Protocol Data Unit

As previously noted, bridges obtain topology information by the use of bridge protocol data unit (BPDU) frames. Once a root bridge is selected, that bridge is responsible for periodically transmitting a "HELLO" BPDU frame to all networks to which it is connected. According to the spanning tree protocol, HELLO frames must be transmitted every 1 to 10 seconds. The BPDU has the group MAC address 800143000000, which is recognized by each bridge. A designated bridge will then update the path cost and timing information and forward the frame. A standby bridge will monitor the BPDUs, but will not update nor forward them. If the designated bridge does not receive a BPDU on its root port for a predefined period of time (default is 20 seconds), the designated bridge will assume that either a link or device failure occurred. That bridge, if it is still receiving configuration BPDU frames on other ports, will then switch its root port to a port that is receiving the best configuration BPDUs.

When a standby bridge is required to assume the role of the root or designated bridge, the HELLO BPDU will indicate that a standby bridge should become a designated bridge. The process by which bridges determine their role in a spanning tree network is iterative. As new bridges enter a network, they assume a listening state to determine their role in the network. Similarly, when a bridge is removed, another iterative process occurs to reconfigure the remaining bridges.

Although the STP algorithm procedure eliminates duplicate frames and degraded intranet performance, it can be a hindrance for situations where multiple active paths between networks are desired. In addition, if a link or device fails, the time required for a new spanning tree to be formed via the transmission of BPDUs can easily require 45 to 60 seconds or more. Another disadvantage of STP occurs when it is used in remote bridges connecting geographically dispersed networks. For example, returning to Figure 6.2, suppose Ethernet 1 were located in Los Angeles, Ethernet 2 in New York, and Ethernet 3 in Atlanta. If the link between Los Angeles and New York were placed in a standby mode of operation, all frames from Ethernet 2 routed to Ethernet 1 would be routed through Atlanta. Depending on the traffic between networks, this situation might require an upgrade in the bandwidth of the links connecting each network to accommodate the extra traffic flowing through Atlanta. Since the yearly cost of upgrading a 56- or 64-Kbps circuit to a 128-Kbps fractional T1 link can easily exceed the cost of a bridge or router, you might wish to consider the use of routers to accommodate this networking situation. In comparison, when using local bridges, the higher operating rate of local bridges in interconnecting local area networks normally allows an acceptable level of performance when LAN traffic is routed through an intermediate bridge.

Protocol Dependency

Another problem associated with the use of transparent bridges concerns the differences between Ethernet and IEEE 802.3 frame field compositions. As noted in Chapter 4, the Ethernet frame contains a type field that indicates the higher-layer protocol in use. Under the IEEE 802.3 frame format, the type field is replaced by a length field, and the data field is subdivided to include logical link control (LLC) information in the form of destination (DSAP) and source (SSAP) service access points. Here, the DSAP and SSAP are similar to the type field in an Ethernet frame: they also point to a higher-level process. Unfortunately, this small difference can create problems when you are using a transparent bridge to interconnect Ethernet and IEEE 802.3 networks.

The top portion of Figure 6.6 shows the use of a bridge to connect an AppleTalk network supporting several Macintosh computers to an Ethernet network on which a Digital Equipment Corporation VAX computer is located. Although the VAX may be capable of supporting DecNet Phase IV, which is true Ethernet, and AppleTalk if both modules are resident, a pointer is required to direct the IEEE 802.3 frames generated by the Macintosh to the right protocol on the VAX. Unfortunately, the Ethernet connection used

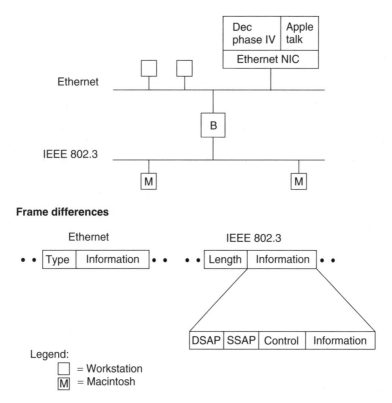

Figure 6.6 Protocol differences preclude linking IEEE 802.3 and Ethernet networks using transparent bridges. A Macintosh computer connected on an IEEE 802.3 network using AppleTalk will not have its frame pointed to the right process on a VAX on an Ethernet. Thus, the differences between Ethernet and IEEE 802.3 networks require transparent bridges for interconnecting similar networks.

by the VAX will not provide the required pointer. This explains why you should avoid connecting Ethernet and IEEE 802.3 networks via transparent bridges. Fortunately, almost all Ethernet NICs manufactured today are IEEE 802.3–compatible to alleviate this problem; however, older NICs may operate as true Ethernets and result in the previously mentioned problem.

Source Routing

Source routing is a bridging technique developed by IBM for connecting Token-Ring networks. The key to the implementation of source routing is the use of a portion of the information field in the Token-Ring frame to carry routing information and the transmission of *discovery* packets to determine the best route between two networks.

The presence of source routing is indicated by the setting of the first bit position in the source address field of a Token-Ring frame to a binary 1. When set, this indicates that the information field is preceded by a route information field (RIF), which contains both control and routing information.

The RIF Field

Figure 6.7 illustrates the composition of a Token-Ring RIF. This field is variable in length and is developed during a discovery process, described later in this section.

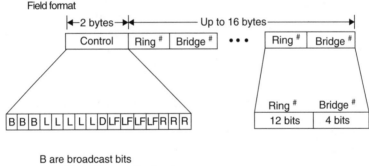

Field format

B are broadcast bits

Bit settings	Designator
0XX	Nonbroadcast
10X	All-routes broadcast
11X	Single route broadcast

L are length bits which denote length of the RIF in bytes
D is direction bit
LF identifies largest frame

Bit settings	Size in bytes
000	516
001	1500
010	2052
011	4472
100	8191
101	Reserved
110	Reserved
111	Used in all-routes broadcast frame

R are reserved bits

Figure 6.7   Token-Ring route information field. The Token-Ring RIF is variable in length.

The control field contains information that defines how information will be transferred and interpreted and what size the remainder of the RIF will be. The three broadcast bit positions indicate a nonbroadcast, all-routes broadcast, or single-route broadcast situation. A nonbroadcast designator indicates a local or specific route frame. An all-routes broadcast designator indicates that a frame will be transmitted along every route to the destination station. A single-route broadcast designator is used only by designated bridges to relay a frame from one network to another. In examining the broadcast bit settings shown in Figure 6.7, note that the letter X indicates an unspecified bit setting that can be either a 1 or 0.

The length bits identify the length of the RIF in bytes, while the D bit indicates how the field is scanned, left to right or right to left. Since vendors have incorporated different memory in bridges which may limit frame sizes, the LF bits enable different devices to negotiate the size of the frame. Normally, a default setting indicates a frame size of 512 bytes. Each bridge can select a number, and if it is supported by other bridges, that number is then used to represent the negotiated frame size. Otherwise, a smaller number used to represent a smaller frame size is selected, and the negotiation process is repeated. Note that a 1500-byte frame is the largest frame size supported by Ethernet IEEE 802.3 networks. Thus, a bridge used to connect Ethernet and Token-Ring networks cannot support the use of Token-Ring frames exceeding 1500 bytes.

Up to eight route number subfields, each consisting of a 12-bit ring number and a 4-bit bridge number, can be contained in the routing information field. This permits two to eight route designators, enabling frames to traverse up to eight rings across seven bridges in a given direction. Both ring numbers and bridge numbers are expressed as hexadecimal characters, with three hex characters used to denote the ring number and one hex character used to identify the bridge number.

Operation Example

To illustrate the concept behind source routing, consider the intranet illustrated in Figure 6.8. In this example, let us assume that two Token-Ring networks are located in Atlanta and one network is located in New York.

Each Token-Ring and bridge is assigned a ring or bridge number. For simplicity, ring numbers R1, R2, and R3 are used here, although as previously explained, those numbers are actually represented in hexadecimal. Similarly, bridge numbers are shown here as B1, B2, B3, B4, and B5 instead of hexadecimal characters.

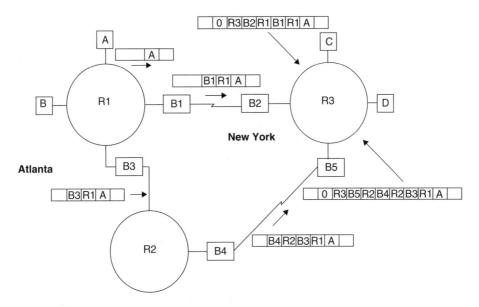

Figure 6.8 Source routing discovery operation. The route discovery process results in each bridge entering the originating ring number and its bridge number into the RIF.

When a station wants to originate communications, it is responsible for finding the destination by transmitting a discovery packet to network bridges and other network stations whenever it has a message to transmit to a new destination address. If station A wishes to transmit to station C, it sends a route discovery packet containing an empty RIF and its source address, as indicated in the upper left portion of Figure 6.8. This packet is recognized by each source routing bridge in the network. When a source routing bridge receives the packet, it enters the packet's ring number and its own bridge identifier in the packet's routing information field. The bridge then transmits the packet to all of its connections except the connection on which the packet was received, a process known as *flooding*. Depending on the topology of the interconnected networks, it is more than likely that multiple copies of the discovery packet will reach the recipient. This is illustrated in the upper right corner of Figure 6.8, in which two discovery packets reach station C. Here, one packet contains the sequence R1B1R1B2R30—the zero indicates that there is no bridging in the last ring. The second packet contains the route sequence R1B3R2B4R2B5R30. Station C then picks the best route, based on either the most direct path or the earliest arriving packet, and transmits a response to the discover packet originator. The response indicates the specific route to use, and station A then enters that route into memory for the duration of the transmission session.

Under source routing, bridges do not keep routing tables like transparent bridges. Instead, tables are maintained at each station throughout the network. Thus, each station must check its routing table to determine what route frames must traverse to reach their destination station. This routing method results in source routing using distributed routing tables instead of the centralized routing tables used by transparent bridges.

Advantages

There are several advantages associated with source routing. One advantage is the ability to construct mesh networks with loops for a fault-tolerant design; this cannot be accomplished with the use of transparent bridges. Another advantage is the inclusion of routing information in the information frames. Several vendors have developed network management software products that use that information to provide statistical information concerning intranet activity. Those products may assist you in determining how heavily your wide area network links are being used, and whether you need to modify the capacity of those links; they may also inform you if one or more workstations are hogging communications between networks.

Disadvantages

Although the preceding advantages are considerable, they are not without a price. That price includes a requirement to identify bridges and links specifically, higher bursts of network activity, and an incompatibility between Token-Ring and Ethernet networks. In addition, because the structure of the Token-Ring RIF supports a maximum of seven entries, routing of frames is restricted to crossing a maximum of seven bridges.

When using source routing bridges to connect Token-Ring networks, you must configure each bridge with a unique bridge/ring number. In addition, unless you wish to accept the default method by which stations select a frame during the route discovery process, you will have to reconfigure your LAN software. Thus, source routing creates an administrative burden not incurred by transparent bridges.

Due to the route discovery process, the flooding of discovery frames occurs in bursts when stations are turned on or after a power outage. Depending upon the complexity of an intranet, the discovery process can degrade network performance. This is perhaps the most problematic for organizations that require the interconnection of Ethernet and Token-Ring networks.

A source routing bridge can be used only to interconnect Token-Ring networks, since it operates on RIF data not included in an Ethernet frame. Although transparent bridges can operate in Ethernet, Token-Ring, and mixed environments, their use precludes the ability to construct loop or mesh topologies, and inhibits the ability to establish operational redundant paths for load sharing. Another problem associated with bridging Ethernet and Token-Ring networks involves the RIF in a Token-Ring frame. Unfortunately, different LAN operating systems use the RIF data in different ways. Thus, the use of a transparent bridge to interconnect Ethernet and Token-Ring networks may require the same local area network operating system on each network. To alleviate these problems, several vendors introduced source routing transparent (SRT) bridges, which function in accordance with the IEEE 802.1D standard approved during 1992.

Source Routing Transparent Bridges

A source routing transparent bridge supports both IBM's source routing and the IEEE transparent STP operations. This type of bridge can be considered two bridges in one; it has been standardized by the IEEE 802.1 committee as the IEEE 802.1D standard.

Operation

Under source routing, the MAC packets contain a status bit in the source field that identifies whether source routing is to be used for a message. If source routing is indicated, the bridge forwards the frame as a source routing frame. If source routing is not indicated, the bridge determines the destination address and processes the packet using a transparent mode of operation, using routing tables generated by a spanning tree algorithm.

Advantages

There are several advantages associated with source routing transparent bridges. First and perhaps foremost, they enable different networks to use different local area network operating systems and protocols. This capability enables you to interconnect networks developed independently of one another, and allows organization departments and branches to use LAN operating systems without restriction. Secondly, also a very important consideration, source routing transparent bridges can connect Ethernet and

Token-Ring networks while preserving the ability to mesh or loop Token-Ring networks. Thus, their use provides an additional level of flexibility for network construction.

Translating Operations

When interconnecting Ethernet/IEEE 802.3 and Token-Ring networks, the difference between frame formats requires the conversion of frames. A bridge that performs this conversion is referred to as a *translating bridge*.

As previously noted in Chapter 4, there are several types of Ethernet frames, such as Ethernet, IEEE 802.3, Novell's Ethernet-802.3, and Ethernet-SNAP. The latter two frames represent variations of the physical IEEE 802.3 frame format. Ethernet and Ethernet-802.3 do not use logical link control, while IEEE 802.3 CSMA/CD LANs specify the use of IEEE 802.2 logical link control. In comparison, all IEEE 802.5 Token-Ring networks either directly or indirectly use the IEEE 802.2 specification for logical link control.

The conversion from IEEE 802.3 to IEEE 802.5 can be accomplished by discarding portions of the IEEE 802.3 frame not applicable to a Token-Ring frame, copying the 802.2 LLC protocol data unit (PDU) from one frame to another, and inserting fields applicable to the Token-Ring frame. Figure 6.9 illustrates the conversion process performed by a translating bridge

Figure 6.9   IEEE 802.3 to 802.5 frame conversion.

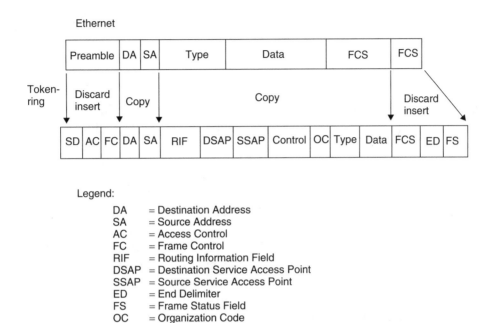

Legend:

DA = Destination Address
SA = Source Address
AC = Access Control
FC = Frame Control
RIF = Routing Information Field
DSAP = Destination Service Access Point
SSAP = Source Service Access Point
ED = End Delimiter
FS = Frame Status Field
OC = Organization Code

Figure 6.10   Ethernet to Token-Ring frame conversion.

linking an IEEE 802.3 network to an IEEE 802.5 network. Note that fields unique to the IEEE 802.3 frame are discarded, while fields common to both frames are copied. Fields unique to the IEEE 802.5 frame are inserted by the bridge.

Since an Ethernet frame, as well as Novell's Ethernet-802.3 frame, does not support logical link control, the conversion process to IEEE 802.5 requires more processing. In addition, each conversion is more specific and may or may not be supported by a specific translating bridge. For example, consider the conversion of Ethernet frames to Token-Ring frames. Since Ethernet does not support LLC PDUs, the translation process results in the generation of a Token-Ring-SNAP frame. This conversion or translation process is illustrated in Figure 6.10.

6.2 Bridge Network Utilization

In this section, we will examine the use of bridges to interconnect separate local area networks and to subdivide networks to improve performance. In addition, we will focus our attention on how we can increase network availability by employing bridges to provide alternate communications paths between networks.

Serial and Sequential Bridging

The top of Figure 6.11 illustrates the basic use of a bridge to interconnect two networks serially. Suppose that monitoring of each network indicates a high level of intranetwork use. One possible configuration to reduce intra-LAN traffic on each network can be obtained by moving some stations off each of the two existing networks to form a third network. The three networks would then be interconnected through the use of an additional bridge, as illustrated in the middle portion of Figure 6.11. This extension results in *sequential* or *cascaded bridging*, and is appropriate when intra-LAN traffic is necessary but minimal. This intranet topology is also extremely useful when the length of an Ethernet must be extended beyond the physical cabling of a single network. By locating servers appropriately within each network segment, you may be able to minimize inter-LAN transmission. For example, the first network segment could be used to connect marketing personnel, while the second and third segments could be used to connect engineering and personnel departments. This might minimize the use of a server on one network by persons connected to another network segment.

A word of caution is in order concerning the use of bridges. Bridging forms what is referred to as a *flat* network topology, because it makes its forwarding decisions using layer 2 MAC addresses, which cannot distinguish one network from another. This means that broadcast traffic generated on one segment will be bridged onto other segments which, depending upon the amount of broadcast traffic, can adversely affect the performance on other segments.

The only way to reduce broadcast traffic between segments is to use a filtering feature included with some bridges or install routers to link segments. Concerning the latter, routers operate at the network layer and forward packets explicitly addressed to a different network. Through the use of network addresses for forwarding decisions, routers form hierarchical structured networks, eliminating the so-called broadcast storm effect that occurs when broadcast traffic generated from different types of servers on different segments are automatically forwarded by bridges onto other segments.

Both serial and sequential bridging are applicable to transparent, source routing, and source routing transparent bridges that do not provide redundancy nor the ability to balance traffic flowing between networks. Each of these deficiencies can be alleviated through the use of parallel bridging. However,

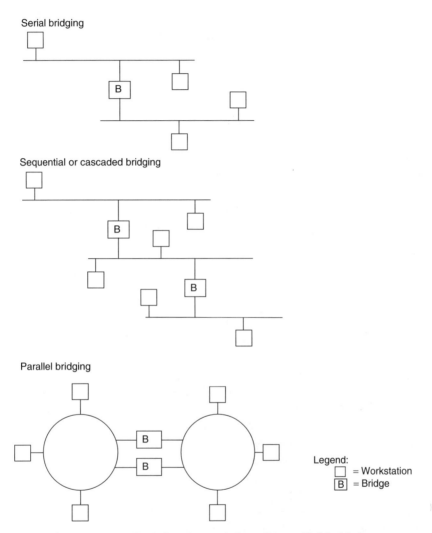

Figure 6.11   Serial, sequential, and parallel bridging.

this bridging technique creates a loop and is only applicable to source routing and source routing transparent bridges.

Parallel Bridging

The lower portion of Figure 6.11 illustrates the use of parallel bridges to interconnect two Token-Ring networks. This bridging configuration permits one bridge to back up the other, providing a level of redundancy for linking the two networks as well as a significant increase in the availability of one network to communicate with another. For example, assume the availability of each bridge used at the top of Figure 6.11 (serial bridging) and bottom of Figure 6.11 (parallel bridging) is 90 percent. The availability through two serially connected bridges would be 0.9×0.9 (availability of bridge 1 $\times$ availability of bridge 2), or 81 percent. In comparison, the availability through parallel bridges would be $1 - (0.1 \times 0.1)$, which is 99 percent.

The dual paths between networks also improve inter-LAN communications performance, because communications between stations on each network can be load balanced. The use of parallel bridges can thus be expected to provide a higher level of inter-LAN communications than the use of serial or sequential bridges. However, as previously noted, this topology is not supported by transparent bridging.

Star Bridging

With a multiport bridge, you can connect three or more networks to form a star intranet topology. The top portion of Figure 6.12 shows the use of one bridge to form a star topology by interconnecting four separate networks. This topology, or a variation on this topology, could be used to interconnect networks on separate floors within a building. For example, the top network could be on floor $N + 1$, while the bottom network could be on floor $N - 1$ in a building. The bridge and the two networks to the left and right of the bridge might then be located on floor N.

Although star bridging permits several networks located on separate floors within a building to be interconnected, all intranet data must flow through one bridge. This can result in both performance and reliability constraints to traffic flow. Thus, to interconnect separate networks on more than a few floors in a building, you should consider using backbone bridging.

Backbone Bridging

The lower portion of Figure 6.12 illustrates the use of backbone bridging. In this example, one network runs vertically through a building with Ethernet *ribs* extending from the backbone onto each floor. Depending upon the amount of intranet traffic and the vertical length required for the backbone network, the backbone can be either a conventional Ethernet bus-based network or a fiber-optic backbone.

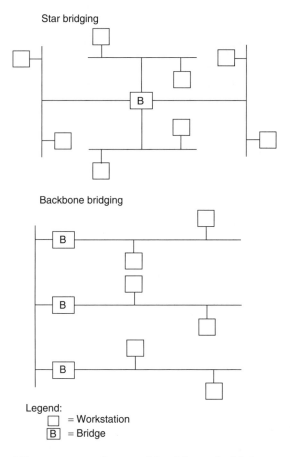

Figure 6.12 Star and backbone bridging.

6.3 Bridge Performance Issues

The key to obtaining an appropriate level of performance when interconnecting networks is planning. The actual planning process will depend upon several factors, such as whether separate networks are in operation, the type of networks to be connected, and the type of bridges to be used—local or remote.

Traffic Flow

If separate networks are in operation and you have appropriate monitoring equipment, you can determine the traffic flow on each of the networks to be interconnected. Once this is accomplished, you can expect an approximate 10- to 20-percent increase in network traffic. This additional traffic represents the flow of information between networks after an interconnection links previously separated local area networks. Although this traffic increase represents an average encountered by the author, your network traffic may not represent the typical average. To explore further, you can examine the potential for intranet communications in the form of electronic messages that may be transmitted to users on other networks, potential file transfers of word processing files, and other types of data that would flow between networks.

Network Types

The types of networks to be connected will govern the rate at which frames are presented to bridges. This rate, in turn, will govern the filtering rate at which bridges should operate so that they do not become bottlenecks on a network. For example, the maximum number of frames per second will vary between different types of Ethernet and Token-Ring networks, as well as between different types of the same network. The operating rate of a bridge may thus be appropriate for connecting some networks while inappropriate for connecting other types of networks.

Type of Bridge

Last but not least, the type of bridge—local or remote—will have a considerable bearing upon performance issues. Local bridges pass data between networks at their operating rates. In comparison, remote bridges pass data between networks using wide area network transmission facilities, which typically provide a transmission rate that is only a fraction of a local area network operating rate. Now that we have discussed some of the aspects governing bridge and intranet performance using bridges, let's probe deeper by estimating network traffic.

Estimating Network Traffic

If we do not have access to monitoring equipment to analyze an existing network, or if we are planning to install a new network, we can spend some time developing a reasonable estimate of network traffic. To do so, we should attempt to classify stations into groups based on the type of general activity performed, and then estimate the network activity for one station per group. This will enable us to multiply the number of stations in the group by the station activity to determine the group network traffic. Adding up the activity of all groups will then provide us with an estimate of the traffic activity for the network.

As an example of local area network traffic estimation, let us assume that our network will support 20 engineers, 5 managers, and 3 secretaries. Table 6.1 shows how we would estimate the network traffic in terms of the bit rate for each station group and the total activity per group, and then sum up the network traffic for the three groups that will use the network. In this example, which for the sake of simplicity does not include the transmission of data to a workstation printer, the total network traffic was estimated to be slightly below 50,000 bps.

TABLE 6.1   Estimating Network Traffic

Activity	Message Size (Bytes)	Frequency	Bit Rate*
Engineering workstations			
Request program	1,500	1/hour	4
Load program	480,000	1/hour	1,067
Save files	120,000	2/hour	533
Send/receive e-mail	2,000	2/hour	9
Total engineering activity			
$= 1,613 \times 20 = 32,260$ bps			1,613
Managerial workstations			
Request program	1,500	2/hour	7
Load program	320,000	2/hour	1,422
Save files	30,000	2/hour	134
Send/receive e-mail	3,000	4/hour	27
Total managerial activity			
$= 1,590 \times 5 = 7,950$ bps			1,590
Secretarial workstations			
Request program	1,500	4/hour	14
Load program	640,000	2/hour	2,844
Save files	12,000	8/hour	214
Send/receive e-mail	3,000	6/hour	40
Total secretarial activity			
$= 3,112 \times 3 = 9,336$ bps			3,112
Total estimated network activity			
$= 49,546$ bps			

*Note: Bit rate is computed by multiplying message rate by frequency by 8 bits/byte and dividing by 3,600 seconds/hour.

To plan for the interconnection of two or more networks through the use of bridges, our next step should be to perform a similar traffic analysis for each of the remaining networks. After this is accomplished, we can use the network traffic to estimate inter-LAN traffic, using 10 to 20 percent of total intranetwork traffic as an estimate of the intranet traffic that will result from the connection of separate networks.

Intranet Traffic

To illustrate the traffic estimation process for the interconnection of separate LANs, let us assume that network A's traffic was determined to be 50,000 bps, while network B's traffic was estimated to be approximately 100,000 bps. Figure 6.13 illustrates the flow of data between networks connected by a local bridge. Note that the data flow in each direction is expressed as a range, based on the use of an industry average of 10 to 20 percent of network traffic routed between interconnected networks.

Network Types

Our next area of concern is to examine the types of networks to be interconnected. In doing so, we should focus our attention on the operating rate of

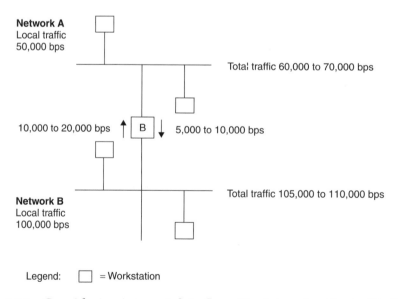

Figure 6.13 Considering intranet data flow. To determine the traffic flow on separate networks after they are interconnected, you must consider the flow of data onto each network from the other network.

each LAN. If network A's traffic was estimated to be approximately 50,000 bps, then the addition of 10,000 to 20,000 bps from network B onto network A will raise network A's traffic level to between 60,000 and 70,000 bps. Similarly, the addition of traffic from network A onto network B will raise network B's traffic level to between 105,000 and 110,000 bps. In this example, the resulting traffic on each network is well below the operating rate of all types of local area networks, and will not present a capacity problem for either network.

Bridge Type

As previously mentioned, local bridges transmit data between networks at the data rate of the destination network. This means that a local bridge will have a lower probability of being a bottleneck than a remote bridge, since the latter provides a connection between networks using a wide area transmission facility, which typically operates at a fraction of the operating rate of a LAN.

In examining the bridge operating rate required to connect networks, we will use a bottom-up and a top-down approach. That is, we will first determine the operating rate in frames per second for the specific example previously discussed. This will be followed by computing the maximum frame rate supported by an Ethernet network.

For the bridge illustrated in Figure 6.13, we previously computed that its maximum transfer rate would be 20,000 bps from network B onto network A. This is equivalent to 2500 bytes per second. If we assume that data is transported in 512-byte frames, this would be equivalent to 6 frames per second — a minimal transfer rate supported by every bridge manufacturer. However, when remote bridges are used, the frame forwarding rate of the bridge will more than likely be constrained by the operating rate of the wide area network transmission facility.

Bridge Operational Considerations

A remote bridge wraps a LAN frame into a higher-level protocol packet for transmission over a wide area network communications facility. This operation requires the addition of a header, protocol control, error detection, and trailer fields, and results in a degree of overhead. A 20,000-bps data flow from network B to network A, therefore, could not be accommodated by a transmission facility operating at that data rate.

In converting LAN traffic onto a wide area network transmission facility, you can expect a protocol overhead of approximately 20 percent. Thus, your actual operating rate must be at least 24,000 bps before the wide area network communications link becomes a bottleneck and degrades communications.

Now that we have examined the bridging performance requirements for two relatively small networks, let us focus our attention on determining the maximum frame rates of an Ethernet network. This will provide us with the ability to determine the rate at which the frame processing rate of a bridge becomes irrelevant, since any processing rate above the maximum network rate will not be useful. In addition, we can use the maximum network frame rate when estimating traffic, because if we approach that rate, network performance will begin to degrade significantly when use exceeds between 60 to 70 percent of that rate.

Ethernet Traffic Estimation

An Ethernet frame can vary between a minimum of 72 bytes and a maximum of 1526 bytes. Thus, the maximum frame rate on an Ethernet will vary with the frame size.

Ethernet operations require a dead time between frames of 9.6 μsec. The bit time for a 10-Mbps Ethernet is $1/10^7$ or 100 nsec. Based upon the preceding, we can compute the maximum number of frames/second for 1526-byte frames. Here, the time per frame becomes:

$$9.6 \ \mu sec + 1526 \ bytes \times 8 \ bits/byte$$

or

$$9.6 \ \mu sec + 12{,}208 \ bits \times 100 \ nsec/bit$$

or

$$1.23 \ msec$$

Thus, in one second there can be a maximum of 1/1.23 msec or 812 maximum-size frames. For a minimum frame size of 72 bytes, the time per frame is:

$$9.6 \ \mu sec + 72 \ bytes \times 8 \ bits/byte \times 100 \ nsec/bit$$

or

$$67.2 \times 10^{-6} \ sec.$$

Thus, in one second there can be a maximum of $1/67.2 \times 10^{-6}$ or 14,880 minimum-size 72-byte frames. Since 100BASE-T Fast Ethernet uses the same frame composition as Ethernet, the maximum frame rate for maximum- and minimum-length frames are ten times that of Ethernet. That is, Fast Ethernet supports a maximum of 8120 maximum-size 1526-byte frames per second and a maximum of 148,800 minimum-size 72-byte frames per second. Similarly, Gigabit Ethernet uses the same frame composition as Ethernet but is 100 times faster. This means that Gigabit Ethernet is capable of supporting a maximum of 81,200 maximum-length 1526-byte frames per second and a maximum of 1,488,000 minimum-length 72-byte frames per second. As you might expect, 10 Gigabit Ethernet expands support by an order of magnitude beyond the frame rate of Gigabit Ethernet. For both Gigabit and 10 Gigabit Ethernet the maximum frame rates are for full-duplex operations. Table 6.2 summarizes the frame processing requirements for a 10-Mbps Ethernet, Fast Ethernet, Gigabit Ethernet, and 10 Gigabit Ethernet under 50 percent and 100 percent load conditions, based on minimum and maximum frame lengths. Note that those frame processing requirements define the frame examination (filtering) operating rate of a bridge connected to different types of Ethernet networks. That rate indicates the number of frames per second a bridge connected to different types of Ethernet local area networks must be capable of examining under heavy (50-percent load) and full (100-percent load) traffic conditions.

In examining the different Ethernet network frame processing requirements indicated in Table 6.2, it is important to note that the frame processing requirements associated with Fast Ethernet, Gigabit Ethernet, and 10 Gigabit Ethernet commonly preclude the ability to upgrade a bridge by simply changing its adapter cards. Due to the much greater frame processing requirements associated with very high speed Ethernet networks, bridges are commonly designed to support those technologies from the ground up to include adapters and a

TABLE 6.2   Ethernet Frame Processing Requirements (Frames per Second)

Average Frame Size (Bytes)	Frame Processing Requirements	
	50% Load	100% Load
Ethernet		
1526	406	812
72	7440	14,880
Fast Ethernet		
1526	4050	8120
72	74,400	148,800
Gigabit Ethernet		
1526	40,600	81,200
72	744,000	1,488,000
10 Gigabit Ethernet		
1526	406,000	812,000
72	7,440,000	14,880,000

central processor to support the additional frame processing associated with their higher operating rate.

We can extend our analysis of Ethernet frames by considering the frame rate supported by different link speeds. For example, let us consider a pair of remote bridges connected by a 9.6-Kbps line. The time per frame for a 72-byte frame at 9.6 Kbps is:

$$9.6 \times 10^{-6} + 72 \times 8 \times 0.0001041 \text{ s/bit} \quad \text{or} \quad 0.0599712 \text{ seconds per frame}$$

Thus, in one second the number of frames is 1/.0599712, or 16.67 frames per second. Table 6.3 compares the frame-per-second rate supported by different link speeds for minimum- and maximum-size Ethernet frames. As expected, the frame transmission rate supported by a 10-Mbps link for minimum- and maximum-size frames is exactly the same as the frame processing requirements under 100 percent loading for a 10-Mbps Ethernet LAN, as indicated in Table 6.2.

In examining Table 6.3, note that the entries in this table do not consider the effect of the overhead of a protocol used to transport frames between two networks. You should therefore decrease the frame-per-second rate by approximately 20 percent for all link speeds through 1.536 Mbps. The reason the 10-Mbps rate should not be adjusted is that it represents a local 10-Mbps Ethernet bridge connection that does not require the use of a wide area network protocol to transport frames. Also note that the link speed of 1.536 Mbps represents a T1 transmission facility that operates at 1.544 Mbps. However, since the framing bits on a T1 circuit use 8 Kbps, the effective line speed available for the transmission of data is 1.536 Mbps.

TABLE 6.3　Link Speed versus Frame Rate

Link Speed	Frames per Second	
	Minimum	Maximum
9.6 Kbps	16.67	0.79
19.2 Kbps	33.38	1.58
56.0 Kbps	97.44	4.60
64.0 Kbps	111.17	5.25
1.536 Mbps	2815.31	136.34
10.0 Mbps	14,880.00	812.00

Predicting Throughput

Until now, we have assumed that the operating rate of each LAN linked by a bridge is the same. However, in many organizations this may not be true, because LANs are implemented at different times using different technologies. Thus, accounting may be using a 10-Mbps LAN, while the personnel department might be using a 100-Mbps LAN.

Suppose we wanted to interconnect the two LANs via the use of a multimedia bridge. To predict throughput between LANs, let us use the network configuration illustrated in Figure 6.14. Here, the operating rate of LAN A is assumed to be R_1 bps, while the operating rate of LAN B is assumed to be R_2 bps.

In one second, R_1 bits can be transferred on LAN A and R_2 bits can be transferred on LAN B. Similarly, it takes $1/R_1$ seconds to transfer one bit on LAN A and $1/R_2$ seconds to transfer one bit on LAN B. So, to transfer one bit across the bridge from LAN A to LAN B, ignoring the transfer time at the bridge:

$$\frac{1}{R_T} = \frac{1}{R_1} + \frac{1}{R_2}$$

or

$$R_T = \frac{1}{(1/R_1) + (1/R_2)}$$

We computed that a 10-Mbps Ethernet would support a maximum transfer of 812 maximum-sized frames per second. If we assume that the second LAN operating at 100 Mbps is also an Ethernet, we would compute its transfer rate to be approximately 8120 maximum-sized frames per second. The throughput in frames per second would then become:

$$R_T = \frac{1}{(1/812) + (1/8120)} = 738 \text{ frames per second}$$

Knowing the transfer rate between LANs can help us answer many common questions. It can also provide us with a mechanism for determining whether

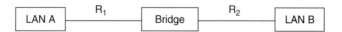

Figure 6.14 Linking LANs with different operating rates. When LANs with different operating rates (R_1 and R_2) are connected via a bridge, access of files across the bridge may result in an unacceptable level of performance.

we should alter the location of application programs on different servers. For example, suppose that a program located on a server on LAN B suddenly became popular for use by workstations on LAN A. If the program required 1024 K of storage, we could estimate the minimum transfer time required to load that program and, depending on the results of our calculation, we might want to move the program onto a server on LAN A. For this example, the data transfer rate would be 738 frames/second × 1500 bytes/frame or 1,107,000 bytes per second. Dividing the data to be transferred by the data transfer rate, we obtain:

$$\frac{1024 \text{ Kbytes} \times 1024 \text{ bytes/k}}{1,107,000 \text{ bytes/seconds}} = .95 \text{ seconds}$$

The preceding computation represents a best-case scenario, in which the use of each network is limited to the user on LAN A loading a program from a server on LAN B. In reality, the average number of users using the resources of each network must be used to adjust the values of R_1 and R_2. For example, suppose that through monitoring you determined that the average number of active users on LAN A was 5 and on LAN B was 10. In that case, you would adjust the value of R_1 by dividing 812 by 5 to obtain 162.4 and adjust the value of R_2 by dividing 8120 by 10 to obtain 812. You would then use the new values of R_1 and R_2 to obtain the average value of R_T, based on the fact that the program loading operation would be performed concurrently with other operations on each network. Thus, you would compute R_T as follows:

$$R_T = \frac{1}{(1/162.5) + (1/812)} = 135.4 \text{ frames per second}$$

6.4 LAN Switches

The incorporation of microprocessor technology into hubs can be considered as the first step in the development of switching hubs, which are now more commonly referred to as LAN switches. Through additional programming, the microprocessor could examine the destination address of each frame; however, switching capability required the addition of a switching fabric design into the hub. Once this was accomplished, it became possible to use the microprocessor to read the destination address of each frame and initiate a switching action based upon data stored in the hub's memory, which associates destination frame addresses with hub ports.

There are several basic types of LAN switches, with the major difference between each type resulting from the layer in the ISO Reference Model where switching occurs. A layer 2 switch looks into each frame to determine the destination MAC address while a layer 3 switch looks further into the frame to determine the destination network address. Similarly, a layer 4 switch looks even further into each frame to focus upon the transport layer header. Depending upon the software that supports switch operations a layer 4 switch may be programmed to make switching decisions based upon two or more criteria, such as destination IP address and port number. Thus, a layer 2 switch operates at the MAC layer and can be considered to represent a sophisticated bridge while a layer 3 switch resembles a router. In comparison, a layer 4 switch that uses multiple metrics in determining where to forward frames could function as a traffic load balancer. Layer 2, layer 3, and layer 4 operations will be covered as we examine the operation and use of LAN switches.

In this section we will first examine the rationale for LAN switches by noting the bottlenecks associated with conventional and intelligent hubs as network traffic grows. Once this is accomplished, we will focus upon the operation and usage of different types of LAN switches.

Rationale

The earliest types of Ethernet LANs were designed to use coaxial cable configured using a bus topology. The development of the hub-based 10BASE-T local area network offered a number of networking advantages over the use of coaxial cable. Some of those advantages included the use of twisted-pair cable, which is easier to use and less expensive than coaxial cable, and the ability to reconfigure, troubleshoot, and isolate network problems. By simply moving a cable connection from one port to another network, administrators can easily adjust the usage of a hub or interconnect hubs to form a new network structure. The connection of test equipment to a hub, either to a free port or by temporarily removing an existing network user, could be accomplished much easier than with a coaxial-based network. Recognizing these advantages, hub manufacturers added microprocessors to their hubs, which resulted in the introduction of a first generation of intelligent Ethernet hubs.

The first generation of intelligent hubs used the capability of a built-in microprocessor to provide a number of network management functions network administrators could use to better control the operation and usage of their network. Those functions typically include tracking the network usage level and providing summary statistics concerning the transmission of frames by different workstations, as well as providing the network administrator with the ability to segment the LAN by entering special commands recognized by the hub.

Bottlenecks

Both conventional and first-generation intelligent hubs simply duplicate frames and forward them to all nodes attached to the hub. This restricts the flow of data to one workstation at a time, since collisions occur when two or more workstations attempt to gain access to the media at the same time.

Conventional hubs, to include the first generation of intelligent hubs, create network bottlenecks, because all network traffic flows through a shared backplane. This results in every workstation connected to the hub competing for a slice of the backplane's bandwidth. For example, consider the hub illustrated in Figure 6.15, in which up to seven workstations and a file server contend for access to the network. Since only one device can transmit at any point in time, the average slice of bandwidth that each device receives is 1.25 Mbps (10 Mbps/8). The actual data transfer capability is less, since attempts by two or more workstations to simultaneously transmit can result in collisions that cause jam signals to be placed on the network, precluding other workstations from transmitting data during the duration of those signals. As more users are added to a network through the interconnection of hubs, network performance will continue to decrease as the potential for congestion increases. Thus, manufacturers of Ethernet products, as well as network administrators, focused their efforts upon developing different tools and techniques to alleviate network congestion.

Congestion-Avoidance Options

There are several techniques you can consider to alleviate network congestion. Those techniques include splitting a network into two, with each segment

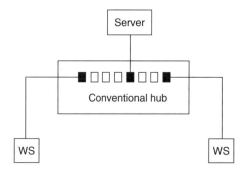

Figure 6.15 When using a conventional hub, congestion occurs when several workstations vie for access to a server.

connected to a separate server port, using bridges and dual servers, employing a router to develop a collapsed backbone network linking multiple network segments, or using one or more intelligent switches.

Network Segmentation

One of the earliest methods used to alleviate network congestion was obtained through the use of a server with an internal bridging capability. Splitting the network infrastructure into two and connecting each resulting segment to an NIC installed in a server provides the capability to reduce traffic on each segment, in comparison to traffic previously carried on a nonsegmented network.

Figure 6.16 illustrates the segmentation of a network into two on one server. NetWare, as well as other LAN operating systems, includes a capability to move packets between cable segments. This enables users on each segment to transmit and receive information from users on other segments, as well as maintain access to a common server. If server usage is low but network usage is high, this method of network subdivision represents a cost-effective method for reducing the effect of network congestion upon LAN performance.

In examining Figure 6.16, note that a workstation on each network segment can simultaneously transmit data to the server or receive data from the server. Thus, segmentation not only reduces network congestion, but in addition can double throughput if the server is capable of supporting sustained transmission to or receiving data from workstations on both segments.

Bridging

The major problem associated with the use of a server for network segmentation is the fact that it must perform internal bridging in addition to its file server operations. This usually limits the ability of the server to support network segments with a large number of workstations. In addition, the workstations on the connected segments still contend for the services of a common server. Thus, the use of a stand-alone bridge is usually the next step to

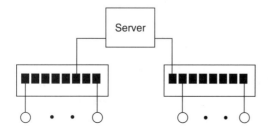

Figure 6.16 Network segmentation using a common server. Through the use of a file server that can move packets between segments, you obtain the ability to subdivide a network.

consider when the level of network usage adversely affects LAN performance, and segmentation through the use of a file server is not a viable option.

Figure 6.17 illustrates the use of a bridge for network segmentation. Although the segmentation shown in Figure 6.17 is similar to the segmentation shown in Figure 6.16, there are several distinct differences between the two methods. First, the stand-alone bridge requires file servers to be located on one or more network segments. Secondly, since a stand-alone bridge is performing the required bridging functions, more workstations can be placed on each network segment than when a file server performs bridging operations. Workstations on each segment can simultaneously access the server on each segment, permitting network throughput to double when such traffic is localized to each segment.

Using a Router

Although primarily thought of as a mechanism to interconnect geographically dispersed networks, routers can be used as switching devices to interconnect network segments located within one geographical area, such as a building or campus. The networking architecture associated with the use of a router in this manner is referred to as a collapsed backbone, since the older bus-structured Ethernet LAN is replaced by LAN segments that communicate with one another through the router. Until 1994, the primary device used in the center of a collapsed backbone network was a router. Since then, LAN switches have gradually taken over the role of routers for reasons we will discuss later in this chapter.

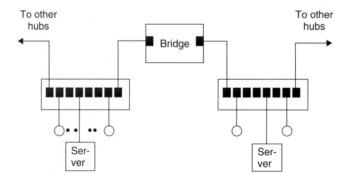

Figure 6.17 Using a bridge for network segmentation. The use of a bridge and one or more servers on each interconnected segment can significantly increase network capacity by localizing more traffic on each segment.

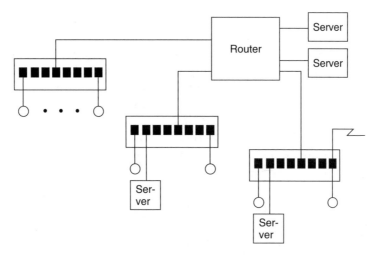

Figure 6.18 Collapsed router-based backbone. A collapsed backbone topology based upon the use of a router enables servers to be distributed based upon network access requirements.

Figure 6.18 illustrates a collapsed backbone formed through the use of a router. Note that you can locate servers on network segments for which server access is limited to workstations on the segment, and connect servers that are accessed by workstations on two or more segments to separate router ports. Thus, a router provides you with the ability to distribute network traffic based upon server access requirements. In addition, the construction of a collapsed backbone offers other benefits over distributed networks. Those advantages include the centralization of complexity and economy of operations. Rather than dispersing routers, locating a single router near a network technical control center can make network management easier. Then, if a routing problem arises, you may not have to send a technician to every location where hubs and servers are installed, since router management software may be able to pinpoint the problem. Since one router may be able to replace a number of less capable devices, you may also obtain some economic benefits from the use of a single router.

Three additional benefits associated with the use of a router for creating a collapsed backbone network are security, protocol support, and the control of broadcast traffic. Many routers have a sophisticated filtering capability, permitting you to program templates that enable only predefined applications from predefined network users to access other network segments or servers connected to the router. Concerning protocol support, many routers can support multiprotocol transmission. Thus, you could connect a router port to a mainframe and pass SNA traffic between the mainframe and workstations on different network segments, as well as switching other protocol traffic between workstations and different types of servers. Since the use of a router results in a hierarchical network structure where frames are transported based upon network addresses, this provides the ability to restrict broadcast traffic generated on one segment to that segment. Thus, service advertisements commonly generated by different types of servers can be localized to the segment where they are located instead of flowing onto other segments where they would consume bandwidth.

Although the advantages associated with the use of routers to create a collapsed backbone are considerable, their use has several disadvantages. Those disadvantages include the complexity and cost of routers, as well as the latency or delay time associated with moving packets from one network segment to another segment. Concerning router latency, although all devices have a degree of latency, the delay associated with routers greatly exceeds that of bridges. The reason for this is the fact that routers operate at the network layer while bridges operate at the data link layer. This means that a bridge can inspect the beginning of each frame to determine its destination. In comparison, a router must look into each frame to determine the destination network address. Thus, the processing rate of a router is generally 50 to 75 percent of the processing rate of a bridge.

Another problem associated with the use of routers is the *eggs in one basket* syndrome, since the failure of the router results in the inability of many network users to access servers or send messages to users on other network segments. The latter problem has been addressed by router manufacturers through redundant logic and power supplies, as well as the use of modular components that can be easily swapped out without bringing down the router when a component failure occurs. Although the latter problem is applicable to LAN switches, this device addresses some of the problems associated with the use of routers, as well as — through improved functionality — permits LAN switches to provide an enhanced level of overall network performance. Thus, let's focus our attention upon the operation and use of LAN switches in the remainder of this chapter.

LAN Switch Operations

LAN switches can be categorized in three main ways — by their method of operation, their support of single or multiple addresses per port, and the layer in the ISO Reference Model where switching occurs. The method of operation is commonly referred to as the switching *technique*, while the address-per-port support is normally referred to as the switching *method*.

The third main way of categorizing a LAN switch is based upon the type of address used as a switching decision criteria — data link layer MAC addresses, network layer network addresses or transport layer port number. Since LAN switches that support layer 3 switching actually represent a switch with a built-in routing capability, we will discuss layer 3 switches as a separate entity. We will also examine how a layer 4 LAN switch can function as an application distributor by making switching decisions based upon the port number within the transport header. Thus, we will first examine layer 2 switching hubs before focusing our attention upon layer 3 and layer 4 switches.

Layer 2 Switching

A switch that operates at the data link layer is a multiport bridge that reads MAC destination addresses and uses those addresses as a decision criterion for determining where to switch each frame. When operating at the data link layer, a LAN switch provides several distinct advantages over the use of conventional and intelligent hubs. First, a LAN switch does not transmit or regenerate data onto every port. Instead, unicast data flow is restricted to a routing from one port to a second port. This precludes a network user from operating a monitor and observing the flow of data on the network. Hence, LAN switches, although not necessarily secure devices, provide a more secure environment than a shared Ethernet LAN.

A second advantage of LAN switches is their ability to support simultaneous communication sessions. For example, consider a simple four-port LAN switch with port numbers 1, 2, 3, and 4. If a user on port 1 is switched to a server on port 3, and another user on port 2 is switched to a server on port 4, you obtain two very short-duration, simultaneous communications sessions. Thus, in this example, bandwidth is double that of a conventional hub. If the LAN switch supports only 10BASE-T operating rates, the four-port switch provides a maximum of two simultaneous cross-connections, doubling potential bandwidth to 20 Mbps. As we will note later in this chapter, many LAN switches incorporate full-duplex, Fast Ethernet, Gigabit Ethernet, and even 10 Gigabit Ethernet technology, providing bandwidth many orders of magnitude beyond that obtainable from the use of a conventional hub.

Switching Techniques There are three switching techniques used by LAN switches — cross-point, also referred to as cut-through or *on the fly*, store-and-forward, and a hybrid method which alternates between the first two methods, based upon the frame error rate. As we will soon note, each technique has one or more advantages and disadvantages associated with its operation.

Cross-Point   A cross-point switch examines the destination address of each packet entering the port. It then searches a predefined table of addresses associated with ports to obtain a port destination. Once the port destination is determined, the switch initiates the cross-connection between the incoming port and the outgoing port. Figure 6.19 illustrates cross-point/cut-through switching.

As previously noted in this chapter, a layer 2 switch can be considered to represent a more sophisticated type of bridge capable of supporting multiple simultaneous cross-connections. Thus, it should come as no surprise that a cross-point switch uses a backward learning algorithm to construct a port-destination address table. That is, the switch monitors MAC source addresses encountered on each port to construct a port-destination address table. If the destination address resides on the same port the frame was received from, this indicates that the frame's destination is on the current network and no switching operation is required. Thus, the switch discards the frame. If the destination address resides on a different port, the switch obtains the port destination and initiates a cross-connection through the switch, transferring the frame to the appropriate destination port where it is placed onto a network where a node with the indicated destination address resides. If the destination address is not found in the table, the switch floods the frame onto all ports other than the port it was received on. Although flooding adversely affects the capability of a switch to perform multiple simultaneous cross-connections, the majority of this type of activity occurs when a switch is powered on and

Figure 6.19   Cross-point/cut-through switching.

its port-address table is empty. Thereafter, flooding occurs periodically after an entry is purged from the table due to aging and a new request to a purged destination occurs, a new station becomes a recipient of traffic, or when a broadcast address is encountered.

Cross-point switching minimizes the delay or latency associated with placing a packet received on one port onto another port. Since the switching decision is made once the destination address is read, this means the full packet is not examined. Thus, a cross-point switch cannot perform error checking on a packet. This limitation does not represent a problem for most networks due to extremely low error rates on local area networks. However, when errored packets are encountered, they are passed from one network segment to another. This results in an unnecessary increase in network use on the destination segment, as a store-and-forward switch would simply discard packets containing one or more bit errors.

Latency Considerations A cross-point switching method only requires a small portion of a frame to be stored until it is able to read the destination address, perform its table lookup operation, and initiate switching to an appropriate output port. Due to this, latency is minimized.

Latency functions as a brake on two-way frame exchanges. For example, in a client/server environment the transmission of a frame by a workstation results in a server response. Thus, the minimum wait time is $2 * \text{latency}$ for each client-server exchange, lowering the effective throughput of the switch. We can compute the minimum amount of latency associated with a cross-point switch as follows. At a minimum, the switch must read 14 bytes (8 bytes for the preamble and 6 bytes for the destination address) before being able to initiate a search of its port-destination address table. At 10 Mbps we obtain:

$$9.6 \ \mu s + 14 \ \text{bytes} * 8 \ \text{bits/byte} * 100 \ \text{ns/bit}$$

or
$$9.6 \times 10^{-6} + 112 * 100 * 10^{-9}$$

or
$$20.8 * 10^{-6} \ \text{seconds}$$

Here 9.6 μs represents the Ethernet interframe gap at an operating rate of 10 Mbps, while 100 ns/bit represents the bit duration of a 10-Mbps Ethernet LAN. Thus, the minimum one-way latency not counting switch overhead of a cut-through layer 2 switch is $20.8 * 10^{-6}$ seconds, while the round-trip minimum latency would be twice that duration.

At 100 Mbps the interframe gap would be reduced to .96 μs, while the bit duration would be 10 ns. Thus, at 100 Mbps the minimum one-way latency for a cross-point switch becomes:

$$.96 \times 10^{-6} + 112 * 10 * 10^{-9}$$

or $\qquad\qquad\qquad$ $2.08 * 10^{-6}$ seconds

For Gigabit Ethernet the minimum one-way latency would be further reduced by an order of magnitude to $.208 * 10^{-6}$ seconds.

Store-and-Forward A store-and-forward LAN switch stores the full incoming packet in a buffer. This enables the switch to perform a CRC check to determine if the received packet is error-free. If it is, the switch uses the destination address of the packet to perform a table lookup to obtain the destination port address. Once that address is obtained, the switch performs a cross-connect operation and forwards the packet to its destination. Otherwise, the frame is considered to have one or more bits in error and will be discarded. Besides checking the CRC a store-and-forward switch will examine the entire frame. This enables other errors, such as runts and extended lengths (giant) frames to be caught and sent to the great bit bucket in the sky instead of being forwarded.

The storage of frames by a store-and-forward switch permits filtering against various frame fields to occur. Although a few manufacturers of store-and-forward LAN switches support different types of filtering, the primary advantage advertised by such manufacturers is data integrity and the ability to perform translation switching, such as switching a frame between an Ethernet network and a Token-Ring network. Since the translation process is extremely difficult to accomplish on the fly due to the number of conversions of frame data, most switch vendors first store the frame, resulting in store-and-forward switches supporting translation between different types of connected networks. Concerning the data integrity capability of store-and-forward switches, whether or not this is actually an advantage depends upon how you view the additional latency introduced by the storage of a full frame in memory as well as the necessity for error checking. Concerning the latter, switches should operate error-free, so a store-and-forward switch only removes network errors, which should be negligible to start with.

When a switch removes an errored frame, the originator will retransmit the frame after a period of time. Since an errored frame arriving at its destination network address is also discarded, many persons question the necessity of error checking by a store-and-forward switch. However, filtering capability, if offered, may be far more useful as you could use this capability, for example, to route protocols carried in frames to destination ports far easier than by frame destination address. This is especially true if you have hundreds or thousands of devices connected to a large switch. You might set up two or three filters instead of entering a large number of destination addresses into the switch. When a switch performs filtering of protocols, it really becomes a router. This is because it is now operating at layer 3 of the OSI Reference Model.

Figure 6.20 illustrates the operation of a store-and-forward switch. Note that a common switch design is to use shared buffer memory to store entire frames, which increases the latency associated with this type of switch. Since the minimum length of an Ethernet frame is 72 bytes, then the minimum one-way delay or latency for a 10 mbps Ethernet operation, not counting the switch overhead associated with the lookup table and switching fabric operation, becomes:

$$9.6 \ \mu\text{sec} + 72 \ \text{bytes} * 8 \ \text{bits/byte} * 100 \ \text{ns/bit}$$

or
$$9.6 * 10^{-6} + 576 * 100 * 10^{-9}$$

or
$$67.2 * 10^{-6} \ \text{seconds}$$

Once again, 9.6 μs represents the 10-Mbps Ethernet interframe gap, while 100 ns/bit is the bit duration of a 10-Mbps Ethernet LAN. Thus, the minimum one-way latency of a store-and-forward Ethernet LAN switch is .0000672 seconds, while a round-trip minimum latency is twice that duration. For a maximum-length Ethernet frame with a data field of 1500 bytes, the

Legend: ① = Packet address read as packet enters RAM

② = Full packet enters RAM; CRC computed

③ = Destination port obtained

④ = Packet forwarded from RAM to destination port

Figure 6.20   Store-and-forward switching.

frame length becomes 1526 bytes. Thus, the one-way maximum latency at 10 Mbps becomes:

$$9.6 \ \mu s + 1526 \ \text{bytes} * 8 \ \text{bits/byte} * 100 \ \text{ns/bit}$$

or
$$9.6 * 10^{-6} + 12208 * 100 * 10^{-9}$$

or
$$.0123404 \ \text{seconds}$$

At a 100 Mbps operating rate associated with Fast Ethernet the interframe gap is reduced to .96 μs while the bit duration becomes 10 ns. Thus, the one way latency for a minimum length frame becomes:

$$.96 * 10^{-6} + 576 * 10 * 10 \ 10^{-9}$$

or
$$6.72 * 10^{-6} \ \text{seconds}$$

Similarly, for a maximum length frame the one way latency at 100 Mbps becomes:

$$.96 * 10^{-6} + 12208 * 10^{-9}$$

or
$$.00123 \ \text{seconds}$$

At a Gigabit Ethernet data rate of 1 Gbps both the interframe gap and bit duration are further reduced by an order of magnitude. This results in the one way latency for a minimum length frame becoming $.672 * 10^{-6}$ seconds while the delay for a maximum length frame becomes:

$$1.23 * 10^{-4} \ \text{seconds}$$

Table 6.4 summarizes the minimum latency for cut-through and store-and-forward switches operating at 10 and 100 Mbps and 1 Gbps. You can use the entries in this table to determine the potential effect upon different applications, such as real-time video, and select a switch that can satisfy organizational requirements.

Hybrid A hybrid switch supports both cut-through and store-and-forward switching, selecting the switching method based upon monitoring the error rate encountered by reading the CRC at the end of each frame and comparing its value with a computed CRC performed on the fly on the fields protected by the CRC. Initially the switch might set each port to a cut-through mode of operation. If too many bad frames are noted occurring on the port the switch will automatically set the frame processing mode to store-and-forward, permitting the CRC comparison to be performed before the frame being forwarded. This permits frames in error to be discarded without having them pass through the switch. Since the switch, no pun intended, between cut-through and store-and-forward modes of operation occurs adaptively, another term used to reference the operation of this type of switch is adaptive.

The major advantages of a hybrid switch are that it provides minimal latency when error rates are low and discards frames by adapting to a store-and-forward switching method so it can discard errored frames when the frame error rate rises. From an economic perspective, the hybrid switch can logically be expected to cost a bit more than a cut-through or store-and-forward switch as its software development effort is a bit more comprehensive. However, due to the competitive market for communications products upon occasion its price may be reduced below competitive switch technologies.

Switching Methods   LAN switches can be classified with respect to their support of single or multiple addresses per port. The support of a single address per port is referred to as *port-based* switching, while the support of multiple addresses per port is referred to as *segment-based* switching.

Port-Based Switching   A port-based LAN switch can be considered to operate similar to an $n \times n$ matrix switch, reading the destination address of incoming frames from a single device connected to the port and using that address through a table lookup process to initiate a cross-connect to a destination port.

Figure 6.21 illustrates an example of port-based switching. Since each connected node is isolated from other nodes except when simultaneously

TABLE 6.4   Cut-through and Store-and-forward Minimum Switch Latency

Switch/Operating Rate	Latency (seconds)	
	Minimum Length Frame	Minimum Length Frame
Cut-through		
10 Mbps	$20.8 * 10^{-6}$	$20.8 * 10^{-6}$
100 Mbps	$2.08 * 10^{-6}$	$2.08 * 10^{-6}$
1 Gbps	$.208 * 10^{-6}$	$.208 * 10^{-6}$
Store-and-forward		
10 Mbps	$67.2 * 10^{-6}$	$1.2304 * 10^{-2}$
100 Mbps	$6.72 * 10^{-6}$	$.12304 * 10^{-2}$
1 Gbps	$.672 * 10^{-6}$	$.012304 * 10^{-2}$

Figure 6.21 Port-based switching. In port-based switching only a single address per port is supported, restricting switching to one device per port.

contending for access to the same destination port, the resulting network throughput can be considerably higher than a shared Ethernet network. For example, user 1 could communicate with server 1, user 2 with server 2, and so on, all simultaneously. In this *best case* example, with n users and n servers, the operating rate through the switch becomes $n \times 10$ Mbps, or n times the operating rate of a conventional Ethernet network.

It is important to compare the maximum potential throughput through a switch with its rated backplane speed. If the maximum potential throughput is less than the rated backplane speed, the switch will not cause delays based upon the traffic being routed through the device. For example, consider a 64-port switch that has a backplane speed of 400 Mbps. If the maximum port rate is 10 Mbps, then the maximum throughput assuming 32 active cross-connections were simultaneously established becomes 320 Mbps. In this example the switch has a backplane transfer capability sufficient to handle the worst-case data transfer scenario. Now let's assume that the maximum backplane data transfer capability was 200 Mbps. This would reduce the maximum number of simultaneous cross-connections capable of being serviced to 20 instead of 32 and adversely affect switch performance under certain operational conditions.

Since a port-based switch only has to store one address per port, search times are minimized. When combined with a pass-through or cut-through switching technique, this type of switch results in a minimal latency to include the overhead of the switch in determining the destination port of a frame.

Segment-Based Switching A segment-based switch permits switched connectivity between multiple LAN segments, by supporting multiple addresses per port. The key difference between a segment-based switch and a port-based switch is in their ability to support multiple addresses per port. A port-based layer 2 switch only supports one MAC address per port. In comparison, a segment-based layer 2 switch supports multiple addresses per port, enabling it to support the direct connection of a single workstation or server as well as the connection of a segment to each port on the switch.

Figure 6.22 illustrates an example of a segment-based switch. Note that ports that support the connection of a segment must support switching for multiple MAC addresses. In examining the segment-based switching example illustrated in Figure 6.22, also note that workstations on each segment contend for access to n servers. Since a group of users is connected to the switch via a conventional hub, throughput is limited by the conventional hubs. In this example, two hubs would limit throughput of the network to 20 Mbps if a user on each segment accessed a different server. In comparison, a port-based switch can provide a higher throughput, since each network user is directly connected to a port on the switch. The primary advantage of a segment-based LAN switch is cost, since a few ports can be used to support network segments containing a large number of LAN users.

Switching Processor The construction of intelligent switches varies both between manufacturers as well as within some vendor product lines. Most switches are based upon the use of either reduced instruction set computer (RISC) microprocessors or application-specific integrated circuit (ASIC) chips, while a few products use conventional complex instruction set computer (CISC) microprocessors.

Although there are a large number of arguable advantages and disadvantages associated with each architecture from the standpoint of the switch

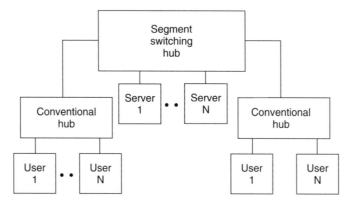

Figure 6.22 Segment-based switching. A segment-based switching technique requires each port to support multiple MAC addresses.

manufacturer that are beyond the scope of this book, there are also some key considerations that warrant discussion with respect to evolving technology, such as virtual LANs. Both RISC and CISC architectures enable switches to be programmed to make forwarding decisions based upon either the data link layer or network layer address information. In addition, when there is a need to modify the switch such as to enable it to support a vLAN standard, this architecture is easily upgradable.

In comparison to RISC- and CISC-based switches, an ASIC-based device represents the use of custom-designed chips to perform specific switch functions in hardware. Although ASIC-based switches are faster than RISC- and CISC-based switches, there is no easy way to upgrade this type of switch. Instead, the vendor will have to design and manufacture new chips and install the hardware upgrade in the switch.

Today most switches use an ASIC architecture, as its speed enables the support of cut-through switching. While ASIC-based switches provide the speed necessary to minimize latency, readers should carefully check vendor upgrade support as support for adding load balancing and other functions to a LAN switch can be expected to require modifications to existing switches.

Now that we have an appreciation for the general operation and use of LAN switches, let's obtain an appreciation for the high-speed operation of switch ports, which enables dissimilar types of networks to be connected and which can result in data flow compatibility problems along with methods used to alleviate such problems.

High-Speed Port Operations There are several types of high-speed port connections switches may support. Those high-speed connections include 100-Mbps Fast Ethernet, 1-Gbps and 10-Gbps Gigabit Ethernet, 100-Mbps FDDI, 155-Mbps ATM, full-duplex Ethernet and Token-Ring, and fat pipes, with the latter referencing a grouping of ports treated as a transmission entity. Another common name used in place of the term fat pipe is trunk group. The most common use of one or more high-speed connections on a switch is to support highly used devices, such as network servers and printers as well as for obtaining a backbone LAN connection capability. Figure 6.23 illustrates the use of an Ethernet switch, with two 100BASE-T Fast Ethernet adapters built into the switch to provide a high-speed connection from the switch to each server. Through the use of high-speed connections the cross-connection time from a server to client when the server responds to a client query is minimized. Since most client queries result in server responses containing many multiples of characters in the client query, this allows the server to respond to more queries per unit of time. Thus, the high-speed connection

Figure 6.23 Using high-speed connections to servers.

can enhance client/server response times through a switch. In examining Figure 6.23, let's assume a small query results in the server responding by transmitting the contents of a large file back to the client. If data flows into the switch at 100 Mbps and flows from the switch to the client at 10 Mbps, any buffer area in the switch used to provide temporary storage for speed incompatibilities between ports will rapidly be filled and eventually overflow, resulting in the loss of frames which, when compensated for by retransmission, compounds the problem. Thus, a mechanism is required to regulate the flow of data into and out of switch ports. That mechanism is known as flow control, and specific methods used to implement flow control will be covered later in this chapter when we discuss switch features.

Thus for now we can note that the LAN switch is a highly versatile device that may support single or multiple devices per port and whose operation can vary based upon its architecture. By providing the capability for supporting multiple simultaneous cross-connections, the LAN switch can significantly increase network bandwidth, and its ability to support high-speed network connections enhances its versatility. Now that we have a basic appreciation for the operational characteristics of generic Ethernet LAN switches, we can use that information as a base and focus our attention upon the operation of Ethernet switches.

Switch Operations Although features incorporated into Ethernet switches considerably differ between vendors as well as within vendor product lines, upon occasion we can categorize this communications device by the operating rate of the ports they support. Doing so results in six basic types of Ethernet switches which are listed in Table 6.5. Switches that are restricted to operating at a relatively low data rate are commonly used for departmental operations, while switches that support a mixed data rate are commonly used in a tiered network structure at a higher layer in the tier than switches that operate at a low uniform data rate. Concerning the latter, when used in a tiered network structure the lower uniform operating rate switch is commonly used at the lower level in the tier. One item that warrants attention in Table 6.5 is the last entry in the table. At the time this book was prepared 10 Gbps ports were restricted to one or two per switch and it could be several years before a switch is available with ports that all operate at 10 Gbps.

Multi-Tier Network Construction

Figure 6.24 illustrates the generic use of a two-tiered Ethernet switch−based network, with the switch at the higher tier functioning as a backbone connectivity mechanism, which enables access to shared servers commonly known as global servers by users across departmental boundaries, while switches in the lower tier facilitate access to servers shared within a specific department. This hierarchical networking structure is commonly used with a higher-speed Ethernet switch such as a Fast Ethernet or Gigabit Ethernet switch, or with other types of backbone switches, such as FDDI and ATM, as well as with other types of lower-tier switches. One common variation associated with the use of a tiered switch−based network is the placement of both departmental and global servers on an upper-tier switch. This placement allows all servers to be colocated in a common area for ease of access and control and is commonly referred to as a server farm. However, if an upper-tier switch should fail,

TABLE 6.5   Types of Ethernet Switches Based upon Port Operating Rates

All ports operate at 10 Mbps.

Mixed 10-/100-Mbps port operation.

All ports operate at 100 Mbps.

Mixed 10-/100-/1000-Mbps port operation.

All ports operate at 1000 Mbps.

Mixed 10-/100-/1000/10000 Mbps port operation.

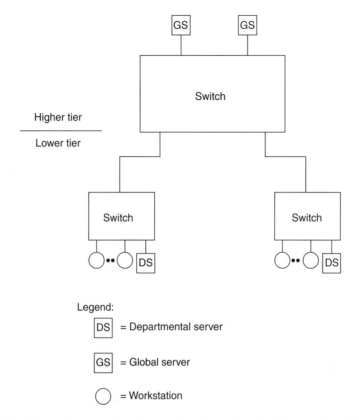

Figure 6.24 Generic construction of a two-tiered Ethernet switch–based network.

access to all servers could be affected, representing a significant disadvantage of this design. A second major disadvantage is the fact that all traffic has to be routed through at least two switches when a server farm is constructed. In comparison, when servers primarily used by departmental employees are connected to a switch serving departmental users, most traffic remains local to the local switch at the bottom of the tier.

With the introduction of Gigabit Ethernet switches it becomes possible to use this type of switch in either a multitier architecture as previously shown in Figure 6.24 or as a star-based backbone. Concerning the latter, Figure 6.25 illustrates the potential use of a Gigabit Ethernet switch that supports a mixture of 100-Mbps and 1-Gbps ports. In this example the Gigabit Ethernet switch is shown being used to support two fat pipes or trunk groups, with one trunk group consisting of four 100-Mbps ports, while the second group

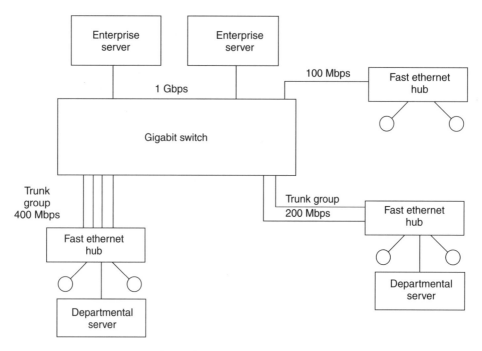

Figure 6.25 Using a Gigabit Ethernet switch as a star-based backbone switch.

consists of two 100-Mbps ports. To enable each grouping requires the use of switches from the same vendor since the establishment of fat pipes or trunk groups is a proprietary feature and not yet standardized.

In examining Figure 6.25 note that enterprise servers are connected to the Gigabit switch, while department servers are connected to 100-Mbps Fast Ethernet hubs. By connecting 10BASE-T LAN switches to Fast Ethernet hubs you could extend the star into a star-tiered network structure.

6.5 Switch Basic Architecture

Regardless of the operating rate of each port on an Ethernet switch, most devices are designed in a similar manner. That is, most switches consist of a chassis into which a variety of cards are inserted, similar in many respects to the installation of cards into the system expansion slots of personal computers.

Components

Modular Ethernet switches that are scalable commonly support CPU, logic, matrix, and port cards.

CPU Card

The CPU card commonly manages the switch, identifies the types of LANs attached to switch ports, and performs self and directed switch tests.

Logic Module

The logic module is commonly responsible for comparing the destination address of frames read on a port against a table of addresses it is responsible for maintaining, and instructing the matrix module to initiate a cross-bar switch once a comparison of addresses results in the selection of a destination port address.

Matrix Module

The matrix module of a switch can be considered to represent a cross-bar of wires from each port to each port as illustrated in Figure 6.26. Upon

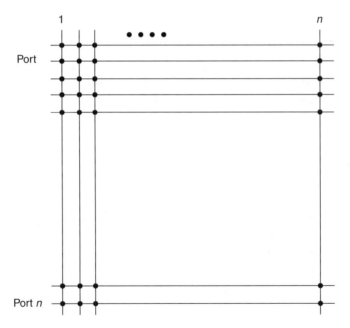

Figure 6.26 The key to the operation of a switch is a matrix module which enables each port to be cross-connected to other ports. The matrix module of a switch with n ports can be considered to represent an $n \times n$ star-wired backplane.

receipt of an instruction from a logic module, the matrix module initiates a cross-connection between the source and destination port for the duration of the frame.

Port Module

The port module can be considered to represent a cluster of physical interfaces to which either individual stations or network segments are connected based upon whether the switch supports single or multiple MAC addresses per port. Some port modules permit a mixture of port cards to be inserted, resulting in, as an example, 10 and 100 Mbps as well as full-duplex connections to be supported. In comparison, other port modules are only capable of supporting one type of LAN connection. In addition, there are significant differences between vendor port modules concerning the number of ports supported. Some modules are limited to supporting two or four ports, while other modules may support six, eight, or ten ports. It should be noted that many switches support other types of LAN port modules such as Token-Ring, FDDI, and even ATM.

Redundancy

In addition to the previously mentioned modules, most switches also support single and redundant power supply modules and may also support redundant matrix and logic modules. Figure 6.27 illustrates a typical Ethernet modular switch chassis showing the installation of 11 modules to include five 8-port modules to form a 40-port switch.

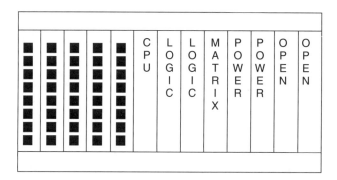

Figure 6.27 A typical Ethernet modular switch chassis containing a mixture of port, CPU, logic, matrix, and power cards.

Switch Features

There are literally an ever expanding number of features being incorporated into Ethernet switches. Those features range from providing such basic functions as port and segment switching to methods developed by some vendors to prevent erroneous frames from being transferred through the switch in a cut-through mode of operation. In this section we will review 19 distinct switch features, which are summarized in alphabetical order in Table 6.6.

The table of features presented was constructed not only to list features you should note, but, in addition, as a mechanism to facilitate the evaluation of switches. That is, you can indicate your requirement for a particular feature and then note whether or not that requirement can be satisfied by different vendor products by replacing *Vendor A* and *Vendor B* by the names of switches you are evaluating. By duplicating this table, you can extend the two rightmost columns to evaluate more than two products. As we examine each feature listed in Table 6.6, our degree of exploration will be based upon whether or not the feature was previously described. If the feature was previously described in this chapter, we will limit our discussion to a brief review of the feature. Otherwise we will discuss its operation in considerable detail.

Address Table Size Support

The ability of a switch to correctly forward packets to their intended direction depends upon the use of address tables. Similarly, the capability of a switch to support a defined number of workstations depends upon the number of entries that can be placed in its address table. Thus, the address table size can be viewed as a constraint that affects the ability of a switch to support network devices.

There are two address table sizes you may have to consider—the number of addresses supported per port and the number of addresses supported per switch. The first address table constraint is only applicable for ports that support the connection of network segments. In comparison, the total number of addresses recognized per switch represents a constraint that affects the entire switch. Many Ethernet switches support up to 1024 addresses per port for segment-based support. Such switches may only support a total of 8192 addresses per switch. This means that a 16-port switch with 8 fully populated segments could not support the use of the 8 remaining ports as the switch would run out of address table entries. Thus, it is important to consider the number of addresses supported per port and per switch as well as match such data against your anticipated requirements.

TABLE 6.6 Ethernet Switch Features

Feature	Requirement	Vendor A	Vendor B
Address table size support			
Addresses/port	_____	_____	_____
Addresses/switch	_____	_____	_____
Aging settings	_____	_____	_____
Architecture			
ASIC-based	_____	_____	_____
CISC-based	_____	_____	_____
RISC-based	_____	_____	_____
Autonegotiation ports	_____	_____	_____
Backplane transfer capacity	_____	_____	_____
Error prevention	_____	_____	_____
Fat pipe and trunk group	_____	_____	_____
Filtering/forwarding rate support	_____	_____	_____
Filtering rate	_____	_____	_____
Forwarding rate	_____	_____	_____
Flow control			
Backpressure	_____	_____	_____
Software drivers	_____	_____	_____
802.3x flow control	_____	_____	_____
No control	_____	_____	_____
Full-duplex port operation	_____	_____	_____
Jabber control	_____	_____	_____
Latency	_____	_____	_____
Management	_____	_____	_____
Mirrored port	_____	_____	_____
Module insertion	_____	_____	_____
Port buffer size	_____	_____	_____
Port module support	_____	_____	_____
Spanning tree support	_____	_____	_____
Switch type			
Port-based switch	_____	_____	_____
Segment-based switch	_____	_____	_____

TABLE 6.6   (*Continued*)

Feature	Requirement	Vendor A	Vendor B
Switching mode			
Cut-through	_____	_____	_____
Store-and-forward	_____	_____	_____
Hybrid	_____	_____	_____
Virtual LAN support	_____	_____	_____
Port-based	_____	_____	_____
MAC-based	_____	_____	_____
Layer 3–based	_____	_____	_____
Rule-based	_____	_____	_____

Aging Settings

As explained earlier in this book when we discussed the operation of bridges, MAC addresses and their associated ports are stored with a time stamp value. This provides the bridge with the ability to purge old entries to make room for new entries in the port-address table. Since a switch is a multiport bridge, it also uses a timer to purge old entries from its port-address table. Some switches provide users with the ability to set the aging time within a wide range of values or to disable aging. Other switches have a series of predefined aging values from which a user can select.

Architecture

As previously noted, there are three basic methods used to construct LAN switches. Those methods include the use of application-specific integrated circuits (ASICs), complex or conventional instruction set computers (CISCs), and reduced instruction set computers (RISCs). Although the use of an ASIC-based architecture commonly results in a very low latency and high level of performance, upgrades are difficult to accomplish as such circuits must be replaced. In comparison, both conventional microprocessor and RISC-based switches use instructions in replaceable ROM. Although the differences may appear trivial, if an ASIC-based switch, for example, requires an upgrade you would probably require a technician to visit your site to perform the upgrade. In comparison, you might be able to simply download a new software release from the vendor's World Wide Web site or electronic bulletin board to update a RISC- or CISC-based switch.

Autonegotiation Ports

To provide a mechanism to migrate from 10 Mbps to 100 Mbps, National Semiconductor developed a chip set known as NWay, which provides an automatic data rate sensing capability as part of an autonegotiation function. This capability enables a switch port to support either a 10- or 100-Mbps Ethernet attachment to the port; however, this feature only works when cabled to a 10-/100-Mbps network adapter card. You may otherwise have to use the switch console to configure the operating rate of the port or the port may be fixed to a predefined operating rate.

Backplane Transfer Capacity

The backplane transfer capacity of a switch provides you with the ability to determine how well the device can support a large number of simultaneous cross-connections, as well as its ability to perform flooding. For example, consider a 64-port 10BASE-T switch with a backplane transfer capacity of 400 Mbps. Since the switch can support a maximum of 64/2 or 32 cross connects, the switch's backplane must provide at least a $32 * 10$ Mbps or 320 transfer capacity. However, when it encounters an unknown destination address on one port, the switch will output or flood the packet onto all ports other than the port the frame was received on. Thus, to operate in a nonblocked mode the switch must have a buffer transfer capacity of $64 * 10$ Mbps or 640 Mbps.

Error Prevention

Some switch designers recognize that the majority of runt frames (frames improperly terminated) result from a collision occurring during the time it takes to read the first 64 bytes of the frame. On a 10-Mbps Ethernet LAN this is equivalent to a time of 51.2 μs. In a cut-through switch environment when latency is minimized, it becomes possible to pass runt frames to the destination. To preclude this from happening, some switch designers permit the user to introduce a 51.2-μs delay, which provides sufficient time for the switch to verify that the frame is of sufficient length to have a high degree of probability that it is not a runt frame. Other switches that operate in the cut-through mode may simply impose a 51.2-μs delay at 10 Mbps to enable this error prevention feature. Regardless of the method used, the delay is only applicable to cut-through switches that support LAN segments, as single user ports do not generate collisions.

Fat Pipe and Trunk Group

A fat pipe is a term used to reference a high-speed port. When 10BASE-T switches were first introduced, the term actually referenced a group of two or more ports operating as an entity. Today a fat pipe can reference a 100-Mbps port on a switch primarily consisting of 10-Mbps operating ports or a 1-Gbps or 10-Gbps port on a switch that contains a mixture of lower-speed and Gigabit or 10 Gigabit Ethernet ports. In addition, some vendors retain the term fat pipe as a reference to a group of ports operating as an entity while other vendors use the term trunk group to represent a group of ports that function as an entity. However, to support a grouping of ports operating as a common entity requires the interconnected switches to be obtained from the same company as the method used to group ports is currently proprietary.

Filtering and Forwarding Rate Support

The ability of a switch to interpret a number of frame destination addresses during a defined time interval is referred to as its filtering rate. In comparison, the number of frames that must be routed through a switch during a predefined period of time is referred to as the forwarding rate. Both the filtering and forwarding rates govern the performance level of a switch with respect to its ability to interpret and route frames. When considering these two metrics, it is important to understand the maximum frame rate on an Ethernet LAN, which was discussed earlier in this book.

Flow Control

Flow control represents the orderly regulation of transmission. In a switched network environment, there are a number of situations for which flow control can be used to prevent the loss of data and subsequent retransmissions, which can create a cycle of lost data followed by retransmissions. The most common cause of lost data results from a data rate mismatch between source and destination ports. For example, consider a server connected to a switch via a Fast Ethernet 100-Mbps connection, which responds to a client query when the client is connected to a switch port at 10 Mbps. Without the use of a buffer within the switch, this speed mismatch would always result in the loss of data. Through the use of a buffer, data can be transferred into the switch at 100 Mbps and transferred out at 10 Mbps. However, since the input rate is 10 times the output rate, the buffer will rapidly fill. In addition, if the server is transferring a large quantity of data the buffer could overflow, resulting in subsequent data sent to the switch being lost. Thus, unless the length of the buffer is infinite, an impossible situation, there would always be some probability that data could be lost.

Another common cause of lost data is when multiple source port inputs are contending for access to the same destination port. If each source and destination port operates at the same data rate, then only two source ports contending for access to the same destination port can result in the loss of data. Thus, a mechanism is required to regulate the flow of data through a switch. That mechanism is flow control.

All Ethernet switches this author is familiar with have either buffers in each port, or centralized memory that functions as a buffer. The key difference between switch buffers is in the amount of memory used. Some switches have 128K, 256 Kbytes, or even 1 or 2 Mbytes per port, whereas other switches may support the temporary storage of 10 or 20 full-length Ethernet frames. To prevent buffer overflow four techniques are used — backpressure, proprietary software, IEEE 802.3x flow control, and no control. Thus, let's examine each technique.

Backpressure   Backpressure represents a technique by which a switch generates a false collision signal. In actuality, the switch port operates as if it detected a collision and initiates the transmission of a jam pattern. The jam pattern consists of 32 to 48 bits that can have any value other than the CRC value that corresponds to any partial frame transmitted before the jam.

The transmission of the jam pattern ensures that the collision lasts long enough to be detected by all stations on the network. In addition, the jam signal serves as a mechanism to cause nontransmitting stations to wait until the jam signal ends before attempting to transmit, alleviating additional potential collisions from occurring. Although the jam signal temporarily stops transmission, enabling the contents of buffers to be output, the signal also adversely affects all stations connected to the port. Thus, a network segment consisting of a number of stations connected to a switch port would result in all stations having their transmission capability suspended, even when just one station was directing traffic to the switch.

Backpressure is commonly implemented based upon the level of buffer memory used. When buffer memory is filled to a predefined level, that level serves as a threshold for the switch to generate jam signals. Then, once the buffer is emptied beyond another lower level, that level serves as a threshold to disable backpressure operations.

Proprietary Software Drivers   Software drivers enable a switch to directly communicate with an attached device. This enables the switch to enable and disable the station's transmission capability. Currently, software drivers are available as a NetWare Loadable Module (NLM) for NetWare servers, and may be available for Windows XP by the time you read this book.

IEEE 802.3x Flow Control   During 1997 the IEEE standardized a method that provides flow control on full-duplex Ethernet connections. To provide this capability, a special pause frame was defined that is transmitted by devices that want to stop the flow of data from the device at the opposite end of the link.

Figure 6.28 illustrates the format of the pause frame. Since a full-duplex connection has a device on each end of the link, the use of a predefined destination address and operation code (OpCode) defines the frame as a pause frame. The value following the OpCode defines the time in terms of slot times that the transmitting device wants its partner to pause. This initial pause time can be extended by additional pause frames containing new slot time values or canceled by another pause frame containing a zero slot time value. The PAD field shown at the end of the pause frame must have each of its 42 bytes set to zero.

Under the 802.3x standard, the use of pause frames is autonegotiated on copper media and can be manually configured for use on fiber links. The actual standard does not require a device capable of sending a pause frame to actually do so. Instead, it provides a standard for recognizing a pause frame as well as a mechanism for interpreting the contents of the frame so a receiver can correctly respond to it.

The IEEE 802.3x flow control standard is applicable to all versions of Ethernet from 10 Mbps to 10 Gbps; however, the primary purpose of this standard is to enable switches to be manufactured with a minimal amount of memory. By supporting the IEEE 802.3x standard, a switch with a limited amount of memory can generate pause frames to regulate inbound traffic instead of having to drop frames when its buffer is full.

No Control   Some switch vendors rely upon the fact that the previously described traffic patterns that can result in buffers overflowing and the loss of

Destination address 01–C2–80–00–00–01 (6 bytes)	Source address (6 bytes)	Type 8808 (2 bytes)	OpCode 0001 (2 bytes)	Pause.time (slot times) (2 bytes)	PAD (42 bytes)

Figure 6.28   The IEEE 802.3x pause frame.

data have a relatively low probability of occurrence for any significant length of time. In addition, upper layers of the OSI Reference Model will retransmit lost packets. Thus, some switch vendors rely upon the use of memory buffers and do not incorporate flow control into their products. Whether or not this is an appropriate solution will depend upon the traffic you anticipate flowing through the switch.

Full-Duplex Port Operation

If a switch port only supports the connection of one station, a collision can never occur. Recognizing this fact, most Ethernet switch vendors now support full-duplex or bidirectional traffic flow by using two of the four wire connections for 10BASE-T for transmission in the opposite direction. Full-duplex support is available for 10BASE-T, Fast Ethernet, and Gigabit Ethernet connections. Since collisions can occur on a segment, switch ports used for segment-based switching cannot support full-duplex transmission.

In addition to providing a simultaneous bidirectional data flow capability, the use of full duplex permits an extension of cabling distances. This extension of cabling distance becomes possible since the CSMA/CD mode of operation is no longer followed. This means we do not need to be concerned about the number of bit times in a collision diameter. Thus, the governing parameter is not the distance a signal can be driven prior to attenuation and distortion rending the signal unrecognizable. For example, at 100 Mbps the use of a fiber cable for full-duplex operations can support a distance of 2000 meters, while only 412 meters is supported using half-duplex transmission via fiber.

Due to the higher cost of full-duplex ports and adapter cards, you should carefully evaluate the potential use of FDX before using this capability. For example, most client workstations will obtain a minimal gain through the use of a full-duplex capability since humans operating computers rarely perform simultaneous two-way operations. Thus, other than speeding acknowledgments associated with the transfer of data, the use of an FDX connection for workstations represents an excessive capacity that should only be considered when vendors are competing for sales, and as such, they provide this capability as a standard. In comparison, the use of an FDX transmission capability to connect servers to switch ports enables a server to respond to one request while receiving a subsequent request. Thus, the ability to use the capability of FDX transmission is enhanced by using this capability on server-to-switch port connections.

Although vendors would like you to believe that FDX doubles your transmission capability, in actuality you will only obtain a fraction of this advertised throughput. This is because most network devices, to include servers that are provided with an FDX transmission capability, only use that capability a fraction of the time.

Jabber Control

A jabber is an Ethernet frame whose length exceeds 1518 bytes. Jabbers are commonly caused by defective hardware or collisions, and can adversely affect a receiving device by its misinterpretation of data in the frame. A switch operating in the cut-through mode with jabber control will truncate the frame to an appropriate length. In comparison, a store-and-forward switch will normally automatically drop a jabbered frame.

Latency

When examining vendor specifications, the best word of advice is to be suspicious of latency notations, especially those concerning store-and-forward switches. Many vendors do not denote the length of the frame used for latency measurements, while some vendors use what might be referred to as creative accounting when computing latency. Thus, let's review the formal definition of latency. Latency can be defined as the difference in time (t) from the first bit arriving at a source port to the first bit output on the destination port. Modern cut-through switches have a latency of approximately 40 μs, while store-and-forward switches have a latency between 80 and 90 ms for a 72-byte frame, and between 1250 and 1300 ms for a maximum-length 1500-byte frame.

For a store-and-forward Ethernet switch an entire frame is first stored. Since the maximum length of an Ethernet frame is 1526 bytes, this means that the maximum latency for a store-and-forward 10-Mbps Ethernet switch is:

$$\frac{1526 \text{ bytes} * 8 \text{ bits/byte}}{10 \text{ Mbps}} \quad \text{or } 1.2208 \text{ ms}$$

plus the time required to perform a table lookup and cross-connection between source and destination ports. Since a 10-Mbps Ethernet LAN has a 9.6-μs gap between frames, this means that the minimum delay time between frames flowing through a cut-through switch is 20.8 μs. At 100 Mbps the total cut-through delay would be 2.08 μs, while at 1 Gbps the total delay would be 0.208 μs. Figure 6.29 illustrates the composition of this delay at a 10-Mbps operating rate. For a store-and-forward 10BASE-T switch, considering the 9.6-μs gap between frames results in a maximum latency of 12304 μs plus the time required to perform a table lookup and initiate a cross-connection between

Figure 6.29 Switch latency includes a built-in delay resulting from the structure of the Ethernet frame.

source and destination ports. As noted earlier in this section, at 100 Mbps the maximum latency would be one-tenth, or 1230.4 μs, while at 1 Gbps the delay would be reduced by another order of magnitude to 123.04 μs.

Management

The most common method used to provide switch management involves the integration of RMON support for each switch port. This enables an SNMP console to obtain statistics from the RMON group or groups supported by each switch. Since the retrieval of statistics on a port-by-port basis can be time-consuming, most switches that support RMON also create a database of statistics to facilitate their retrieval.

Mirrored Port

A mirrored port is a port that duplicates traffic on another port. For traffic analysis and intrusive testing, the ability to mirror data exiting the switch on one port to a port to which test equipment is connected can be a very valuable feature.

Module Insertion

Modular switches support two different methods of module insertion — switch power down and hot. As their names imply, a switch power down method requires you to first deactivate the switch and literally bring it down. In comparison, the ability to perform hot insertions enables you to add modules to an operating switch without adversely affecting users.

Port Buffer Size

Switch designers incorporate buffer memory into port cards as a mechanism to compensate for the difference between the internal speed of the switch and the operating rate of an end station or segment connected to the port. Some switch designers increase the amount of buffer memory incorporated into port cards to use in conjunction with a flow control mechanism, while other switch designers may use port buffer memory as a substitute for flow control. If used only as a mechanism for speed compensation, the size of port buffers may be limited to a few thousand bytes of storage. When used in conjunction with a flow control mechanism or as a flow control mechanism, the amount of buffer memory per port may be up to 64, 128, or 256 Kbytes, perhaps even up to 1 or 2 Mbytes. Although you might expect more buffer memory to provide better results, this may not necessarily be true. For example, assume a workstation on a segment is connected to a port that has a large buffer with just enough free memory to accept one frame. When the workstation transmits a sequence of frames only the first is able to be placed into the buffer. If the switch then initiates flow control as the contents of its port buffer is emptied, subsequent frames are barred from moving through the switch. When the switch disables flow control, it is possible that another station with data to transmit is able to gain access to the port before the station that sent frame one in a sequence of frames. Due to the delay in emptying the contents of a large buffer, it becomes possible that subsequent frames are sufficiently delayed as they move through a switch to a mainframe via a gateway that a time-dependent session could time out. Thus, you should consider your network structure in conjunction with the operating rate of switch ports and the amount of buffer storage per port to determine if an extremely large amount of buffer storage could potentially result in session time-outs. Fortunately, most switch manufacturers limit port buffer memory to 128 Kbytes, which at 10 Mbps results in a maximum delay of

$$\frac{128 * 1024 * 8 \text{ bits/byte}}{10 \text{ Mbps}}$$

or .10 seconds. At 100 Mbps, the maximum delay is reduced to .01 second, while at 1 Gbps the delay becomes .001 second.

Port Module Support

Although many Ethernet switches are limited to supporting only Ethernet networks, the type of networks supported can considerably differ between vendor products as well as within a specific vendor product line. Thus, you may wish to examine the support of port modules for connecting 10BASE-2, 10BASE-5, 10BASE-T, 100BASE-T LANs, and Gigabit and 10 Gigabit Ethernet devices. In addition, if your organization supports different types of LANs or is considering the use of switches to form a tier-structured network using a different type of high-speed backbone, you should examine port support for FDDI, full-duplex Token-Ring, and ATM connectivity. Many modular Ethernet switches include the ability to add translating bridge modules, enabling support for several different types of networks through a common chassis.

Spanning Tree Support

Ethernet networks use the spanning tree algorithm to prevent loops that, if enabled, could result in the continuous replication of frames. In a bridged network, spanning tree support is accomplished by the use of bridge protocol data units (BPDUs), which enable bridges to select a root bridge and agree upon a network topology that preclude loops from occurring. Since a switch in effect represents a sophisticated bridge, we would want to preclude the use of multiple switches from forming a loop. For example, consider Figure 6.30, which illustrates the use of two switches to interconnect two LANs. If both switches were active, a frame from the client connected on LAN A destined to the server on LAN B would be placed back onto LAN A by switch S1, causing a packet loop and the replication of the packet, a situation we want to avoid. By incorporating spanning tree support into each switch, they can communicate with one another to construct a topology that does not contain loops. For example, one switch in Figure 6.30 would place a port in a blocking

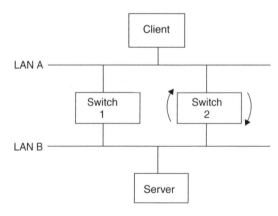

Figure 6.30   The need for loop control.

mode while the other switch would have both ports in a forwarding mode of operation.

To obtain the ability to control the spanning tree, most switches permit a number of parameters to be altered from their management console. Those parameters include the forwarding delay that governs the time the switch will wait before forwarding a packet, the aging time the switch waits for the receipt of a hello packet before initiating a topology change, the Hello time interval between the transmission of BPDU frames, and the path cost assigned to each port.

Switch Type

As previously discussed, a switch will either support one or multiple addresses per port. If it supports one address per port, it is a port-based switch. In comparison, if it supports multiple addresses per switch, it is considered to be a segment-based switch, even if only one end station is connected to some or all ports on the switch.

Switching Mode

Ethernet switches can be obtained to operate in a cut-through, store-and-forward, or hybrid operating mode. As previously discussed in this section, the hybrid mode of operation represents toggling between cut-through and store-and-forward based upon a frame error rate threshold. That is, a hybrid switch might initially be set to operate in a cut-through mode and compute the CRC for each frame on-the-fly, comparing its computed values with the CRCs appended to each frame. When a predefined frame error threshold is reached, the switch would change its operating mode to store-and-forward, enabling erroneous frames to be discarded. Some switch vendors reference a hybrid switch mode as an error-free cut-through operating mode.

Virtual LAN Support

A virtual LAN can be considered to represent a broadcast domain created through the association of switch ports, MAC addresses, or a network layer parameter. Thus, there are three basic types of vLAN creation methods you can evaluate when examining the functionality of an Ethernet switch. In addition, some vendors now offer a rules-based vLAN creation capability, which enables users to have an almost infinite number of vLAN creation methods with the ability to go down to the bit level within a frame as a mechanism for vLAN associations. Although port-based vLANs were standardized by the IEEE under the 802.1Q specification during the late 1990s, other vLAN creation methods currently represent proprietary vendor-specific solutions.

Switched-Based Virtual LANs

As briefly mentioned in our review of switch features, a virtual LAN or vLAN can be considered to represent a broadcast domain. This means that transmission generated by one station assigned to a vLAN is only received by those stations predefined by some criteria to be in the domain. Thus, to understand how vLANs operate requires us to examine how they are constructed.

Construction Basics

A vLAN is constructed by the logical grouping of two or more network nodes on a physical topology. To accomplish this logical grouping you must use a vLAN-aware switching device. Those devices can include intelligent switches, which essentially perform bridging and operate at the MAC layer, or routers, which operate at the network layer, or layer 3, of the OSI Reference Model. Although a switching device is required to develop a vLAN, in actuality it is the software used by the device that provides you with a vLAN capability. That is, a vLAN represents a subnetwork or broadcast domain defined by software and not by the physical topology of a network. Instead, the physical topology of a network serves as a constraint for the software-based grouping of nodes into a logically defined network.

Implicit versus Explicit Tagging   The actual criteria used to define the logical grouping of nodes into a vLAN can be based upon implicit or explicit tagging. Implicit tagging, which in effect eliminates the use of a special tagging field inserted into frames or packets, can be based upon MAC address, port number of a switch used by a node, protocol, or another parameter that nodes can be logically grouped into. Since many vendors offering vLAN products use different construction techniques, interoperability between vendors may be difficult, if not impossible. In comparison, explicit tagging requires the addition of a field into a frame or packet header. This action can result in incompatibilities with certain types of vendor equipment as the extension of the length of a frame or packet beyond its maximum can result in the inability of such equipment to handle such frames or packets. As noted in Chapter 4 when we examined different types of Ethernet frames, under the IEEE 802.1Q standard a four-byte field is inserted into the frame header behind the source address field. This field contains a two-byte tag protocol identifier that is set to a value of hex 8100 and three additional subfields. A 3-bit priority subfield enables eight levels of priority to be assigned to a frame and permits 802.1p compliant switches and routers to place prioritized traffic into predefined queues as a mechanism to expedite traffic. A 1-bit canonical format identifier subfield when set indicates that a Token-Ring frame is being transported encapsulated within an Ethernet frame. The last subfield is a 12-bit vLAN ID field. This field contains a value that identifies the vLAN to which the frame belongs. After we examine the generic operation of port-based vLANs, we will focus our attention upon the 802.1Q operations.

Port-Grouping vLANs

As its name implies, a port-grouping vLAN represents a virtual LAN created by defining a group of ports on a switch or router to form a broadcast domain. Thus, another common name for this type of vLAN is a port-based virtual LAN.

Operation Figure 6.31 illustrates the use of a LAN switch to create two vLANs based upon port groupings. In this example the switch was configured to create one vLAN consisting of ports 0, 1, 5, and 6, while a second vLAN was created based upon the grouping of ports 2, 3, 4, and 7 to form a second broadcast domain.

Legend : $\boxed{n}$ = port n

$\perp$ = network segment

vLAN1 = ports 0, 1, 5, 6
vLAN2 = ports 2, 3, 4, 7

Figure 6.31   Creating port-grouping vLANs using a LAN switch.

Advantages associated with the use of LAN switches for creating vLANs include the ability to use the switching capability of the switch, the ability to support multiple stations per port, and intranetworking capability. A key disadvantage associated with the use of a port-based vLAN is the fact they are commonly limited to supporting one vLAN per port. This means that moves from one vLAN to another affect all stations connected to a particular switch port.

Supporting Inter-vLAN Communications   The use of multiple NICs provides an easy-to-implement solution to obtaining an inter-vLAN communications capability when only a few vLANs must be linked. This method of inter-vLAN communications is applicable to all methods of vLAN creation; however, when a built-in routing capability is included in a LAN switch, you would probably prefer to use the routing capability rather than obtain and install additional hardware.

Figure 6.32 illustrates the use of a server with multiple NICs to provide support to two port-based vLANs. Not only does this method of multiple vLAN support require additional hardware and the use of multiple ports on a switch or wiring hub, but, in addition, the number of NICs that can be installed in a station is typically limited to two or three. Thus, the use of a large switch with hundreds of ports configured for supporting three or more vLANs may not be capable of supporting inter-vLAN communications unless a router is connected to a switch port for each vLAN on the switch.

IEEE 802.1Q Operations

When the IEEE developed the 802.1Q specification for supporting port-based vLANs, it recognized that vLAN aware switches would have to interoperate

Figure 6.32 Overcoming the port-based constraint where stations can only join a single vLAN. By installing multiple network adapter cards in a server or workstation, a LAN device can become a member of multiple vLANs.

with "legacy" devices that are not aware of vLANs. Due to this, the 802.1Q specification provides support for both tagged and untagged frames, with each type of frame associated with different vLANs.

Initially, all switch ports in an 802.1Q environment belonged to a single port-based vLAN referred to as a port vLAN ID (PVID). The PVID has a numeric value, with a default of 1. Any untagged frame that enters the switch generated by a non-aware vLAN device would thus become a member of the vLAN identified by the PVID for the port through which the frame entered the switch. If the frame was generated by a vLAN-aware network adapter card, it would contain a vLAN tag in its header that would identify the vLAN to which the frame belongs. That value is the vLAN ID or VID.

Each switch port can have one or more VIDs. Those VIDs identify all of the vLANs that a specific port is a member of. Thus, when a frame enters a switch port it is identified as belonging to a vLAN either by the VID within its frame or via the port on which the frame entered the switch. The switch then consults its vLAN-port table and forwards the frame onto all ports that correspond to the VID.

Figure 6.33 illustrates an example of the manner by which an 802.1Q aware LAN switch could be configured to support tagged and untagged frames. In this example assume the workstation UT transmits an untagged frame into the switch on port 0. By default the PVID value of 1 is used to tag the frame,

Figure 6.33   IEEE 802.1Q PVID and VID illustrative example.

resulting in it being forwarded to port 1. Now let's assume station T transmits a tagged frame with a VID value of 2 into the switch on port 1. In this example, the frame would be forwarded onto ports 0 and 3.

MAC-Based vLANs

Figure 6.34 illustrates the use of an 18-port switch to create two virtual LANs. In this example, 18 devices are shown connected to the switch via six ports, with four ports serving individual network segments. Thus, the LAN switch in this example is more accurately referenced as a segment switch with a

Legend:

$\boxed{n}$ = Port n

$\bigcirc\!\!n$ = MAC address

Figure 6.34 Layer 2 vLAN. A layer 2 vLAN uses MAC addresses to construct broadcast domains that form a virtual LAN.

MAC or layer 2 vLAN capability. This type of switch can range in capacity from small 8- or 16-port devices capable of supporting segments with up to 512 or 1024 total addresses to large switches with hundreds of ports capable of supporting thousands of MAC addresses. For simplicity of illustration we will use the 6-port segment switch to denote the operation of layer 2 vLANs as well as their advantages and disadvantages.

In turning our attention to the vLANs shown in Figure 6.34, note that we will use the numeric or node addresses shown contained in circles as MAC addresses for simplicity of illustration. Thus, addresses 1 through 8 and 17 would be grouped into a broadcast domain representing vLAN1, while addresses 9 through 16 and 18 would be grouped into a second broadcast domain to represent vLAN2. At this point in time you would be tempted to say "so what," as the use of MAC addresses in creating layer 2 vLANs resembles precisely the same effect as if you used a port-grouping method of vLAN creation. For example, using a LAN switch with vLAN creation based upon port grouping would result in the same vLANs as those shown in Figure 6.34 when ports 0, 1, and 4 are assigned to one vLAN and ports 2, 3, and 5 to the second.

To indicate the greater flexibility associated with the use of equipment that supports layer 2 vLAN creation, let's assume users with network node addresses 7 and 8 were just transferred from the project associated with vLAN1 to the project associated with vLAN2. If you were using a port-grouping method of vLAN creation, you would have to physically recable nodes 7 and 8 to either the segment connected to port 2 or the segment connected to port 3. In comparison, when using a segment switch with a layer 2 vLAN creation capability, you would use the management port to delete addresses 7 and 8 from vLAN1 and add them to vLAN2. The actual effort required to do so might be as simple as dragging MAC addresses from one vLAN to the other when using a graphical user interface (GUI) to entering one or more commands when using a command line management system. The top of Figure 6.35 illustrates the result of the previously mentioned node transfer. The lower portion of Figure 6.35 shows the two vLAN layer 2 tables, indicating the movement of MAC addresses 7 and 8 to vLAN2.

Although the reassignment of stations 7 and 8 to vLAN2 is easily accomplished at the MAC layer, it should be noted that the partitioning of a segment into two vLANs can result in upper-layer problems. This is because upper-layer protocols, such as IP, normally require all stations on a segment to have the same network address. Some switches overcome this problem by dynamically altering the network address to correspond to the vLAN on which the station resides. Other switches without this capability restrict the creation of

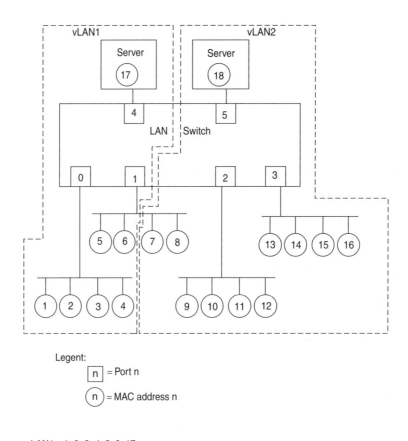

Figure 6.35 Moving stations when using a layer 2 vLAN.

MAC-based vLANs to one device per port, in effect limiting the creation of vLANs to port-based switches.

Interswitch Communications Similar to the port-grouping method of vLAN creation, a MAC-based vLAN is normally restricted to a single switch; how-ever, some vendors include a management platform that enables multiple switches to support MAC addresses between closely located switches. Unfor-tunately, neither individual nor closely located switches permit an expansion of vLANs outside of the immediate area, resulting in the isolation of the virtual LANs from the rest of the network. This deficiency can be alleviated in two ways. First, for inter-vLAN communications you could install a second adapter card in a server and associate one MAC address with one vLAN while the second address is associated with the second vLAN. While this method is appropriate for a switch with two vLANs, you would require a different method to obtain interoperability when communications are required between a large number of virtual LANs. Similar to correcting the interoperability problem with the port-grouping method of vLAN creation, you would have to use routers to provide connectivity between MAC-based vLANs and the rest of your network.

Router Restrictions   When using a router to provide connectivity between vLANs, there are several restrictions you must consider. Those restrictions typically include a requirement to use a separate switch port connection to the router for each virtual LAN and the inability to assign portions of segments to different vLANs. Concerning the former, unless the LAN switch either internally supports layer 3 routing or provides a trunking or aggregation capability that enables transmission from multiple vLANs to occur on a common port to the router, one port linking the switch to the router will be required for each vLAN. Since router and switch ports are relatively costly, intranetworking of a large number of vLANs can become expensive. Concerning the latter, this requirement results from the fact that in a TCP/IP environment routing occurs between segments. An example of inter-vLAN communications using a router is illustrated in Figure 6.35.

When inter-vLAN communications are required, the layer 2 switch transmits packets to the router via a port associated with the virtual LAN workstation requiring such communications. The router is responsible for determining the routed path to provide inter-vLAN communications, forwarding the packet back to the switch via an appropriate router-to-switch interface. Upon receipt of the packet the switch uses bridging to forward the packet to its destination port.

Returning to Figure 6.36, a workstation located in vLAN1 requiring communications with a workstation in vLAN2 would have its data transmitted by the switch on port 5 to the router. After processing the packet the router would return the packet to the switch, with the packet entering the switch on port 6. Thereafter, the switch would use bridging to broadcast the packet to ports 2, 3, and 7 where it would be recognized by a destination node in vLAN2 and copied into an appropriate NIC.

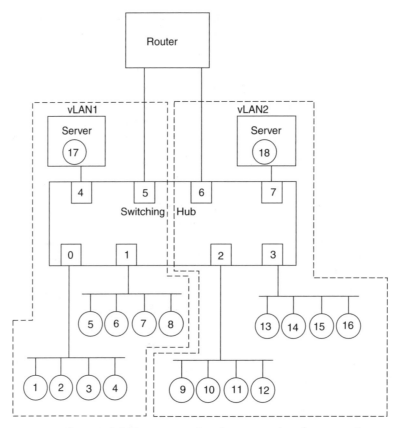

Figure 6.36 Inter-vLAN communications require the use of a router.

Layer 3–Based vLANs

A layer 3–based vLAN is constructed using information contained in the network layer header of packets. As such, this precludes the use of LAN switches that operate at the data link layer from being capable of forming layer 3 vLANs. Thus, layer 3 vLAN creation is restricted to routers and LAN switches that provide a layer 3 routing capability.

Through the use of layer 3 operating switches and routers, there are a variety of methods that can be used to create layer 3 vLANs. Some of the more common methods supported resemble the criteria by which routers operate, such as IPX network numbers and IP subnets, AppleTalk domains, and layer 3 protocols.

The actual creation options associated with a layer 3 vLAN can vary considerably based upon the capability of the LAN switch or router used to form the vLAN. For example, some hardware products permit a subnet to be formed across a number of ports and may even provide the capability to allow more than one subnet to be associated with a network segment connected to the port of a LAN switch. In comparison, other LAN switches may be limited to creating vLANs based upon different layer 3 protocols.

Subnet-Based vLANs Figure 6.37 illustrates the use of a layer 3 LAN switch to create two vLANs based upon IP network addresses. In examining the vLANs created through the use of the LAN switch, note that the first vLAN is associated with the subnet 198.78.55, which represents a Class C IP address, while the second vLAN is associated with the subnet 198.78.42, which represents a second Class C IP address. Also note that since it is assumed that the LAN switch supports the assignment of more than one subnet per port, port 1 on the switch consists of stations assigned to either subnet. While some LAN switches support this subnetting capability, it is also important to note that other switches do not. Thus, a LAN switch that does not support multiple subnets per port would require stations to be recabled to other ports if it was desired to associate them to a different vLAN.

vLAN1 = Subnet 198.78.55
vLAN2 = Subnet 198.78.42

Figure 6.37 vLAN creation based upon IP subnets.

Protocol-Based vLANs In addition to forming vLANs based upon a network address, the use of the layer 3 transmission protocol as a method for vLAN creation provides a mechanism that enables vLAN formation to be based upon the layer 3 protocol. Through the use of this method of vLAN creation, it becomes relatively easy for stations to belong to multiple vLANs. To illustrate this concept, consider Figure 6.38, which illustrates the creation of two vLANs based upon their layer 3 transmission protocol. In examining the stations shown in Figure 6.38, note that the circles with the uppercase *I* represent those stations configured for membership in the vLAN based upon the use of the IP protocol, while those stations represented by circles containing the uppercase X represent stations configured for membership in the vLAN that uses the IPX protocol as its membership criteria. Similarly, stations represented by circles containing the characters I/X represent stations operating dual protocol stacks, which enable such stations to become members of both vLANs.

Two servers are shown at the top of the LAN switch illustrated in Figure 6.38. One server is shown operating dual IPX/IP stacks, which results

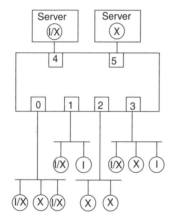

I = vLAN1 membership X = vLAN2 membership
I/X = Membership in both LANs

Legend:

⬚ n ⬚ = Port n

Ⓘ = IP protocol used by station

Ⓧ = IPX protocol used by station

(I/X) = IPX and IP protocols used by station

Figure 6.38   vLAN creation based upon protocol.

in the server belonging to both vLANs. In comparison, the server on the upper right of the switch is configured to support IPX and could represent a NetWare file server restricted to membership in the vLAN associated with the IPX protocol.

Rule-Based vLANs

A recent addition to vLAN creation methods is based upon the ability of LAN switches to look inside packets and use predefined fields, portions of fields, and even individual bit settings as a mechanism for the creation of a vLAN.

Capabilities   The ability to create vLANs via a rule-based methodology provides, no pun intended, a virtually unlimited vLAN creation capability. To illustrate a small number of the almost unlimited methods of vLAN creation, consider Table 6.7, which lists eight examples of rule-based vLAN creation methods. In examining the entries in Table 6.7, note that in addition to creating vLANs via the inclusion of specific field values within a packet, such as all IPX users with a specific network address, it is also possible to create vLANs using the exclusion of certain packet field values. The latter capability is illustrated by the next to last example in Table 6.7, which forms a vLAN consisting of all IPX traffic with a specific network address but excludes a specific node address.

Multicast Support   One rule-based vLAN creation example that deserves a degree of explanation to understand its capability is the last entry in Table 6.7. Although you might be tempted to think that the assignment of a single IP address to a vLAN represents a typographical mistake, in actuality it represents

TABLE 6.7   Rule-Based vLAN Creation Examples

All IP users with a specific IP subnet address.
All IPX users with a specific network address.
All network users whose adapter cards were manufactured by the XYZ Corporation.
All traffic with a specific Ethernet-type field value.
All traffic with a specific SNAP field value.
All traffic with a specific SAP field value.
All IPX traffic with a specific network address but not a specific node address.
A specific IP address.

the ability to enable network stations to dynamically join an IP multicast group without adversely affecting the bandwidth available to other network users assigned to the same subnet, but located on different segments attached to a LAN switch. To understand why this occurs, let me digress and discuss the concept associated with IP multicast operations.

IP multicast references a set of specifications that allows an IP host to transmit one packet to multiple destinations. This one-to-many transmission method is accomplished by the use of Class D IP addresses (224.0.0.0 to 239.255.255.255), which are mapped directly to data link layer 2 multicast addresses. Through the use of IP multicasting, a term used to reference the use of Class D addresses, the need for an IP host to transmit multiple packets to multiple destinations is eliminated. This, in turn, permits more efficient use of backbone network bandwidth; however, the arrival of IP Class D–addressed packets at a network destination, such as a router connected to an internal corporate network, can result in a bandwidth problem. This is because multicast transmission is commonly used for audio and/or video distribution of educational information, videoconferencing, news feeds, and financial reports, such as delivering stock prices. Due to the amount of traffic associated with multicast transmission, it could adversely affect multiple subnets linked together by a LAN switch that uses subnets for vLAN creation. By providing a registration capability that allows an individual LAN user to become a single-user vLAN associated with a Class D address, Class D packets can be routed to a specific segment even when several segments have the same subnet. Thus, this limits the effect of multicast transmission to a single segment.

Switch Usage

The basic use of a stand-alone switch is to support a workgroup that requires additional bandwidth beyond that available on a shared bandwidth LAN. Figure 6.39 illustrates the use of a switch to support a workgroup or small organizational department. As a workgroup expands or several workgroups are grouped together to form a department, most organizations will want to consider the use of a two-tiered switching network. The first or lower-level tier would represent switches dedicated to supporting a specific workgroup to include local servers. The upper tier would include one or more switches used to interconnect workgroup switches as well as to provide workgroup users with access to departmental servers whose access crosses workgroup boundaries. Since the upper-tier switch or switches are used to interconnect workgroup switches, the upper-tier switches are commonly referred to as

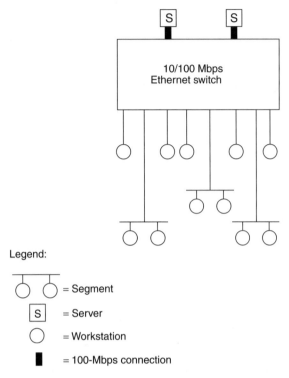

Legend:

○ ○ = Segment

S = Server

○ = Workstation

■ = 100-Mbps connection

Figure 6.39   Support for a small department or workgroup.

backbone switches. Figure 6.40 illustrates a possible use of one backbone switch to interconnect two workgroup switches.

Since the backbone switch provides an interconnection between workgroup switches as well as access to departmental servers, the failure of a backbone switch would have a much more significant effect upon communications than the failure of a workgroup switch. Thus, you should consider using a backbone switch with redundant power supplies, common logic, and other key modules. Then, the failure of one module at worst would only make one or a few port connections inoperative. If you acquire one or a few additional port modules you would then have the ability to recable around a port failure without having to wait for a replacement module to be shipped to your location.

When using one or more backbone switches, it is important to note that these switches directly affect the throughput between workgroups as well as the transfer of information to and from departmental servers. Due to this, most organizations will use dedicated 100-Mbps or Gigabit Ethernet

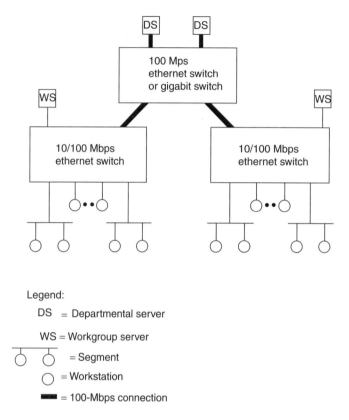

Figure 6.40 Creating a two-tiered switch-based network.

switches for backbone operations. If this type of switch is not available at an economical cost, an alternative is to use a 10-/100-Mbps switch with enough 100-Mbps ports to provide connections from workgroup switches as well as to departmental servers.

Organizational Switching

Building upon the departmental switching previously illustrated in Figure 6.40, you can use routers to interconnect geographically dispersed departments. Doing so can result in an organizational Ethernet switching network that could span different locations in the same city, different cities, one or more states, a country, or the entire globe. Figure 6.41 illustrates the attachment of one router to a backbone switch, connecting the backbone at one location to a wide area network. Although the actual use of one

Figure 6.41 Interconnecting geographically dispersed switch-based networks.

or more routers will be governed by our specific networking requirements, Figure 6.41 illustrates how you can connect one switch-based network to other switch-based networks.

As you design your network infrastructure you should consider the use of one or more Ethernet switch features previously discussed in this chapter to enhance the performance of your network. For example, you may wish to use full-duplex ports for local and departmental server connections. In addition, by the time you read this book economical 10-Gigabit switches should be available whose use could provide you with another option to consider when constructing a tiered network structure.

Layer 3 and Layer 4 Switching

In concluding this chapter we will briefly turn our attention to LAN switching at layer 3 and layer 4 in the OSI Reference Model. In a TCP/IP environment this requires the LAN switch to look further into each frame to locate the IP header and the TCP or UDP header and then a particular field in each header. This results in more processing being required to locate the applicable header and field within the header that is used as a switching decision criterion.

The key advantage associated with the use of layer 3 and layer 4 LAN switches is the fact that they enable an organization to use the switch to tailor their network to a specific operational requirement. For example, assume your organization operates several Web servers. Through the use of a layer 3 LAN switch you could direct traffic to different servers based upon the destination IP address. Using a layer 4 LAN switch you could route traffic based upon IP address, TCP port, or both metrics. Doing so could provide your organization with the ability to perform a load balance operation.

chapter seven

Routers

In Chapter 5, we examined the basic operation and use of a variety of local area networking components, including routers. Information presented in that chapter will serve as a foundation for the more detailed discussion of the operation and use of routers presented in this chapter.

7.1 Router Operation

By operating at the ISO Reference Model network layer, a router becomes capable of making intelligent decisions concerning the flow of information in a network. To accomplish this, routers perform a variety of functions that are significantly different from those performed by bridges. Unlike bridges, routers are addressable. Routers examine frames that are directly addressed to them by looking at the network address within each frame to make their forwarding decisions. In an IP environment you would configure the IP address of the router serving your network in a TCP/IP properties dialog box if you are using Microsoft Windows. However, because routers were originally referred to as gateways and the latter term is still used as a reference to a router, you would enter the IP address of the "gateway" serving your network. Thus, if your workstation needs to transmit a packet to an IP address on a different network, it will use the preconfigured gateway address to literally route the packet to the router, which will then send it off the network towards its ultimate destination.

IP Support Overview

The most popular network layer protocol supported by routers is the Internet Protocol (IP), whose packet format was described in Chapter 5. Each IP network has a distinct network address, and each interface on the network has a unique host address that represents the host portion of a 32-bit address.

Since the IP address occurs at the network layer while frames that move data on a LAN use MAC addresses associated with the data link layer, a translation process is required to enable IP-compatible devices to use the transport services of a local area network. Thus, any discussion of how routers support IP requires an overview of the manner by which hosts use the services of a router.

When a host has a packet to transmit, it will first determine if the destination IP address is on the local network or a distant network, with the latter requiring the services of a router. To accomplish this, the host will use the subnet mask bits set in its configuration to determine if the destination is on the local network. For example, assume the subnet mask is 255.255.255.128. This means the mask extends the network portion of an IP address to 11111111.11111111.11111111.1, or 25 bit positions, resulting in 7 (32−25) bit positions being available for the host address. This also means you can have two subnets, with subnet 0 containing host addresses 0 to 127 and subnet 1 having host addresses 128 to 255, with the subnet defined by the value of the 25th bit position in the IP address. However, we need to note that restrictions concerning IP network addresses mentioned in Chapter 5 are also applicable to subnets. That is, you cannot have a subnet address that consists of all 0's or all 1's. Noting these restrictions, the host addresses allowable on subnet 0 then range from 1 to 126 while the allowable host addresses on subnet 1 range from 129 to 254.

If we assume the base network IP address is 193.56.45.0, then the base network, two subnets, and the subnet mask are as follows:

```
Base network: 11000001.00111000.00101101.00000000 = 193.56.45.0
Subnet 0:     11000001.00111000.00101101.00000000 = 193.56.45.0
Subnet 1:     11000001.00111000.00101101.10000000 = 193.56.45.128
Subnet mask:  11111111.11111111.11111111.10000000 = 193.56.45.128
```

In examining the above base network, subnets and subnet mask, it is important to remember that you cannot have a subnet of all 0's or all 1's. Thus, as previously noted, the allowable hosts on subnet 0 range from 1 to 126 while the allowable hosts on subnet 1 range from 129 to 254. Now suppose a host with the IP address 193.56.45.21 needs to send a packet to the host whose address is 193.56.45.131. By using the subnet mask, the transmitting host notes that the destination, while on the same network, is on a different subnet. Thus, the transmitting host will require the use of a router in the same manner as if the destination host was on a completely separate network.

Figure 7.1 illustrates the internal and external network view of the subnetted network. Note that from locations exterior to the network, routers forward

Exterior view

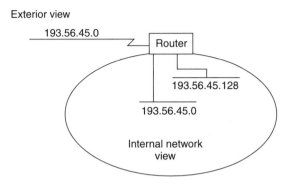

Figure 7.1   Using subnet masks to subdivide a common IP network address.

packets to the router connecting the two subnets as if no subnetting existed. The corporate router is configured via the use of subnet masks to differentiate hosts on one subnet from those on the other subnet. From an interior view, packets originating on one subnet must use the resources of the router to reach hosts on the other subnet as well as hosts on other networks.

Once the transmitting host notes that the destination IP address is either on a different network or different subnet, it must use the services of a router. Although each host will be configured with the IP address of the router, the host will transport packets via the data link layer, which requires knowledge of the 48-bit MAC address of the router port connected to the segment the transmitting host resides on.

The translation between IP and MAC addresses is accomplished by the use of the Address Resolution Protocol (ARP). To obtain the MAC address of the router's LAN interface the host will broadcast an ARP request. This request will be received by all stations on the segment, with the router recognizing its IP address and responding by transmitting an ARP response.

Because a continuous use of ARP would rapidly consume network bandwidth, hosts normally maintain the results of ARP requests in cache memory. Thus, once the relationship between an IP address and MAC address is learned, subsequent requests to transmit additional packets to the same destination can be accomplished by the host checking its cache memory.

When packets arrive at the router destined for a host on one of the subnets, a similar process occurs. That is, the router must obtain the MAC addresses associated with the IP address to enable the packet to be transported by data link layer frames to its appropriate destination. Thus, in addition to being able to correctly support the transmission of packets from one interface to another, an IP-compatible router must also support the ARP protocol. Later in this chapter we will discuss and describe additional protocols routers can support.

Basic Operation and Use of Routing Tables

To see the basic operation of routers, consider the simple mesh structure formed by the use of three routers labeled R1, R2, and R3 in Figure 7.2a. In this illustration, three Ethernet networks are interconnected through the use of three routers.

The initial construction of three routing tables is shown in Figure 7.2b. Unlike bridges, which learn MAC addresses, routers are initially configured, and either routing tables are established at the time of equipment installation or the configuration process informs the router of addresses associated with each of its interfaces and the attachment of networks and subnets, enabling the device to construct its routing table. Thereafter, periodic communication between routers updates routing tables to take into consideration any changes in internet topology and traffic.

In examining Figure 7.2b, note that the routing table for router R1 indicates which routers it must communicate with to access each interconnected Ethernet network. Router R1 would communicate with router R2 to reach network 2, and with router R3 to reach network 3.

Figure 7.2c illustrates the composition of a packet originated by station S2 on Ethernet 1 that is to be transmitted to station S12 on Ethernet 2. Router R1 first examines the destination network address and notes that it is on another network. The router searches its routing table and finds that the frame should be transmitted to router R2 to reach Ethernet network 2. Router R1 forwards the frame to router R2. Router R2 then places the frame onto Ethernet network 2 for delivery to station S12 on that network.

Since routers use the network addresses instead of MAC addresses for making their forwarding decisions, it is possible to have duplicate locally administered MAC addresses on each network interconnected by a router. The use of bridges, on the other hand, requires you to review and then eliminate any duplicate locally administered addresses. This process can be time-consuming when large networks are connected.

Another difference between bridges and routers is that a router can support the transmission of data on multiple paths between local area networks. Although a multiport bridge with a filtering capability can perform intelligent routing decisions, the result of a bridge operation is normally valid for only one point-to-point link within a wide area network. In comparison, a router

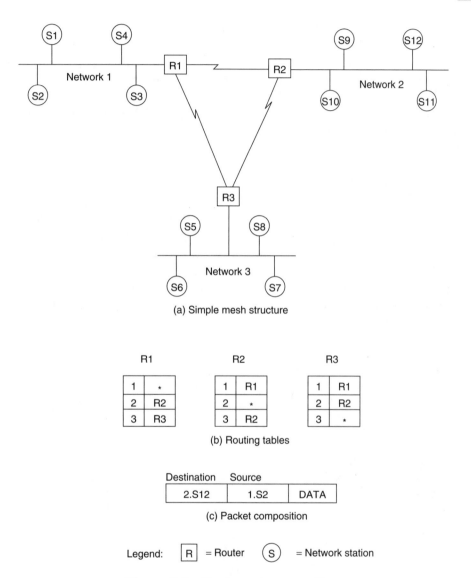

(a) Simple mesh structure

(b) Routing tables

(c) Packet composition

Legend: R = Router   S = Network station

Figure 7.2   Basic router operation.

may be able to acquire information about the status of a large number of paths and select an end-to-end path consisting of a series of point-to-point links. In addition, most routers can fragment and reassemble data. This permits packets to flow over different paths and to be reassembled at their final destination. With this capability, a router can route each packet to its destination over the best possible path at a particular instant in time, and change paths dynamically to correspond to changes in network link status on traffic activity.

For example, each of the routing tables illustrated in Figure 7.2b can be expanded to indicate a secondary path to each network. While router R1 would continue to use the entry of R2 as its primary mechanism to reach network 2, a secondary entry of R3 could be established to provide an alternative path to network 2 via routers R3 and R2, rather than directly via router R2.

Networking Capability

For an illustration of the networking capability of routers, see Figure 7.3. It shows three geographically dispersed locations that have a total of four Ethernet and three Token-Ring networks, interconnected through the use of four routers and four wide area network transmission circuits or links. For simplicity, modems and DSUs on the wide area network are not shown. This figure will be referred to several times in this chapter to illustrate different types of router operations.

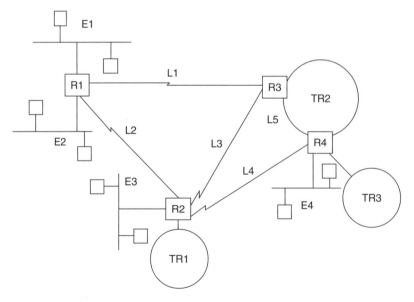

Figure 7.3 Router operation. Routers enable the transmission of data over multiple paths, alternate path routing, and the use of a mesh topology that transparent bridges cannot support.

In addition to supporting a mesh structure that is not obtainable from the use of transparent bridges, routers offer other advantages in the form of addressing, message processing, link utilization, and priority of service. A router is known to stations that use its service. Packets can thus be addressed directly to a router. This eliminates the necessity for the device to examine in detail every packet flowing on a network, and results in the router having to process only messages that are addressed to it by other devices.

Assume that a station on E1 transmits to a station on TR3. Depending on the status and traffic on network links, packets could be routed via L1 and use TR2 to provide a transport mechanism to R4, from which the packets are delivered to TR3. Alternatively, links L2 and L4 could be used to provide a path from R1 to R4. Although link availability and link traffic usually determine routing, routers can support prioritized traffic, and may store low-priority traffic for a small period of time to allow higher-priority traffic to gain access to the wide area transmission facility. Because of these features, which are essentially unavailable with bridges, the router is a more complex and more expensive device.

7.2 Communication, Transport, and Routing Protocols

For routers to be able to operate in a network, they must normally be able to speak the same language at both the data link and network layers. The key to accomplishing this is the ability to support common communication, transport, and routing protocols.

Communication Protocol

Communication protocols support the transfer of data from a station on one network to a station on another network; they occur at the OSI network layer. In examining Figure 7.4, which illustrates several common protocol implementations with respect to the OSI Reference Model, you will note that Novell's NetWare uses IPX as its network communications protocol, while IBM LANs use the PC LAN Support Program, and Microsoft's LAN Manager uses the Internet Protocol (IP). Also note that when a TCP/IP stack is used, certain applications are transported by TCP while others are transported using UDP; however, both TCP and UDP obtain their routing via the use of IP. This means that a router linking networks based on Novell, IBM, and Microsoft LAN operating systems must support those three communication protocols. Thus, router communication protocol support is a very important criterion

OSI layer | Common protocol implementation

OSI layer	Common protocol implementation				
Application	Application programs				
	Application protocols				
Presentation	Novell Network File Server Protocol (NFSP)	IBM Server Message Block (SMB)	Microsoft LAN manager	TCP/IP applications	
Session	Xerox Networking System (XNS)	NetBIOS	NetBIOS advanced peer-to-peer communications		
Transport	Sequenced Packet Exchange (SPX)	PC LAN support program	Transmission Control Protocol (TCP) Transport Protocol Class 4 (TCP4)	TCP	UDP
Network	Internetwork Packet Exchange (IPX)		Internet Protocol (IP)	Internet Protocol (IP)	
Data link	Logical link control 802.2				
	Media access control				
Physical	Transmission media: twisted pair, coax, fiber optic				

(Note: The column between Session and Transport contains the vertical text "NetBIOS")

Figure 7.4 Common protocol implementations. Although Novell, IBM, and Microsoft LAN operating system software support standardized physical and data link operations, they differ considerably in their use of communication and routing protocols.

in determining whether a particular product is capable of supporting your networking requirements.

Routing Protocol

The routing protocol is the method used by routers to exchange routing information; it forms the basis for providing a connection across an internet. In evaluating routers, it is important to determine the efficiency of the routing protocol, its effect upon the transmission of information, the method used and memory required to construct routing tables, and the time required to adjust those tables. Examples of router-to-router protocols include Xerox Network Systems' (XNS) Routing Information Protocol (RIP), TCP/IP's RIP, Open Shortest Path First (OSPF), and Hello routing protocols.

Handling Nonroutable Protocols

Although many mainframe users consider IBM's System Network Architecture (SNA) as a router protocol, in actuality it is nonroutable in the traditional sense of having network addresses. This means that for a router to support SNA or another nonroutable protocol, such as NetBIOS, the router cannot compare a destination network address against the current network address as there are no network addresses to work with. Instead, the router must be capable of performing one or more special operations to handle nonroutable protocols. For example, some routers may be configurable such that SNA addresses in terms of physical units (PUs) and logical units (LUs) can be associated with pseudonetwork numbers, enabling the router to route an unroutable protocol. Another common method employed by some routers is to incorporate a nonroutable protocol within a routable protocol, a technique referred to as *tunneling.* A third method, and one considered by many to be the old reliable mechanism, is to use bridging. Later in this chapter when we cover protocol-independent routers, we will describe methods that can be used to route nonroutable protocols, to include SNA traffic.

Transport Protocol

The transport protocol guarantees the delivery of information between two points. Here, the transport protocol represents the fourth layer illustrated in Figure 7.4. Examples of transport protocols include SPX, TCP, UDP, X.25, and Frame Relay.

There is a wide variety of communication and transport protocols in use today. Some of these protocols, such as Apple Computer's AppleTalk, were designed specifically to operate on local area networks. Other protocols, such as X.25 and Frame Relay, were developed as wide area network protocols.

Fifteen popular communication and transport protocols are listed below. Many routers support only a subset of these protocols.

- AppleTalk
- Apple Domain
- Banyan VINES
- CHAOSnet
- DECnet Phase IV
- DECnet Phase V
- DDN X.25
- Frame Relay
- ISO CLNS
- HDLC
- Novell IPX
- SDLC

- TCP/IP
- Xerox XNS
- X.25

7.3 Router Classifications

Depending upon their support of communication and transport protocols, routers can be classified into two groups: protocol-dependent and protocol-independent.

Protocol-Dependent Routers

To understand the characteristics of a protocol-dependent router, consider the network illustrated in Figure 7.3. If a station on network E1 wishes to transmit data to a second station on network E3, router R1 must know that the second station resides on network E3, and it must know the best path to use to reach that network. The method used to determine the destination station's network also determines the protocol dependency of the router.

If the station on network E1 tells router R1 the destination location, it must supply a network address in every LAN packet it transmits. This means that all routers in the intranet must support the protocol used on network E1. Otherwise, stations on network E1 could not communicate with stations residing on other networks, and vice versa.

NetWare IPX Example

To illustrate the operation of a protocol-dependent router, let us assume that networks E1 and E3 use Novell's NetWare as their LAN operating system. The routing protocol used at the network layer between a station and server on a Novell network is known as IPX. This protocol can also be used between servers.

Under NetWare's IPX, a packet addressed to a router will contain the destination address in the form of network and host addresses, and the origination address in the form of the source network and source host addresses. Here, the IPX term *host* is actually the physical address of a network adapter card.

Figure 7.5a illustrates in simplified format the IPX packet composition for workstation A on network E1, transmitting data to workstation B on network E3, under Novell's NetWare IPX protocol.

After router R1 receives and examines the packet, it notes that the destination address E3 requires the routing of the packet to router R2. It converts the first

(a) Packet from workstation A, network E1 to router R1

(b) Router (R1) to router (R2) packet

(c) Router R2 converts packet for placement on network E3

Figure 7.5   NetWare IPX routing.

packet into a router (R1) to router (R2) packet, as illustrated in Figure 7.5b. At router R2, the packet is again examined. Router R2 notes that the destination network address (E3) is connected to that router, so it reconverts the packet for delivery onto network E3. It does this by converting the destination router address to a source router address and transmitting the packet onto network E3. This is illustrated in Figure 7.5c.

Addressing Differences

In the preceding example, note that each router uses the destination workstation and network addresses to transfer packets. If all protocols used the same format and addressing structure, routers would be protocol-insensitive at the network layer. Unfortunately, this is not true. For example, TCP/IP addressing conventions are very different from those used by NetWare. This means that networks using different operating systems require the use of multiprotocol routers configured to perform address translation. Each multiprotocol router must maintain separate routing tables for each supported protocol, requiring additional memory and processing time.

Other Problems

Two additional problems associated with protocol-dependent routers are the time required for packet examination and the fact that not all LAN protocols are routable. If a packet must traverse a large network, the time required by a series of routers to modify the packet and assure its delivery to the next router can significantly degrade router performance. To overcome this problem, organizations should consider the use of a frame relay service.

In addition to providing an enhanced data delivery service by eliminating error detection and correction within the network, the use of a frame relay service can significantly reduce the cost of routers. Consider, for example, the network in Figure 7.3, in which four routers are interconnected through the use of five links. To support transmission on five links, the routers require ten ports. Normally, each router port is obtained as an adapter card installed in a high-performance computer. If a frame relay service is used, the packet network providing that service also provides the routing paths to interconnect routers, as illustrated in Figure 7.6. This reduces the number of required router ports to four. This reduction can result in a considerable hardware savings.

In addition to using a frame relay service provider, another method that can reduce the cost of router hardware and communications circuits is obtained from establishing a virtual private network (VPN) through the Internet. In doing so, you would need to consider encryption of data as the Internet represents an open, public network. However, the physical topology associated with connecting geographically separated locations would remain similar to that shown in Figure 7.6, with the frame relay packet network service being replaced by the Internet.

A second problem associated with protocol-dependent routers is the fact that some LAN protocols cannot be routed using that type of device. This is because some LAN protocols, such as NetBIOS and IBM's LAN Server—and unlike NetWare, DECnet, and TCP/IP—do not include routing information

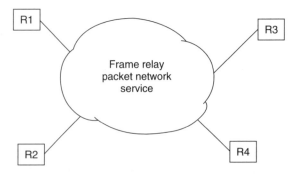

Figure 7.6 Using a frame relay service. If a frame relay service is used, the packet network provides the capability for interconnecting each network access port to other network access ports. Thus, only one router port is required to obtain an interconnection capability to numerous routers connected to the network.

within a packet. Instead, those protocols employ a user-friendly device-naming convention instead of using network and device addresses. This convention permits such names as "Gil's PC" and "Accounting Printer" to be used. For example, IBM's NetBIOS was designed to facilitate program-to-program communication by hiding the complexities of network addressing from the user. Thus, NetBIOS uses names up to 16 alphanumeric characters long to define clients and servers on a network. Unfortunately, NetBIOS does not include a facility to distinguish one network from another, since it lacks a network addressing capability. Such protocols are restricted to using the physical addresses of adapter cards, such as Ethernet source and destination addresses. Since a protocol-dependent router must know the network on which a destination address is located, it cannot in a conventional sense route such protocols. A logical question, then, is how a router interconnects networks using an IBM LAN protocol or a similar nonroutable protocol. The answer to this question will depend upon the method used by the router manufacturer to support nonroutable protocols. As previously discussed, such methods can include bridging, tunneling, or the configuration of a router that enables pseudonetwork addresses to be assigned to each device.

Protocol-Independent Routers

A protocol-independent router functions as a sophisticated transparent bridge. That is, it addresses the problem of network protocols that do not have network addresses. It does this by examining the source addresses on connected networks to learn automatically what devices are on each network. The protocol-independent router assigns network identifiers to each network whose operating system does not include network addresses in its network protocol. This activity enables both routable and nonroutable protocols to be serviced by a protocol-dependent router.

In addition to building address tables automatically like a transparent bridge, a protocol-independent router exchanges information concerning its routing directions with other internet routers. This enables each router to build a map of the interconnected networks. The method used to build the network map falls under the category of a link state routing protocol, which is described later in this chapter.

Advantages

There are two key advantages to using protocol-independent routers. Those advantages are the abilities of routers to learn network topology automatically and to service nonroutable protocols. The ability to learn network topology automatically can considerably simplify the administration of an internet. For example, in a TCP/IP network, each workstation has an IP address and must know the IP addresses of other LAN devices it wants to communicate with.

IP addresses are commonly assigned by a network administrator, and they must be changed if a station is moved to a different network, or if a network is segmented because of a high level of traffic or other reason. In such situations, LAN users must be notified about the new IP address, or they will not be able to locate the moved station. Obviously, the movement of stations within a building between different LANs could become a considerable administrative burden. The ability of a protocol-independent router to learn addresses automatically removes the administrative burden of notifying users of changes in network addresses.

An exception to the preceding occurs through the use of the Dynamic Host Configuration Protocol (DHCP). Through the use of a DHCP server and appropriate client software, stations are dynamically assigned IP addresses for a relatively short period of time. Once they complete an application the server can reassign the address to a new station. Although the use of the DHCP can ease the administrative burden of configuring and reconfiguring IP workstations, it requires the use of a server and client software. Thus, there continues to be no free lunch in networking.

The ability to route nonroutable protocols can be of considerable assistance in integrating IBM SNAs into an enterprise network. Otherwise, without the use of protocol-independent routers, organizations may have to maintain separate transmission facilities for SNA and LAN traffic.

Supporting SNA Traffic

Figure 7.7 illustrates an example of the use of protocol-independent routers to support both inter-LAN and SNA traffic. In this example, an IBM SNA network, a 3174 control unit with a Token-Ring adapter (TRA) at a remote site provides communications connectivity to an IBM 3745 communications controller at a central site. Routers must be capable of routing both SNA and LAN traffic to enable the use of a common transmission facility between the central and remote site.

Methods to Consider

There are essentially three methods by which SNA and LAN traffic can be combined for routing over a common network: encapsulation, conversion, and protocol-independent routing. Under the encapsulation method, SNA packets are modified so that another protocol's header, addressing,

Remote site   **Central site**

Figure 7.7 Supporting SNA traffic. A protocol-independent router can support SNA traffic and other LAN traffic over a common transmission facility.

and trailer fields surround each SNA packet. For example, a TCP/IP protocol–dependent router would encapsulate SNA into TCP/IP packets for routing through a TCP/IP network. Since a TCP/IP packet has over 60 bytes of overhead, and the average SNA packet is 30 bytes in length, encapsulation can reduce performance considerably when transmission occurs over low-speed WAN links. A second disadvantage of encapsulation is that it requires the existence of a corporate network using the encapsulation protocol. Otherwise, you would have to build this network to obtain an encapsulation capability.

The second method used for integrating SNA traffic with LAN traffic occurs through the use of protocol conversion. This technique eliminates the need for adding network headers and enhances the efficiency of the protocol integration efforts.

The third method by which an SNA network can be integrated with LAN traffic is through protocol-independent routing. Protocol-independent routers assign a LAN device address to each SNA control unit and communications controller. Then, SNA packets are prefixed with source and destination addresses to permit their routing through the internet. At the destination router, the addressing information is removed, and the SNA packets are delivered to their destination in their original form. Since the addition of source and destination addresses adds a significantly lower number of bytes than an encapsulation process, overhead is reduced. This, in turn, enables you to consider using lower-speed circuits to interconnect locations.

Another advantage of protocol-independent routing over encapsulation relates directly to the operation of SNA networks, with several SNA operational characteristics warranting attention. They will help us appreciate the advantages of protocol-independent routing, and they will explain the rationale for such routers' requiring a traffic priority mechanism to support SNA traffic efficiently.

Need for Priority Mechanism

In its original incarnation, SNA represents a hierarchically structured network, as shown in Figure 7.8. Here, the communications controller communicates with control units, which in turn communicate with attached terminal devices. The communications controller periodically polls each control unit, and the control unit periodically polls each terminal device. If there is no data to transmit in response to a poll, each polled device indicates this fact to the higher-level device by responding negatively to the poll. Thus, the communications controller expects to receive a response to each poll it generates. In fact, if it does not receive a response within a predefined period of time (typically less than five seconds), the communications controller will assume that the control unit has malfunctioned, terminate any

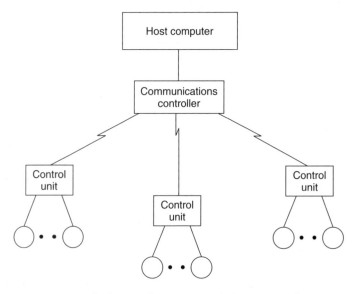

Figure 7.8 SNA network hierarchy. In an SNA network, communications controllers poll control units, which in turn poll attached devices.

active sessions to devices attached to the control unit, and then attempt to reestablish communications by sending an initialization message to the control unit.

When SNA and LAN traffic is integrated into a common router-based network, the operation of routers can adversely affect SNA traffic because of the time delays associated with routing and encapsulation. For example, routers may alter the path used to transmit data, depending on internet traffic and circuit availability. If path switching makes the SNA traffic exceed its timeout threshold, the communications controller will terminate sessions and reinitialize control units that fail to respond to its poll within the predefined time period. Similarly, delays caused by encapsulation can also result in unintended timeouts.

To prevent unintended timeouts caused by path switching, some vendors have added a traffic priority mechanism to their protocol-independent routing capability. This priority mechanism enables users to assign a higher priority to SNA traffic than to LAN traffic, thus enabling SNA data to be forwarded across wide area networks ahead of other inter-LAN traffic. This can considerably reduce or even eliminate the potential for LAN traffic to obstruct the flow of SNA data; it may also result in unintended timeouts, inadvertently causing session terminations.

7.4 Routing Protocols

The routing protocol is the key element to transferring information across an internet in an orderly manner. The protocol is responsible for developing paths between routers, using a predefined mechanism.

Types of Routing Protocols

There are two types of routing protocols: interior and exterior domain. Here, we use the term *domain* to refer to the connection of a group of networks to form a common entity, such as a corporate or university enterprise network.

Interior Domain Routing Protocols

An *interior domain routing protocol* is used to control the flow of information within a series of separate networks that are interconnected to form an internet. Thus, interior domain routing protocols provide a mechanism for the flow of information within a domain and are also known as *intradomain* routing protocols. Such protocols create routing tables for each autonomous system within the domain, using such metrics as the hop count or time delay to develop routes from one network to another within the domain. Examples of interior domain routing protocols include RIP, OSPF, and Hello.

Exterior Domain Routing Protocols

Exterior domain routing protocols are used to connect separate domains together. Thus, they are also referred to as *interdomain* routing protocols. Examples of interdomain routing protocols include the Exterior Gateway Protocol (EGP), the Border Gateway Protocol (BGP), and the Inter-Domain Routing Protocol (IDRP). Unlike interior domain routing protocols, which are focused on the construction of routing tables for data flow within a domain, interdomain routing protocols specify the method by which routers exchange information concerning what networks they can reach on each domain.

Figure 7.9 illustrates the use of interior and exterior domain routing protocols. In this example, OSPF is the intradomain protocol used in Domain A, while RIP is the intradomain protocol used in Domain B. Routers in Domains A and B use the interdomain routing protocols EGP and/or BGP to determine what networks on other domains they can reach.

Exterior Gateway Protocol

There are four basic functions performed by the Exterior Gateway Protocol. First, the EGP performs an acquisition function, which enables a router in one domain to request information exchange with a router on another domain. Since routers also serve as gateways to the domain, they are sometimes referred to as *gateways.* A second function performed by the router gateway is to test periodically whether its EGP neighbors are responding. The third and most important function performed by the EGP is to enable router gateways to exchange information concerning the networks in each domain by transmitting routing update messages. The fourth function involves terminating an established neighbor relationship between gateways on two domains.

To accomplish its basic functions, EGP defines nine message types. Figure 7.10 illustrates EGP message types associated with each of the three basic features performed by the protocol.

Under the EGP, once a neighbor is acquired, Hello messages must be transmitted at a minimum of 30-second intervals. In addition, routing updates must be exchanged at a minimum of two-minute intervals. This exchange of information at two-minute intervals can result in the use of a considerable

Figure 7.9 Interior and exterior routing protocols. An interior routing protocol controls the flow of information within a collection of interconnected networks known as a *domain*. An exterior routing protocol provides routers with the ability to determine what networks on other domains they can reach.

amount of the bandwidth linking domains when the number of networks on each domain is large, or when the circuits linking domains consist of low-speed lines. The Border Gateway Protocol was developed to alleviate those potential problems.

Border Gateway Protocol

The Border Gateway Protocol represents a follow-on to the EGP. Unlike the EGP, in which all network information is exchanged at two-minute or shorter intervals, the BGP transmits incremental updates as changes occur. This can significantly reduce the quantity of data exchanged between router gateways, thus freeing up a considerable amount of circuit bandwidth for the transmission of data. Both the EGP and the BGP run over TCP/IP and are standardized by Internet documents RFC904 and RFC1105, respectively.

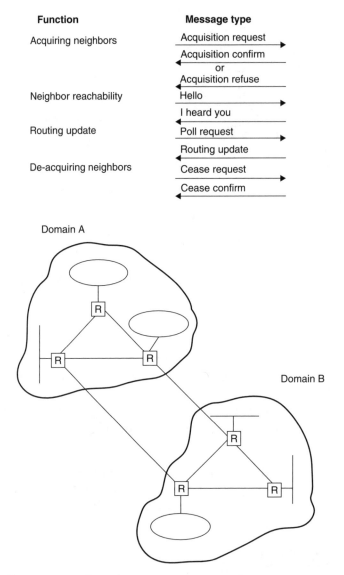

Function	Message type
Acquiring neighbors	Acquisition request →
	← Acquisition confirm
	or
	Acquisition refuse ←
Neighbor reachability	Hello →
	← I heard you
Routing update	Poll request →
	← Routing update
De-acquiring neighbors	Cease request →
	← Cease confirm

Domain A

Domain B

Figure 7.10 Exterior gateway protocol message types.

Types of Interior Domain Routing Protocols

As previously discussed, interior domain routing protocols govern the flow of information between networks. This is the type of routing protocol that is of primary interest to most organizations. Interior domain routing protocols can be further subdivided into two broad categories, based on the method they use for building and updating the contents of their routing tables: vector distance and link state.

Vector Distance Protocol

A vector distance protocol constructs a routing table in each router, and periodically broadcasts the contents of the routing table across the internet. When the routing table is received at another router, that device examines the set of reported network destinations and the distance to each destination. The receiving router then determines whether it knows a shorter route to a network destination, finds a destination it does not have in its routing table, or finds a route to a destination through the sending router where the distance to the destination changed. If any one of these situations occurs, the receiving router will change its routing tables.

The term *vector distance* relates to the information transmitted by routers. Each router message contains a list of pairs, known as vector and distance. The *vector* identifies a network destination, while the *distance* is the distance in hops from the router to that destination.

Figure 7.11 illustrates the initial distance vector routing table for the routers R1 and R2 shown in Figure 7.3. Each table contains an entry for each directly connected network and is broadcast periodically throughout the internet. The distance column indicates the distance in hops to each network from the router.

At the same time router R1 is constructing its initial distance vector table, other routers are performing a similar operation. The lower portion of Figure 7.11 illustrates the composition of the initial distance vector table for router R2. As previously mentioned, under a distance vector protocol, the contents of each router's routing table are periodically broadcast. When routers R1 and R2 broadcast their initial distance vector routing tables, each router uses the received routing table to update its initial routing table. Figure 7.12

a. Router R1

Destination	Distance
E1	0
E2	0

b. Router R2

Destination	Distance
E3	0
TR1	0

Figure 7.11   Initial distance vector routing tables.

a. Router R1

Destination	Distance	Route
E1	0	direct
E2	0	direct
E3	1	R2
TR1	1	R2

b. Router R2

Destination	Distance	Route
E1	1	R1
E2	1	R1
E3	0	direct
TR1	0	direct

Figure 7.12   Initial routing table update.

illustrates the result of this initial routing table update process for routers R1 and R2.

As additional routing tables are exchanged, the routing table in each router will converge with respect to the internet topology. However, to ensure that each router knows the state of all links, routing tables are periodically broadcast by each router. Although this process has a minimal effect upon small networks, its use with large networks can significantly reduce available bandwidth for actual data transfer. This is because the transmission of lengthy router tables will require additional transmission time in which data cannot flow between routers.

Popular vector distance routing protocols include the TCP/IP Routing Information Protocol (RIP), the AppleTalk Routing Table Management Protocol (RTMP), and Cisco's Interior Gateway Routing Protocol (IGRP).

Routing Information Protocol

Under RIP, participants are either active or passive. *Active* participants are normally routers that transmit their routing tables, while *passive* machines listen and update their routing tables based upon information supplied by other devices. Normally, host computers are passive participants, while routers are active participants.

Operation

Under RIP, an active router broadcasts its routing table every 30 seconds. Each routing table entry contains a network address and the hop count to the network. To illustrate an example of the operation of RIP, let's redraw the network previously shown in Figure 7.3 in terms of its links and nodes,

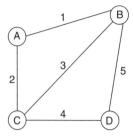

Figure 7.13 Redrawing the network in Figure 7.3 in terms of its links and nodes.

replacing the four routers by the letters A, B, C, and D for simplicity of illustration. Figure 7.13 contains the revised network consisting of four nodes and five links.

When the routers are powered up they only have knowledge of their local conditions. Thus, each routing table would contain a single entry. For example, the table of router n would have the following value:

From n to	Link	Hop Count
n	local	0

For the router represented by node A, its table would then become:

From A to	Link	Hop Count
A	local	0

Thirty seconds after being turned on, node A will broadcast its distance vector (A = 0) to all its neighbors, which, in Figure 7.13 are nodes B and C. Node B receives on link 1 the assistance vector A = 0. Upon receipt of this message, it updates its routing table as follows, adding one to the hop count associated with the distance vector supplied by node 1:

From B to	Link	Hop Count
B	Local	0
A	1	1

Node B can now prepare its own distance vector (B = 0, A = 1) and transmit that information on its connections (links 1, 3, and 5).

During the preceding period node C would have received the initial distance vector transmission from node A. Thus, node C would have updated its routing table as follows:

From C to	Link	Hop Count
C	Local	0
A	2	1

Once it updates its routing table, node C will then transmit its distance vector (C = 0, A = 1) on links 2, 3, and 4.

Assuming the distance vector from node B is now received at nodes A and C, each will update their routing tables. Thus, their routing tables would appear as follows:

From A to	Link	Hop Count
A	Local	0
B	1	1

From C to	Link	Hop Count
C	Local	0
A	2	1
B	3	1

At node D, its initial state is first modified when it receives the distance vector (B = 0, A = 1) from node B. Since D received that information on link 5, it updates its routing table as follows, adding one to each received hop count:

From D to	Link	Hop Count
D	Local	0
B	5	1
A	5	2

Now, let's assume node D receives the update of node C's recent update (C = 0, A = 1, B = 1) on link 4. As it does not have an entry for node C, it will add it to its routing table by entering C = 1 for link 4. When it adds 1 to the hop count for A received on link 4, it notes that the value is equal to the current hop count for A in its routing table. Thus, it discards the information about node A received from node C. The exception to this would be if the router maintained alternate routing entries to use in the event of a link failure. Next, node D would operate upon the vector $B = 1$ received on link 4, adding one to the hop count to obtain $B = 2$. Since that is more hops than the current entry, it would discard the received distance vector. Thus, D's routing table would appear as follows:

From D to	Link	Hop Count
D	Local	0
C	4	1
B	5	1
A	5	2

The preceding example provides a general indication of how RIP enables nodes to learn the topology of a network. In addition, if a link should fail, the condition can be easily compensated for as similar to bridge table entries, those of routers are also time stamped and the periodic transmission of distance vector information would result in a new route replacing the previously computed one.

One key limitation of RIP is the maximum hop distance it supports. This distance is 16 hops, which means that an alternative protocol must be used for large networks.

Configuration Example

Because Cisco Systems manufactures over 70 percent of all routers we will use its Internetworking Operating System (IOS) to illustrate an example of the router configuration process. In doing so we will assume that during the router setup process you entered the name of the router as Cisco, an enable password which governs access to the router's privileged mode of operation as "wxyz," and agreed to configure IP on a serial and Ethernet interface. Figure 7.14 illustrates the interfaces of the router and the assignment of IP addresses to each router interface.

Router Modes

Cisco routers support two modes of operation — user and privileged. The user mode is the default mode when you reboot a router and access it via a direct

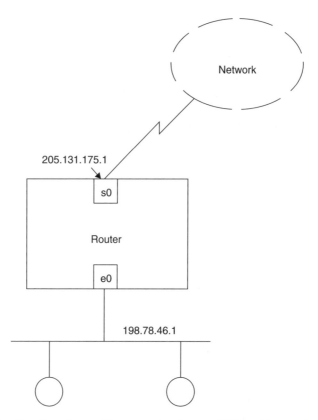

Figure 7.14 Configuring a Cisco router to use RIP as its routing protocol.

console connection or access the router via Telnet. When you access a router and are in its user mode this fact is denoted by the router name followed by the greater than (>) sign. If your router name is Cisco, the user mode prompt becomes:

Cisco >

Once in user mode you can display many items concerning the router to include its configuration; however, you cannot configure the router. To obtain the ability to configure the router you need to be in its privileged mode. To do so, you need to type "enable" at the user mode prompt and then press Enter. You will then be prompted to enter the enable password, after which the prompt changes to the router name followed by the pound sign (#) — called a hash sign in the UK. The following example illustrates how you would move from the user mode into the privileged mode when using a Cisco router:

Cisco > enable

Cisco > Password : wxyz

Cisco#

Cisco's IOS uses a command interpreter to execute commands you enter. That interpreter is referred to as the Exec and user and privileged modes can be considered to represent different levels of the Exec. Assuming you are in the privileged mode, you can obtain the ability to configure a router by entering the command "configure," or if you want to eliminate a prompt, enter the command "config t" to denote you are configuring the router from a terminal as opposed to configuring it from memory or the network. To configure the s0 (serial 0) interface with the IP address 205.131.175.1, you would enter the following IOS statements:

Cisco#config t

Enter configuration commands, one per line, End with CNTL/Z

Cisco(config)#interface s0

Cisco(config-if)#ip address 205.131.175.1 255.255.255.0

Once you define the IP addresses for each interface you need to configure a routing protocol, so let's do so. Since RIP is limited to 16 hops (0 through 15), which makes it suitable for small to medium networks, let's assume you will use this routing protocol. To configure RIP you would type "config t" at the privileged prompt. At the configuration prompt you would enter "router rip" to select RIP as the routing protocol. Next you would enter the keyword "network" followed by what is referred to as the major network number at the next config prompt. Here Cisco uses the term major network number to reference the IP network address for a Class A, B or C network directly connected to the router. From Figure 7.14 you would note that there is only one network connected to the router. Thus, you would configure RIP as follows:

Cisco#config t

Enter configuration commands, one per line. End with CNTL/Z.

Cisco(config)#router rip

Cisco(config-router)#network 198.78.46.0

If you had more than one network connected to the router you would repeat using the keyword "network" followed by the IP address for each network connected to the router. Once you finish entering the directly connected networks you would press CNTL + Z to end the configuration session. Now that we have an appreciation of how we would configure RIP in a Cisco environment, let's continue our examination of a few additional routing protocols.

Routing Table Maintenance Protocol

The Routing Table Maintenance Protocol (RTMP) was developed by Apple Computer for use with that vendor's AppleTalk network. Under RTMP, each router transmits messages to establish routing tables and update them periodically. The update process, during which information on an internet is exchanged between routers, also serves as a mechanism for implementing alternate routing. This is because the absence of update information for a greater than expected period of time converts the status of an entry in other router routing tables from "good" to "suspect" and then to "bad."

RTMP is delivered by AppleTalk's Data Delivery Protocol (DDP), which is a network layer connectionless service operating between two upper-layer processes referred to as *sockets*. Four types of packets are specified by RTMP: data, request, route data request, and response. Routing updates are transmitted as data packets. End nodes transmit request packets to acquire information about the identity of the internet routers (IRs) to which they can transmit nonlocal packets. Internet routers respond to route request packets with response packets, while end nodes that want to receive an RTMP data packet indicate this by sending a route data request packet. The latter packet type is also used by nodes that require routing information from IRs not directly connected to their network.

Routing Process

In the AppleTalk routing process, the source node first examines the destination network number. If the packet has a local network address, it is passed to the data link layer for delivery. Otherwise, the packet is passed to any of the IRs that reside on a network segment. The IR will examine the destination address of the packet and then check its routing tables to determine the next hop, routing the packet on a specific port that enables it to flow toward the next hop. Thus, a packet will travel through the internet on a hop-by-hop basis. When the packet reaches an IR connected to the destination network, the data link layer is used to deliver the packet to its local destination.

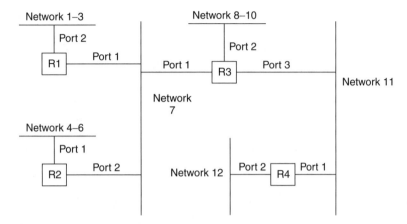

Rounting Table for Router R1

Network Range	Distance	Port	Next IR	Entry State
1–3	0	2	0	Good
7–7	0	1	0	Good
4–6	1	1	R2	Good
8–10	1	1	R3	Good
11–11	1	1	R3	Good
12–12	2	1	R3	Good

Figure 7.15 AppleTalk routing table example.

Figure 7.15 illustrates a sample AppleTalk network and the routing table for one router. Each AppleTalk routing table has five entries, as indicated. The *network range* defines the range of network numbers assigned to a particular network segment. The *distance* entry specifies the number of routers that must be traversed prior to the destination being reached, and *port* defines the router port used to provide access to a destination location. The *next IR* entry indicates the identifier of the next IR on the internet, and *entry state* defines the status of receiving routing updates. An entry state can go from "good" to "suspect" to "bad" if routing updates are not received within predefined time intervals.

Interior Gateway Routing Protocol

Cisco's proprietary Interior Gateway Routing Protocol is a distance vector protocol in which updates are transmitted at 90-second intervals. Each IGRP gateway operates on a local basis to determine the best route for forwarding data packets. Unlike protocols that require each router to have a complete routing table, each IGRP router computes only a portion of the routing table, based on its perspective of the Intranet. This enables the IGRP to support distributed routing without requiring each router to have a complete view of the internet.

Other features of the IGRP include the ability to establish routes automatically, perform load balancing dynamically over redundant links, and detect and remove bad circuits from the internet routing tables it develops. Routes are declared inaccessible if an update is not received within three update periods (270 seconds). After five update periods (450 seconds), the route is removed from the routing table.

IGRP, unlike RIP, supports a wide range of metrics that can be used to govern routing. Both reliability and load can be considered as well as inter-network delay and the bandwidth on a link. The use of IGRP occurs within an autonomous system (AS) that represents a group of routers connecting networks that use a common routing protocol. This makes it possible for a network administrator to set weighting factors for each routing metric or to allow the protocol to use default weights. An enhanced IGRP (EIGRP) was introduced by Cisco that incorporates the capabilities of link-state protocols into distant vector protocols. Under EIGRP a router stores all of its neighbors' routing tables so it can rapidly adapt to alternate routes. Other improvements under EIGRP include support for variable-length subnet masks and the transmission of partial table entries when the metric for a route changes in place of full periodic updates. As you might expect, in a large AS, this considerably reduces the overhead and the adverse effect of bandwidth congestion due to table updates.

Link State Protocols

A link state routing protocol addresses the traffic problem associated with any large networks that use a vector distance routing protocol. It does this by transmitting routing information only when there is a change in one of its links. A second difference between vector difference and link state protocols concerns the manner in which a route is selected when multiple routes are available between destinations. For a vector distance protocol, the best path is the one that has the fewest intermediate routers on hops between destinations. A link state protocol, however, can use multiple paths to provide traffic balancing between locations. In addition, a link state protocol permits routing to occur based on link delay, capacity, and reliability. This provides the network manager with the ability to specify a variety of route development situations.

SPF Algorithms

Link state routing protocols are implemented by a class of algorithms known as Shortest Path First (SPF). Unfortunately, this is a misnomer, since routing is not based on the shortest path.

The use of SPF algorithms requires each participating router to have complete knowledge of the intranet topology. Each router participating in an SPF algorithm then performs two tasks: status testing of neighboring routers and periodic transmission of link status information to other routers.

To test neighboring routers, a short message is periodically transmitted. If the neighbor replies, the link is considered to be up. Otherwise, the absence of a reply after a predefined period of time indicates that the link is down.

To provide link status information, each router will periodically broadcast a message indicating the status of each of its links. Unlike the vector distance protocol, in which routes are specified, an SPF link status message simply indicates whether communications are possible between pairs of routers. Using information in the link status message, routers are able to update their network maps.

Unlike vector distance protocols, in which tables are required to be exchanged, link state protocols such as SPF algorithms exchange a much lower volume of information in the form of link status queries and replies. Then, SPF participating routers simply broadcast the status of each of their links, and other routers use this information to update their intranet maps. This routing technique permits each router to compute routes independently of other routers, and eliminates the potential for the table flooding that can occur when a vector state protocol is used to interconnect a large number of networks.

To illustrate the operation of a link state routing protocol, let us return to the internet configuration previously illustrated in Figure 7.15. Figure 7.16 indicates the initial network map for router R1. This map lists the destination of all networks on the intranet from router R1, with their distances and routes. Note that if multiple routes exist to a destination, each route is listed. This defines a complete network topology, and allows alternate routes to be selected if link status information indicates that one or more routes cannot be used.

Destination	Distance	Route	Status
E1	0	direct	up
E2	0	direct	up
E3	1	R2	up
E3	2	R3,R2	up
E3	3	R3,R4,R2	up
E4	2	R2,R4	up
E4	2	R3,R4	up
E4	3	R3,R2,R4	up
TR1	1	R2	up
TR1	2	R3,R2	up
TR1	3	R3,R4,R2	up
TR2	1	R3	up
TR2	2	R2,R3	up
TR2	2	R2,R4	up
TR3	2	R3,R4	up
TR3	2	R2,R4	up
TR3	3	R3,R2,R4	up

Figure 7.16 Router R1 initial network map.

R1 link status

Link	Status
L1	Up
L2	Up

R2 link status

Link	Status
L2	Up
L3	Down
L4	Up

R3 link status

Link	Status
L1	Up
L3	Down

R4 link status

Link	Status
L4	Up
L5	Up

Figure 7.17 Link status messages.

Let us suppose that at a particular point in time, the link status messages generated by the routers in the intranet are as indicated in Figure 7.17. Note that both routers R2 and R3 have determined that link L3 is down. Using this information, router R1 would then update the status column for its network map. Since link L3 is down, all routes that require a data flow between R2 and R3 would have their status changed to "down." For example, for destination E3 via route R3, R2 would have its status changed to "down." Since the minimum distance to E3 is 1 hop via router R2, the failure of link L3 would not affect data flow from router R1 to network E3. Now consider the effect of link L2 becoming inoperative. This would affect route R2, which has the minimum distance to network E3. It would still leave route R3 = R4 = R2, although this route would have a distance of three hops. Of course, when a new link status message indicates that a previously declared down link is up, each router's network map is updated accordingly.

Examples of link state protocols include Open Shortest Path First (OSPF), OSI Intermediate System to Intermediate System (IS-IS), DECnet Phase V, and IBM's Advanced Peer-to-Peer Networking (APPN). Due to space limitations, we will review briefly the operational features of only the first of these link state protocols.

Open Shortest Path First Protocol

The OSPF protocol is an interior domain routing protocol that uses the SPF algorithm. Like the EGP, the OSPF protocol consists of a small core of different types of messages. Under the OSPF protocol, five message types are defined.

A Hello message is used to test the reachability of other devices. A database description message passes the topology. The remaining message types include a link status request, a link status update, and a link status acknowledgement message.

Initially, OSPF generates database description messages to initialize its network topology database. These messages are flooded through the domain. However, once a topological database is formed, routing table updates are transmitted at 30-minute intervals unless there is a change in the network, in which case there is an immediate update.

Like the EGP, OSPF routers use a Hello message to discover their neighbors. One of the key features of the OSPF protocol is its ability to authenticate messages. This means that you can't entice routers to transmit packets to a specific computer for examination or interception by generating low-cost routes. Another key feature of the OSPF protocol is its ability to support multiple active paths of equal weight: it selects each path in a round-robin manner. Table 7.1 provides a summary of 16 common routing protocol abbreviations, their meanings, and a short description of each protocol.

TABLE 7.1 Common Routing Protocols

AURP	AppleTalk Update Routing Protocol. This routing protocol is implemented in Apple networks and sends changes to routing tables via updates.
BGP	Border Gateway Protocol. This is a TCP/IP interdomain routing protocol.
CLNP	Connectionless Network Protocol. This is the OSI version of the IP routing protocol.
DDP	Datagram Delivery Protocol. This routing protocol is used in Apple's AppleTalk network.
EGP	Exterior Gateway Protocol. This TCP/IP protocol is used to locate networks on another domain.
IDRP	Inter-Domain Routing Protocol. This is the OSI interdomain routing protocol.
IGP	Interior Gateway Protocol. This TCP/IP protocol is used by routers to move information within a domain.
IGRP	Interior Gateway Routing Protocol. This is a proprietary routing protocol developed by Cisco Systems.
IP	Internet Protocol. This is the network layer protocol of the TCP/IP (Transmission Control Protocol/Internet Protocol) suite of protocols.
IPX	Internet Packet Exchange. This routing protocol is based on Xerox's XNS, was developed by Novell, and is implemented in Novell's NetWare.
IS-IS	Intermediate-Station-to-Intermediate-Station. This is an OSI link-state routing protocol that routes both OSI and RIP traffic.
NCP	NetWare Core Protocol. This is Novell's NetWare specific routing protocol.
OSPF	Open Shortest Path First. This is a TCP/IP link-state routing protocol that provides an alternative to RIP.
RIP	Routing Information Protocol. This routing protocol is used in TCP/IP, XNS, and IPX. Under RIP, a message is broadcast to find the shortest route to a destination based on a hop count.
RTMP	Routing Table Maintenance Protocol. This is Apple's distance-vector protocol.
SPF	Shortest Path First. This link-state routing protocol uses a set of user-defined parameters to find the best route between two points.

7.5 Filtering

The filtering capability of routers is primarily thought of as a mechanism to implement security. Although filtering does indeed provide a mechanism to implement network security, it also provides a mechanism to regulate network traffic. Through the regulation of network traffic you may be able to predefine routes for particular types of packets, protocols, and addresses, as well as different combinations of the preceding.

Another area where filtering has achieved a considerable degree of use is in providing a mechanism to differentiate the service provided to different classes of traffic. This is accomplished by associating filters with different router queues and enabling a specific router queuing method. Figure 7.18 illustrates how you could use an outbound filter to place all UDP traffic using a predefined destination port number or IP address into queue 1, while all other traffic is routed into queue 2. If queue 1 is always serviced when it is occupied, this would prioritize UDP traffic over all other traffic. If UDP is used to transport digitized voice, in effect this filtering and queuing scheme provides a Quality of Service (QoS) capability from the router into the network.

The filtering capability of routers is highly dependent upon this functionality as well as the ingenuity of the router manager or administrator. To illustrate the latter, we will define a few generic router filtering functions to illustrate how those functions can be applied to achieve a variety of filtering results that could satisfy different organizational requirements. Although the router filtering functions we will define are not applicable to a specific router, most routers will support the functions we will cover. Thus, the filtering examples presented in this section represent practical examples that illustrate how you can control network traffic. In Chapter 9, when we devote an entire chapter to the issue of security, we will turn our attention to the creation and operation of Cisco router access lists. Until then, we will conclude this chapter with generic examples of the use of router filtering.

The key to the functionality of a router's filtering capability is the router's ability to *look* inside the composition of packets. Most routers, at a minimum, provide filtering based upon the examination of the contents of the destination and source addresses transported by a packet. Other routers provide a filtering capability based upon the Ethernet protocol value carried in the type/length field, and the DSAP and SSAP values carried in the data field. This additional capability provides you with the ability, for example, to enable or disable Novell IPX traffic between certain router ports, enable or disable TCP/IP traffic

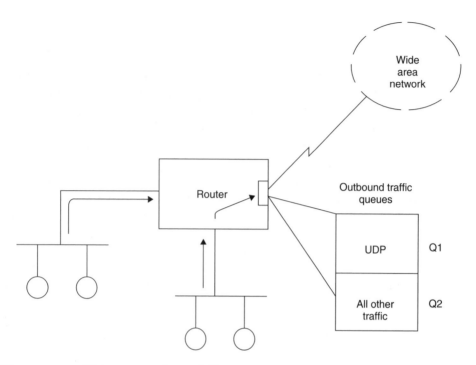

Figure 7.18 Using an outbound filter to prioritize UDP traffic with a prede-fined destination port.

between the same or different router ports, and regulate other protocols that may be carried to and from an Ethernet LAN.

Another common filtering capability associated with routers that support the TCP/IP protocol stack is the ability to filter based upon TCP and UDP well-known ports. For example, by blocking outbound packets with a TCP port address of 80 an organization could bar HTTP traffic, in effect prohibiting employees from surfing the World Wide Web.

Figure 7.19 illustrates the connection of an Ethernet network to a four-port router. In this example, ports 1, 2, and 3 can represent connections to other routers via wide area network transmission facilities or to other LANs a short distance away. Since we are primarily interested in how we can use filtering as a mechanism to regulate traffic, it is more important to focus upon the flow of data between router ports than the devices connected to each hub. However, since we need a point of reference, we will discuss traffic routed to and from the Ethernet network connected to port 0 in Figure 7.19.

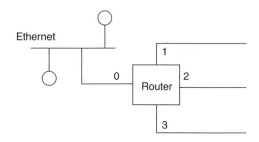

Ethernet

Figure 7.19 Through filtering you can implement security as well as regulate network traffic.

Filtering Expressions

Most routers perform filtering based upon specified patterns linked by logical operators. Thus, you would first specify one or more patterns to be filtered, and then link multiple patterns or prefix a single pattern with an appropriate logical operator. Before actually creating a filter pattern, it is important to note how the manufacturer of the router implements filtering. Some vendors enable everything, requiring you to preclude certain data flows by filtering. Other vendors inhibit everything, only permitting data flow based upon positive filters. For our examples, we will presume the manufacturer of our router permits or enables all data flow unless it is specifically precluded.

Filtering Examples

For our first example, let's assume you have a UNIX server connected to the Ethernet LAN and do not want IP traffic from port 2 to flow to the server. Assuming P1 (pattern 1) = IP, originating port is PORT2, and destination port is PORT0, you would set up the filter as follows:

Originate	Destination
P1 AND PORT2	PORT0

Thus, any IP frames received on port 2 and destined for port 0 would be filtered or blocked.

Now let's assume you do not want to transfer Ethernet broadcast packets beyond that network. To do so you would set the pattern (P1) to recognize a destination address of FF-FF-FF-FF-FF-FF, which is the Ethernet broadcast address. Then, you would set up the filter as follows:

Originate	Destination
P1 AND PORT0	PORT1 OR PORT2 OR PORT3

For another example, let's assume router filtering patterns and ports support the use of the logical NOT operator. Then, you could set up the filter for the preceding example as follows:

Originate	Destination
P1 AND PORT0	NOT PORT0

Router Access Lists

To illustrate the use of filtering for protecting stations on an internal corporate network from potential hackers lurking on the Internet, consider Figure 7.20. In that illustration several workstations and a server are shown connected to an Ethernet LAN, which in turn is shown connected via a router to an ISP, which in turn is connected to the Internet. Assuming the corporate Ethernet is assigned the IP network address 206.172.31.0, let's assume the workstations and server have host addresses of .2, .3, and .4, as indicated in the lower portion of Figure 7.20.

Many routers use what are referred to as access lists to enable filtering operations on an inbound and outbound basis. To illustrate the potential use of an access list, let's assume we are using that list with the TCP/IP protocol and each list entry has the following format:

Operation direction from IP address/port to IP address/port

Here "operation" is either *enable* or *disable,* while "direction" is either *inbound* or *outbound.*

Let's further assume that you can use the global asterisk character (∗) to reference *all*. Then, assuming you want to restrict inbound traffic to the server to Telnet operations from any IP address, you would code the following access list entry:

ENABLE INBOUND ∗/23 206.172.31.3/23

The preceding entry allows Telnet (port 23) from any IP address to the server running Telnet at address 206.172.31.3 to its Telnet port. The reason a port

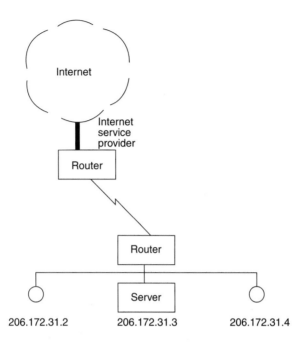

Figure 7.20 Connecting a corporate LAN to the Internet exposes each corporate computer to a virtually unlimited number of hackers. Through programming router access lists this exposure can be minimized.

address is required at the destination results from the fact that both workstations and servers can support multiple simultaneous TCP/IP applications. For example, a Web server can also support FTP as well as ping, finger, and other TCP/IP applications.

For a second example of the use of an access list, let's assume you wish to bar all employees on your local LAN from sending Internet mail. Since SMTP uses port 25, your access list entry would appear as follows:

DISABLE OUTBOUND 206.172.31 ∗ /25 ∗ /25

In this example we used the global character (∗) to replace the last digit in the 206 network dotted decimal position, in effect barring all stations (1 to 254) on the network from sending data on port 25 to any IP address.

Although the preceding examples illustrate but a fraction of router filtering capability, they illustrate several important concepts. First, by filtering on source and/or destination addresses and protocols, it becomes possible to enable or disable traffic. Secondly, by reaching into the frame router, filtering permits you to enable or disable the flow of specific protocols. The latter is an important consideration when connecting a LAN to the Internet, since many organizations do not wish to provide access to their computer systems connected to the LAN by anyone that has Internet access.

Through the packet filtering capability of a router you obtain the ability to control the flow of data between and through router interfaces. As indicated in this section, this control can be used to expedite traffic or as a security mechanism. Concerning the latter, readers are referred to Chapter 9 for specific information concerning security, including an examination of the types of access lists supported by Cisco routers.

7.6 Performance Considerations

Regardless of the type of router and its protocol support and routing algorithm, the processing required for its operation is considerably more than that required for a bridge. This means that you can expect the packet processing capability of routers to be considerably less than that of bridges.

High-capacity bridges can be expected to provide a forwarding rate between 100,000 and 200,000 packets per second. In comparison, most routers have a forwarding capacity rated under 100,000 packets per second. Although this may appear to indicate a poor level of performance in comparison to bridges, note that only when functioning as a local bridge will a high-capacity bridge actually use its full capacity. Otherwise, when used to interconnect remote networks via a wide area transmission facility, a remote bridge will be able to use only a fraction of its packet-processing capability for the forwarding of packets over a relatively slow-speed WAN transmission facility. Similarly, when routers are connected to a T1 or E1 line or to a frame relay service, they may not be able to use their full packet forwarding capability. To see this, refer to Table 7.2, which indicates the maximum packets-per-second transfer capability of a router connected to five types of transmission lines, based on five packet sizes. Note that a T1 line operating at 1.544 Mbps supports a maximum transfer of 3015 64-byte packets per second. In actuality, since the wide area network transmission facility results in the use of a WAN protocol to wrap LAN packets, the actual PPS rate obtainable is normally 15 to 20 percent less than that indicated in Table 7.2. Thus, the forward rate of most routers greatly exceeds the capacity of a single WAN connection. This means that only a requirement for the use of multiple router ports should make the forwarding rate of the router into a key equipment acquisition issue.

TABLE 7.2 Maximum Packet Transfer Rates (Packets per Second)

Packet Size (bytes)	Wide Area Network Transmission Facility				
	56 Kbps	128 Kbps	256 Kbps	512 Kbps	1.544 Mbps
64	109	250	500	1000	3015
128	54	125	250	500	1508
500	14	32	64	128	386
1000	7	16	32	64	193
1518	5	10	20	40	127

Otherwise, the communication, transport, and routing protocols supported are more important criteria for determining whether a vendor's product can support the requirements of an organization.

One key exception to the preceding involves the use of routers connected to very high-speed transmission facilities, such as a T3 line operating at approximately 45 Mbps or a synchronous optical network (SONET) connection operating at 155 Mbps. In such situations, the forwarding rate of the router would be an extremely important consideration.

chapter eight

Wireless Ethernet

The purpose of this chapter is to make readers familiar with a relatively new method of constructing or expanding an Ethernet network using the "ether" as the transmission media. Referred to as wireless Ethernet, the technology we will examine in this chapter is also commonly known as wireless LANs, 802.11 networks and "Wi-Fi," with the latter a term used to denote wireless fidelity, a new term used for fast wireless LAN technology that is a play of words on a stereo system.

8.1 Overview

The IEEE 802.11 standard for wireless LANs represents a base that has evolved over the years. The original 802.11 standard dates to 1997 and resulted in three physical layers being standardized to transport Ethernet frames over the air. One physical layer is for infrared transmission, while the other two physical layers provide support for radio frequency (RF) communications through the use of Frequency Hopping Spread Spectrum (FHSS) and Direct Sequence Spread Spectrum (DSSS) that were originally developed to resist jamming in a military environment.

Figure 8.1 illustrates the architecture associated with the original IEEE 802.11 standard in comparison with the lower two layers of the ISO OSI Reference Model. In examining Figure 8.1 you will note that the media access control method used by the IEEE 802.11 standard is not the basic CSMA/CD access protocol used by wired Ethernet. Instead, a protocol referred to as Carrier Sense Multiple Access with Collision Avoidance (CSMA/CA) is used. Later in this chapter we will turn our attention to how CSMA/CA operates.

The original IEEE 802.11 standard supports operations at either 1 Mbps or 2 Mbps under each of the three physical layers. Recognizing that infrared is rarely used and data rates of 1 Mbps and 2 Mbps are not sufficient for many modern applications in a shared over-the-air environment resulted in

ISO OSI
Reference Model   IEEE 802.11 layers

	Logical link control
Data link layer	
	Media access control (CSMA/CA)
Physical layer	FHSS	DSSS	IR

Legend:

FHSS Frequency Hopping Spread Spectrum
DSSS Direct Sequence Spread Spectrum
IR   Infrared

Figure 8.1   IEEE 802.11 architecture.

several additions to the IEEE standard. One addition was the IEEE 802.11b specification, which extended the operating rate of DSSS to 5.5 Mbps and 11 Mbps and which represented the most popular type of wireless LAN when this book revision occurred. Both the basic 802.11 and the 802.11b specifications operate in the 2.4 GHz unlicensed Industrial Scientific and Medical (ISM) band. While the Federal Communications Commission (FCC) in the U.S. regulates the maximum power and transmission method, the fact that the ISM band is unlicensed means that a user does not have to obtain a license to use equipment in that frequency band.

A second addendum to the IEEE 802.11 standard is the 802.11a specification. This specification defines the use of a multi-carrier frequency transmission method in the 5 GHz ISM band. The multi-carrier frequency method is referred to as orthogonal frequency division multiplexing (OFDM), which results in a large number of carriers being used, each of which operates at a low data rate, but cumulatively they support a high data rate up to 54 Mbps. Because higher frequencies attenuate more rapidly than lower frequencies, the range of 802.11a-compatible devices is significantly less than that of 802.11b devices. This results in a requirement to install additional access points to obtain the same area of wireless LAN coverage and increases the cost of a very high speed wireless LAN. Because many network operators require more speed than that provided by the 802.11b specification but a higher range than that supported by the 802.11a specification, the IEEE has been working on a new standard, referred to as 802.11g, which doubles the data rate of 802.11b networks to 22 Mbps in the 2.4 GHz frequency band.

Network Topology

The IEEE 802.11 wireless LAN standards support two types of network topology, referred to as ad hoc and infrastructure. Figure 8.2 illustrates an example of an ad hoc network. An ad hoc network consists of two or more wireless nodes or stations that recognize one another and communicate on a peer-to-peer basis within their area of RF or IR coverage. The term ''ad hoc'' is assigned as this type of network environment is commonly formed when two wireless devices come into the range of one another and communicate on a temporary basis until one or more devices depart the area.

A second type of wireless LAN topology is known as a network infrastructure. In its most basic form a wireless network infrastructure consists of an access point (AP) connected to a wired LAN and one or more client stations. Figure 8.3 illustrates an example of a wireless network infrastructure. In this example an access point is shown connected to a hub on a wired LAN. The access point can be considered to represent a bridge between the wired and wireless LANs. However, in addition to providing bridging between the wired and wireless networks, an access point also interconnects wireless clients. That is, when an access point is present, client stations communicate with one another through the AP and not on a peer-to-peer basis.

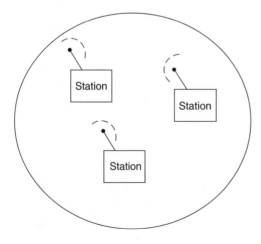

Figure 8.2 A wireless ad hoc network infrastructure.

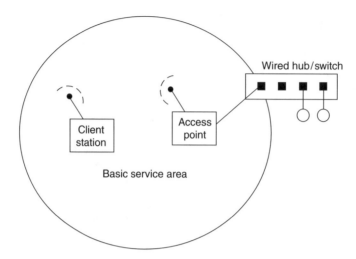

Figure 8.3 A wireless network infrastructure contains at least one access point and one wireless station, referred to as a Basic Service Set.

When two or more mobile nodes come together to communicate or if one mobile client comes into close proximity to an access point, this action results in the formation of a Basic Service Set (BSS). Each BSS has an identification that typically corresponds to the 48-bit MAC address of the wireless network adapter card. That identification is referred to as a Basic Service Set Identification (BSSID) and the area of coverage within which members of a BSS can communicate is referred to as a Basic Service Area (BSA).

When wiring an office, college campus or government agency, you will more than likely need to install multiple access points. When this is done, the basic service areas of coverage from multiple Basic Service Sets form what is referred to as an Extended Service Set (ESS). The wired LAN infrastructure functions as a distribution system, which enables clients to roam and be serviced by different APs. Figure 8.4 illustrates an Extended Service Set formed by the use of two access points interconnected by a wired LAN used as a Distribution System (DS). Each BSS within a DS is said to be operating in an infrastructure mode.

In examining Figure 8.4 it should be noted that the Basic Service Sets may or may not overlap. In addition, each station associates itself with a particular access point based upon selecting the one with the greatest received signal strength. Each access point in the Extended Service Set will have an ESSID (Extended Service Set Identifier) programmed into it. The ESSID can be considered to represent the subnet the access point is connected to. You can

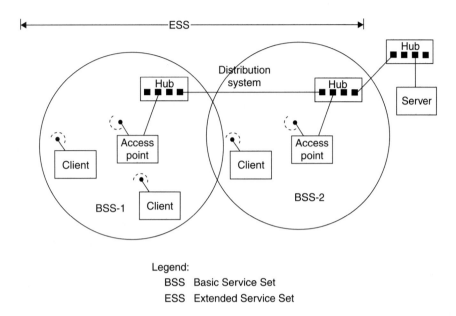

Figure 8.4 An extended service set consists of one or more basic service sets connected via a distribution system.

also program the ESSID into a station, which then requires it to connect to a like programmed access point.

When creating an extended service set it is also important to consider the frequency of operation of each access point. This is due to the need to minimize the overlapping of frequency use by adjacent access points. Because FHSS and DSSS operating access points have different restrictions concerning frequency overlap, you must also consider the transmission scheme used when you design a large wireless infrastructure.

Roaming

In examining Figure 8.4 note that the movement of a client from BSS-1 to BSS-2 or vice versa represents a roaming action. Although IEEE 802.11 wireless LANs support roaming, a wireless operational LAN environment is commonly a fixed-location environment in comparison to cellular telephones, which are used anywhere from a reception area, to the office, and even in the powder room. Thus, while 802.11 wireless LANs support roaming, the actual degree of this activity is limited in comparison to a cellular telephone.

As a mobile client moves from one access-point service area to another, a mechanism is required for one AP to drop the user while the other begins servicing the user. A mobile client will typically monitor the signal-to-noise ratio (SNR) as it moves and, if required, scan for available access points and connect to a desired AP. APs periodically transmit a beacon frame that enables clients to note the presence of one or more APs and select the one with the best SNR. However, the actual method used depends upon a vendor's implementation method. For example, in a Cisco wireless LAN roaming environment a client will become associated with a new access point when three conditions occur. First, the signal strength of the new access point must be at least 50 percent. Second, the percentage of time the client's transmitter is active is less than 20 percent of the present access point. The third condition requires the number of users on the new access point to be four fewer than on the present access point. If the first two conditions are not met, then the client will not change access points regardless of the number of users associated with the AP.

Physical Layer Operations

As discussed earlier in this chapter, the original IEEE 802.11 wireless LAN standard supports a choice of three physical layers — infrared and two radio-frequency layers. The infrared physical layer is based upon the use of pulse position modulation (PPM) at peak data rates of 1 Mbps, with an optional 2 Mbps rate. Because infrared is limited to use within a single room without barriers, its use is severely limited. In fact, this author is not aware of any infrared-based 802.11 LANs. Because of this, in this section we will focus our attention upon the RF physical layers. Both Frequency Hopping Spread Spectrum (FHSS) and Direct Sequence Spread Spectrum operate in the 2.4 GHz ISM band, which represents a worldwide-recognized unlicensed band. However, it should be noted that the actual frequencies for the 2.4 GHz band can vary from country to country, as noted in Table 8.1.

FHSS

Under Frequency Hopping Spread Spectrum data is transmitted for a short duration, referred to as dwell time at a single frequency. At the end of that time duration the transmitter shifts to a new frequency and resumes transmission. Thus, a FHSS system uses narrow-band data transmission but changes its frequency periodically to create a wide-band transmission system.

Figure 8.5 illustrates an example of how an FHSS system hops for predefined time intervals using different center frequencies based upon a predefined

TABLE 8.1 2.4 GHz ISM Frequency Allocation

Region	Allocated Frequency
United States	2.400–2.4835
Europe (except France/Spain)	2.400–2.4835
Japan	2.4710–2.4970
France	2.4465–2.4835
Spain	2.4450–2.4750

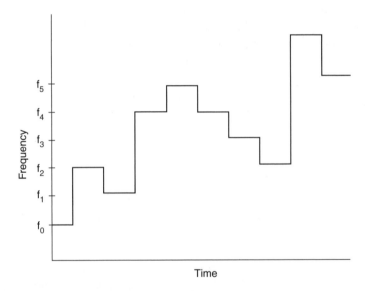

Figure 8.5 A frequency hopping spread spectrum system hops at a fixed time interval, known as the dwell time, around a wide band using different center frequencies in a predefined sequence.

algorithm. By only dwelling at one frequency for a short time duration, an FHSS system can alleviate the effect of narrow-band noise occurring in portions of the transmission band.

Although a military system based upon FHSS keeps the algorithm used for hopping a secret, in the wonderful world of wireless LANs the hopping sequence is well known. In fact, both the frequencies at which hopping occurs as well as the number of hops within an assigned ISM band are commonly regulated to prevent a wireless LAN from interfering with other electronic equipment. In the United States FHSS uses 79 channels, each 1 MHz wide. In Japan, the number of channels is reduced to 23. For both locations channels are selected according to a pseudo-random selection algorithm that requires a dwell time of 20 ms per channel and all channels to be used prior to being able to reuse a channel. Under the IEEE 802.11 standard 78 different hopping sequences are defined. Each hopping sequence is referred to as a channel, which can cause a degree of confusion if you scan the standard without noting this relationship. At the physical layer FHSS uses two- or four-level Gaussian Frequency Shift Keying (GFSK) modulation. Under two-level FSK modulation each bit is encoded by the transmission of a distinct frequency from two available frequencies. Thus, the bit rate is the same as the baud or signaling rate and the 1 MHz bandwidth used for each short transmission supports a data rate of 1 Mbps. When four-level GFSK is used, each pair (dibit) of bits is encoded into one of four frequencies. Thus, the bit rate is twice the baud rate, resulting in a data rate of 2 Mbps. The term "Gaussian" prefixes FSK because the wave form is Gaussian filtered.

Now that we have an appreciation for FHSS let us turn our attention to how DSSS operates.

DSSS

Under Direct Sequence Spread Spectrum (DSSS) a spreading code is used to spread each bit to be transmitted such that a number of bits representing each bit are actually transmitted. The spreading code used under the 802.11 standard is referred to as a Barker code and its use results in each bit being replaced by 11 bits. At 1 Mbps Differential Binary Phase Shift Keying (DBPSK) is used for modulation, resulting in each bit being represented by one of two possible phase changes. Because 11 bits replace each data bit, the resulting signal is spread over 11 MHz. At 2 Mbps Differential Quadrature Phase Shift Keying (DQPSK) is employed as the modulation method, which results in two bits being encoded into one phase change. When this modulation method is used, the bit rate becomes twice the baud rate, which results in a 2 Mbps data rate.

Table 8.2 gives an example of DSSS coding using a five-bit sequences from a pseudo-random bit generator. Note that data for transmission is simply logically modulo-2 added to obtain the data stream to be modulated.

Upon demodulation the same pseudo-random bit sequence is modulo-2 subtracted to obtain the original setting of the bit that was spread. If a transmission error occurs, the receiver simply selects the most popular bit

TABLE 8.2 DSSS Bit Spreading Example using a Five-bit Spreading Code

Data bits	1	0
Five-bit spreading code	10110	01001
Modulo-2 addition (data to be modulated)	01001	01001
Demodulated data	01001	01001
Five-bit spreading code	10110	01001
Modulo-2 subtraction	11111	00000

setting. That is, a if a five-bit spreading code was used and as a result of the modulo-2 subtraction process at the receiver, three bits were set to a value of 1 while two were set to a value of 0, the bit setting would be assumed to be 1.

Similar to FHSS, the use of DSSS can vary by location. Under the IEEE 802.11 standard the use of 13 DSSS channels is defined for transporting an 11-bit Barker-coded 22 MHz signal. For operation in the United States the 802.11 standard defines the use of 11 independent channels. Although Europe and many Asian countries permit the use of 13 channels, in Japan the small amount of available bandwidth (see Table 8.1) results in the support of a single channel. Table 8.3 lists the carrier-frequency channel assignments. As previously noted, depending upon the physical location of a DSSS system a subset of available channels may be required to be used.

In the United States and Europe DSSS channel definitions permit three frequency-isolated channels available for co-location. An example of channel co-location is illustrated in Figure 8.6. This frequency isolation enables organizations to operate up to three DSSS functioning access points within close proximity to one another without one access point interfering with another.

High-Speed Wireless LANs

There are two extensions to the basic IEEE 802.11 standard for which equipment had reached the market when this book revision was performed. Those extensions are the IEEE 802.11b specification, for which equipment conforming to that standard dominates the market, and the IEEE 802.11a specification. Although the modulation methods differ for each method, they use the same

TABLE 8.3   2.4 GHz DSSS Channels

Channel	Frequency (MHz)
1	2412
2	2416
3	2422
4	2427
5	2432
6	2437
7	2442
8	2447
9	2452
10	2457
11	2462
12	2467
13	2473

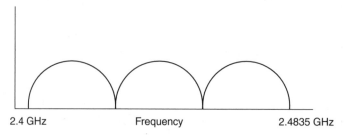

2.4 GHz   Frequency   2.4835 GHz

Figure 8.6 DSSS supports up to three non-overlapping channels in the 2.4 GHz band.

access protocol, a topic we will focus our attention upon once we obtain an appreciation of the two extensions to the basic IEEE 802.11 standard.

802.11b

Under the 802.11b extension to the IEEE 802.11 standard the data rate was increased to 5.5 Mbps and 11 Mbps under DSSS operations. At the higher data rates of 5.5 Mbps and 11 Mbps DSSS transmitters and receivers use different pseudo-random codes. Collectively, the higher modulation rates are referred to as Complementary Code Keying (CCK).

802.11a

Under the 802.11a extension to the IEEE 802.11 standard orthogonal frequency division modulation (OFDM) is employed in the 5 GHz frequency band. Under OFDM multiple-modulated carriers are used instead of a single carrier, as illustrated in Figure 8.7. Here each modulated signal is orthogonal to the other modulated signals.

The term orthogonal describes the axis of the signals and the fact that they do not interfere with one another. Because multiple signals are transmitted by a single user, the carriers can be said to be multiplexed. Thus, the transmission of multiple carriers at 90 degree angles to one another was given the term OFDM. However, if you are familiar with the operation of DSL modems or one of the first 9600 BPS analog dial modems, you are also probably aware of the term "multitone" used to denote the use of multiple carriers. Thus, OFDM can be considered to represent a multitone transmission scheme.

Under the 802.11a standard 48 data and four pilot carriers or a total of 52 carriers are transmitted within a 20 MHz channel. This action makes use of the three blocks or bands of frequency allocated by the FCC for unlicensed operations in the 5 GHz band. A 200 MHz band from 5.15 GHz to 5.35 MHz has two sub-bands. The first 100 MHz in the lower section is restricted to a maximum power output of 50 mW, while the second 100 MHz has a more generous 250 mW maximum power output. A third band at 5.725 MHz to 5.825 MHz is designed for outdoor applications and supports a maximum of 1 W of power output.

Because the 5 GHz band has almost four times the bandwidth of the ISM band, the developers of the 802.11a specification turned to OFDM to make

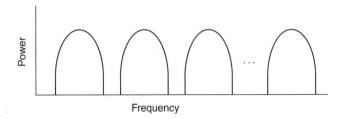

Figure 8.7 Orthogonal frequency division multiplexing results in the transmission of multiple carriers, each modulating a small amount of data.

better use of available bandwidth. As previously mentioned, each 20 MHz channel consists of 48 data subchannels and four used for pilot tones and error correction, with each subchannel approximately 300 kHz wide.

Several different modulation methods are supported under the 802.11a standard. Binary Phase Shift Keying (BPSK) is used to encode 125 kbps of data per channel, resulting in a 6 Mbps data rate. When Quadrature Phase Shift Keying (PSK) is used, the amount of data encoded increases to 250 kbps per channel, which results in a 12 Mbps data rate. A 16-level quadrature amplitude modulation method that encodes four bits per signal change permits a data rate of 24 Mbps. At the "top end of the line" a 64-level QAM modulation method is supported. 64 QAM can operate encoding either 8 or 10 bits per signal change, permitting a maximum data rate of 1.125 Mbps per 300 Hz channel. Because 48 data subchannels are supported per channel, this results in a maximum data rate of 54 Mbps.

Although the 802.11a specification supports a much higher data rate than the 802.11b specification, it is important to remember that higher frequencies attenuate much more rapidly than lower frequencies. As a result of this, the range of 802.11a equipment is probably half that of 802.11b products, which means the radius of coverage of an 802.11a access point will be one-fourth that of an 802.11b access point.

Access Method

Unlike wired Ethernet, which uses the CSMA/CD access protocol, wireless Ethernet LANs use what is referred to as a distributed coordination function (DCF). DCF represents a modification of the Carrier Sense Multiple Access/Collision Avoidance (CSMA/CA) protocol. Under the CSMA/CA protocol each station listens to the air for activity of other users. If the channel it is tuned to is idle, the station can transmit. However, if the channel has activity, the station will wait until transmission ceases and then enter a random back-off procedure. This action is designed to prevent multiple stations from seizing the channel immediately after the completion of an in-progress transmission. Under the distribution coordination function access method a period of time referred to as the DCF interframe space (DIFS) determines if a packet can be transmitted. That is, if the medium is sensed to be available for a duration of time that exceeds the DIFS, a packet can be immediately transmitted.

A second time interval that comes into play under the DCF access method is the short interframe space (SIFS). Under the IEEE 802.11 standard a receiver must transmit a positive acknowledgement (ACK) to the transmitter when a packet is received error free. An ACK will be transmitted after the SIFS, which is of less duration than the DIFS. This ensures that an ACK is transmitted prior to any new frame being transmitted. If an ACK is not received within a period of time, the transmitter will assume the frame was corrupted and will re-transmit the frame at the first opportunity to do so.

Figure 8.8 illustrates the relationship of the DIFS and SIFS to the transmission of data. At the top of the illustration the transmitting device is assumed to listen to the channel and observe no activity for at least one DCF Interframe Space (DIFS) prior to transmitting a frame. The receiving device must then wait one Short Interframe Space (SIFS) prior to acknowledging the frame.

A second device requiring the ability to transmit is shown in the lower portion of Figure 8.8. This device is assumed to need to transmit a frame, but listens to the channel and hears the transmission of the first device or the acknowledgement of the receiver. The time from the frame being placed onto the channel through the DIFS following the receiver's ACK represents a deferred access time. Because a transmission was sensed to be in progress, the second device must wait a random period after the deferred access time. The second transmitter sets an internal time to an integer number of slot times and observes when the DIFS time expires. Upon the expiration of the DIFS time the timer of the second transmitter decrements towards zero. If the channel is still available when the timer decrements to zero, the second station can

Figure 8.8 The CSMA/CA access protocol is based upon two key timers and a back-off algorithm.

commence transmission. Otherwise, if the channel is used by another station prior to the timer reaching zero, its setting is retained at its current value for future use.

The Hidden Node Problem

Because radio-frequency communications can be easily blocked by obstructions, it becomes possible for one node to be placed in a situation where it doesn't hear another. When this situation occurs, another node would listen to a channel and an obstruction hiding the transmission of another station would make the node think it is available for use when it is actually occupied. The result of this action would be a propagation of two radio waves that at a distant point collide, preventing other nodes from using the channel. To reduce the probability of collisions, a derivative of the CSMA/CA protocol referred to as Virtual Carrier Sense (VSC) is used by the 802.11 standard. Under VCS a station that needs to transmit information will first transmit a Request to Send (RTS) frame. The RTS frame represents a relatively short control frame that contains the source and destination address and the duration of the following transmission. The duration is specified in terms of the time for the transmission of a frame carrying data and the acknowledgement of the frame by the receiver. The receiver responds to the RTS frame with a Clear To Send (CTS) control frame that indicates the same time duration information as contained in the RTS control frame.

A station that receives either an RTS or CTS control frame will set its virtual carrier sense indicator for the duration of the transmission. The VSC indicator is referred to as the Network Allocation Vector (NAV) by the 802.11 standard and serves as a mechanism to alert all other stations on the air to back off or defer their transmission.

If a station transmitting an RTS frame does not receive a corresponding CTS frame within a predefined period of time, the originator will assume a collision has occurred. Then, the originator will listen to the channel and, upon noting it is free, transmit another RTS frame. Once a CTS frame is received, the originator will send a data frame. The receiver will then return an ACK frame to acknowledge a successful transmission.

The use of RTS and CTS frames, while reducing the probability of collisions occurring at a receiver from a station "hidden" from the transmitter, adds overhead to the media access operation. Due to this, most manufacturers disable this option by default, requiring network managers to enable it on both client stations and access points.

8.2 Frame Formats

Similar to wired Ethernet, where there is one basic frame format, wireless LANs also have a basic data frame format. However, wireless LANs also support two additional types of frames. One type, referred to as control frames, was briefly mentioned when we discussed the hidden node. The third type of frame supported by wireless LANs is management frames, which are used to exchange management information between stations at layer 2 but which are not forwarded to upper layers in the protocol suite.

Data Frame

Figure 8.9 illustrates the format of the MAC data frame which is used to transmit information between stations. This basic data frame contains nine fields, with two fields subdivided into additional fields. As we will note later in this section, several fields from this frame are used in other types of frames.

In examining Figure 8.9, you will note that the 802.11 frame permits a body that can be up to 2312 bytes in length. Because the maximum length Ethernet frame has a 1500-byte Information field, the wireless LAN frame can transport a maximum wired Ethernet frame. However, because the bit error rate on a radio link can considerably exceed that of a wired LAN, this

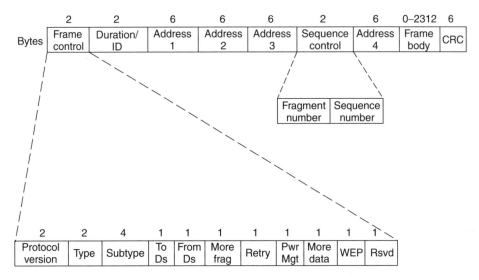

Figure 8.9   The basic 802.11 MAC data frame format.

means that the probability of a bit error increases as the length of the wireless frame increases. To compensate for this higher wireless bit error probability, a simple fragmentation and re-assembly mechanism is included in the 802.11 standard and we will shortly examine this. To obtain an appreciation of the manner by which the MAC data frame conveys information, let us turn our attention to the use of the fields and subfields in the frame.

Control Field

The 16-bit control field consists of 11 subfields, with eight representing one-bit fields whose setting indicates whether a specific feature or function is enabled or disabled. In this section we will examine the use of each subfield in the order they appear in the control field.

Protocol Version Subfield

The two-bit Protocol Version subfield provides a mechanism to identify the version of the IEEE 802.11 standard. In the initial version of the standard the value of the Protocol Version subfield is set to 0.

Type and Subtype Subfields

The Type and Subtype subfields consist of six bits that identify the type of frame and its function or subtype. Bits 2 and 3 denote the type of frame. Although the use of two bits permits four types of frames to be defined, at the present time only three types are defined—management, control, and data. The Subtype subfield consists of bits 4 through 7 and defines the function of a specific type of frame. Table 8.4 lists the Type and Subtype subfield values to include a description of what the values of the y-bit positions indicate.

In examining the entries in Table 8.4 note that the previously mentioned RTS, CTS and ACK functions represent the frames we briefly described earlier and the format of which we will investigate later in this section. The Beacon frame represents the frame an access point periodically generates to indicate its presence to stations while probe frames are used to query the status of a device.

ToDS

This 1-bit field is set to a value of 1 when the frame is addressed to an access point for forwarding to the distribution system. Otherwise, the bit is set to a value of 0.

TABLE 8.4   Type and Subtype Values

Type Value b3 b2	Type Description	Subtype Value b7 b6 b5 b4	Subtype Description
00	Management	0000	Association Request
00	Management	0001	Association Response
00	Management	0010	Association Request
00	Management	0011	Association Response
00	Management	0100	Probe Request
00	Management	0101	Probe Response
00	Management	0110–0111	Reserved
00	Management	1000	Beacon
00	Management	1001	ATM
00	Management	1010	Disassociation
00	Management	1011	Authentication
00	Management	1100	De-authentication
00	Management	1101–1111	Reserved
01	Control	0000–0001	Reserved
01	Control	1010	PS-Poll
01	Control	1011	RTS
01	Control	1100	CTS
01	Control	1101	ACK
01	Control	1110	CF End
01	Control	1111	CF End + CF-ACK
10	Data	0000	Data
10	Data	0001	Data + CF-ACK
10	Data	0010	Data + CF-Poll
10	Data	0011	Data + CF-ACK + CF-Poll
10	Data	0100	Null Function (no data)
10	Data	0101	CF-ACK (no data)
10	Data	0111	CF-Poll (no data)

TABLE 8.4 (*Continued*)

Type Value b3 b2	Type Description	Subtype Value b7 b6 b5 b4	Subtype Description
10	Data	0111	CF-ACK + Cf + Poll (no data)
10	Data	1000–1111	Reserved
10	Data	0000–1111	Reserved
11	Reserved	0000–1111	Reserved

FromDS

This field is used to indicate whether or not a frame was received from the distribution system. If the frame was received from the distribution system this 1-bit field is set to 1. Otherwise, this field is set to 0.

More Fragments Subfield

This subfield is one bit in length and denotes if more fragments follow the current fragment. If the value of this field is set to 1, then one or more fragments follow. If the value of this field is set to 0, then no fragments follow. Thus, this field permits the originator to note whether or not a frame represents a fragment and enables a receiver to reconstruct a series of fragments into a complete frame.

To illustrate the frame fragmentation process, consider Figure 8.10. This example shows a frame consisting of four fragments. To identify that the frame was fragmented as well as to let the receiver reconstruct the fragmented

Figure 8.10 An example of frame fragmentation.

frame, fragments 0, 1 and 2 would have their More Fragments subfield values set to 1 in the MAC header in each frame.

Under the IEEE 802.11 standard the fragmentation process is based upon a simple send-and-wait algorithm. Under this algorithm the transmitting station cannot send a new fragment until it either receives an ACK for the prior segment or decides that the fragment was retransmitted a predefined number of times and drops the entire frame.

Retry Subfield

The value of this one-bit subfield is set to 1 to indicate that the frame is a fragment representing the retransmission of a previously transmitted fragment. The receiving station uses this field to recognize duplicate transmissions that can occur if an ACK frame is lost.

Power Management Subfield

The IEEE 802.11 standard defines two power modes that a station can be in — Power Save or Active. A station that is Active when transmitting a frame can change its power status from Active to Power Save.

The Power Management setting is used by access points, which continuously maintain a record of stations working in the Power Saving mode. The access point will buffer frames addressed to those stations until either they specifically request them via the transmission of a polling request or they change their power status.

A second technique employed to transmit buffered frames to a station in its Power Save mode of operation is obtained through the use of Beacon frames. An access point periodically broadcasts frames that includes information concerning which stations operating in a Power Saving mode have frames buffered by the access point. The station uses the Beacon of information to wake up and remains in an Active power mode while it transmits a polling message to the AC to retrieve those buffered frames.

More Data Subfield

The purpose of the More Data subfield is to indicate if there are more frames following the current frame. This one-bit field is set by an access point to indicate that there are more frames buffered to a particular station. The destination station will use this bit setting to decide if it should continue polling or if it should change its power management state.

WEP Subfield

The Wired Equivalent Privacy (WEP) subfield indicates whether or not the body of the frame is encrypted. WEP uses the RC4 encryption algorithm, which is a stream cipher. As a reminder, a stream cipher operates by expanding a short key into an infinite pseudo-random key stream. The transmitter XORs (modulo-2 adds) the key stream to the plain text, resulting in the generation of encrypted ciphertext. The receiver uses the same key to generate the same sequence of pseudo-random bits, which are then modulo-2 subtracted from the received ciphertext to reconstruct the plain text.

As we will note later in this chapter when we examine some wireless equipment configurations, the WEP algorithm uses a pseudo-random number generator that is initialized by a 40-bit key. Through the use of a 40-bit key and a 24-bit initialization vector a 64-bit key is generated that, according to many reports, is relatively easy to break. Although some products support 128-bit WEP keys, papers have been published that appear to indicate that the extended key is also susceptible to being broken. Because only one bit is used in the field to indicate whether WEP is enabled or disabled, all stations within a BSS must be configured similarly with respect to WEP. That is, either all stations and the access point within a BSS must have WEP disabled or they must be configured to use the same key.

Order Subfield

The last position in the Control field is the one-bit Order subfield. The setting of this bit is used to indicate that the frame is being transmitted using the Strictly Ordered service class. This bit position was added to accommodate the DEC LAT protocol, which cannot accept change of ordering between unicast and multicast frames. Because the DEC LAT protocol is not exactly a popular one for the vast majority of wireless applications, this subfield is ignored.

Now that we have an appreciation of the subfields within the control field, let us continue our tour of the MAC data frame.

Duration/ID Field

This two-byte field indicates either the station identification (ID) or the duration in microseconds requested to transmit a frame and its interval to the next frame. The actual interpretation of the value stored in this field depends upon the type of the frame. In a Power-Save Poll message this field indicates the station ID. In all other types of frames the value in this field indicates the duration in milliseconds requested to transmit a frame and its interval to the next frame.

Address Fields

If you examine Figure 8.9 you will note the presence of four address fields, labeled Address 1 through Address 4. This enables a frame to transport four addresses, with the address carried in each address field based upon the settings of the ToDS and From DS bits in the Control field.

Table 8.5 summarizes the type of address transported in each address field based upon the values of the ToDS and From DS bits in the Control field. In examining Table 8.5 note that Address 1 always indicates the recipient, which can be the destination address (DA), Basic Service Set ID (BSSID), or the Recipient Address (RA). If the ToDS bit is set, Address 1 contains the AP address. When the ToDS bit is not set, the value of the Address 1 field contains the station address. All stations filter on the Address 1 field as it always indicates the recipient address.

Address 2 is always used to identify the station transmitting the frame. If the From DS bit is set, the value contained in the Address 2 field is the AP address. Otherwise the address represents the station address.

Moving on to the Address 3 field, you will note from Table 8.5 that it also depends upon the ToDS and From DS bit settings. When the FromDS bit is set to a value of 1, the Address 3 field contains the Source Address (SA). If the frame has the ToDS bit set, then the Address 3 field contains the Destination Address (DA).

The fourth and last address field, which is Address 4, is used for the special situation where a wireless distribution system is employed and a frame is being transmitted from one access point to another. In this situation both the ToDS and FromDS bits are set. Thus, neither the original destination address

TABLE 8.5 The Settings of the ToDS and From DS Bits in the Control Field Govern the Use of the Address Fields

ToDS	FromDs	Address 1	Address 2	Address 3	Address 4
0	0	DA	SA	BSSID	N/A
0	1	DA	BSSID	SA	N/A
1	0	BSSID	SA	DA	N/A
1	1	RA	TA	DA	SA

Legend:
TA = Transmitter Address
RA = Receiver Address
BSSID = Basic Service Set

nor the original source address is applicable and Address 4 is then limited to identifying the source of the wireless DS frame.

Sequence Control Field

The two-byte Sequence Control field provides a mechanism to represent the order of different fragments that are part of a frame. As previously illustrated in Figure 8.9, the Sequence Control field consists of two subfields — Fragment Number and Sequence Number. Those subfields are used to define the frame and the number of the fragment that is part of a frame.

Frame Body Field

The Frame Body field is the field that transports information between stations. As indicated in Figure 8.9, this field can vary in length up to 2312 bytes.

CRC Field

The last field in the MAC data frame is the CRC field. This field is four bytes in length and is used to contain a 32-bit CRC.

Now that we have an appreciation of the composition of the MAC data frame, let us turn our attention to the composition of several control frames.

Control Frames

As previously noted in this chapter, the IEEE 802.11 standard defines the use of several types of control frames that govern access to the media as well as provide acknowledgement of a received frame. In this section we will examine the format and utilization of three control frames — RTS, CTS and ACK. Figure 8.11 indicates the format of each frame.

RTS Frame

The RTS and CTS frames have a similar format, with the MAC header contained in the Frame Control field for each frame. Concerning the RTS frame, the Receiver Address represents the address of the wireless network station that is the intended immediate recipient of the next data or management frame. The transmitted address (TA) represents the address of the station transmitting the RTS frame, while the Duration field contains the time in microseconds required to transmit the next data or management frame plus one CTS frame, one ACK frame, and three interval periods between frames.

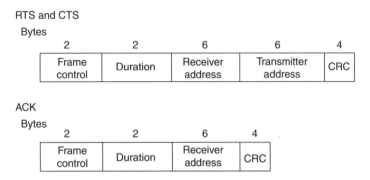

Figure 8.11 Common control frames.

Because the RTS frame is generated by a transmitter requesting access to the medium, it will be responded to by a CTS frame.

CTS Frame

The CTS frame has the same format as the RTS frame and the entry of data in the fields of the frame forms a relationship between the two. That is, the Receiver Address (RA) of a CTS frame is copied from the Transmitter Address (TA) field of the received RTS frame. The value of the duration field is obtained from the duration field of the previously received RTS frame less the time, in microseconds, required to transmit the frame and the Short Interframe Space (SIFS) interval. The Receiver Address and Transmitter Address for both RTS and CTS frames are 48 bits in length and represent the address length used by IEEE 802.3 wired LANs.

ACK Frame

A third commonly used control frame is the ACK frame, the format of which is shown in the lower portion of Figure 8.11.

Similar to the CTS frame, several fields in the ACK frame contain values based upon a previously received frame. For example, the Receiver Address field value of the ACK frame is copied from the Address 2 field of the previously received frame that the ACK acknowledges. A second example of field relationships between frames concerns the setting of the More Fragment bit in the Frame Control field of the previous frame. If that bit was set to 0, the Duration field in the ACK frame is set to 0. Otherwise, the Duration field value is obtained from the Duration field of the previous frame minus the time in microseconds required to transmit the ACK frame and its SIFS interval.

Management Frames

As noted in Table 8.4, there are 10 defined management frames. Two of the more popular types of management frames are Beacon and Probe frames, both of which we will examine in this section.

The Beacon Frame

Figure 8.12 illustrates the basic format of the body of a Beacon and Probe frame as well as the Capability field included in each frame.

When a client comes in range of an access point it will hear the periodic broadcast of Beacon frames transmitted by the access point to indicate its presence. In addition to notifying stations of the presence of the access point, Beacon frames provide all stations within a BSS with synchronization information and power management support. Concerning the latter, as previously noted clients can be in a Power Save or Awake mode. In the Awake mode stations are fully powered on and can receive frames at any time. If a node goes into a Power Save mode it must first inform the access point. Once in the Power Save mode a station will periodically wake up to listen for beacons that indicate that the AP has queued messages for it.

In examining the Parameter Set shown in Figure 8.12, note that a particular parameter, such as FH, is only present if a station is using the applicable physical layer. The IBSS parameter set is only present within Beacon frames generated by stations within an IBSS, while TIM information is only present within Beacon frames generated by an access point. Here the term IBSS references an independent basic service set, which is a single BSS that operates independently within an area.

Probe Response Frame

The Beacon can be considered to represent an advertisement that tells stations an access point is alive. If a station notes the presence of a Beacon frame and wants to join an existing cell it will transmit a Probe Request frame to an access point.

The response to a Probe Request is conveyed by a Probe Response frame, whose body is shown in the middle portion of Figure 8.12. Note that the body is similar to the Beacon frame body; however, the TIM information element is not present.

Capability Information Field

Within both Beacon and Probe frames is a capability information field. This field consists of two bytes, with the first used to define eight one-bit subfields

Beacon frame

Information	Timestamp	Beacon interval	Capability	SSID	Supported rates	Parameter set			IBSS	TIM
						FH	DS	EF		

Probe response

Information	Timestamp	Beacon interval	Capability information	SSID	Supported rates	Parameter set			IBSS parameter set
						FH	DS	EF	

Capability information field

B0	B1	B2	B3	B4	B5	B6	B7	B15
ESS	IBSS	CF pollable	CF poll request	Privacy	Short preamble	PBCC	Channel agility	Reserved

Figure 8.12 Beacon and probe frame bodies.

as indicated in the lower portion of Figure 8.12. The function of the capability information field is to indicate requested or advertised capabilities. Under the current Draft 8 version of changes to the 802.11 standard the second byte remains to be defined.

Physical Protocol Data Units

The transfer of information in an IEEE 802.11 environment occurs using Physical Protocol Data Units (PPDUs). The composition and format of the PPDU varies based upon the physical layer used. Thus, because the 802.11 standard supports three physical layers, as you might expect there are three PPDU frame formats. Because practical wireless LANs are restricted to RF communications, we will focus our attention upon the protocol frames for FHSS and DSSS.

FHSS

Figure 8.13 illustrates the frame format for the FHSS physical layer. This frame consists of an 80-bit preamble of synchronization bits in the repeating

Legend:
PLCP   Physical Layer Convergence Protocol
PPDU   Physical Protocol Data Unit
SFD   Start of Frame Delimiter

Figure 8.13   The FHSS frame format.

pattern of 0101…01. This pattern is used for signal detection and is followed by a 16-bit Start of Frame Delimiter (SFD). The SFD field is followed by a Physical Layer Convergence Procedure (PLCP) header, which includes three subfields. The length subfield denotes the length of the payload in bytes, a four-bit Signaling field that denotes the operating rate and a 16-bit CRC that is used to detect errors in the header. Under FHSS, initial transmission occurs at a 1 Mbps data rate until the signaling field value is read. As a refresher, a 1 Mbps data rate is obtained by using two-level GFSK while a 2 Mbps data rate occurs through the use of four-level GFSK.

DSSS

In comparison to the FHSS frame format, the format for the DSSS frame is slightly more complex. That frame format, which is illustrated in Figure 8.14, uses a 144-bit Physical Layer Convergence Procedure (PLCP) preamble divided into a 128-bit sequence used for signal detection and a Start of Frame Delimiter (SFD).

The PLCP header consists of four fields. Those fields include an eight-bit Signal field, which indicates the data rate. Currently this field supports four

Legend:
PLCP   Physical Layer Convergence Protocol
PPDU   Physical Protocol Data Unit

Figure 8.14   DSSS frame format.

values that correspond to operating rates of 1, 2, 5.5, and 11 Mbps. Three bits in the Service field are used to support a high-rate extension, indicating the modulation method, if transmit frequency and symbol clocks are derived from the same oscillator and if an extension to the Length field is in effect. Concerning the Length field, that 16-bit field indicates the number of bytes in the MAC layer Protocol data Unit (PDU). The fourth field is the CRC field, which protects the Signal, Service and Length fields.

8.3 Deployment

When considering the deployment of wireless LAN technology, there are four key hardware products you need to consider. Those products include wireless PC network adapter cards, access points, a combined router–access point, and a bridge.

Wireless PC Network Adapter Cards

The purpose of the wireless PC network adapter card is to turn a computer into a participant on a wireless LAN. There are three common form factors by which wireless LAN network adapter cards are fabricated. Those form factors include manufacture as a Type II PCMCIA card (now referred to as a PC card), as a PCI adapter card designed for insertion into the system unit of a desktop computer, and as a self-contained unit. When fabricated as a self-contained unit, the network adapter includes a USB connector, which facilitates its use with the growing number of computers manufactured with such ports instead of legacy parallel and serial ports.

Figure 8.15 shows a picture of the SMC Networks EZ Wireless PC Card. The left portion of the card slides into a PC Card slot in a laptop or notebook. The dark area on the right of the card represents a self-contained antenna that protrudes from the card slot. This PC card is designed for use in an IEEE 802.11b ad hoc or infrastructure network environment and supports DSSS radio frequency communications at 1, 2, 5.5, and 11 Mbps. As we will note later in this chapter, this adapter supports wired equivalent privacy (WEP).

The installation of a wireless LAN adapter card or the cabling of a self-contained network adapter via a USB bus cable turns a computer into a wireless LAN client or station. Once software drivers are installed, you can normally tailor the operation of the adapter card. Depending upon the manufacturer of the adapter card, you may be able to select an ad hoc or infrastructure mode of operation, enable or disable a power-saving mode of operation, select one of 13 RF channels for DSSS operation, and enable or disable WEP. Typically,

Figure 8.15   The SMC networks EZ wireless PC card is designed for insertion into a Type II PC slot in a notebook or laptop computer.

default values are selected for each option that minimize or eliminate the need for user configuration; however, accepting default settings can result in certain problems. For example, the default setting for WEP is disabled, which means that all transmission is in the clear, a topic we will examine later in this chapter.

Access Point

A second network component associated with wireless LANs is designed to interconnect wired and wireless LANs. That network component is the access point, which functions as a bridge between wired and wireless LANs.

Figure 8.16 illustrates a dual-antenna access point manufactured by SMC Networks. The use of dual antennas permits the device to select a stronger received signal at a particular point in time. This can be important, because in a wireless LAN environment transmitted signals will hit different objects that result in RF signals being reflected in different directions. Such reflections result in a spread of signals being received over many paths, which is referred to as multipath transmission. Through the use of dual antennas it becomes possible to discriminate among reflected signals and select the most applicable signal at a point in time.

The SMC Networks EZ Connect wireless access point shown in Figure 8.16 has an operating range up to approximately 1800 feet. However, the exact range that can be obtained, as well as the data rate, depends upon the number of obstructions between a client and an access point. In an office environment

Figure 8.16 The SMC networks 11 Mbps wireless access point supports up to 64 users at a maximum range of 1800 feet.

where cubicles, doors and corridors may be fabricated out of metal it may be difficult to achieve the stated maximum operating range.

The use of an access point resembles a two-port Ethernet wired bridge. However, instead of two wired ports, the access point has one. For the SMC Networks EZ Connect access point shown in Figure 8.16 a built-in RJ-45 port provides cabling for a connection to an IEEE 802.3 10 Mbps network or a 10/100 Mbps auto-negotiation port on a hub or switch. The other port on the access point is its dual antenna, which provides an IEEE 802.11b network connection. According to the vendor, the access point can support up to 64 wireless users and, like its wired cousin, the access point is a "plug-and-play" device that automatically learns MAC addresses on the wired and wireless sides.

Combined Router/Access Point

Recognition of the growth in the use of DS Land Cable modems as a mechanism to access the Internet resulted in many hardware developers combining a router and access point into a common housing. Through the use of this combined housing it becomes possible to extend a single Internet connection for use by multiple wireless clients.

Figure 8.17 illustrates the SMC Networks Barricade broadband router, which combines an access point, a router, and a three-port 10/100 Mbps Ethernet switch into one housing. A fourth Ethernet port is used to provide a connection to a DSL or cable modem. The use of this device or similar products from other vendors provides a high degree of networking flexibility. For example, you could cable this device to a DSL or cable modem and use it to provide clients with wireless access to the Internet. As an alternative, you could cable one of the built-in switch ports to your existing wired hub or switch and obtain the capability for wireless clients to access the Internet or your wired infrastructure. In addition to supporting both wired and wireless LANs, the Barricade broadband router includes an asynchronous interface that enables an ISDN dial connection to the Internet to be shared. Because wireless clients commonly do not have their own printer, the Barricade also functions as a print server and includes a printer interface on the device.

Network Address Translation

Because Internet Service Providers (ISPs) only issue one IP address per DSL or cable modem connection, a mechanism is required to share that address

Figure 8.17 The SMC Networks Barricade broadband router consists of an access point, a router and a three-port 10/100 Mbps Ethernet switch in a common housing.

among many wireless clients as well as any devices wired to the router. The mechanism used is referred to as Network Address Translation (NAT). The SMC Networks Barricade router is similar to other products used by this author in that it uses a Class C network address defined in RFC 1918 behind the router as a mechanism for translating to and from the single IP address assigned to the DSL or cable modem connections.

RFC 1918 defines Class A, B, and C address blocks that are reserved for private network use. Because two or more organizations can use those addresses, they are not unique and cannot be directly used on the Internet. However, they can be used internally to an organization and only require a translation mechanism to provide clients with the ability to access the Internet. That translation mechanism is performed by the router by mapping each RFC 1918 Class C IP address into a high-value TCP or UDP source port number but not altering the single IP address allocated to the DSL or cable modem connection. When a response occurs, the source port value is returned as a destination port value that enables the router performing NAT to change the IP address to an applicable RFC 1918 Class C address.

Figure 8.18 illustrates an example of the use of a wireless router/access point in an office environment. In this example the wireless router/access point is shown connected to a DSL modem that provides access to the Internet.

The wireless router/access point is cabled to the wired network. Thus, the wireless router/access point provides NAT to wireless clients as well as

Figure 8.18 Using a wireless router/access point.

wired clients on the existing wired LAN. Because most wireless router/access point devices perform NAT using a single RFC 1918 network address, you are limited to supporting a total of 253 stations for translation purposes. This is because host addresses of 0 and 255 are not usable and one Class C address is used by the router/access point.

Wireless Bridge

While an access point represents a bridge between wired and wireless Ethernet networks, a wireless bridge represents a facility used to interconnect two wired LANs via wireless transmission at line-of-sight distances up to approximately 10 miles. A wireless bridge consists of two components — an access point that is cabled to the wired LAN and a directional antenna, which is commonly mounted on the roof of a building and which is cabled to the access point located in the building.

Now that we have an appreciation of the four common types of wireless LAN devices, we will conclude this chapter by focusing our attention upon the configuration of a wireless router/access point and wireless client station.

Router/Access Point Configuration

To illustrate the configuration possibilities when using a wireless router/access point, this author used the SMC Networks Barricade broadband router. Figure 8.19 illustrates the system status menu of the Barricade when viewed through the Microsoft Internet Explorer browser. If you look at the address entered in the browser, you will note that it is an RFC 1918 Class C address. That IP address is 192.168.123.254 and represents one of 254 total Class C addresses that will be mapped to the IP address assigned by the Internet Service Provider (ISP) to the Internet connection.

If you focus your attention on the System Status portion of the display in Figure 8.19, you will note under the column labeled Item the first row labeled Remaining Lease Time and an associated value. This indicates that the IP address on the Internet connection represents leased addresses provided by the ISP using the Dynamic Host Configuration Protocol (DHCP). The other entries in the system status area indicate the IP address that is leased, the subnet mask, the gateway for the ISP and two DNS addresses. This initial screen provides system status information; however, until you enter a correct password and log into the device you cannot perform any configuration operations. Thus, let us log into the router/access point by entering a system password, which after the initial installation should be changed from the default of "admin."

Figure 8.19 The SMC Networks Barricade broadband router system status screen.

Figure 8.20 The primary setup entry permits a user to define how the SMC Networks Barricade broadband router will be connected to the Internet.

Figure 8.20 illustrates one of several Barricade screens you can use to configure the router/access point once you have logged into the system. After you successfully log into the system, the left panel changes from a Status entry and the password request shown in Figure 8.19 to a series of selection items. In Figure 8.20 the Primary Setup entry was selected, which results in the display of a screen that enables you to select the type of Wide Area Network (WAN) connection. Note that you can select a static or dynamic IP address, PPP over Ethernet or dial-up, the latter enabling wireless clients to share a common modem or ISDN connection to the Internet.

In concluding our brief examination of the Barricade's configuration let us turn our attention to its access list capability. Figure 8.21 illustrates the Router Access Control menu. This graphic user interface provides you with the ability to enable or disable (block or permit) three groups and a default group for all hosts not defined in a numbered group.

Blocking or permitting is based upon the entry of one or more port numbers, such as 80 for HTTP and group members. The latter is defined by entering the last digit or range of digits for the host portion of the RFC 1918 address assigned to a wireless client. For example, to block Telnet for all hosts whose IP address is in the range 192.168.123.100 to 192.168.123.199 you would enter 23 as the port value and 100–199 as the member value for a group number.

Client Configuration

In concluding this chapter we will examine several wireless client configuration screens, primarily focusing our attention upon security issues. Figure 8.22 illustrates the advanced display during the installation of software drivers for an SMC Networks Wireless PC Card. Although there are seven entries you

Figure 8.21 The SMC Networks Barricade broadband router access control configuration screen.

Figure 8.22 The SMC networks advanced client setup screen provides users with the ability to modify the settings for seven properties.

can configure, the default settings are designed to get an organization up and running without having to perform any configuration changes. However, from a security viewpoint this can be dangerous, as we will shortly note.

The first entry in the property box in Figure 8.22 is Authentication Algorithm and its setting defines how stations authenticate themselves. If you select the default of Shared Key, this means that users authenticate one another by using the same WEP encryption key. Unfortunately, by default the Use WEP property value is set to "disabled," which means that if you select all defaults you have no authentication and no transmission security.

If you accept all of the default values during the setup of the adapter card, you can use a utility program provided by the vendor to reconfigure one or more settings at a later date. The main display of this utility program is shown in Figure 8.23 and warrants a discussion as its Link Info tab provides both valuable information for site selection of an access point and a mechanism to enhance security.

If you examine the lower portion of Figure 8.23, you will note that the utility program displays both Link Quality and Signal Strength information. If you use a laptop or battery power to roam over an office area, you can determine

Figure 8.23 The utility program provided with SMC networks wireless PC cards provides a mechanism to monitor link quality and signal strength.

if the location of an access point is sufficient to provide a good-quality signal to various station locations or if the access point should be moved. Because wireless LAN transmission can easily "leak" out of a building, you can take your laptop outside to determine if a snooper setting in the parking lot can obtain a good signal. If so, you could consider shielding a portion of the walls facing the parking lot or move the access point to a location where radiated signals into the parking lot do not represent a problem.

In concluding our examination of the SMC Networks utility program let us focus our attention on the WEP key. By default WEP is disabled, which explains the reason why two men in a van were able to travel from one Silicon Valley parking lot to another and "read" wireless LAN traffic. Figure 8.24 illustrates the default setting of WEP, which as indicated results in no encryption. SMC Networks, like other vendors, provides users with the ability to define up to four shared keys. Thus, you might use one key when in one office, another key when you travel to a remote office, a third key for home use and perhaps a fourth key when you stay overnight at a hotel with a wireless Internet portal.

Assuming you check the box to the left of Enable Data Security, your screen display will appear similar to that shown in Figure 8.25. In this example the SMC Networks utility program permits users to enter a pass phrase to generate up to four WEP key settings. Other vendors require users to enter alphabetic or hex values for key settings.

Figure 8.24 The default setting for WEP is disabled.

Figure 8.25 The SMC networks wireless adapter card utility program supports the entry of a pass phrase to create a WEP key.

There are two WEP settings that warrant discussion. A 64-bit key is generated by entering 10 hex digits, which are extended by a 24-bit initialization vector (IV) into the 64-bit key. Several papers have noted that this key is relatively insecure as the IV is transmitted in the clear and capturing when it repeats permits a frequency analysis to decipher the encoded text. A second key, which is 128 bits in length, is proprietary to vendors. Thus, extended security could lock your organization to a single vendor. Because many organizations cannot wait for new security solutions, a bit of common sense and the appropriate location of clients and access points can reduce the risk of interception of data. First, enabling WEP makes it harder for interceptions to read your traffic. Second, placing access points and clients so as to minimize radiation into the parking lot can make it difficult, if not impossible, for an unauthorized person to sit in a van during the day and monitor an organization's wireless traffic. Third, if you notice a van in the parking lot with a directional antenna pointed towards your building you should realize something is amiss.

chapter nine

Security

As indicated previously in this book, Ethernet primarily represents a layer 2 data link protocol used to transport information in a local environment. As such, the design of Ethernet is focused upon the lower two layers of the OSI Reference Model. This means that the basic structure of Ethernet is not secure and an Ethernet network has a variety of vulnerabilities. Thus, it is incumbent upon the higher layers in the protocol stack to provide security to an Ethernet network.

In this chapter we will turn our attention to the general topic of security and techniques that can be used to protect an Ethernet network. Because we briefly described and discussed wireless LAN security in the form of Wired Equivalency Privacy (WEP) in Chapter 8, our primary focus in this chapter is upon wired Ethernet. However, because wireless Ethernet LANs are commonly used to provide a connection to a wired infrastructure, our discussion of security will be applicable to protecting wireless devices accessing a corporate network or the Internet. In this chapter we will first examine the role of the router, as it represents the first line of defense of a network. This will be followed by discussing the operation of a firewall and virus scanners.

9.1 The Security Role of the Router

Because a router functions as a gateway between networks, it also represents your first line of network defense. In this section we will turn our attention to the security role of this vital communications device. In the first portion of this section we will focus our attention upon router access control. The rationale for this coverage is based upon the fact that most routers are remotely administered. Thus, they can be remotely accessed by persons with evil intentions as well as by authorized employees.

In the second portion of this section we will turn our attention to router access lists, examining how they are created, their use, and limitations.

Because Cisco Systems has approximately 70 percent of the market for routers, we will primarily describe and discuss access control and access lists with respect to Cisco routers.

Access Control

Cisco's Internetworking Operating System (IOS) controls the operation of that vendor's communications devices to include routers and switches. IOS support a command line interface that can be accessed via the router console port, a modem connection, or a Telnet connection. Of the three methods only the first can offer the possibility of being truly secure as it requires a directly connected terminal device, which can be co-located with the router in a secure, locked area. Because the other two methods support remote access, they theoretically permit a virtually unlimited number of persons to attempt to access a router's operating system and represent potential vulnerabilities that you need to consider. However, prior to giving an explanation of the three methods, a brief discussion of one of the reasons it is relatively simple to attack a router is in order.

Address and Message Identity

Many organizations employ an IP addressing scheme which results in the assignment of a .1 (dot one) network address to a router's interface. Thus, if you can use ping or nslookup to determine the IP address of a host, it is then relatively easy to replace the host address with a "dot 1" address to determine if the device at that address is a router.

A second technique that enables the location of a router is to ping a host for which pings onto the host network are blocked. This action results in a router returning a "destination net unreachable" message. If the previous methods do not yield results, another popular method is to develop a Telnet scanner to search for the prompt "User Access Verification," which is returned by Cisco routers when you Telnet to a router's IP address that supports remote access. You can note this by examining Figure 9.1, which indicates an attempted access to a router whose IP address is 205.131.176.1. Note the prompt "User Access Verification."

Cisco routers provide you with three tries to enter a password. If you do not enter a correct password the router displays the message "% bad passwords" and terminates the Telnet session. This results in the display of the dialog box shown in the middle of the display that informs the user that the "connection

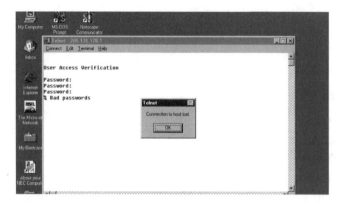

Figure 9.1   Attempting to use Telnet to gain access to a Cisco router.

to host lost." At this time you can manually reconnect and try another series of passwords.

Although we did not break into the router in Figure 4.1, we had three tries to do so. If we write a program to continuously try different combinations of characters over a long weekend, it may be possible to gain access to the router. Thus, let's examine router access in detail.

Cisco EXEC Sessions

Access to a Cisco router results in a command line session that is referred to as an EXEC session. For those familiar with UNIX, an EXEC session is similar to a UNIX shell process.

There are two different types of EXEC sessions supported by Cisco routers—user EXEC and privileged EXEC. A user EXEC session allows a person to perform a limited number of functions, such as displaying interface information, but does not allow the user to change the router's configuration. In a privileged EXEC session you obtain the ability to perform router configuration operations as well as all of the functions available to the user EXEC session mode of operation.

All logins to a Cisco router first result in an entry into the router's user EXEC mode. When this occurs you will encounter a greater-than sign (>) prompt. That prompt follows the name configured for the router or, if no name was assigned, the default "Router" is displayed. To enter the privilege EXEC mode a person first enters the command "enable." This action results in the prompt "Password:" which, when a password is successfully entered, places the user in the privileged EXEC mode. When this occurs, the prompt changes to a pound (#) sign — called a hash sign in the UK — as illustrated by the following sequence for a router named Macon.

Macon > enable

Password:

Macon #

Password Protection

If you have initial access to a Cisco router you can assign a password for initial access to the router with the password line command. The format of this commands is:

Password text

Where "text" can contain any string of alphanumeric characters to include spaces up to 80 characters in length. The alphabetic characters are case sensitive, which provides a router administrator with the ability to create passwords that would be extremely difficult and time-consuming to guess via a dictionary or brute-force attack method. Unfortunately, in a haste to configure a router for remote access and to keep things simple, many administrators use such classic passwords as "bingo," "tiger," "router," and even "Cisco."

To assign a password for the privileged command level you would use a router's enable password global configuration command. This means you must first enter the privileged command level via the enable command. If a password for the privileged mode was not previously set, you will not be prompted for one. Unfortunately, this is a common omission when some organizations receive their first few routers and rush to establish an Internet connection. The absence of router passwords can be equated to walking barefoot. While you might reach your destination unharmed, there is also a distinct chance of a serious reversal of fortune! Once you enter the privileged mode, you could use the enable password command as shown below to set the password to supersecret.

enable-password supersecret

Telnet Access

Each Telnet port on a router is referred to as a virtual terminal (vty). Cisco routers support a maximum of five vty ports that are numbered 0 through 4. You can configure nonprivileged passwords for Telnet access via the use of the password command. The following example illustrates the assignment of the password 4hard2guess to vty ports 0 through 4.

line vty 0 4

login

password 4hard2guess

When a user Telnets to the router's IP address, the router will prompt the user to enter a password. The user–router interaction will be similar to that shown below:

%telnet 198.78.46.1

Trying. . . .

Connected to 198.78.46.1

Escape character is '^]'

User Access Verification

Password:

Once the user enters the correct nonprivileged password, the following prompt is displayed:

Router>

At this point the remote user can use the enable command in an attempt to access the router's EXEC privileged mode.

Password Encryption

By default anyone who has privileged access to a router can view all of the passwords set on the router. For example, suppose you assigned usernames techman and investor the passwords good4me and notgood4u as shown below:

username techman good4me

username investor notgood4u

Without encrypting passwords anyone with privileged access to the router can view each user's password as well as the general user and enable passwords. This means that it becomes possible for one user to access the router as another user. If you configured your router to log activity to a server, you might be tempted to blame the wrong party for the mess he or she creates, either on purpose or inadvertently.

Prior to discussing password encryption, a few words about usernames are in order. The use of the username command allows you to assign separate, unique, personalized login names for each administrator. By assigning usernames to virtual terminal (vty) liens you can require persons attempting to gain remote access to a router to know both a username and associated password, which makes it more difficult for an uninvited user to gain access to a router.

To encrypt router passwords you would use the **service password-encryption** global configuration command. The format of that command is:

service password-encryption

It should be noted that Cisco's password encryption scheme produces what is referred to as a type 7 password because this digit is used as a prefix to the encrypted password scheme. It should also be noted that a search of the Web using "type 7 passwords" or "Cisco router password encryption" will provide several references to the fact that the encryption scheme used is more accurately a simple scrambling method and that the resulting scrambled passwords can be decoded quite easily. Due to this it is suggested that the **enable secret** command should be used to better protect the enable password.

Using the Enable Secret Command

The use of the **enable secret** command uses Message Digest 5 (MD5), a one-way cryptographic hash function to encrypt the password. This means that simple re-scrambling will not suffice to obtain the source of the password. Instead, someone must use a password generation program against the algorithm and compare the result against the MD5 result to determine the clear value of the password. This is obviously much more difficult than simply viewing stored passwords. The following example illustrates the use of the enable secret global configuration command:

Macon (config) #enable secret bingo7

Macon (config) #exit

Macon#show running-config

Building configuration...

enable secret 5 eK3ghM$ 4X...

Note that a prefix of "5" is used to identify the use of MD5. Because of this, the resulting encrypted password is also referred to as a type 5 password. You should also note that, because MD5 is a one-way hash algorithm, it cannot be used to encrypt all passwords, such as those used by the Network Time Protocol (NTP) and similar protocols that require access to clear text strings.

You can considerably preclude dictionary and brute-force attacks by selecting applicable length passwords with an appropriate mix of characters. By encrypting passwords you make it more difficult for one person to use the access privileges of another. While each of these techniques is recommended to provide a barrier to unauthorized persons gaining access to your organizational routers, you can also limit access via the use of an applicable access list.

Access List Restrictions

Although we will discuss the use of Cisco access lists in considerable detail in the second portion of this section, we can note that you can limit access or even block all Telnet access. To do so you would use several IOS commands. For example, you can use the **transport** command in conjunction with a line command to disable the Telnet listener on your router. The following example turns off the Telnet listener on all vty lines:

```
line vty 0 4

transport input none
```

You can also use the **access-list** and **access-class** commands to limit access from specific IP addresses. For example, assume you want to restrict vty access to your router to users on the 198.78.46.0 network. To do so you would use the following IOS statements:

```
access-list 1 permit 198.78.46.0 0.0.0.255

!

line vty 0 4

access-class 1 in
```

In this example, the access-list statement permits packets with a source address on the 198.78.46.0 network. As we will note when we examine access lists in detail in the second portion of this section, 0.0.0.255 represents a wildcard mask that functions in a reverse manner to a subnet mask, requiring matches for "0" bit positions and a don't care for "1" bit positions.

The **access-class** statement provides you with the capability to define the access checks made in a particular direction. The format of this command is shown below:

access-class list number {**in**|**out**}

where the list number is an integer between 1 and 99 and references the direction an access list is applied. Because the list number is between 1 and 99, this also means that the access-class statement is only applicable to a standard access list. The keyword "in" applies to incoming connections, such as virtual terminals. In comparison, the keyword "out" applies to outgoing Telnet connections, such as a person who gains access to your router's EXEC mode and attempts to initiate a Telnet connection to another host. Thus, the preceding series of three IOS commands restricts the ability to connect to the virtual terminals on the router (terminal lines 0 through 4) to hosts on the 198.78.46.0 network.

Protecting the Hardwired Connection

Because a connection to the console is accomplished by directly cabling a terminal device to the port, it is assumed that the person operating the terminal is authorized. Due to this, this type of connection is by default provided EXEC mode access without a password. Because it is quite possible for an unauthorized person to experiment with gaining full router access, it is a good idea to set a user EXEC password on those ports. To do so you would enter the following statements:

line console 0

login

password hard2guess4

exec-timeout 5 0

When you log onto the router its login prompt would be as follows:

User Access Verification

Password:

At this point you would have to enter the password to gain access to the router. Because the default timeout for an unattended console is 10 minutes, you may wish to lower this value. To do so you would use the **exec-timeout** command whose format is shown below:

    exec-timeout m s

where m is the time in minutes and n is the time in seconds of no activity that forces a session timeout. In the above example we lowered the timeout to 5 minutes.

Table 9.1 provides a summary of Cisco security management related commands that we previously examined. While the exec-timeout command can technically be applicable to supporting a policy to prevent persons from connecting and hogging access to the router throughout the day, this author also considers the command to enhance security management. Thus, this command is included in the referenced table.

Considering SNMP

The Simple Network Management Protocol (SNMP) represents a potential vulnerability because it uses community names that are test strings for access control. All too often the default community name of "public" is used and provides a mechanism for persons to attempt to exploit an opening in your router's defense.

TABLE 9.1   Cisco Security Management Commands

Command	Operational Effect
line console 0	Establish a password on the console terminal.
line vty 0 4	Establish a password for Telnet connections.
enable-password	Establish a password for access to the privileged EXEC mode.
enable secret	Establish an enable secret password using MD5 encryption.
exec-timeout m s	Establish an idle timeout period in minutes and seconds, which when reached terminates the connection.
password text	Establish a password for access to user EXEC mode.
service password-encryption	Scramble the display of passwords to protect them from view by the use of the show running-config command.

You can use the **snmp-server community** command to assign a community name as well as restrict SNMP operations to read only. The format of this command is shown below:

snmp-server community name {**ro|rw**} list number

where "name" represents a community name, "ro" represents read only, and "rw" represents read/write capability, so certain Management Information Base (MIB) objects can be changed. "List number" represents an integer between 1 and 99 that references a standard access list. Readers are referred to Chapter 10 for detailed information concerning SNMP.

To illustrate an example of the use of the snmp-server community statement, let's assume you want to restrict access to SNMP reads to one host on the 198.78.46.8. To do so you would code the following IOS commands:

snmp-sever community yo4mo52be ro 1

access-list 1 permit host 198.78.46.8

Note that in the first statement we changed the default community name to you4mo52be. Because you can configure the management station with the changed community name, you should always use a hard to guess name. In addition, note that we used the "ro" option to restrict access to the MIB to read-only and used a list number of 1 to associate the first command with the access list that only permits access from the hosts we previously defined.

A second SNMP-related area you need to consider is the transmission of traps. Although most SNMP commands are initiated by a management station to an agent, an agent can be configured to transmit unsolicited packets to the management station where certain predefined conditions occur. These unsolicited packets represent SNMP traps.

There are three SNMP-related commands you can use to control traps. The first is **snmp-server trap-authentication**, which enables a router to transmit a trap message when it receives a packet with an incorrect community string. This is a highly recommended command to use as it will alert the management station to mistaken access attempts as well as brute force and dictionary based attacks.

The second command is **snmp-server trap-source**, which indicates the interface where traps originate. The third command, **snmp-server host**, permits you to associate an IP address or host name with a community name. For example, assume you want to send traps to the host at 198.78.46.8 from interface Ethernet1 using the community name yo4mo52be. You would then code the following IOS statements:

snmp-server trap-authentication

snmp-server trap-source Ethernet1

snmp-server host 198.78.46.8 yo4mo52be

Now that we have an appreciation of router access control methods including SNMP, let's turn our attention to a more formal and detailed examination of access lists.

Access Lists

An access list can be defined as "an ordered set of statements that permit or deny the flow of packets across an interface." As such, an access list represents a filtering mechanism since the list parameters are matched against applicable information in each packet.

Interface Considerations

The creation of an access list represents the first in a two-part process. The second step is to apply the access list to a specific direction on an interface. Concerning the direction, it is important to note that the flow of packets from a router is considered to represent an outbound direction while the flow of packets toward a router represents the inbound direction. This means you must carefully consider the direction of packet flow in conjunction with the devices whose packets you wish to filter. To understand this concept better, consider Figure 9.2, which illustrates the direction of inbound and outbound packet flow with respect to a router that has one serial and two Ethernet ports.

In examining Figure 9.2 note that if you want to block certain types of packets arriving from the Internet you would apply an access list to the s0 (serial 0) port in the inbound direction. In comparison, let's assume you want to block certain users on the Ethernet1 (e1) network from accessing the Internet. You could apply an access list to either the e1 or s0 interface. If you apply the access list to the e1 interface you would apply it in the inbound direction. In comparison, if you wanted to use the s0 interface you would apply the access list in the outbound direction.

Also note that if you want to block traffic from the 198.78.46.0 network from flowing to the 205.131.175.0 network, you could either filter packets inbound to interface e1 or outbound from interface e0. In comparison, if you

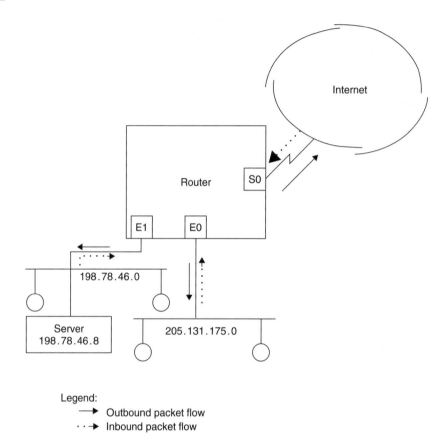

Legend:
→ Outbound packet flow
··→ Inbound packet flow

Figure 9.2 Inbound and outbound packet flow.

wanted to block traffic on the 198.78.46.0 and 205.131.175.0 networks from flowing to the Internet, you could apply an appropriate access list to interface s0. This illustrates an important concept concerning access lists. That is, you must carefully consider both the interface and the direction an access list is applied to an interface, topics which we will examine in additional detail as we expand our coverage of access lists.

Types of Access Lists

Cisco routers support two types of access lists—standard and extended. In the first portion of this section we briefly looked at the use of a standard access list to control hosts that could gain vty access to a router. Now we will examine the format and use of access lists in much more detail. In doing so we will primarily focus our attention upon IP access lists since IP is the only protocol supported for use on the Internet.

Standard IP Access Lists

The format of a standard IP access list is shown below:

access-list [list #] [permit|deny] [source address] [wild-card-mask] [log]

In examining the format of a standard IP access list a few items require a degree of elaboration. First, the term "access-list" requires a hyphen between the two words. Second, the list number is a numeric between 1 and 99 for the IP protocol and is used to identify the access list statements belonging to a common access list. Because a standard IP access list number must be within the range 1 to 99, the list number also defines the protocol that the access list operates upon.

Keywords

The **permit** or **deny** keyword identifies whether filtering permits or prohibits packets that match the source address and wildcard mask from flowing through an interface. The keyword **permit** allows packets that match the address criteria to flow through an interface, while the keyword **deny** sends packets matching the specified source address into the bit bucket.

Source Address

For a standard IP access list the source address represents the IP address of a host or group of hosts specified using dotted decimal notation. In actuality, the specification of a group of hosts is accomplished through the use of a wildcard-mask. Thus, let's turn our attention to this topic prior to examining several examples of the use of standard IP access list statements.

The Wildcard Mask

As previously noted in this section, the wildcard mask functions in a reverse manner to a subnet mask. That is, this mask uses a binary 0 to represent a match and a binary 1 to represent a don't care condition.

To illustrate the use of a wildcard mask, assume your organization has the Class C network address of 205.131.175.0. If no subnets were configured for that network, each station would have a subnet mask of 255.255.255.0.

Here each binary 1 (255 is a byte of all 1's) represents a match, while a 0 bit represents a don't care condition. Thus, specifying 255 in each of the first three positions of the four position subnet mask field results in the TCP/IP protocol stack matching the network address in each packet and not caring about the host address. Because the Cisco wildcard mask functions in an opposite manner with respect to binary 1s and 0s, the mask required to allow all packets with a source network address of 205.131.175.0 would be 0.0.0.255. Then, a standard access-list statement that would enable all packets with a source network address of 205.131.175.0 would be coded as follows:

        access-list 1 permit 205.131.175.0 0.0.0.255

Because the wildcard-mask represents the complement of the subnet mask, you can determine the subnet mask and take its inverse. For example, a subnet mask of 255.255.0.0 results in a wildcard mask of 0.0.255.255.

        As another example of a standard access list, suppose you wish to permit packets from hosts on the previously mentioned network as well as the 198.78.46.0 network but preclude hosts from the 198.78.22.0 network. Your access list would be as follows:

        access-list 1 permit 205.131.175.0 0.0.0.255

        access-list 1 permit 198.78.46.0 0.0.0.255

Wait! Where is the deny statement, you ask? While you could add the appropriate statement, each access list has an implicit "deny everything" at the end of the list. Because access lists are processed top down, we only need to permit what we want to permit as all else is denied. For those of us who get tired of typing network addresses and wildcard masks, Cisco access lists support two keywords that can simplify the address specification process. A third keyword provides a logging function. Although most access-list keywords are only applicable to extended access lists, these three are also applicable to standard access lists; so let's examine them now.

The Host Keyword

Host is used to denote an exact match and represents a shorthand notation for a mask of 0.0.0.0. For example, assume you want to permit packets from the host address 205.131.175.1. To do so you could code the following access list statement:

        access-list 1 permit 205.131.175.1 0.0.0.0

Because the keyword **host** signifies an exact match you can re-code the previous access list statement as follows:

        access-list 1 permit host 205.131.175.1

The Any Keyword

A second keyword supported by a standard access list is **any**. This keyword is used as an abbreviation for a source address and wildcard mask of 0.0.0.0 255.255.255.255. To illustrate the use of **host** and **any** keywords, let's assume you want to deny packets from source address 205.131.175.1 and permit all other addresses. The standard access-list statements to accomplish this would be as follows:

        access-list 1 deny host 205.131.175.1

        access-list 1 permit any

If you observe the order of the two statements, we first explicitly deny packets from the specified host. This is because processing occurs top down. If we reversed the order, the effect would be to permit all packets, a condition we would not want to occur in this situation.

The Log Keyword

The keyword **log** represents an addition to access lists that occurred in IOS Version 11.3. When you include this keyword in an access list it results in the logging of packets that match permit and deny statements in the access list.

After you apply an access list with the **log** keyword to an interface the first packet that meets a condition in the list causes an immediate logging message to occur. Thereafter, packets matching the access-list conditions are either displayed on the console or logged to memory every five minutes. Logged messages include the access-list number, whether the packet was permitted or denied, the source IP address and the number of packets that were matched during the five-minute interval succeeding the first match. For example, assume the following standard IP access-list statement:

        access-list 1 permit host 205.131.175.1 log

        access-list 1 deny host 205.131.175.2 log

Assume that over a five-minute period host 205.131.175.2 issued 10 packets. When the first match occurred, the following would be displayed on the router console or logged to memory, with the actual logging controlled by the "logging console" command:

list 1 deny 205.131.175.2 1 packet

Then, five minutes later the following display or logged message to memory would occur:

list 1 deny 205.131.175.2 9 packets

The ability to log access-list matches provides you with both a testing and alert capability. You can use logging to test the development of different access lists by observing the resulting match of packets as different activities are attempted. When used as an alert facility, you would scan the display to locate repeated attempts to perform an activity you designed an access list to deny. In this situation, repeated attempts to perform an activity the access-list statement was developed to deny would more than likely indicate a potential attack.

In examining the standard access-list format, you will note it only provides a mechanism to filter based upon source address. In comparison, an extended access list, as its name implies, extends the packet filtering capability.

Extended IP Access Lists

Through the use of an extended IP access list you obtain the ability to filter based upon source and destination address, protocol, source and destination port, as well as other options that significantly enhance your ability to permit or deny packets flowing across an interface. The general format of an extended IP access list is shown below:

access-list [list#] **[permit|deny]** [protocol] [source address source-wildcard] [source port] [destination address destination-wildcard] [destination port] [log] [options]

To obtain an appreciation of the operation of an extended IP access list, let's examine the use of each of the fields in the above format to include some of the options supported by this statement.

The List Number Field

The **list number** field identifies statements that make up an access list as well as the type of access list. An extended IP access list uses numbers 100 through 199, which enables 100 unique extended IP access lists to be defined.

The Protocol Field

The **protocol field** entry defines the protocol to be filtered. You can filter on IP, TCP, and UDP, as well as on different routing protocols. When creating an extended IP access-list statement, it is important to remember the relationship of protocols within the TCP/IP protocol suite that form IP datagrams. That is, an IP header is used to transport ICMP, TCP, UDP and various routing protocols. This means that if you specify IP as the protocol to be filtered, all matches against other fields will cause the packet to be either permitted or denied regardless of whether the packet represents an application transported by TCP or UDP, an ICMP message, or a routing protocol. This also means that if you intend to filter based upon a specific protocol you need to specify that protocol. Thus, you need to specify more specific entries prior to less specific entries. For example, assume the following statements:

    access-list 101 permit ip any any

    access-list 101 deny tcp any host 198.78.46.8

Because the first statement permits IP from any host to any host, this means you could not block TCP from any host to the host whose IP address is 198.78.46.8 as the second statement would never take effect. You would need to reverse the order of statements, which is why more specific entries should be placed ahead of less specific entries.

Source Address and Wildcard Mask Fields

The source address and wildcard mask for an extended IP access list function in the same manner as for a standard IP access list. This means that you can use the keywords "host" and "any" and avoid specifying a mask.

Source Port Number Field

You can use either an integer or a mnemonic to specify a port number. For example, to specify the Web's HyperText Transmission Protocol (HTTP) you can either use 80 or http. In addition, for TCP and UDP you can use the keyword operators lt (less than), gt (greater than), eq (equal), and neq (not equal).

Destination Address and Wildcard Mask Fields

The destination address and wildcard mask have the same structure as the source address and wildcard mask. Thus, you can use the keywords "host" and "any" to specify a specific address or any destination address without having to specify a mask.

Destination Port Number

Similar to the source port you can specify the destination port as a numeric or a mnemonic. You can also use an operator to specify a range. The following example illustrates the use of both a numeric and a mnemonic to block Web surfing from any source to the 198.78.46.0 network:

access-list 101 deny tcp any 198.78.46.0 0.0.0.255 eq 80

access-list 101 deny tcp any 198.78.46.0 0.0.0.255 eq http

Options

Extended IP access lists support a wide range of options. One commonly used option is "log," which was described when we examined standard IP access lists. Another commonly used option is "established." This option is only applicable to the TCP protocol and is employed to restrict TCP traffic in one direction as a response to sessions initiated in the opposite direction. To accomplish this, an access-list statement that contains the word "established" results in each packet being examined to determine if its ACK or RST bit is set. If so, this condition indicates that the packet is part of a previously established TCP connection.

To illustrate the use of the keyword "established" in an extended IP access-list statement, let's assume that the Ethernet network shown in Figure 9.2 has the IP address 205.131.175.0. To restrict TCP packets flowing from the Internet to those in response to packets originating on the Ethernet network, you would use the following access list statement:

access-list 101 permit tcp any 205.131.175.0 0.0.0.255 established

In examining the use of the keyword "established" there are several points to note. First, although its use provides a mechanism to control access from a router's untrusted side based upon traffic originated from the trusted side, the method used is rather primitive. That is, packets are considered to be kosher if their ACK or RST bit is set, a condition easy for a hacker to overcome. Second, "established" is only applicable to TCP as there is no field in a UDP header to indicate that a UDP Segment is a response packet. As we will note later in this section, reflexive access lists and Context Based Access Control (CBAC) provide more powerful mechanisms for controlling access via the untrusted side of a router, based upon the flow of packets from the trusted side of the router.

To facilitate the use of Cisco extended IP access lists, Table 9.2 provides a list of commonly used keywords and a brief description of their use. As we continue our examination of the use of IP access lists in this section, we will examine the use of most of the keywords listed in this table. However, one keyword deserves a brief mention now as it provides a mechanism to add comments to an access list. That keyword is remark, which is placed after an

TABLE 9.2   Extended IP Access List Keywords

Keyword	Utilization
any	An abbreviation for an address and wildcard-mask value of 0.0.0.0 255.255.255.255. This keyword is applicable to both source and destination address fields.
established	Causes a match if the ACK or RST bits are set in the TCP header.
host	An abbreviation for a wildcard-mask of 0.0.0.0. This keyword is applicable to both source and destination address fields.
icmp-type	Provides a mechanism for filtering ICMP messages by their message type. You can also specify the ICMP message code (0 to 255).
port	Provides a mechanism to define the decimal number or name of a TCP or UDP port.
protocol	Provides a mechanism to define a specific protocol for filtering. The specified protocol can include one of the keywords eigrp, gre, icmp, igmp, igrp, ip, ipinip, nos, ospf, tcp or udp, or an integer between 0 and 255, which represents an IP protocol.
precedence *precedence*	Provides a mechanism for filtering by the precedence level name or number (0 to 7) in the IP Type of Service field.
remark	Provides a mechanism for adding text comments for an access list.
TOS *tos*	Provides a mechanism for filtering based upon the name or service level in the IP Type of Service field.

access-list number and allows you to place a comment in an access list. The following example illustrates its use:

access-list 101 remark allow TCP to our network

access-list 101 permit tcp any any

Rules and Guidelines

There are several general "rules" and guidelines you should consider when creating and applying Cisco access lists. The rules we will examine represent factual information, while the guidelines represent informative suggestions. The factual information is based upon the manner by which access-list processing occurs, while the information suggestions are based upon the experience of this author.

Top Down Processing   The evaluation of an access list results in a sequential examination of statements, commencing at the top of the list. This means you must carefully consider the order in which you place statements in an access list.

Access List Additions   New entries are automatically placed at the bottom of an access list. This means it may be difficult or even impossible to change the functionality of an access list. If so, you will then have to consider creating a new list, deleting the existing list, and applying the new list to an interface.

Access List Placement   You should consider placing extended access lists as close as possible to the source being filtered. This minimizes the potential effect of filtering on the dataflow on other interfaces. In comparison, consider placing standard access lists as close as possible to the destination. This results from the fact that a standard access list is limited to filtering on source addresses. Thus, if you place the list too close to the source, it could block the flow of packets to other ports.

Statement Placement   Because an IP datagram is used to transport ICMP, TCP, UDP, and various routing protocols, you should place more specific entries in an access list before less specific entries. This ensures that the placement of one statement before another does not negate the effect of a statement appearing later in the list.

Access List Application   An access list does not go into effect until it is applied to an interface via an access-group command. Remember, until the access list is applied to an interface, the list has no effect upon the flow of packets.

Filtering Direction Use the filtering direction to define whether inbound or outbound packets are filtered. Remember that packets flowing away from a router's interface are outbound, while packets flowing towards a router are inbound.

Router-Generated Packets Packets generated by a router, such as a "destination net unreachable" message or a routing table update, cannot be filtered by an access list applied to outbound traffic. However, you can control such packets, either by filtering their arrival via an access list applied in an inbound direction or by turning their generation off via an applicable IOS command.

Creating and Applying an Access List

Cisco routers support the creation of an access list via several methods. You can create an access list directly from the console, via a vty connection, or via a word processor or text editor. If you use a word processor or text editor you would store the resulting file as ASCII text and use the computer on which you stored the file as a server. To accomplish this you need to install on your computer a trivial file transfer program (TFTP) that operates as a server. You would then use the router as a client to upload or retrieve the previously created file. Figure 9.3 illustrates the Cisco TFTP Server screen with its option dialog box displayed. Note that this is a relatively simple program that allows you to specify the TFTP server root directory and the name and location of a log file, as well as whether or not the progress of file transfers is displayed and logging is enabled.

To apply an access list to a router requires a three-step process. First, you need to create an access list. Once it is created, you need to apply it to an interface. Finally, you need a method to define the direction that the access list will be applied to an interface.

Specifying an Interface You specify a router interface through the use of the "interface" command. For example, to apply an access list to serial port 0 (previously shown in Figure 9.2), you would define the interface with the following command:

    interface serial 0

Similarly, to apply an access list to a router port connected to a LAN, you would use the interface command with the name and port identifier of the

Figure 9.3 Cisco's TFTP server program permits you to create access lists that can be uploaded from a PC by a router.

connection. For example, assuming the router port was e0 shown in Figure 9.2, you could enter the following:

    interface ethernet0

Because you can abbreviate most keywords in a command, you could also use e0 in the command as shown below.

    interface e0

Using the IP Access-group Command   The third step in the three-step process is to define the direction of the interface that the access list works on. To do so you would use the **ip access-group** command whose format is shown below:

ip access-group [list number] [**in|out**]

Similar to other commands, the list number identifies a particular access list. The keywords "in" and "out" identify the direction that the access list will be applied. That is, if packets are flowing towards the router you would use the keyword "in," while you would use the keyword "out" if they are flowing out of a particular router interface.

To illustrate an example of the three-step process, let's create an access list. In doing so, let's assume our network configuration is that shown in

Figure 9.2. Let's further assume that we want to restrict data originating from the Internet to Web traffic bound for the host whose IP address is 198.78.46.8. In addition, we want to allow users on the 205 and 198 networks shown in Figure 9.2 to initiate Telnet and Web-based queries to hosts on the Internet and allow the results of those queries to return via the Internet. To do so our access list would be as follows:

interface serial0

ip access-group 110 in

access-list 110 remark allow TCP with ACK or RST bit set

access-list 110 permit TCP any any established

access-list 110 remark allow Web access to server

access-list 110 permit TCP any host 198.78.46.8

access-list 110 remark block everything else

access-list 110 deny ip any any

In this example the "interface" command is first used to define serial port 0. Next, the "ip access-group" command is used to apply the access list statements we will enter as access list number 110 in the inbound direction on the serial interface. This is followed by the entry of six access list statements that form the actual access list. Note that for internal documentation three statements include remarks. Thus, let's focus our attention upon the other three statements in the access list.

The first non-remark statement permits TCP traffic that responds to queries initiated from the internal Ethernet networks. This is due to the keyword "established" in the statement. The second non-remark statement permits Web traffic (port 80) from any host on the Internet to the server whose IP address is 198.78.46.8. The third non-remark statement is not really necessary as an access list has a "deny all" implicitly placed at the end of the list.

In examining this access list it is important to note that it could create a problem for Web surfers and other persons using the Internet. This is because, although TCP traffic is permitted, all other traffic is blocked. This means your internal network users cannot use DNS as it is carried via UDP, nor can they use ping as ICMP messages are not permitted.

To allow UDP we could add the following statement before the "deny" statement:

access-list 110 permit UDP any any eq 53

In this statement port 53 represents DNS. Thus, instead of opening all UDP access we will just allow DNS.

To allow pings we can permit echo replies to echo requests. Thus, we could add either of the following statements to our access list:

access-list 110 permit icmp any any echo-reply

or   access-list 110 permit icmp any any eq 0

Here the value 0 represents the ICMP type number for echo reply.

Limiting ICMP   To make your TCP connection more secure you should consider limiting the types of ICMP messages allowed to flow through your router. As previously indicated in our short extended IP access list example addendum, you can include a permit statement to allow a specific type of ICMP message. If you do not allow any ICMP and do not include a permit for the IP protocol, then all ICMP messages will be blocked. Before you block all ICMP messages there are certain ICMP messages you should consider permitting and others you may wish to block. Thus, let's focus our attention upon those messages. In doing so we will again assume the access list will be applied to the serial interface in Figure 9.2 in the inbound direction to the 205.131.175.0 network. You will obviously add an additional permit statement if you wish to allow applicable traffic to the other Ethernet network.

Permitting Echo-reply   If you have no outbound restrictions, then you are only filtering an inbound packets. Thus, echo requests transmitted from either Ethernet result in an echo-reply. To allow responses to those pings you could code the following statement into your access list:

access-list 101 permit icmp any 198.78.46.0 0.0.0.255 echo-reply

Permitting Pings   Although ping can be used as a discovery weapon to probe your network to discover information about your organization's resources, it can also be helpful for determining the status of certain devices. For example, if your organization administers a remote Web server, you might wish to permit pings to that server from your IP address. Assuming your IP address is 192.36.25.11, to permit pings to the server at 198.78.46.8 you would enter the following statement:

access-list 101 permit icmp host 192.36.25.11 host 198.78.46.8 echo

Considering Destination Unreachable   By default, when an access list sends a packet to the great bit bucket in the sky the router will return a type 3 ICMP message that has a code value of 13. This message, which is displayed as "Destination net unreachable," informs the person issuing the packet that the router on the path to that target address is performing access list filtering. There is a special router statement you can use to prevent this information from being determined by a potential hacker. After all, why make their job easier? That statement is:

    no ip unreachables

which you would enter for each router interface providing an Internet connection. The reason you cannot use an access-list statement is due to the fact that router-generated packets are not checked by an access list applied in an outbound direction. Thus, to turn off the previously mentioned message, you need to enter the **no ip unreachables** statement.

Anti-Spoofing Statements

Regardless of the type of access list employed, one of the first series of statements in your list should be anti-address spoofing statements. Because hackers like to use RFC 1918 addresses, you should deny all packets with a source address in three address blocks in RFC 1918. In addition, you should block all packets with an IP address of all zeros, all ones, and the IP loopback address of 127.0.0.0. If your organization does not support multicast (Class D) nor any experimental access via Class E addresses, there is also no reason to allow packets with Class D or class E source addresses. Finally, because some hackers think it is funny to use a source address on the network they are attacking, you should block all packets with a source address associated with your network. If we assume that the internal network to be protected has the network address 198.78.46.0, then the initial anti-spoofing statements at the beginning of your access list would be as follows:

    !Anti-spoofing statements
    !
    !Deny RFC 1918 addresses
       access-list 101 deny 10.0.0.0 0.255.255.255 any
       access-list 101 deny 172.16.0.0 0.31.255.255 any
       access-list 101 deny 192.168.0.0 0.0.255.255 any
    !
    !Deny address all zeros, all ones, loopback
       access-list 101 deny 0.0.0.0 0.255.255.255 any
       access-list 101 deny host 255.255.255.255 any
       access-list 101 deny 127.0.0.0 0.0.255.255 any

```
!
!Deny Class D and Class E addresses
    access-list 101 deny 224.0.0.0 15.255.255.255 any
    access-list 101 deny 240.0.0.0 7.255.255.255 any
!
!Deny source address of your network
    access-list 101 deny 198.78.46.0 0.0.0.255 any
```

Now that we have an appreciation of the operational capabilities of standard and extended IP access lists, let's turn our attention to new features that were added over the past few years that significantly enhance the capability of router packet filtering technology.

New Capabilities in Access Lists

In tandem with several relatively recent updates to the Cisco Internetwork Operating System (IOS) were improvements to the functionality and capability of access lists. Six additions to access lists that warrant attention include named access lists, dynamic access lists, reflexive access lists, time-based access lists, TCP intercept and Context Based Access Control (CBAC). In actuality, these additions represent new capabilities added to access lists and do not literally represent new types of access lists.

Named Access Lists

Because standard and extended access lists have a limited range of acceptable numbers, it is theoretically possible, although highly unlikely, that you could run out of numbers when configuring an enterprise router. Perhaps a more important reason for the use of named access lists is the fact that a name can be more meaningful than a number. In addition, as we will shortly note, you can delete statements in a named access list while a numbered list does not provide this capability.

Overview

Named access lists were introduced in IOS Version 11.2. As its name implies, a named access list is referred to by a name instead of a number.

Standard Named IP Access List

Named access lists are applicable to both standard and extended lists. The format of a standard named IP access list is shown below.

ip access-list standard name

where "name" represents the name you would assign to the standard named IP access list. The preceding statement is then followed by one or more permit or deny statements that define the filtering to take place. The following example illustrates the creation of a standard named access list to which we assigned the name "inbound" to denote that it will be applied in the inbound direction. In this access list we only permit traffic from two defined network addresses:

```
ip access-list standard inbound

permit 205.131.175.0 0.0.0.255

permit 198.78.46.0 0.0.0.255
```

To apply a named access list we use a modified version of the previously described ip access-group command. That modified version includes the name of a named access list and has the following format:

ip access-group name [**in**|**out**]

where "name" represents the name of the named access list. Thus, to apply the previously created named access list to the serial0 interface to filter inbound packets, our IOS statements would appear as follows:

```
interface serial0

ip access-group inbound in

!

ip access-list standard inbound

permit 205.131.175.0 0.0.0.255

permit 198.78.46.0 0.0.0.255
```

Now that we have an appreciation for the creation of standard named IP access lists, let's turn our attention to extended named IP access lists.

Extended Named IP Access Lists

An extended named IP access list is similar to a standard named IP access list. The format of the extended named IP access list command is shown below:

ip access-list extended <name>

where "name" represents the name assigned to the access list.

You can use an extended named IP access list in the same manner as a standard named IP access list. However, because extended access lists provide considerably greater filtering capability, you can perform more functions with this access list. To illustrate an example of the use of an extended named IP access list, assume you only want to allow http access to the server shown in Figure 9.2, whose IP address is 198.78.46.8. Let's further assume you will name the access list "security." Because you want to filter packets flowing from port 31, you would apply the access list in the outbound direction. Based upon the preceding, the extended named IP access list statements would be as follows:

    interface ethernet1

    ip access-group security out

    !

    ip access-list extended security

    ip permit tcp any host 198.78.46.8 eq 80

In examining this extended named access list, you may be puzzled as to the selection of the ethernet1 interface instead of the serial0 interface. The reason we apply the access list to the ethernet1 interface instead of the serial0 interface is that selecting the latter would block all Internet traffic flowing into the router other than Web traffic flowing to the specified server. Also note that we specify the direction of the list as being applied to outbound (out) traffic. This is because packets leave the ethernet1 interface to flow to the specified network.

Editing Capability

We previously mentioned that one advantage of a named access list is the fact you can remove previously entered list statements. To do so you would reenter the configuration mode and enter a "no" prefix for the statement you previously entered. It should be noted that you cannot delete specific entries in a numbered access list. One other point that deserves mentioning is the fact that you cannot selectively add statements to any type of access list other than to the bottom of the list. To add statements to a numbered or a named access list you must delete an existing list and reapply a new or modified list with appropriate entries. Now that we have an appreciation for the operation and utilization of named access lists, let's continue our exploration of additional list features and turn our attention to dynamic access lists.

Dynamic Access Lists

As the name of this access list implies, dynamic access lists create dynamic entries in a list. Those dynamic entries represent temporary openings in an access list that occur in response to a user authentication process.

Rationale for Use

The primary use of a dynamic access list is to obtain the ability to authenticate users attempting to access your network. To accomplish this you would first set up user accounts on your router. Next, you would create and apply a dynamic access list to the serial port of your router in the inbound direction, assuming you wish to authenticate users transmitting in that direction. Users then open a Telnet session to your router and authenticate themselves, normally by providing a user ID and password. Once the user is authenticated, the router will close the Telnet session and place a dynamic entry in an access list, which permits packets with a source IP address of the authenticated user's workstation.

One of the key advantages associated with the use of a dynamic access list is that it can be used for certain situations where it is not possible to use a static access list. For example, many Internet Service Providers (ISPs) assign dynamic IP addresses to subscribers. This means that there is no way to create a static access list entry to allow authorized users who have dynamically assigned addresses to access your network via an ISP connection other than to allow all ISP network addresses. Because this would result in a potentially large security gap and is not recommended, you would more than likely turn to the use of a dynamic access list for this situation.

Utilization

The dynamic access list is very similar to an extended IP access list, with a key difference being the inclusion of the keyword "dynamic" in an extended access-list statement. The format of a dynamic access-list entry is shown below:

access-list <list number> **dynamic** <name> [timeout n] [**permit|deny**] <protocol> **any** <destination address> <destination mask>

The first variable field, "list number," follows the same format as a traditional extended access list and represents a number between 100 and 199. The second variable field, "name," represents the designated name of the dynamic access list. The optional timeout variable can be used to specify an absolute timeout for a particular dynamic entry. The "protocol" parameters represent any one of the TCP/IP protocols, such as IP, TCP, UDP, and ICMP. Because the source IP address is always replaced by the IP address of the authenticating host, the keyword "any" should be used for the source IP address field. The last two variable fields, "destination address" and "destination mask" are used in the same manner as in an extended IP access list.

Prior to examining an example of the use of a dynamic access list, a few additional details warrant discussion. First, you cannot specify more than one dynamic access-list statement per access list. This means you need to consider carefully which protocols you want to create dynamic openings for in an access list. Second, you need to permit users to Telnet to your router or they will not be able to authenticate themselves and proceed to create dynamic openings in the access list. Third, to allow dynamic entries to be created, you must use the "autocommand" parameter under the vty line configuration. An example of the use of this command parameter is shown below:

line vty 0 3

login local

autocommand access-enable host timeout 5

In this example the "host" parameter enables the source IP address of the authenticating host to be substituted into the dynamic entries that will be created. The "timeout" parameter is optional and when included specifies an idle timeout. If you use both absolute and idle timers, the idle timer value should be set to a value less than the absolute timer. As a minimum, at least one timer value should be configured. This is because without a timer the dynamic entries will remain until the router is reinitialized.

One additional point deserves mention prior to illustrating the utilization of a dynamic access list. This point is of key importance because its omission can become a network administrator's nightmare if he or she is remotely administrating a router. Because a Telnet session is immediately closed after authentication, this action will prevent you from managing a router via Telnet. If you configure your virtual terminal lines as previously described you would be literally up the creek without a paddle. The way around this problem is to specify the "rotary 1" command beneath one or more vty ports as this command enables normal Telnet access to a router on port 3001. For example, to enable normal Telnet access on port 3001 for vty 4, you would enter the following commands:

line vty 4

login local

rotary 1

Once the preceding occurs, you would set your Telnet application to use port 3001. For example, if your router's IP address is 205.131.176.1, you would enter the following command:

telnet 205.131.176.1 3001

Now that we have an appreciation of the details concerning a dynamic access list, let's focus our attention upon an example. In doing so, let's assume your router is connected to the Internet as shown in Figure 9.4. The serial port of your router has the IP address 205.131.175.1 and you only want to allow

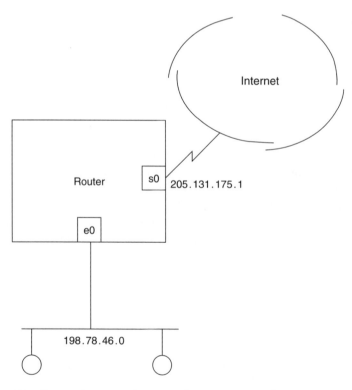

Figure 9.4 Configuration to reference for creating a dynamic access list that permits authenticated users access to the 198.78.46.0 network.

persons with predefined user IDs on the router to access your private network. In addition, we will assume you wish to permit remote administration of the router via Telnet. To accomplish the preceding you would enter the following IOS commands. Note that only the relevant portions of the configuration commands are listed:

```
username gxheld password gizmo87
!
interface serial0
    ip address 205.131.175.1 255.255.255.0
    ip access-group 101 in
!
access-list 101 permit tcp any host 205.131.175.1 eq 23
access-list 101 dynamic gxheld 10 permit ip any 198.78.46.0 0.0.0.255
!
line vty 0 3
    login local
    autocommand access-enable host timeout 5
line vty 4
    login local
    rotary 1
```

In this example note that we create the user name gxheld and reference it in the second access-list statement. This makes it harder for an attack since a person must specify both a user name and password to gain access. Also note that the first access-list statement restricts access to the router to Telnet (port 23). The second access-list statement contains the keyword "dynamic." This statement creates dynamic openings in the access list, substituting the source address of the authenticated Telnet user for all IP traffic with a destination address on the 198.78.46.0 network. Now that we have an understanding of the operation and utilization of dynamic access lists, let's turn our attention to reflexive access lists.

Reflexive Access Lists

When we previously discussed the use of the keyword "established" in an extended IP access list, we noted that it is only applicable to TCP. If you wish to control other upper-layer protocols, such as UDP and ICMP, you would have to either permit all incoming traffic or define a large number of permissible source/destination host/port addresses. In addition to representing a time-consuming and tedious task, the resulting access list could conceivably require more memory than available on your router. Perhaps in recognition of this problem, Cisco introduced reflexive access lists in IOS Version 11.3.

Overview

A reflexive access list creates a dynamic, temporary opening in an access list, based upon a mirror image of an IP traffic session originated from inside your network to an external network. The temporary opening is always a permit entry and specifies the same protocol as the original outbound packet. This opening also swaps source and destination IP addresses and upper-layer port numbers and remains in existence until either the session initiated on the trusted network is closed or an idle timeout value is reached.

Rationale for Use

The rationale behind the use of a reflexive access list is to enable employees on the trusted internal side of the router to control openings in the access list that occur from the untrusted side of the network. An example of the operation of a reflexive access list is shown in Figure 9.5. In examining Figure 9.5 note that the inbound opening reverses source and destination IP addresses and port numbers. Also note that the initial Telnet session uses a destination port of 23 and a random source port number greater than 1023. Thus, the opening results in a source port value of 23 and a destination port value greater than 1023.

Creation

There are four general tasks associated with the creation of a reflexive access list. The first task is to create an extended named access list. In an IP environment you would use the following command format:

ip access-list extended name

where "name" represents the name of the access list.

The second task is to create one or more permit entries to establish reflected openings. Because you normally apply a reflexive access list to outbound traffic, it will result in an inbound access list. When defining permit statements for your outbound access list, you use a slightly modified format of the permit statement. This modified format is shown below:

permit protocol **any any reflect** name [**timeout** seconds]

Here the protocol represents the protocol for which you want reflexive openings created. Because you normally want any user behind the router to create

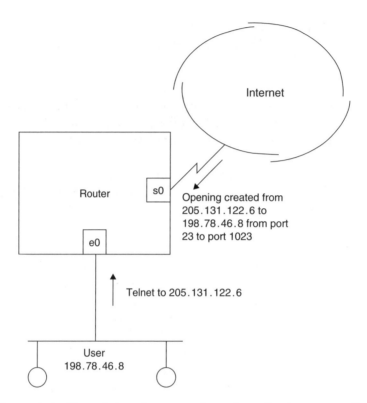

Figure 9.5 Examining the operation of a reflexive access list.

dynamic openings, the keyword "any" is used for the source address. Similarly, because reflexive results can represent any swapped addresses and port numbers, you would also use the keyword "any" for the destination address. The keyword "reflect" identifies the statement as a reflexive statement, while "name" represents the name of the access list. The optional keyword "timeout" is used to assign a timeout period to each reflexive entry created in the inbound direction. If this option is omitted, a default timeout value of 300 seconds is used.

You can also place a global timeout value that will be applicable to all reflexive statements. To do so you would use the **ip reflexive-list timeout** global command, whose format is shown below:

ip reflexive-list timeout value

where "value" represents the global timeout value in seconds.

The third task associated with the creation of a reflexive access list is to create an access list for inbound filtering. This is required as dynamic reflexive entries will be added to this access list.

The last task in the reflexive list creation process is to conclude your list with the **evaluate** command whose format is shown below:

> **evaluate** name

where the variable "name" represents the name of the access list and determines which packets are to be evaluated by reflexive entries.

To illustrate the use of a reflexive access list, let's assume we want to limit reflected openings to 240 seconds of idle time. Let's also assume your inbound access list will initially be coded to perform anti-spoofing operations by sending RFC 1918 addresses as well as "all 0's," loopback and "all 1's" source addresses to the bit bucket. The following example illustrates the creation of the applicable statements for the previously described reflexive access list. In examining the statements, note that the six deny statements in the extended access list named "inbound" are conventional statements that are not reflected but indicate where reflexive statements will be dynamically added.

```
ip reflexive-list timeout 240
!
ip access-list extended outbound
    permit tcp any any reflect my-session
    permit udp any any reflect my-session
    permit icmp any any reflect my-session
!
ip access list extended inbound
    deny ip 127.0.0.0 0.255.255.255 any
    deny ip host 255.255.255.255 any
    deny ip 0.0.0.0 255.255.255.255 any
    deny ip host 255.255.255.255 any
    deny ip 10.0.0.0 0.255.255.255 any
    deny ip 172.16.0.0 0.31.255.255 any
    deny ip 192.168.0.0 0.0.255.255 any
evaluate my_session
```

Limitations

Although the use of reflexive access lists considerably enhances the ability to secure the flow of packets from an untrusted side of a router, their key limitation is the fact that they are limited to supporting single-channel connections. This means that applications such as file transfer protocol (ftp) that use multiple port numbers or channels cannot be supported by reflexive access lists. To obtain support for multi-channel applications, Cisco initially provided a special release of IOS referred to as the Firewall Feature Set (FFS), which was limited with respect to the platforms it operated upon. During 1999 FFS was incorporated into IOS Release 12.0 under the name Context Based Access Control (CBAC). CBAC not only supports multi-channel applications but, in addition, adds a Java blocking capability as well as denial-of-service prevention and detection, real-time alerts, and audit trails. Because CBAC represents the most sophisticated variation of access lists, we will defer an examination of this access list to the end of this section. Thus, we will continue our examination of access lists by turning our attention to time-based access lists.

Time-Based Access Lists

Until the release of IOS Version 12.0 there was no easy method to establish different security policies based upon the time of day or date. Although you could create multiple access lists and apply them at different times of the day, doing so could entail a work effort that might be less than desirable. For example, to implement a new security policy to enable Web surfing after 6:00 p.m., you would either have to stay in the office until that time or Telnet from home and revise your access list. If your organization decides that the policy should also revert back to blocking Web surfing at 5:00 a.m., it might not be very appealing to get up before your pet to go to work. With the introduction of IOS Version 12.0 you can now use time-based access lists to obtain the ability to implement different security policies based upon the time of day.

Creation

The creation of a time-based access list is a relatively straightforward two-step process. First, you define a time range. Once this is accomplished you reference the time range in an access-list entry.

The specification of a time range is accomplished through the use of a time-range statement whose format is shown below:

time-range time-range-name

where the "time-range-name" represents the name you assign to the time range. Once this task is accomplished you can specify a time range in one of two ways. You can use an "absolute" statement or you can use a "periodic" statement. The format of each statement is shown below:

absolute [**start** time date] [**end** time date]

periodic days-of-the-week hh:mm to [days-of-the-week] hh:mm

The "time" parameter in an absolute statement is entered in the format hh:mm, where hours (hh) are expressed in a 24-hour format. For the periodic statement you can list the days of the week separated by spaces or use the keywords "daily" or "weekend." Once you create a time range, you can reference it through the optional keyword "time-range" in a conventional access-list entry.

Example

Since the old adage "the proof of the pudding is in the eating" holds true today, let's focus our attention upon an example. The following example illustrates the creation of a time-based access list that restricts Web access to Saturday and Sunday from 9:00 a.m. until 5:00 p.m.:

```
time range allow-http
!
periodic weekend 09:00 to 17:00
!
access-list 101 permit tcp any any eq 80 time-range allow-http
```

TCP Intercept

TCP intercept represents a feature that was added in IOS Version 11.3 as a mechanism to minimize the effect of a special type of denial-of-service attack referred to as SYN flooding and which is also known as a Smurf attack, after the cartoon character. With the release of IOS Version 12.0, TCP intercept was incorporated into Context Based Access Control. Thus, we can literally cover two topics at the same time by deferring a discussion of TCP intercept and covering it as we examine context based access control.

Context Based Access Control

Context Based Access Control (CBAC) represents the latest addition to Cisco router packet filtering capabilities. Introduced during 1999, CBAC provides a router administrator with the ability to create dynamic entries in a router's access list for both single- and multi-channel applications. In addition, CBAC provides the ability to control the flow of Java applets, as well as the ability to minimize the effect of certain types of denial-of-service attacks.

Overview

Until 1999 CBAC was a special feature referred to as the firewall feature set (FFS), which was only available for use on the Cisco series 1600 and 2500 router platforms. During 1999 the release of Cisco's Internetwork Operating System (IOS) Release 12.0T expanded the availability of FFS, which is now referred to as CBAC, to Cisco 800, uBR900, 1600, 1700, 2500, 2600, 3600, 7100, and 7200 series platforms.

CBAC operates similarly to reflexive access lists, which were previously covered in this chapter. As we noted earlier, a reflexive access list is used to create dynamic openings in an inbound access list in response to an outbound data transmission. A key limit of a reflexive access list is its inability to support multi-channel applications, such as FTP, CU-SeeMe, H. 323, and similar transmissions that use two or more TCP or UDP ports. CBAC overcomes this limitation, providing you with the ability to extend the capability of reflexive access lists to multi-channel applications.

Table 9.3 provides a list of representative applications that CBAC can securely support. Concerning that support, CBAC functions by examining packets that enter or exit a specified interface. Key information contained in the packet, such as IP addresses and layer 4 port numbers, is placed in a state table. The contents of that table are then used by CBAC to create temporary openings in an access list for returned traffic. Although the operation is similar to that of a reflexive access list, CBAC does this for both single and multi-channel applications. In addition, CBAC tracks the sequence numbers used in a TCP conversation to ensure that they are within the expected range, which can prevent a sophisticated attack by someone monitoring a conversation and attempting to piggyback onto it to break into a network resource.

In addition to extending the ability of reflexive access lists, CBAC adds several new features that result in much more than an access-list enhancement. These additional features include Java blocking, denial-of-service prevention and detection, and the ability to provide real-time alerts and audit trails. Thus, CBAC can be considered to represent a comprehensive set of security tools, even though it is enabled in a manner similar to other types of Cisco access lists.

TABLE 9.3   Examples of Applications Supported by CBAC

Single-channel TCP (i.e., Telnet)
Single-channel UDP (i.e., DNS)
CU-SeeMe (White Pine Software version)
FTP
H. 323 (NetMeeting, ProShare)
IP fragments
Java (applets embedded in HTTP)
Unix r commands (rlogin, rexec, etc.)
RealAudio
RPC (Sun version)
SMTP
SQL*Net
TFTP

Operation

As previously noted, CBAC extends the capability of reflexive access lists to multi-channel applications in addition to adding several new features. Because CBAC monitors outbound traffic to create applicable inbound access-list entries, two access lists are required. One CBAC access list will define the packets that will be inspected by CBAC. The second access list will include the entries that CBAC dynamically creates as it compares outbound packets against the statements you will code into an access list that will be applied to a particular interface in the outbound direction.

The actual CBAC configuration process is similar to the manner by which a reflexive access list is created. That is, you first select an interface and then configure the applicable access lists on the interface. In doing so you use one or more "ip inspect" statements in the access list you are configuring, which informs IOS that it should perform CBAC operations.

CBAC Example

To illustrate the creation of an access list with CBAC capability, let's assume your organization has a branch office with a connection to the Internet as

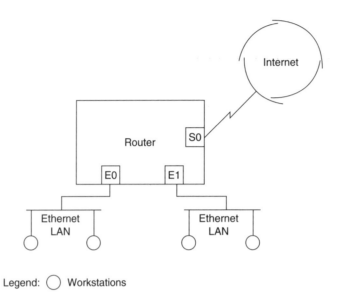

Figure 9.6 A sample network to be used for illustrating the configuration and operation of Context-Based Access Control (CBAC).

illustrated in Figure 9.6. In this example we will assume the branch office operates two Ethernet LANs, connected to ports #0 and E1 on the router, while port S0 provides a serial interface to the Internet.

Interface Because the first step in creating any type of access list is to select an appropriate interface, let's do so. Assuming we are attempting to protect internal users on the two Ethernet LANs from the virtually unlimited Internet user population, we configure CBAC on the external interface, S0. This will result in any traffic attempting to reach either internal Ethernet networks being inspected by CBAC. Now that we have selected an interface, a few words about the type and direction of the access lists to be applied to the interface are in order.

Since we want to protect internal users from traffic flowing inbound from the Internet, we create an outbound access list that specifies the traffic to be inspected by CBAC. This access list can be either a standard or extended IP access list. As CBAC examines outbound packets it will dynamically create openings in an inbound access list that governs the flow of traffic from the Internet that can reach either Ethernet network located behind the router. This access list must be an extended access list.

One aspect of CBAC that requires elaboration is the fact that it is important to remember that its use creates dynamic openings in an inbound access list based upon the IP address and layer 4 ports used in packets flowing in the outbound direction that match your defined criteria. This means that unless you supplement your CBAC-related statements with permissions for different types of data originated from the Internet, your organization's Internet connection will block all inbound traffic originated on the distrusted side of the router. While this may represent your intention, suppose one of the Ethernet networks shown in Figure 9.6 is connected to a Web server you wish to allow the general Internet population to access. To do so you must include an applicable permission in the inbound access list to enable traffic to flow through the router to the Web server. Another aspect of CBAC that warrants attention is the fact that it does not protect your organization from certain types of HTTP application-layer attacks, such as the exploitation of cgi scripts. Thus, it is important to note that CBAC is not a total barrier to security problems. Instead, it represents a sophisticated tool that adds to the capability of your organization's total security policy. That said, let's turn our attention to the statements that add CBAC capability to your access list.

The Inspect Statement

The ip inspect statement represents the key IOS command associated with configuring a monitored connection for inspection by CBAC. The format of this command for all protocols other than Java and RPC (remote procedure call) is shown below:

> **ip inspect name** inspection-name protocol [**alert** {**on|off**}] [**audit-trail**] [**on|off**] [**timeout seconds**]

In this format, the ip inspect command's optional keyword "alert" causes CBAC to generate messages to a syslog server or the router's buffer whenever it detects a violation in the monitored application. For example, if you configure CBAC to monitor TCP and an illegal TCP operation is detected when audit is enabled, the router will send an alert to the syslog server.

The keyword "audit-trail" enables CBAC to track the connections for a protected application. When this keyword is used, the router will log information for each permitted application to include source and destination IP addresses, ports used, and the number of bytes transferred. Although the audit trail was probably developed to enable network managers to obtain information on the traffic characteristics of network applications, it also enables managers to determine the locations employees are accessing. Thus, it also provides a database that could be used to determine if employees are viewing the stock market, accessing Web auction locations, or performing other activities that management may not particularly support.

The keyword "timeout" provides you with the ability to specify the duration of inactive sessions. In addition to being able to specify a general inactive timeout for specific protocols, CBAC also supports the capability to prevent denial-of-service (DOS) attacks by monitoring the number and frequency of half-open connections. For TCP a half-open connection represents a session that has not completed the initial three-way (syn–syn–ack) handshake. Because UDP has no handshake, a UDP half-open session is one for which CBAC has not detected return traffic.

You can control the number of TCP and UDP half-open connections through the use of ten ip inspect related statements that assign a timeout or threshold value. Table 9.4 lists those commands, their default values, and a brief description of each statement.

To obtain an appreciation of the entries in Table 9.4, a brief review of the operation of denial-of-service (DOS) is warranted. Under a DOS attack a hacker floods a network with either TCP or UDP requests and does not answer responses to those requests. This action rapidly consumes all available resources on the target host, which is then forced to deny service to legitimate users. While using a router to intercept and control DOS attacks ensures that computer resources on the network are available for legitimate use, the router could easily have its resources consumed. To prevent this situation from occurring there are timeout and threshold defaults associated with CBAC as indicated in Table 9.4. You can either elect to accept those defaults and do nothing, or modify one or more of those defaults through the use of the ip inspect commands listed in Table 9.4.

To illustrate the use of the basic ip inspect command, let's assume you want to create dynamic openings in the inbound direction from the Internet for TCP and UDP applications originating on the trusted side of the router. Let's further assume you want to assign a 60-second timeout for TCP connections and a 30-second timeout for UDP connections. To do so you would use the following ip inspect commands:

ip inspect name firewall tcp 60

ip inspect name firewall udp 30

To complete our discussion of ip inspect command formats, let's turn our attention to the two previously mentioned variations in the command format

TABLE 9.4 IP Inspect Commands Used to Configure Time-out and Threshold Values Used by CBAC

Command	Default Value	Description
ip inspect tcp synwait-time seconds TCP	30 s	Length of time to wait for session to be established.
ip inspect tcp finwait-time seconds	5 s	Length of time TCP is managed after FIN exchange.
ip inspect tcp idle-time seconds	3600 s	TCP idle time-out
ip inspect udp idle-time seconds	30 s	UDP idle time-out
ip inspect dns-timeout seconds	5 s	DNS lookup idle timer
ip inspect max-incomplete high number	500 sessions	Maximum number of half-open connections permitted before CBAC begins closing connections.
ip inspect max-incomplete low number	400 sessions	Number of half-open connections causing CBAC to stop closing connections.
ip inspect one-minute high number	500 sessions	Rate of half-open sessions per minute before CBAC begins closing connections.
ip inspect one-minute low number	400 sessions	Rate of half-open sessions per minute causing CBAC to stop deleting connections.
ip inspect tcp max-incomplete host Number block-time seconds	50 sessions	Number of existing half-open sessions with the same destination address before CBAC begins closing sessions.

for RPC and Java. For RPC the format of the command is slightly different as illustrated below:

ip inspect name inspection-name **rpc program-number** number [**wait-time** minutes] [**alert** {**on**|**off**}] [**audit-trail** {**on**|**off**}] [**timeout** seconds]

As an example of a CBAC inspect statement for RPC, assume you want to allow RPC program number 14000 and effect a 60-second idle timeout. To do so you would use the following inspect command:

ip inspect name firewall rpc program-number 14000 timeout 60

To use CBAC for Java blocking you need to associate a list of permitted IP addresses via the use of a standard IP access list to a slightly modified inspect command. This modified inspect command format is shown below:

ip inspect name inspection-name **http[java-list** access-list#] **[alert{on|off}]]** **[audit-trail {on|off}]** **[timeout** seconds]

In this format the access-list# represents the standard IP access-list number you wish to associate with Java blocking. If you should reference an undefined access list in the java-list definition, the default behavior will result in all Java applets being denied since there are no permitted IP addresses associated with the ip inspect command.

As an example of the use of CBAC to block Java applets, let's assume the network address of a parent Ethernet network located on the other side of the Internet in Figure 9.6 is 198.78.46.0. Then, to block all Java applets other than those from the parent network, you would code the following commands:

access-list 1 permit 198.78.46.0 0.0.0.255

ip inspect name firewall http java-list 1

Although these commands block all Java applets other than those originating from the 198.78.46.0 network, it should be noted that in its current incarnation CBAC does not block ActiveX. At the present time Cisco recommends the use of a dedicated content-filtering product if you need to perform an extensive amount of content filtering or if you need to filter one or more applications not presently supported by Cisco access list features to include CBAC.

Applying the Inspection Rules

Similar to other types of access lists, once you create your CBAC inspection rules you need to apply those rules to an interface. To do so you would use an ip inspect command that indicates the direction of inspection. The format used to apply an inspection rule is shown below:

ip inspect inspection-name **{in|out}**

Note that when applying the inspection you should apply them to the direction of outbound traffic to ensure that CBAC checks inbound traffic. This means that if you are configuring inspection on an internal interface, the outbound traffic from the network is entering the interface. Thus, in this situation the inspection rules should be applied inbound. If you are configuring inspection on an external router interface, the outbound traffic is leaving the interface. In this situation the inspection rules should be applied in the outbound direction. While the preceding may appear a bit confusing, you can avoid potential confusion by remembering that you would apply the inspection rule to packets leaving the interface to be guarded to insure that return packets are checked.

Using CBAC

Since the proof of the pudding is in the eating, let's illustrate the manner in which we can use CBAC. For our example, let's assume our organization has a two-port router with the serial port providing a connection to an Internet Service Provider, while the Ethernet interface provides a connection to the internal Ethernet network. Let's further assume you want to allow the internal users on your Ethernet LAN to have access to the Internet for Web browsing, FTP and electronic mail. Let's also further assume that your parent organization, whose network address is 205.131.175.0, should be the only network from which Java applets will be allowed to flow through your router onto your network. In addition, we will assume that you would like to use the alerting capability of CBAC to provide information concerning when Java applets are blocked or permitted and the auditing capability of CBAC to provide you with information concerning FTP traffic. Last but not least, you want to enable your internal Ethernet users to perform ping and traceroute operations to hosts on the Internet.

The specific coding we would use to implement the previously stated network requirements are listed below:

```
interface ethernet0
    ip address 198.78.46.1 255.255.255.0
    ip access-group 101 in
!
!
interface serial0
    ip address 198.78.40.5 255.255.255.0
    ip inspect firewall out
    ip access-group 102 in
```

```
!
!
ip inspect alert-off
ip inspect name firewall http java-list 1 alert on
ip inspect name firewall ftp audit-trail on
ip inspect name firewall smtp
ip inspect name firewall tcp
ip inspect name firewall udp
!
ip access-list 1 permit 205.131.175.0 0.0.0.255
!
ip access-list 101 permit ip any any
!
ip access-list 102 permit icmp any any echo-reply
ip access-list 102 permit icmp any any time-exceeded
ip access-list 102 permit icmp any any packet-too-big
ip access-list 102 permit icmp any any unreachable
ip access-list 102 permit icmp any any administratively-prohibited
```

In examining the coding, note that the IOS commands are grouped into several areas. First, we configure the Ethernet interface by assigning an IP address to the interface and then associating access list number 101 in the inbound direction with the interface through the use of an ip access-group statement. This is followed by the configuration of the serial interface.

Because we will apply CBAC inspection to the serial interface we include an ip inspect command under the serial interface. Note that the ip inspect command is set up to inspect packets flowing in the outbound direction as we want CBAC to create temporary openings in the inbound direction. Because we use the ip access-group command under the serial interface, CBAC will create temporary openings at the bottom of access list 102 whose statements we will shortly review.

After the two interfaces have been configured, you will note a block of six ip inspect commands. The first ip inspect command disables global alerting, permitting us to selectively enable this feature for http in the second ip inspect command. Note that the second ip inspect command specifies that CBAC should use access list number 1 to selectively permit Java applets. Also note that after the six ip inspect commands we define a standard access list number 1 that only allows traffic from the 205.131.175.0 network. Because the second ip inspect statement is linked to access list number 1, this means that only Java applets from the 205.131.175.0 network will be permitted inbound through our router. Also note that, because we previously mentioned that we wanted to be alerted concerning the permission or blocking of Java applets, the second ip inspect command includes an "alert on" option.

The third ip inspect command configures inspection for ftp, while the fourth command provides inspection for sending email. Because we mentioned a requirement to audit ftp, the third ip insert command contains an "audit-track on" option. The fifth and sixth ip inspect commands provide generic TCP and UDP inspection to allow return traffic for queries using different protocols from your internal network. For example, by specifying generic TCP permissions, your employees could use call control protocols required for voice over IP (VoIP) session setup. TCP also allows the use of the post office protocol (POP), which enables your internal users to retrieve their email from an ISP's mail server. In comparison, we explicitly specify smtp in an ip inspect command since it is used for sending email and, if we did not specify a generic tcp, our employees would be limited to sending, but not receiving, email. This obviously would not be particularly useful. The use of a generic UDP permits the actual transfer of VoIP packets that applications transfer using the connectionless operation of UDP. In addition, the generic UDP command permits employees to use DNS and SNMP as both are transported as UDP datagrams.

After the block of six ip inspect commands we include two access-list statements. The first is a standard access-list statement which, as previously noted, is linked with our Java applet blocking. The second access list, list 101, permits all IP traffic to flow in the inbound direction to the router from the Ethernet network. This access list is not required, but has been included as a reference point in the event that we later expand the router and wish to block certain types of traffic from the Ethernet network into the router. Because the access list permits all IP traffic from any source address to any destination address, its current effect is the same as if we did not associate an access list with the Ethernet port in the inbound direction.

The last four statements in our router configuration listing consist of four access-list statements. These statements make up an IP extended access list numbered 102, which is applied in the inbound direction on the serial interface. Because CBAC only inspects TCP and UDP traffic, we must explicitly permit other types of IP traffic through the serial port in the inbound direction. Since part of our previously defined requirement was to permit employees to perform ping and traceroute operations, we need to explicitly enable the IP traffic required to allow these operations. Thus, we have coded several ICMP permissions. The permission of echo-reply allows internal users to ping hosts on the Internet and receive a reply. The permission of the time-exceeded and unreachable ICMP statements allows traceroute to function. Although not part of our requirement, we have added permissions for packet-too-big and administratively prohibited ICMP messages. These messages enable MTU (maximum transmission unit) discovery and messages indicating possible access lists on Internet sites our users may attempt to reach. If we had not included these ICMP permissions, it is possible that our internal users might experience significant delays when attempting to access some locations and might be prevented from reaching other locations. Because CBAC will ensure that TCP and UDP entries are automatically created for return traffic, once traffic from the internal Ethernet network flows toward the Internet we do not have to explicitly enable other protocols. Thus, in addition to creating dynamic openings, CBAC permits us to simplify our access-list creation process.

9.2 The Role of the Firewall

In the first section in this chapter we noted that the router represents the initial line of defense of an organization's private network when that network is connected to the Internet. The key method of defense is the creation of applicable access lists that perform packet filtering. While there are several types of access lists and access-list features you can employ by themselves, they are not sufficient to prevent many types of undesirable operations against hosts residing behind a router. One solution to this security gap is to use another communications device that provides additional capability beyond packet filtering. That device is the firewall, which is the focus of this section.

Access-List Limitations

Although Cisco routers support many new access-list features, including dynamic lists that provide an authentication capability and reflexive and context-based access control that create dynamic openings in an inbound access list based upon outbound activity from the trusted side of a network, they all have one serious limitation. That limitation is the fact that all access lists are relatively blind with respect to the operation being performed. This results from the inability of router access lists to look further into the contents of a packet as a mechanism to determine whether or not an apparently harmful operation is occurring, and if so, to either stop the operation or generate an appropriate alert message to one or more persons in the form of an audio signal, email message, or pager alert, or a combination of such mechanics.

Repeated Logon Attempts

Assume you permit employees to use FTP, email, and Web surfing and to perform other Internet activities. Thus, it is possible for a hacker to attempt to gain access to your hosts, have some fun, and lock out legitimate users from accessing one or more servers. The hacker could also perform a combination of activities harmful to the health of your employees' ability to use organizational computational equipment. For example, by transmitting repeated logins, a person may be able to either break into a host or lock out a legitimate user. For either situation the hacker repeats a sequence of login actions. Because an access list does not check the contents of packets, it is possible that the repeated actions continue until a break in occurs or the lock-out value for a particular valid user ID on a server is reached. One solution to this problem is to examine the contents of each packet and note repeating patterns, which are then blocked. Because this action requires a considerable amount of processing power, it is normally performed by a firewall. In performing this function the firewall maintains a state table of operations between a particular source and destination address, with the examination of packets occurring in an attempt to both determine and prohibit certain activities, with the process referred to as stateful inspection.

Application Harm

A second example of an activity that illustrates a limitation of access lists can be obtained by discussing certain operations associated with the file transfer protocol (FTP). Although we will focus our attention upon the manner by which the FTP application can be hazardous to the health of a remote computer, it should be noted that other TCP and UDP applications can at times also be harmful when used in certain manners.

When using a router's access list, you can enable or deny ftp sessions based upon the source IP address and/or the destination IP address contained in each packet transporting FTP information. Suppose that your organization operates an FTP server supporting anonymous access, allowing any person connected to the Internet to access and retrieve information from the FTP server, a relatively common occurrence on the Internet. Let's further assume that your organization has a large number of files on the server available for downloading. This means that a person could either intentionally or unintentionally use the FTP mget (multiple get) command to retrieve a large number of files with one ftp command line entry. In fact, if the person accessing your organization's ftp server issued the mget command using the wildcard operator of an asterisk (*) in the filename and file extension position to form the command line entry mget *.* then this command would result in your organization's FTP server downloading every file in the directory, one after another, to the remote user. If your organization has a large number of files whose aggregate data storage represents several gigabytes of data and a low-speed connection to the Internet, such as a 56 kbps, 64 kbps or fractional T1 connection, the use of an mget *.* command could tie up the outbound use of the Internet connection for many hours and possibly days. If your organization operates a World Wide Web (WWW) server as well as an FTP server and provides Internet access to employees over a common access line, the use of mget on an intentional basis can be considered to represent an unsophisticated but effective denial-of-service (DOS) attack method. This type of attack is perfectly legal as the person employing the mget command is performing a perfectly valid operation, even though the result of the operation could tie up your organization's connection to the Internet for hours or even days. Similarly, letting a person have the ability to download data to your organization's FTP server means they could consider using the reverse of mget, which is the mput command. Through the use of mput with wildcards they could set up an antiquated 286 processor-based machine and pump gigabytes of data to your FTP server, clogging the inbound portion of your organization's Internet access line. Recognizing the need to examine application-layer operations and provide organizations with the ability to control applications resulted in the development of a proxy services capability, which is included in many firewalls.

Proxy Services

Proxy services represents a generic term associated with the use of a proxy server. The proxy server is normally implemented as a software coding module on a firewall and supports one or more applications, for which the server acts as an intermediary or proxy between the requestor and the actual server that provides the requested service. When implemented in this manner all requests for a specific application are first examined by the proxy service operating on the proxy server. If the proxy service has previously been configured to enable or disable one or more application features for a specific TCP/IP application, then the proxy service examines the contents of each packet and possibly a sequence of packets and compares the contents against the proxy service configuration. If the contents of the packet or sequence of packets that denote a specific operation are permitted by the configuration of the proxy service, then the service permits the packet to flow to the appropriate server. Otherwise the packet is either directly sent to the great bit bucket in the sky or possibly permitted with the server generating a warning message and an alert or alarm message to the firewall administrator or other designated personnel.

Operation

To illustrate the use of a proxy service let's return to our ftp server access example. A common FTP proxy service permits a firewall administrator to enable or disable different FTP commands. Using this feature, the firewall administrator can control the ability of FTP users to issue different types of FTP commands, such as mget and mput.

In a Microsoft Windows environment you can use mget in either a streaming or an interactive mode. Concerning the latter, FTP will prompt you through the use of a question mark (?) whether or not the next file should be transferred. An example of the use of mget is illustrated in Figure 9.7. Note that by simply entering a carriage return in response to the ? prompt the next file is transferred. Thus, it is relatively easy for a hacker to write a script to stream files when using mget under Windows' interactive mode and a no-brainer under its streaming mode.

If you are familiar with the manner in which an FTP server is configured, you probably realize that the FTP server administrator is limited to assigning read and/or write permissions to directories and possibly, depending upon

Figure 9.7 Using mget under Windows NT requires a response to each file prompt, which can be simply a carriage return.

the operating system used, to files within a directory for either anonymous or non-anonymous users, with the latter a term used to denote persons who have an account on the server. However, there is no mechanism that this author is aware of that enables an FTP server administrator or a router administrator to selectively enable or disable individual FTP commands. Thus, an FTP proxy service provides the FTP server administrator with a significantly enhanced capability, which can be used to configure the capability and features of ftp services that other users can access.

Firewall Location

The capability to employ proxy services is based on the use of a firewall located between a router and network servers connected to a LAN behind the router.

To illustrate the common placement of a firewall, as well as a term associated with its use, let's assume we wish to add protection to an Ethernet LAN connected to the Internet. One common method used to protect an internal private network from packets flowing from the Internet is to place a firewall between the router and the network to be protected. In doing so you would install an essentially non-populated hub, whose only connections would be to the router and firewall as illustrated in Figure 9.8. Because there are no workstations, servers or any other device except the router and firewall connections on this hub, it is referred to as a DMZ LAN. Here the term DMZ is an acronym for "demilitarized" and originated from a strip of land where no military activity occurred. If you examine Figure 9.8, you will note that this network configuration insures that the flow of packets to and from the Internet has to pass through the firewall before the packets can effect a host located either on the public Internet or on the private network.

The firewall illustrated in Figure 9.8 represents a generic device, the functionality of which is highly dependent upon the product selected. Just about all firewalls support packet filtering similar to the filtering performed by router access lists as a basic capability. Thereafter, the functionality of firewalls can vary based upon functions and features incorporated into different vendor products. These functions and features can include proxy services for different applications that allow administrators to control different application commands, limiting the rate of pending connections to counter different types of denial-of-service attacks. They also provide network address translation to hide internal host addresses from direct attack via the Internet, perform authentication, virus scanning, and even encryption of data, which is a necessity when creating a virtual private network (VPN). It should again be noted

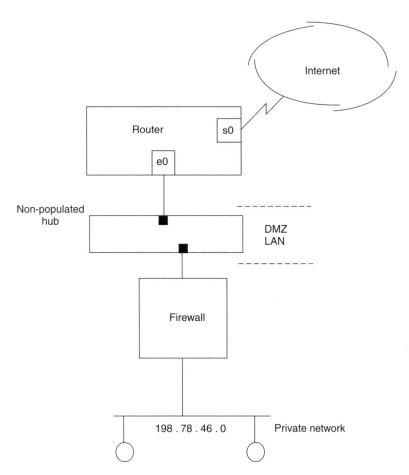

Figure 9.8   Using a firewall to protect a private network.

that the specific features and functions performed by a firewall considerably vary between vendor products, a situation we will note when we turn our attention to two vendor products later in this section.

For organizations that support public access to a Web server, a second common network configuration method is to separate the public and private networks and limit firewall protection to the private network. An example of this network configuration is illustrated in Figure 9.9. In this example a public Web server is located on the 205.131.175.0 network while the firewall is used to protect organizational hosts on the 198.78.46.0 network. If the Web server is the only network device on the 205.131.175.0 network you would more than likely create a router access list to limit inbound traffic to the HTTP protocol

Figure 9.9 Protecting a private network with a firewall while protecting a public access-list capability.

to the address of the Web server. You should also consider programming TCP intercept to minimize the effect of SYN flooding to the Web server and block commonly used spoofed addresses in your access list.

Another popular alternative configuration used with firewalls is to connect both public- and private-access organizational networks behind the firewall as illustrated in Figure 9.10. In this configuration the firewall is used to protect both network segments. This action permits you to reduce or eliminate the

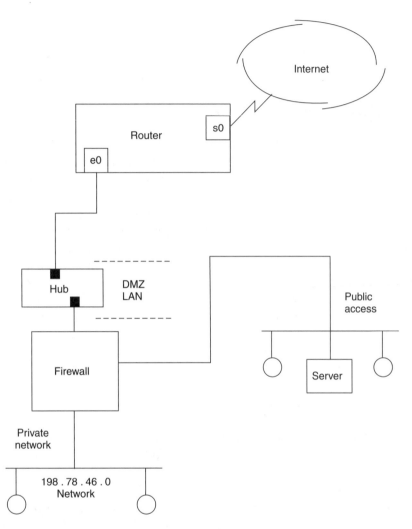

Figure 9.10 Protecting both public- and private-access network segments with a firewall.

access-list processing activity on the router as well as a router port. Because many firewalls use PC-based platforms, it is normally much less expensive to add an additional firewall in the form of a LAN adapter card than to add a port to a router.

While it is possible to protect the public-access server by connecting the network it is located on to another firewall port, the decision to do so is usually based upon the operations supported by the public-access host or hosts. If the server only provides HTTP support, usually protection via a router's access list should be sufficient. If your organization supports public access for HTTP, FTP, Telnet and other applications, you would then probably elect to connect the public-access network to the firewall as shown in Figure 9.10.

Types of Proxy Services

The type of proxy services that can be provided is only limited by the requirements of an organization and the programming capability of firewall programmers. Some of the more popular types of proxy services include remote terminal Telnet and TN3720 proxy services, Simple Mail Transport Protocol (SMTP) proxy service, HyperText Transport Protocol (HTTP) proxy service, the previously discussed FTP proxy service and ICMP proxy service. The last represents a special type of proxy service, which deserves a degree of elaboration due to the enhanced security capability it provides against certain types of hacker attacks.

The Internet Control Message Protocol (ICMP) represents a layer 3 protocol within the TCP/IP protocol suite. ICMP is used to transmit error messages as well as status queries and responses to those queries. ICMP packets are formed by the use of an Internet Protocol (IP) header that contains an appropriate numeric in its Type field, which identifies the packet as an ICMP packet. Although the use of ICMP is primarily oriented towards transporting error messages between devices operating a TCP/IP protocol stack and is transparent to users of a network, the protocol is also popularly used by many individuals who are probably unaware that they are using transmitting ICMP packets. This is because two of the more popular types of ICMP packets are Echo Request and Echo Reply, which are better known to most persons as a ping operation or application.

The use of ping is primarily designed as a mechanism to allow a user to determine if a remote host is operational and using a TCP/IP protocol stack. Pinging a distant host with an ICMP Echo Request packet results in the distant host returning an ICMP Echo Reply packet if the distant host is reachable, if it is operational and if its TCP/IP stack is functioning. While the use of ping can indicate if a distant host is reachable, a ping timeout does not necessarily mean that the distant host is not operational, because one or more communications devices in the path to the distant host could be down while the distant host is operational. However, in most cases ping represents the first troubleshooting method to use when it appears that a host is not responding to a query.

In addition to indicating that a host is potentially reachable and operational, the use of ping provides information concerning the round-trip delay to a remote host. This information results from the ping application on the originator setting a clock and noting the time until a response is received or a timeout period occurs and no response is received. The time between the transmission of the ping and the receipt of a response represents the packet round-trip delay and can provide valuable information about why time-dependent operations, such as Voice over IP (VoIP), produce reproduce a voice that sounds like a famous mouse instead of a person.

Although continuous pinging may appear innocent, in actuality it represents a method for a hacker to initiate a denial-of-service attack. This is because the pinged host must stop what it is doing, even if only for a few milliseconds, and respond to the ping with an Echo Reply ICMP packet. If the person that sets the ping application to continuous pinging also sets the packet size beyond its default size of 32 or 64 bytes, depending upon implementation, that person forces the destination to respond with responses of increased length, which requires the use of additional network resources. Thus, although the use of the ping application may not bring the destination host completely to its knees, ping can be configured to operate in a manner that can significantly interfere with the ability of the destination to perform its intended operations.

Another problem associated with the unrestricted use of ping is that it can be used as a mechanism to discover hosts on a distant network as a prelude for attacking those hosts. For example, a hacker could write a script to cycle though all 254 possible addresses on a Class C IP network as a mechanism to discover which addresses are currently operational.

Based upon the preceding, many organizations may wish to control the operation of ping and other types of ICMP messages. While many router access lists provide administrators with the ability to filter ICMP packets based upon source and/or destination IP address and the type of ICMP message, such access-list filtering is an all or nothing operation. That is, a router access list cannot selectively examine and note that a sequence of ICMP Echo Requests from the same source address occurred after a predefined number of requests flowed through the router and determine that subsequent requests should be prohibited. In comparison, on some firewalls an ICMP proxy service feature can be configured to differentiate between a single sequence of Echo Request packets and the intentional or unintentional setting of a ping application to continuously ping a host. Similarly, an ICMP proxy service capability can be employed to distinguish between a person who may have difficulty accessing a server and another person who is using the ping application in an attempt to discover all hosts on your organization's network. Thus, ICMP proxy service represents an important type of proxy service, the use of which can enhance the security of a network.

Limitations

Although proxy services can provide a considerable degree of security enhancement to networks, there are certain limitations associated with their use that warrant discussion. First and foremost, a proxy service requires a detailed examination of the contents of individual and sequences of individual but related packets, forcing the application to look deeper into each packet. This results in an additional degree of processing occurring on each packet, which introduces a degree of delay. Second, a sequence of packets may have to be examined to determine if it is acceptable to enable those packets to flow to their destination. This means that one or more packets in each sequence may have to be buffered or temporarily stored until the proxy service can determine if the packets can proceed to their destination or should be sent to the great bit bucket in the sky. This also means that additional buffer storage in the proxy server or firewall will be required and the temporary storage of packets adds to the latency of remote requests flowing to servers operated by your organization. In fact, according to tests performed by several communications testing laboratories, as a result of proxy delay, using proxy services from different vendor firewalls results in between 20 and 40 percent of the bandwidth of an Internet connection at the proxy server side being unused during the full utilization on the other side. This also results in a packet loss of between 20 and 40 percent, resulting in additional remote transmissions to the desired site. Thus, you must consider the effect of proxy service delays and balance the potential need to upgrade your Internet access line against the potential enhancements to the security of your organization's network.

Operational Examples

Now that we have an appreciation of the capabilities of a proxy firewall, we will turn our attention to an examination of the capabilities of two firewalls. First, we will examine several configuration screens generated by the Interceptor firewall, a product of Technologic of Atlanta, GA. Once this is accomplished, we will turn our attention to FireWall-1, a product of Check Point Software Technologies Ltd of Ramat Gan, Israel and Redwood City, CA.

The Technologic Interceptor

Similar to most modern firewalls, the Technologic Interceptor supports its configuration via a Web browser. Figure 9.11 illustrates the Interceptor's Advanced Policy Options screen, in which the cursor is shown pointed to the toggled check associated with the FTP Put command to block FTP uploads. In

Figure 9.11 Using the Technologic Interceptor firewall configuration screen to block all FTP Put commands.

examining Figure 9.11 and subsequent Interceptor screen displays, you will note they represent HTML screens displayed using a Netscape browser. The Technologic Interceptor firewall generates HTML forms to enable network managers to view, add, and modify firewall configuration data. To secure such operations the firewall uses encryption and authentication by supporting the Secure Sockets Layer (SSL) protocol for encrypting all traffic between the firewall and a Web browser used to configure the firewall while passwords are used for authentication. This means network managers can safely configure the firewall via the World Wide Web.

Using Classes

The Technologic Interceptor firewall includes a class definition facility, which provides users with a mechanism to replace address patterns, times of day, or URLs by symbolic names. Classes are initiated by selecting the Classes button on the left portion of the configuration screen. By using an equal sign (=) as a prefix, they are distinguished from literal patterns.

Through the use of classes you can considerably facilitate the configuration of the Technologic Interceptor firewall. For example, suppose you want to control access from users behind the firewall to Internet services. To do so you would first enter the IP addresses of computers that will be given permission to access common services you wish them to use. Then you would define a class name that would be associated with the group of IP addresses and create a policy that defines the services the members of the class are authorized to use.

Figure 9.12 illustrates the use of the Technologic Interceptor Edit Policy configuration screen to enable inbound traffic for FTP, HTTP, Telnet, and SNMP. Note that this policy uses the classname "= ALL-Internal-Hosts" in

Figure 9.12 Using the Technologic Interceptor firewall to create a policy allowing outbound FTP, HTTP, Telnet, and SMTP traffic from all users in the previously defined class "All_Internal-Hosts.".

the box labeled "From." Although not shown, you would have first used the class configuration to enter that class name and the IP addresses you want associated with that class. Then, this new edit policy would allow those IP addresses in the predefined class = ALL-Internal-Hosts to use FTP, HTTP, Telnet, and SMTP applications.

Alert Generation

The capability of a firewall is significantly enhanced by an alert generation capability, enabling a firewall to alert a network manager or administrator to a possible attack on their network. Figure 9.13 illustrates the Technologic Interceptor Add Alert screen display with the IP-Spoof pattern shown selected.

In the example shown in Figure 9.13 the IP Spoof alert is used as a mechanism to denote a connection request occurring from a host claiming to have an IP address that does not belong to it. In actuality, it can be very difficult to note

Figure 9.13   Using the Technologic Interceptor firewall Add Alert configuration screen.

the occurrence of IP spoofing. Although it is relatively easy to consider such source IP addresses as those in RFC 1918, all zeros, all ones, loopback and your network as spoofed IP addresses, others are difficult, if not impossible, to detect. This is because unless the firewall previously obtained information about IP addresses, such as their locations on segments whose access is obtained via different firewall ports, or notes restrictions on service by IP address, it will assume an IP address is valid. In comparison, other patterns such as refused connections or failed authentication are much easier to note. For each alert you would first specify a name for the alert definition, such as IP-Spoof for that pattern. After selecting the pattern, you can specify the days and times of day and the frequency of occurrence that, when matched, should generate an alert. The Interceptor supports two methods of alert generation — via either email or pager. If you select the use of a pager to transmit an alert you can include a message, such as a numeric alert code, to inform the recipient of the type of alert.

Packet Filtering

In concluding our brief examination of the operation of the Interceptor firewall, we will examine the initiation of packet filtering. Although the packet filtering capability of firewalls functions in a manner similar to that router feature, the firewall is usually easier to configure and provides more flexibility in enabling or disabling access based upon the set of rules that can be developed.

Figure 9.14 illustrates the Technologic Interceptor Network Services display, which lists the protocols for which this firewall accepts connections. Note that the HTTP protocol is shown selected as we will edit that service. Also note the columns labeled "Max" and "Rate." The column labeled "Max" indicates the maximum number of simultaneous connections allowed for each service, while the column labeled "Rate" indicates the maximum rate of new connections for each service on a per minute basis. By specifying entries for one or both columns, you can significantly control access to the network services you provide as well as balance the loads on heavily used services.

Figure 9.15 illustrates the Technologic Interceptor Edit Service display configuration screen. In this example, HTTP service is enabled for up to 256 connections, and a queue size of 64 was entered, limiting TCP HTTP pending connections to that value. The Max Rate entry of 300 represents the maximum rate of new connections that will be allowed to an HTTP service. Once this rate is exceeded, the firewall will temporarily disable access to that service for a period of one minute. If you allow both internal and external access to an internal Web server, the ability to control the maximum rate of incoming

Figure 9.14 Using the Technologic Interceptor firewall configure screen to edit HTTP network services.

connections to a particular service can be an important weapon in the war against so-called denial-of-service attacks. Under this technique, a malicious person or group of hackers program one or more computers to issue bogus service initiation requests using RFC 1918, loopback addresses, or random IP addresses that more than likely do not exist. Since each access request results in a server initiating a handshake response, the response is directed to a bogus address that does not respond. The server will typically keep the connection open for 60 or 120 seconds, which represents a period of time a valid user may not be able to access the server when its connection capability is at the maximum. If you compare this method of limiting HTTP requests to the TCP intercept capability of Cisco routers presented in the first section in this chapter, you will note that the latter represents a better weapon against SYN flooding when compared to earlier versions of Cisco's IOS. This illustrates an important concept. That is, there are certain security features that a firewall

Figure 9.15 Using the Technologic Interceptor firewall Edit Service configuration display to set a series of rules to govern access to HTTP.

provides that may not be available from routers and vice versa. Thus, it is important to carefully consider the capabilities of each device.

CheckPoint FireWall-1

FireWall-1 represents a scaleable, modular product from CheckPoint Systems that runs on a variety of platforms ranging from Microsoft's Windows NT to Sun's Solaris, HP-UX and IBM's AIX version of UMX. FireWall-1 consists of a troika of components, including a Graphical User Interface client that operates on the previously mentioned platforms as well as on Windows 95 and Windows 98, a management server onto which security policies created via the GUI are saved, and a FireWall module. The last represents software that operates on a device that performs actual packet examination. The device that operates the FireWall module is normally considered as a firewall and is located at network choke points, where it can examine all packets flowing between a public and a private network or another network access location.

The Graphic User Interface

The Graphic User Interface provides the mechanism for defining an organization's security policy. To accomplish this, you would first review your network configuration and devise a security policy that corresponds to your organization's security requirements and its network configuration. For example, let's assume your organization plans to place public-access devices, such as mail servers and Web servers, on a separate LAN behind a firewall, while placing your organization's private network resources onto a separate connection behind the firewall. Figure 9.16 illustrates this network configuration. Note that in this example the public network resources placed on a segment located behind the firewall are referred to as a DMZ.

For the configuration illustrated in Figure 9.16 the security policy that could be developed can vary considerably from organization to organization. One possible policy for illustrative purposes would be to allow external users to

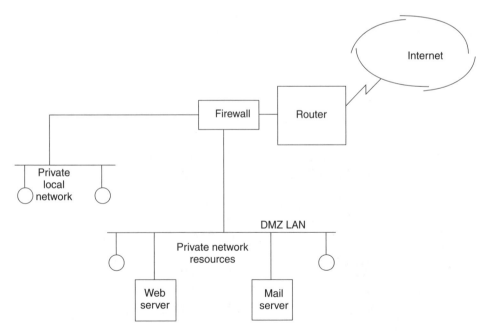

Figure 9.16 Protecting both private and publicly accessible network segments through the use of a firewall.

access the local network facilities only to surf the organization's public Web server or to send mail. In the outbound direction let's assume internal users will be provided with the ability to access all network resources to include the servers on the DMZ LAN as well as the Internet. Note that this policy protects private network resources from the untrusted side of the network represented by the Internet but does not place any restriction on local users on the private network segment.

Network Objects

Once you have developed a proposed security policy, you would use FireWall-1's object manager to define one or more network objects that are used by the program's rule base. Network objects can represent any device that has an IP address, such as a router interface, a Web server, or the hosts on an internal or external network.

From the Rule Base Editor you can invoke the program's Network Properties and Router Properties dialog boxes to define various types of network objects. Figure 9.17 illustrates the entry of configuration information into the two previously mentioned dialog boxes during the network object definition process. The box on the left illustrates the entry of general network properties, including the name assigned to a local network, its IP address, network mask, and applicable comment. Note that, by a simple cursor click, you can define the location as either internal or external and either permit or deny broadcasts. The right dialog box provides a similar network object definition process for a router.

Figure 9.17 Assigning network object definitions for a local network and a router.

For our previously described example, the firewall, Web server, mail server, and the private local network would represent network objects to be defined. Once this action has been accomplished, you would define the services to be used to implement your organization's security policy. In doing so you would create individual rules that form a rule base.

Firewall-1 Rules

The individual rules supported by Firewall-1 includes seven fields and follows the format shown in the column headings of Table 9.5. In this format both source and destination fields can be set to represent a specific object or any device. For example, let's assume that you previously used the program's object manager to assign the label web-server to that server. If you want to provide any internal or external user with the ability to access the Web server, you would develop a rule with "any" in the source field and "web-server" in the destination field. Because the Web server supports HTTP, you would configure the rule for that service. Concerning the action field, since you want to allow traffic you would configure that field to "accept." In comparison, if you wish to block packet flow to the Web server the action field would be set to "drop." The track field can be used to log information or to generate alerts. The field labeled "Install On" denotes the platform upon which the rule being developed will operate. Finally, the field labeled "Time" provides you with the ability to control when the rule remains in effect. The first two rules given in Table 9.5 permit external users to send requests to the Web server and mail to the mail server at any time.

Because we also want to allow users on the internal private network to access both the Internet and the organization's public accessible network, we need the third rule given in Table 9.5.

Similar to router access lists, FireWall-1 will drop all packets that are not explicitly permitted by a security policy. Also similar to our discussion of access lists, rules like access-list statements are examined sequentially and

TABLE 9.5 Setting Rules in Firewall-1

Source	Destination	Service	Action	Track	Install On	Time
Any	Web-server	http	Accept	Log	Gateways	Any
Any	Mail-server	smtp	Accept	Log	Gateways	Any
Localnet	Any	Any	Accept	Log	Gateways	Any
Any	Any	Any	Reject	Long Log	Gateways	Any

the first rule that matches a connection is applied. Although the implicit rule at the end of the FireWall-1 rule base is to drop all connections that do not match the previous rules, on occasion you may wish to log such connection attempts. To do so you could enter the final rule in Table 9.5 to terminate your rule base.

Once you complete the creation of one or more rules necessary to establish your organization's security policy, you would load the code generated by the rules onto one or more gateways.

One of the more interesting aspects of FireWall-1 is that it can convert your general rules into a series of access-list statements that can be installed on any router that supports the Open Security Extension (OSE). This means that you can install your policy on a pure firewall as well as on certain router products.

Figure 9.18 illustrates an example of the use of the CheckPoint Software policy editor to create a series of six rules. Note that the last rule in effect represents an implicit deny all; however, instead of simply sending such traffic to the bit bucket, its occurrence will be used to generate alert messages.

Management Functions

Although the previous rule creation example reminds us of access lists, in actuality you can assign a sophisticated series of properties to one or more rules. Properties are assigned through the use of a Properties Setup dialog

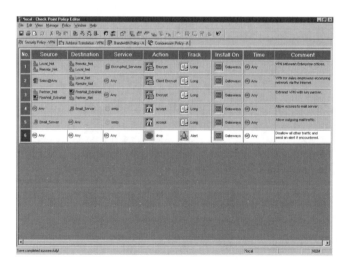

Figure 9.18 The CheckPoint Policy editor uses six fields to define rules that are evaluated top to bottom similar to an access list.

box and specify both general and specific aspects associated with the flow of information. For example, through the Properties Setup dialog box you can define the direction by which gateway rules will be applied as well as the length of TCP session timeouts, encryption, authentication and whether or not to allow RIP, DNS, and ICMP packets.

Figure 9.19 illustrates the Properties Setup dialog box. At the top of the box are a series of tabs that enable you to perform the indicated functions labeled on each tab. In the foreground the Security Policy tab was activated. As you can note from the display, you can use a drop-down menu to select the direction of packet filtering as well as a simple click to enable numerous functions similar to an applicable router access-list permit statement.

Concerning authentication, the FireWall-1 supports eight authentication schemes, which range from password to S/Key, SecurID Tokens, RADIUS server and digital certificates. In addition, FireWall-1 also supports the creation of virtual private networks by providing a mechanism to encrypt communications destined for other networks attached to the Internet, while passing packets flowing to non-VPN locations in clear. While many of the functions performed by this firewall are similar to the capabilities performed by a router's access list, it is important to note two key differences between the two. First, as a stand-alone device a firewall provides more security-related

Figure 9.19 Examining the CheckPoint FireWall-1 Properties Setup dialog box.

functions than commonly available through router access lists. For example, FireWall-1 can provide content checking for HTTP, SNMP and FTP to include anti-virus checking. Second, by off-loading communications security checking to a firewall you should obtain a higher level of router performance.

9.3 The Role of the Virus Scanner and Encryption

In concluding this chapter we will become acquainted with a key network security-related area — virus scanning. In this section we will briefly review some of the methods by which malicious code can adversely affect the operation of a computer. Once this is accomplished, we will describe and discuss the use of virus scanners to protect hosts on a network from receiving malicious code.

Virus Overview

A virus represents a program that reproduces its own code, placing its code in other programs so that, when those programs are executed, the infection spreads. Although not technically viruses, there are three additional types of malicious software that a good virus scanner will check for and which we should note. Those additional types of malicious software are logic bombs, worms, and Trojan horses.

Logic Bombs

A logic bomb represents a program that lies dormant until it is triggered by a specific event. The trigger can range in scope from a specific date and time encoded in the software to the receipt of a command to initiate its predefined operation. Once activated, the logic bomb will normally perform some type of insidious operation, such as changing the value of data previously stored on disk, altering the value of a RAM memory location, or attacking a third party. Concerning the latter, the distributed denial-of-service (DDoS) attack employed against such popular Internet sites as Yahoo and EBay resulted from code placed on third-party hosts that were activated by command.

Worms

A work is a program that reproduces itself. Unlike a virus that both adversely infects and reproduces, the worm is relatively benign as it does not alter or destroy data. However, each copy of the worm creates additional copies, which can rapidly consume all available computer resources.

Worms are usually planted on networks and in multi-processing operating systems where they can do the most harm. In fact, the well-known "Internet virus" that brought several thousand computers connected to that network to a halt during the early 1990s was actually a worm.

Trojan Horse

A Trojan horse represents a program that functions as a delivery vehicle for destructive code that will adversely affect the operation of a computer. Named after the Trojan horse that hid soldiers, a Trojan program will appear useful but when executed can function as a logic bomb, worm, or virus.

Virus Effect

According to several virus-scanning programs with a built-in database describing different malicious software, there are thousands of identified codes that perform different types of malicious functions. Thus, it is a bit difficult to attempt to categorize the effect of a virus. However, we can note that the actual effect of a virus can vary from humorous to catastrophic. Some viruses may simply display the message "X Shopping Days till Christmas," while other viruses can alter your hard drive's boot sector, resulting in the apparent inability to access information previously stored on your hard drive.

One of the most popular methods used by virus developers to replicate their code is to name their program as an external command file with the extension .COM when the real command program has the same name but the extension .EXE. The reason for doing so is that the entry of a command name results in the operating system executing the file with the extension .COM if it encounters both .COM and .EXE file extensions with the same file name. A smartly constructed virus using the .COM extension will also execute the actual .EXE command as it spreads its infection. Thus, for a period of time until the cumulative effect of the virus becomes noticeable it will be hidden because the command entered by the user will execute as expected. This type of virus is referred to as a .COM infection.

Types of Viruses

The types of viruses you can encounter depend upon the ingenuity of the hackers and pranksters who typically develop these programs. Although the types of viruses are virtually unlimited, they can be categorized by the most common areas they attempt to infect. These areas are the boot sector and file allocation table (FAT), system files, and operating system commands.

Boot and FAT Infectors

There are two locations that many viruses commonly attack due to the harm their alterations can cause. Those locations are the boot sector and the file allocation table. By changing information in the boot sector, a virus can make your hard disk appear to be unusable. By changing data in the FAT, a virus can make portions of your disk literally "disappear" simply by marking good sectors as bad or changing a pointer to the next cluster used by a file to an end-of-file cluster value. A few viruses have been known to swap the starting FAT entry address in the root directory, which when performed on a database file can result in the subsequent execution of a database processing program using an output file as an input file and vice versa, a truly insidious trick!

System File Infectors

A system file virus infector changes one of the operating system files. Since system files are always executed upon power-on, their modification functions as an easy mechanism to replicate a virus. The most popular method to develop a system file infector is for the virus developer to attach their program code to a system file. A virus scanner can easily note the occurrence of this type of file by comparing its size to the size of the legitimate system file. Far more difficult to detect is the virus that rearranges system file code so it can insert itself into the file without altering the size of the file. Fortunately, very few persons have the knowledge and are willing to devote the time required to develop this type of virus. Even if someone does, many virus scanners can be configured to prevent any executable system file from being sent over a corporate network.

Command Infectors

As previously noted, a command (.COM) infector virus either attaches itself to an external command file or hides itself by naming itself after an .EXE file using the extension .COM. since operating system commands are frequently executed many times during the day by many computer users, a command infector achieves the ability to replicate itself frequently by pretending to be a command. Now that we have a basic knowledge of the types of software attacks we can encounter and the manner in which most viruses designed to cause harm operate, let's focus our attention upon methods we can consider to prevent a software attack and, if unsuccessful in our prevention methods, recover from the effect of an attack.

Infection Prevention

According to an article published in a recent edition of a national magazine, over 5000 types of worms, logic bombs, and viruses have been identified. This means that it is highly probable that no one prevention and detection strategy or virus scanning program can be expected to represent an absolute guarantee against infection. However, such programs do represent a good starting point to protect your computer.

Infection prevention software functions as a filter, examining computer operations susceptible to modification by different types of attack software. Most infection prevention software monitors all I/O operations and disallows any attempt by code to modify critical disk areas, such as the boot sector, FAT and areas where executable programs that are part of the operating system reside.

Typically, you load the infection prevention software on your hard drive and either modify your AUTOEXEC.BAT file to load the program each time you use the computer or place the program for automatic startup under Windows. For either method the infection program functions as a barrier to most of the commonly used attack software techniques known to result in destructive operations.

Since infection prevention software is designed to detect attack software once it begins to operate, such methods are normally used to locate dormant infections. To identify previously stored attack software commonly requires the use of detection software.

Detection Software

A detection program, now commonly referred to as a virus scanner, searches your disk looking for identifying attributes associated with different types of attach software. Such software may examine the names and size of files to determine if they are disguised executable files, look for replication code, and search system files and the contents of memory looking for any suspicious alterations.

Virus Scanning

Today both infection prevention and detection of malicious code is commonly performed by one program referred to as a virus scanner. To obtain an appreciation of the role of a virus scanner, we will turn our attention to two types of products. One type of product operates as a stand-alone program on a desktop, while the second type of program guards the hosts on a network from malicious email, typically by examining inbound email.

Desktop Scanning

To illustrate the operation of a desktop virus scanner, this author will use Command Software System's Command AntiVirus program. Figure 9.20 illustrates the main window of this program. Note that this program is installed with five predefined tasks, which are listed within the window. To illustrate the operation of this program, this author will use it to scan his computer's hard drives. However, note that the program is also capable of scanning network drives. In addition, you can also create new tasks by clicking on the button with that label. Once you do so you can enter a name for the task and use a resulting dialog box labeled Properties to specify the type of scanning to be performed by the task. Later in this section we will examine the dialog box labeled Properties and the properties that can be configured for a new task.

General Features

One of the key features of the Command AntiVirus program is its ability to schedule a virus scan as well as send a message when an infection is found. Through the use of the program's Preferences menu you can send a message. Figure 6.2 illustrates the program's Network dialog box, which is selected from the Preferences menu. In examining Figure 9.21, note that it provides you with the ability to display a message when an infection is found as well as to send an email. This program integrates very well with Microsoft's Outlook, allowing a user to email a report as well as, if desired, the infected files discovered by the scanning process. Thus, you can configure the program to execute at predefined times and transmit via email any encountered infections to a help desk or another central location.

When you use the program dynamically, you can control both the scanning process and the action when an infection is noted. To do so you would return

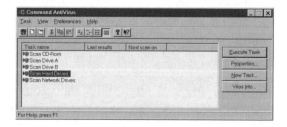

Figure 9.20   The main window of Command Software's Command AntiVirus program includes predefined tasks as well as allows the user to create new tasks.

Figure 9.21   The Command AntiVirus program supports a messaging option, which enables other members of an organization to be alerted when a scan indicates the discovery of the infection of a computer.

to the Preferences menu and select the entry labeled Active Protection. This action will result in the display of a dialog box labeled Active Protection, which contains two tabs labeled Dynamic Virus Protection and Memory Scanning. Figure 9.22 illustrate this dialog box with the tab labeled Dynamic Virus Protection in the foreground.

In examining Figure 9.22 note that the checkbox next to enable DVP must be selected to enable Dynamic Virus Protection. When enabled, the program will operate in the background and dynamically scan the computer resources selected as well as perform the selected action when an infection is encountered. Concerning the latter, note that the right column provides you with five options concerning the action to be performed in the event an infection is encountered.

Figure 9.22   The Dynamic Virus Protection tab in the Active Protection dialog box provides users with the ability to specify what computer resources will be scanned and the action to be performed if an infection is determined.

Figure 9.23 The Memory Scanning tab in the Active Protection dialog box provides users with the ability to control the scanning of the first 640 kbytes of computer RAM.

The second tab in the Active Protection dialog box is labeled Memory Scanning. Figure 9.23 illustrates the tab, which is now located in the foreground of the dialog box. Note that the version of the Command AntiVirus program used by this author was limited to allowing a scan of the first 640 KB of memory.

File Scanning Control

If you are scanning a large-capacity hard drive or many network drives, the scanning process can require a considerable amount of time. Perhaps recognizing this fact, the Command AntiVirus program provides users with the ability to specify the types of files to be included or excluded from a scan. To do so you would return to the program's Preferences menu and select the Files to Include/Exclude option. Figure 9.24 illustrates the dialog box labeled Files to Include/Exclude. Note that in addition to predefining file extensions you can add new file extensions for inclusion or exclusion in a scan.

The Scanning Process

Since the old adage "the proof of the pudding is in the eating" holds true today, this author decided to run a scan. To do so, the task labeled "Scan Hard Drives," previously shown in Figure 9.20, was first selected. The box in the right portion of the display labeled "Execute Task" was then click on. Figure 9.25 illustrates the initial execution of the Command AntiVirus program at a point in time where 856 files were scanned. As the program

Figure 9.24   The dialog box labeled Files to Include/Exclude provides users with the ability to specify files via predefined or entered extensions for inclusion or exclusion in a subsequent scan.

Figure 9.25   Viewing the progress of a virus scan.

scans your hard drive it displays a running progress of the scanning activity as a horizontal bar chart as well as by informing you of the path to the file being scanned. Note that at the particular point in time when the screen was captured no viruses were found.

Virus Information

One of the more interesting tutorial aspects of the Command AntiVirus program is its database of virus information. This database is arranged alphabetically by virus name, as is illustrated in Figure 9.26. As you select a virus

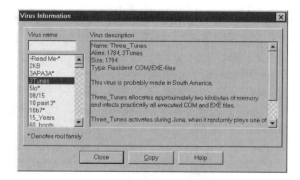

Figure 9.26 Using the Command AntiVirus program to display information about a virus.

in the left portion of the screen, the right portion of the screen will display information about the selected virus. This information can be very helpful in allowing one to sleep at night. For example, assume a virus scan performed once a week located the 3Tunes virus, which you then deleted. You would now more than likely want to know the potential effect of the virus. Although you could more than likely guess its action from the name of the virus in this example, this is not always the case. Thus, the ability to view a description of encountered viruses can be an important consideration when selecting a virus scanner in addition to the number of viruses in its scanning database and other program features.

Controlling the Virus Scan

In concluding our examination of the Command AntiVirus program we will turn our attention to its Properties dialog box, which represents the key to controlling program scans. Figure 9.27 illustrates the Properties dialog box after the Scan Hard Drives task was selected.

In examining Figure 9.27 note that you can specify the action to be taken if an infected file is encountered. You can also specify the drive and paths to be scanned, the types of files to be scanned, and other information, which you can note by examining the screen. The Properties dialog box also includes a button labeled Schedule. As you might expect, you can select that button to have scans automatically performed at predefined times. Now that we have an appreciation of the operation of a typical virus scanning program, let's turn our attention to the scanning of email.

Figure 9.27 The Command AntiVirus Properties dialog box provides users with the ability to control both when and how a virus scan is performed as well as the actions to occur if infected files are discovered.

Email Scanning

According to several surveys of Internet users, one of the highest ranking reasons for the use of the "mother of all networks" is email. While email is certainly a key productivity enhancement method for both residential and business oriented persons, it also represents a mechanism for the introduction of viruses. To facilitate the checking of email for attached files that could cause harm you can consider several options. These options include placing a virus scanner on each desktop, precluding inbound email or attachments to email, adding virus scanning capability to your firewall, or installing a separate virus scanner. The first solution, providing client-based email scanning, can be relatively expensive to deploy due to the need to install and configure software on each desktop. Precluding inbound email or inbound email with attachments defeats the purpose of providing employees with this productivity tool. Thus, if your organization requires protection from email-based attacks, your realistic choice is between a software module on a router that will scan inbound email or a separate server that operates scanning software.

Protecting the Enterprise

Figure 9.28 illustrates the relationship of an enterprise email scanner server to other network components. In examining Figure 9.28 note that an email destined for any client on the local area network will first flow through the router and firewall (1), assuming the datagram(s) transporting the email and any attachments satisfy any constraints imposed by the router's access list or firewall configuration. The firewall can be configured to function as a proxy for the Post Office Protocol (POP) server and send the email and attachments directly to the enterprise virus scanner server, where it is scanned and returned (2) to the firewall. The firewall then forwards the email to the POP server (3). The POP server then forwards the message to the applicable client (4). Note that as an alternative to the dataflow previously described, it is possible to direct emails to the virus scanner and the scanner can then direct scanned email to the POP server.

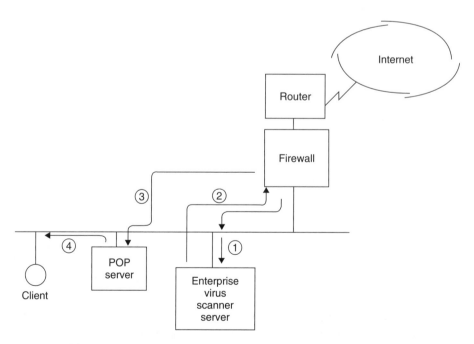

Figure 9.28 Using an enterprise virus scanner server.

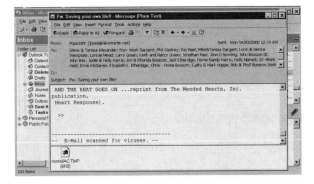

Figure 9.29 Many enterprise virus scanners denote that they operated upon an inbound email by placing an appropriate message at the bottom of the email.

Figure 9.29 illustrates the receipt of an email message that was scanned for viruses. If you examine the lower portion of the email dialog box you will note that the scanner used informs the recipient that the email was scanned. Although many scanners only scan inbound email, other products support a bi-directional scan. The use of a bi-directional scan may assist your organization in stopping the inadvertent infection of another organization from a file downloaded at home by an employee who took the file to work and decided to share it with a friend at another organization.

Optional Features

During the past two years several vendors have introduced virus scanning software oriented towards the enterprise that includes several features within and beyond virus scanning. Concerning additional virus scanning, some programs add scanning for FTP and HTTP in addition to the scanning of SMTP and mail attachments. Concerning features beyond virus scanning, some enterprise software programs now support spam blocking as well as the ability to look inside the contents of email messages. In doing so some programs provide the administrator with the ability to define inappropriate words, such as obscenities, racist hate words, or other terms that should trigger alarms or block messages. Other programs have a database of terms the administrator can use as is or modify. For either method, the ability to stop inappropriate messages from flowing to their destination could save an organization a legal problem, possible embarrassment, along with bad feelings among employees.

Because the best plans and efforts taken to prevent a virus infection could be overridden by the development of a new strain, it is important to be prepared for the worst. Thus, in concluding this section, which was focused on viruses, we will describe and discuss the common symptoms of attack software and the steps you can perform to minimize the effect of an attack.

Recognizing Infection Symptoms

A number of symptoms serve as a warning that your computer is under attack. Some are quite obvious, such as the display of a message that may contain profanity, attack a politician, or display a similar unexpected and unwarranted message. Other symptoms, such as the activation of a disk drive for no apparent reason and the illumination of the drive's light emitting diode, may be much more difficult to note as an indication that your computer is under attack.

Table 9.6 lists nine of the more common indicators that your computer has an unexpected visitor. If one or more of these symptoms should occur, there are several actions you should perform and other actions you may wish you had performed unless you were fortunate enough to prepare yourself to recover from different types of disasters.

Recovery Operations

One of the most important things to understand when you observe an indication that unwanted software is operating on your computer is that whatever

TABLE 9.6 Common Infection Indicators

♦ Programs take longer to load or execute than before.

♦ Disk accesses appear to be excessive for normal tasks.

♦ Disk drives are activated for no apparent reason.

♦ Programs that worked before do not work.

♦ Programs or data files appear to disappear mysteriously.

♦ The use of a utility program shows the presence of mysterious hidden files.

♦ You notice an unexpected reduction in available disk space.

♦ You notice the appearance of an inappropriate message on your screen or strange sounds come from your speaker.

♦ Less memory appears to be available for program execution than normal.

---

harm that can happen has already occurred and your actions from this point onward can prevent further harm from occurring. Unless the unwanted program has taken control of your computer and is writing continuously to disk, do not power off your computer. If you were not using a virus scanner and have a program available for use, run it. The chances are high that, if you have a virus or another type of attack program, its techniques may be recognized and the scanner can locate the program. If a scanner is not available or fails to locate any abnormal software, reboot your system using an original system diskette, which loads a good write-protected copy of the operating system, since the original system diskette is permanently write-protected.

Using the newly loaded operating system, attempt to examine the files you used during the operating that resulted in an infection indicator. For example, did you previously execute a command stored as an .EXE file and a directory listing shows both .COM and .EXE files? If so, the obvious cause of the problem is now apparent. However, what happens if you cannot access your hard drive owing to the modification of your boot sector, FAT, or directory structure?

Although it is probably preferable to have used a disk recover program which keeps an image of your key hard-drive sectors on another area of your drive to facilitate data recovery, you can also attempt to use an operating system command, such as the DOS command SYS C:, which will rewrite your DOS boot sector on your hard drive if that area was modified.

If this still does not fix the problem and persons you consult shrug their shoulders when asked what you should do next, you may be faced with having to reformat your drive and reload your software, which was hopefully backed up on a regular basis. Although this represents a situation most of us will rarely have to encounter, if you have to reload previously backed-up software it is important to recognize that the cause of your problem may also have been placed on your backup tape during your last backup operation. However, since you were able to notice an infection symptom, you also noted an operation you performed which caused the symptom. Thus, after you reload your software, reboot from an original version of the operating system and attempt to locate and eliminate the cause of your problem.

chapter ten

Managing the Network

With a little bit of luck, a small network without a significant amount of usage may require a limited amount of effort by the network manager or administrator to tailor the network to the requirements of the organization. As networks grow in complexity, the necessity to manage the network increases to the point where network management tools and techniques become indispensable for obtaining an efficiently and effectively run network.

This chapter will focus upon the tools and techniques required to effectively manage a network. First, we will examine the Simple Network Management Protocol (SNMP) and its Remote Monitoring (RMON) management information base (MIB). Once this is accomplished, we will focus upon the use of products that can provide us with some of the tools we may require to both effectively manage the transmission of information on the network, as well as observe the operation of file servers attached to the network.

Although an Ethernet network is a layer 2 transport facility, it is commonly used to transport a variety of higher-layer protocols. Thus, any discussion focused upon the management of Ethernet would be remiss if it did not cover at least one tool you can use to observe the state of higher-layer activity on an Ethernet network. Recognizing this fact, we will conclude this chapter by examining the use of several software products that can be used to provide a valuable insight concerning the utilization of an Ethernet network to include the type of traffic transported and status of different devices on the network.

10.1 SNMP

The Simple Network Management Protocol (SNMP) was originally developed as a mechanism for managing TCP/IP and Ethernet networks. Since the first SNMP Internet Draft Standard was published in 1988, the application and utilization of SNMP has considerably expanded, and an enhanced version, which was originally intended to add several security functions, but due to conflicts among members of the standardization committee wound up tailoring features in the first version of SNMP, was introduced in 1993. That version of SNMP is referred to as SNMPv2. A third version of SNMP, referred to as SNMPv3, was introduced during 2000 and added such security features as authentication and access control. Through the use of SNMP, you can address queries and commands to network nodes and devices that will return information concerning the performance and status of the network. Thus, SNMP provides a mechanism to isolate problems, as well as analyze network activity, which may be useful for observing trends that if unchecked could result in network problems.

Basic Components

SNMP is based upon three components—management software, agent software, and management information bases (MIB), the latter representing databases for managed devices. Management software operates on a network management station (NMS) and is responsible for querying agents using SNMP commands. Agent software represents one or more program modules that operate within a managed device, such as a workstation, bridge, router, or gateway. Each managed agent stores data and provides stored information to the manager upon the latter's request. The MIB represents a database that provides a standard representation of collected data. This database is structured as a tree and includes groups of objects that can be managed. Concerning the latter, the first MIB, referred to as MIB-I, included 114 objects organized into eight groups. Table 10.1 lists the groups supported by the first MIB defined by the Internet Standards Organization to include a brief description of each group.

In examining the MIB-I groups listed in Table 10.1, it is important to note that SNMP represents an application layer protocol. That protocol runs over the User Datagram Protocol (UDP), which resides on top of the Internet Protocol (IP) in the TCP/IP protocol stack. Figure 10.1 illustrates the relationship of SNMP protocol elements to Ethernet with respect to the OSI Reference Model.

In examining Figure 10.1, note that SNMP represents the mechanism by which remote management operations are performed. Those operations are transported via UDP, which is a connectionless service that can be viewed as providing a parallel service to the Transmission Control Protocol (TCP), which also operates at layer 4 of the ISO Reference Model. At layer 3, the Internet Protocol provides for the delivery of SNMP, controlling fragmentation and

TABLE 10.1   MIB-I Groups

Group	Description
System	Provides vendor identification to include configuration in information and time since the management portion of the system was last reinitialized.
Interfaces	Provides single or multiple network interfaces that can be local or remote, and designates the operating rate of each interface.
AddressTranslation Table	Provides a translation between the network address and physical address equivalences.
Internet Control Message Protocol (ICMP)	Provides a count of ICMP messages and errors.
Transmission Control Protocol (TCP)	Provides information concerning TCP connections, transmissions, and retransmissions to include maintaining a list of active connections.
User Datagram Protocol (UDP)	Provides a count of UDP datagrams transmitted, received, or undelivered.
Exterior Gateway Protocol (EGP)	Provides a count of interrouter communications, such as EGP locally generated messages, EGP messages received with and without error, and information on EGP neighbors.

reassembly of datagrams, the latter a term used to reference portions of a message. Located between IP and layer 4 is the Internet Control Message Protocol (ICMP). ICMP is responsible for communicating control messages and error reports between TCP, UDP, and IP.

In addition to being transported via UDP, SNMP can be transported via Novell's IPX, within Ethernet frames and through the use of AppleTalk and OSI transports. In 1992, a new MIB, referred to as MIB-II, became an Internet standard. MIB-II included the eight groups of MIB-I previously listed in Table 10.1, as well as two new groups — Common Management Information and Services Over TCP (CMOT) and SNMP. When the effort to run ISO's management on top of TCP/IP was abandoned, CMOT was essentially dropped as an active group. The addition of an SNMP group permits SNMP to track everything to include its own traffic and errors.

Figure 10.1 Relationship of SNMP protocol elements to Ethernet.

Operation

SNMP has a core set of five commands referred to as protocol data units (PDUs). Those PDUs include GetRequest, GetNextRequest, SetRequest, GetResponse, and Trap.

The Network Management Station (NMS) issues a GetRequest to retrieve a single value from an agent's MIB, while a GetNextRequest is used to *walk* through the agent's MIB table. When an agent responds to either request, it does so with a GetResponse.

The SetRequest provides a manager with the ability to alter an agent's MIB. Under SNMP Version 1, there was no method to restrict the use of this command, which if used improperly could corrupt configuration parameters and impair network services. Recognizing this problem, many vendors elected not to support the SetRequest command in their SNMP agent software. The introduction of SNMP Version 3 added authentication as well as encryption, resulting in a network management message received by an agent to be recognized if it was altered, as well as to be verified that it was issued by the appropriate manager. This permits the SetRequest to be supported without fear of an unauthorized person taking control of a portion of a network, or an agent returning false information.

Since SNMP is a polling protocol, a mechanism was required to alert managers to a situation that requires their attention. Otherwise, a long polling interval could result in the occurrence of a serious problem that might go undetected for a relatively long period of time on a large network. The mechanism used to alert a manager is a Trap command, issued by an agent to a manager.

Under SNMP Version 2, two additional PDUs were added — GetBulkRequest and InformRequest. The GetBulkRequest command supports the retrieval of multiple rows of data from an agent's MIB with one request. The InformRequest PDU enables one manager to transmit unsolicited information to another manager, permitting the support of distributed network management, which until SNMP V2, was performed in a proprietary manner.

One of the problems associated with the development of MIBs was the provision within the standard that enables vendors to extend their database of collected information. Although the tree structure of the MIB enables software to be developed by one vendor to read another vendor's extension, doing so requires some effort and on occasion results in interoperability problems. To reduce a degree of interoperability, the Remote Monitoring (RMON) MIB was developed as a standard for remote-LAN monitoring. RMON provides the infrastructure that enables products from different vendors to communicate with a common manager, permitting a single console to support a mixed vendor network.

10.2 Remote Monitoring

Remote Monitoring (RMON) represents a logical evolution of the use of SNMP. RMON provides information required for managing network segments that can be located in your building or on the other side of the world.

Operation

RMON operations are based upon software or firmware operating either in managed devices or managed stand-alone hardware probes. Managed devices can include such programmable hardware products as bridges, routers, gateways, hubs, workstations, minicomputers, and mainframes that are connected to a network. Through appropriate software, each managed device responds to network management station (NMS) requests transported via the SNMP protocol. Although a stand-alone probe can be considered to represent a managed device, it differs slightly from the previously mentioned devices in that it is firmware-based and is restricted to performing one set of predefined tasks — RMON operations.

Whether an RMON agent is a managed device or managed stand-alone probe, it captures predefined data elements and will either send statistics and alarms to a network management station upon request for statistics, or generate a trap command upon occurrence of a preset threshold being exceeded, resulting in the generation of an alarm condition that the NMS will then pool.

Figure 10.2 illustrates the relationship between a network management station and a series of managed devices consisting of RMON agents or probes. The MIB provides a standard representation of collected data, as well as defines groups of objects that can be managed. At the NMS, one or more application programs control the interaction between the NMS and each managed device, as well as the display of information on the NMS and generation of reports. Other functions performed by NMS applications can include password protection to log on to and take control of the NMS, support for multiple operators at different locations, forwarding of critical event information via e-mail or beeper to facilitate unattended operations, and similar functions.

The RMON MIB

Remote network monitoring devices or probes represent hardware and software designed to provide network managers and administrators with information about different network segments to which they are attached. The remote networking monitoring MIB was originally defined in RFC 1271, which was obsoleted by RFC 1757, issued in 1995. Under both RFCs the MIB consists of objects arranged into nine groups.

Figure 10.2 RMON operation.

The key difference between RFCs is the size of the counters, which were expanded from 32 to 64 bits under RFC 1757. This expansion was in recognition of the fact that, as users installed faster Ethernet networks, counters would reach their maximum value in a shorter period of time. Table 10.2 lists each MIB group and provides a brief description of the function of each group. All groups in the MIB listed in Table 10.2 are optional and may or may not be supported by a managed device.

Both the statistics and history groups can provide valuable information concerning the state of the Ethernet segment being monitored. The statistics group contains 17 entries for which countervalues are maintained, while the history group contains 11 entries for which countervalues are maintained. In

TABLE 10.2 Remote Network Monitoring MIB Groups

Group	Description
Statistics	Contains statistics measured by the RMON probe for each monitored interface.
History	Records statistical samples from a network for a selected time interval and stores them for later retrieval.
Alarm	Retrieves statistical samples on a periodic basis from variables stored in a managed device, and compares their values to predefined thresholds. If the monitored variable exceeds a threshold, an alarm event is generated.
Host	Contains statistics associated with each host discovered on a network.
HostTopN	A group used to prepare reports that describe the hosts that had the largest traffic or error counts over an interval of time.
Matrix	Stores statistics of traffic and errors between sets of two addresses.
Filter	Permits packets to be matched based upon a filter equation.
Packet Capture	Permits packets to be captured after they flow through a channel.
Event	Controls the generation and notification of events from the managed device.

addition, the history group includes the real-time maintenance of an integer value that denotes the mean physical layer network utilization in hundredths of a percent.

Table 10.3 provides a comparison of the measurements performed by the statistics and history RMON groups. Although both groups provide essentially the same information, there are some significant differences between the two. The first major difference is the fact that the statistics from the statistics group take the form of free-running counters that start from zero when a valid entry is received, and provide information concerning the recent operational state of the segment. In comparison, the statistics in the history group provide

TABLE 10.3 Comparing Statistics and History Group Measurements

	Statistics	History
Drop Events	Yes	Yes
Octets	Yes	No
Packets	Yes	Yes
Broadcast Packets	Yes	Yes
Multicast Packets	Yes	Yes
CRC Alignment Errors	Yes	Yes
Undersize Packets	Yes	Yes
Oversize Packets	Yes	Yes
Fragments	Yes	Yes
Jabbers	Yes	Yes
Collisions	Yes	Yes
Packets 64 octets in length	Yes	No
Packets 65–127 octets in length	Yes	No
Packets 128–255 octets in length	Yes	No
Packets 256–511 octets in length	Yes	No
Packets 512–1025 octets in length	Yes	No
Packets 1024–1518 octets in length	Yes	No
Utilization	No	Yes

information more useful for long-term segment trend analysis. Recognizing these differences, the statistics group tracks different packet lengths, while the history group ignores packet lengths and tracks network utilization.

Since a managed device or probe is essentially useless if a segment becomes isolated from the organizational network due to a router or bridge failure or cabling problem, some vendors provide Ethernet RMON probes with redundant access capability. This capability is normally provided through the use of a built-in backup modem or ISDN support. Another common feature offered with some stand-alone probes is a multisegment support capability. This feature enables a single probe to be used to provide support for up to four network segments, assuming cabling distances permit. Figure 10.3 illustrates the use of a multisegment RMON probe to capture and report statistics for two Ethernet segments at one location to an NMS at a remote location.

Managing Remote Networks

To illustrate the use of a network management platform to remotely monitor two Ethernet LANs, this author used Network General's Foundation

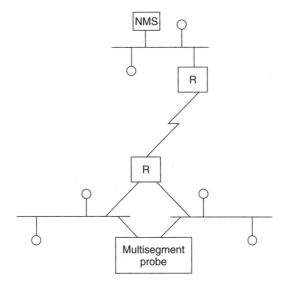

Legend:

NMS = Network management station
R = Router

Figure 10.3   Using a multisegment RMON probe.

Manager program. It should be noted that Network General was one of several companies that were acquired by Network Associates during the past few years. Figure 10.4 illustrates the selection of this program's Remote Quick-Stats bar, which enables you to specify an IP address of a probe on the remote network you wish to monitor. Once this is accomplished, the program will use that address to access the probe and retrieve predefined MIB elements such as the distribution of packet lengths shown in the upper left portion of Figure 10.4. In fact, if you compare the last seven entries in Table 10.3 with the contents of Figure 10.4, you will note that the packet distribution shown in Figure 10.4 and the usage meters in that illustration correspond to those seven statistics entries in the table.

One of the key features of Foundation Manager is its ability to provide users with the capability to remotely monitor up to eight networks at one time and simply click on an icon to change the display of statistics from one monitored network to another. This capability is shown in Figure 10.5 where the first two of eight QuickStat buttons are darkened to indicate two remote

Figure 10.4 Using Network General's Foundation Manager QuickStats feature enables you to view key statistics concerning the operational state of a remote network.

Figure 10.5 Through the use of up to eight QuickStat buttons, Foundation Manager can be used to monitor up to eight remote networks.

LANs are being monitored. Here the second QuickStat button is associated with an Ethernet LAN in San Antonio, and clicking on the first button would immediately bring up the statistics screen for Sacramento that was previously shown in Figure 10.4.

In examining the screens shown in Figures 10.4 and 10.5, you will note both provide the same key metrics for each monitored network. Those metrics include the distribution of packets, network usage, traffic in terms of frames, and bytes and broadcasts. In addition, the lower portion of each screen provides a graph over time of the percentage of network utilization and broadcast traffic. Thus, at a glance you can visually note the current use of the monitored network and whether or not a metric indicates a potential or existing problem that requires closer examination.

10.3 Other Network Management Functions

Now that we have an appreciation for SNMP and RMON, we can turn our attention to a detailed discussion of a core set of network management functions you can use as a mechanism to evaluate the suitability of different vendor products. As we will shortly note, upon occasion no one product will satisfy all of your management requirements and you may have to turn to multiple products to view network operations. Thus, we will conclude this chapter by examining the use of several network management tools you can use to observe network performance.

There is a core set of five functions associated with network management. Those functions are configuration, performance, fault, accounting, and security management. Each functional area manages a set of activities.

Figure 10.6 illustrates the functional areas commonly associated with network management and the set of activities managed by each area.

Configuration Management

The process of configuration management covers both the hardware and software settings required to provide an efficient and effective data transportation highway. Thus, configuration management consists of managing the physical hardware — including cables, computers, and network adapters — along with the logical network configuration governed by the installation of the network operating system, the selection of a network protocol or stack of protocols, and the manner in which users can access server facilities. The latter concerns the setup of the network, including permissions and routings that enable users to access different servers. Although this may appear to involve security management, it is mainly focused on the setting and distribution of network

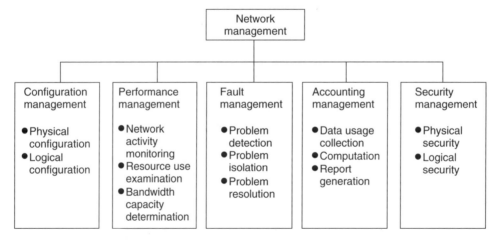

Figure 10.6   Network management functional areas.

passwords and the assignment of file permissions. Thus, logical configuration management permits a user to reach a network facility once he or she is connected to the network, while security management involves the ability of a user to gain access to the network and to different facilities made available by configuration management.

Performance Management

Performance management involves those activities required to ensure that the network operates in an orderly manner without unreasonable service delays. This functional area is concerned with the monitoring of network activity to ensure there are no bottlenecks to adversely affect network performance.

Monitored network activity can include the flow of data between stations and between stations and servers; the use of bridges, routers, and gateways; and the utilization of each network segment with respect to its total capacity. By performing these tasks, you will obtain information that will enable you to adjust the use of network hardware and software, as well as to consider a variety of network segmentation options that can eliminate potential network bottlenecks before they occur.

Fault Management

Networks have their less desirable moments in which components fail, software is configured incorrectly, and other problems occur. *Fault management* is the set of functions required to detect, isolate, and correct network problems.

A large number of hardware and software products are now marketed to provide a fault management capability for cables, hardware, and network software. The most common type of diagnostic device is a *time domain reflectometer*, which generates a pulse and uses its reflected time delay (or absence of a reflection) to isolate cable shorts and opens. LAN protocol analyzers allow you to test individual Ethernet adapters, and to monitor network performance and isolate certain types of network problems, such as jabbering. Both hardware-based LAN protocol analyzers and many software products provide a LAN frame decoding capability. This helps you determine whether the flow of frames and frame responses provides an insight into network problems. For instance, a station might be rejecting frames because of a lack of buffer space, which could easily be corrected by reconfiguring its software.

Accounting Management

Accounting management is a set of activities that enables you to determine network usage, generate usage reports, and assign costs to individuals or groups of users by organization or by department. Normally, the network operating system provides a raw set of network usage statistics, and you will need one or more other software packages to generate appropriate reports and assign costs to usage. While cost assignment is commonly used in wide area networks and for electronic mail usage, it is not commonly used to distribute the cost of using local area networks. Instead, accounting management is normally employed to answer such questions as, "What would be the effect on the network if the engineering department added five new employees?" In this situation, accounting management data might provide you with network usage statistics for the engineering department, including total department usage as well as individual and average station usage data. Using these statistics in conjunction with performance monitoring, you could then determine the probable effect of the addition of new employees to the network.

Security Management

As discussed in our overview of configuration management, security management involves primarily the assignment of network access passwords and access permissions to applications and file storage areas on the network. Other aspects of security management involve the physical placement of stations in areas where access to those stations is restricted, and the selection and control of specialized hardware and software security products. These products can range in scope from programs used to encipher and decipher electronic mail messages to network modems that can be programmed to perform a series of operations: prompt users for a code when they dial into the network, disconnect the user, and then dial a number predefined as associated with the user code.

Most network management products provide excellent coverage of a subset of the five core functional areas, but few products actually cover all functional areas. Most users will normally consider the use of two or more products to perform all five network management functions.

10.4 Representative Network Management Programs

In this section we will turn our attention to obtaining an appreciation of the operational capability of three programs that can be used to monitor an

Ethernet network. The first program we will look at is EtherVision, marketed by Triticom. EtherVision is a layer 2 monitor whose operation is restricted to primarily looking at the Ethernet frame header and computing layer 2 information. The other two programs we will examine, WebXRay from Cinco Systems (now part of Network Associates) and EtherPeek from WildPackets (formerly known as the AG Group), look deeper into each frame and have the ability to provide statistics at layers 2 through 4 of the OSI Reference Model.

Triticom EtherVision

One of the earliest Ethernet software monitors is a program marketed by Triticom of Eden Prairie, Minnesota, under the trademark EtherVision. This program is designed to operate on a workstation, and must be used with a specific type of Ethernet/IEEE 802.3 adapter—a Novell NE/2, NE1000, or NE2000, a 3Com Etherlink II, a Western Digital EtherCard, or a Pure Data PDI8023, PDI 8023-16, or PDUC8023. At the time this book was written, EtherVision supported 14 adapter cards and Triticom was in the process of adding program support for additional vendor adapter cards. Only the workstation executing EtherVision requires a specific Ethernet/IEEE 802.3 adapter card; all other workstations, servers, and other devices on the network can use any vendor adapter card. EtherVision's rationale for requiring a specific vendor's adapter card is based on the necessity to write software that accesses MAC layer buffers in the adapter, so that the program can read frames transmitted on the network. These frames form the basis for numerous network-operation statistics generated by the program.

Main Menu

The starting point for the use of EtherVision is the program's main menu. This menu contains a list of eight actions; these can be selected either by pressing the first letter of the listed options or by moving a highlight bar over an action and pressing the Enter key.

Options you can select from the main menu enable you to perform a variety of operations:

- Monitor network traffic
- Enable and disable a variety of alarms
- Assign names, alarms, and filters to station addresses
- Enable and disable network event logging
- Test the cable connected to the workstation's adapter
- Control the configuration options of the program

♦ Generate different types of reports

♦ Quit to DOS

By examining the use of several program options, we can obtain an appreciation for how EtherVision can assist you in managing your network.

Traffic Monitoring

By selecting the Monitor Traffic option from the program's main menu, you can monitor either source or destination addresses on a real-time basis. Figure 10.7 shows the screen display when the monitoring of source addresses is selected.

The main area of the display lists the source addresses of stations identified on the network and the number of frames counted for each station. At the time this screen display was printed, EtherVision was in operation for 40 seconds and had identified 22 stations on the network. Although station addresses are shown in Figure 10.7 in hexadecimal format, by pressing the F2 key you can toggle the station address display to its logical name or the vendor-adapter address. The highlighted bar over the top source address indicates that information about that address is displayed in the third area on the screen display, which shows the hexadecimal address, logical name, and vendor-ID for the address highlighted. Note that in the first 40 seconds of monitoring, the station named Sleepy was anything but, accounting for 86.3 percent of all

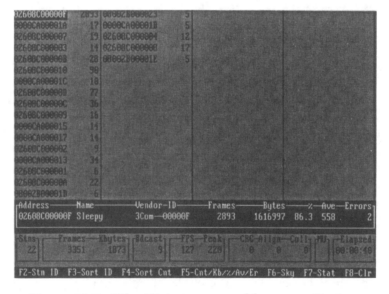

Figure 10.7 EtherVision source address monitoring.

network traffic. If the network utilization continued to be relatively high for a long monitoring period and some users complained about poor response time, you would probably want to determine what the user with the logical name of Sleepy was doing. Perhaps a one-time download of a large file occurred and there is no cause for alarm.

The next area of the screen shown in Figure 10.7 provides summary information concerning all stations that have been identified. Here, we see 22 stations were identified, and together they transmitted 3351 frames and 1873 K of information. A total of nine frames were broadcast to all stations, and the frames per second (FPS) and peak frames per second activity were 127 and 220, respectively. During the monitoring period there were no CRC errors, frame alignment errors, or collisions, nor were there any missed or unprocessed (MU) frames.

A missed or unprocessed frame typically results from data arriving too fast for the adapter to keep up with network traffic. The adapter used by a station running EtherVision must function in a promiscuous mode of operation. This means that the adapter must pass every frame read from the network to the higher-level network layers, instead of passing only frames that have the adapter's destination address. This is required since EtherVision must process each frame to compute a variety of network statistics.

When one or more stations on the network request a long file transfer, it becomes possible that the processor of the computer running EtherVision may not be able to process frames as they are read from the network. Thus, missed or unprocessed frames may indicate the need to operate EtherVision on a workstation that has a faster microprocessor to obtain more reliable statistics.

The bottom area of the display shown in Figure 10.7 indicates the function keys and their assignments, and enables you to select different action options. For example, pressing the F2 key changes the display of identified network adapters to logical names or a vendor-ID display format, while pressing the F8 key clears the display and resets all counters and the elapsed time to zero.

Skyline Displays

To obtain detailed information about network utilization, you would press the F6 key from the traffic monitoring display. This provides you with the ability to view the program's skyline display of network utilization and the FPS carried by the monitored network.

Figure 10.8 shows the EtherVision skyline display of network utilization, and Figure 10.9 shows the skyline display with respect to the FPS rate of data flow on the network. In examining Figure 10.8, note that the display shows

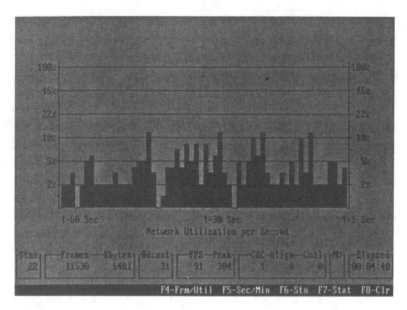

Figure 10.8 EtherVision network utilization skyline display.

Figure 10.9 EtherVision frames per second skyline display.

intervals for a 60-second monitoring period. By pressing the F5 key, you can change the monitoring period of the display to one hour—a more realistic period for examining network utilization. Since the network utilization in Figure 10.8 only slightly exceeded 10 percent, if this low level of utilization continued for a longer period of time it would indicate that you could expand your network through the addition of workstations before considering the use of bridges to subdivide the network.

The FPS display shown in Figure 10.9 provides you with a general indication of traffic flow on your network. However, by itself this display does not provide you with meaningful information, because it does not indicate the average frame size nor the distribution of frames by their length. This information can be obtained by pressing the F7 key to generate the program's statistics screen.

Statistics Display

Figure 10.10 illustrates the display of EtherVision's Statistics screen. Note that this screen provides you with summary information concerning frame counts, distribution of frame sizes, network utilization, and frame errors. Although this screen provides information similar to Foundation Manager's QuickStats display previously shown in Figures 10.4 and 10.5, there are key differences

Figure 10.10 EtherVision statistics display.

between that program and EtherVision that deserve a brief discussion. Foundation Manager is an SNMP RMON manager, capable of monitoring up to eight remote LANs. In comparison, EtherVision requires you to run the program on a station on the network to be monitored and does not support remote monitoring. Thus, you would use Foundation Manager or a similar product if you need to monitor remote networks while EtherVision or a similar product could be used to monitor a local network. Returning to our discussion of EtherVision, note that in the Frame Counts window, the average computed frame size is displayed, while the Frames Per Second window displays the average and peak frames per second monitored on the network. By using this data, you can compute and verify the data in the Network Utilization window and compute the effect of adding additional workstations to the network. For example, the peak FPS rate is 304 for 22 stations, or approximately 14 FPS per workstation. Adding 10 workstations with similar operational characteristics to existing workstations can be expected to increase the network traffic flow by 140 FPS. Since the average frame size is 561 bytes, 10 additional workstations can be expected to result in 561 bytes × 8 bits per byte × 140 FPS, or less than 630,000 bps of network traffic.

Alarms

The key to the effective management of a network is the ability to generate alarms when important predefined events occur. EtherVision provides network administrators with the ability to generate several key alarms, without which you would have to monitor several screens constantly. You can avoid this cumbersome process by using the program's Network Alarms/Options screen, illustrated in Figure 10.11. The Network Alarms/Options screen illustrated in Figure 10.11 allows you to enable or disable five alarms and to set the threshold value for three alarms. When an alarm is enabled and the event occurs or an alarm threshold is exceeded, the alarm status will be displayed on the top line of any EtherVision screen you are using, as well as being written to the program's Network Event Log.

The network idle time alarm will be triggered when EtherVision senses no traffic for the specified period of time. Since NetWare file servers periodically transmit IPX frames to make servers aware of each other, a Novell-based Ethernet LAN will always have at least some traffic at periodic intervals. Thus, the occurrence of a network idle time alarm can inform you of a serious network problem, such as the failure of a server or a faulty adapter in the computer operating EtherVision.

The network utilization alarm allows you to determine whether your network is approaching or has reached a level of saturation that warrants its

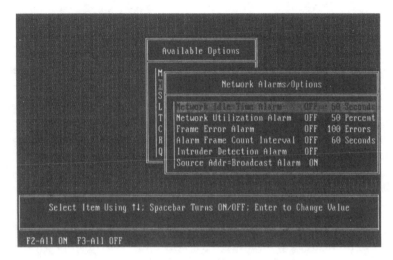

Figure 10.11   EtherVision network alarms/options screen.

subdivision. Normally, a utilization level that periodically exceeds 50 percent on an Ethernet/IEEE 802.3 network indicates a level of use that warrants the subdivision of the network and its connection via a bridge.

The frame error alarm goes off when it reaches a specified number of frame errors. Since the error rate on a LAN is typically 1 in a billion bits, or 1×10^{-9}, you can use this alarm to determine whether your network has an acceptable error level. To do so, you would view the Statistics screen when a frame error alarm occurs to determine the number of bits that have been transmitted during the time it took until the frame error alarm was generated. With this information, you could determine whether your LAN's bit error rate (BER) is at an acceptable level. For example, assume the total number of frames in the frame count window in the Statistics display was 100,000,000 when the frame error count reached 100 and generated an alarm. Also assume, for simplicity, that the average frame size in the Statistics display was 1000 bytes. An average of 100,000,000/100, or 1,000,000 frames, flowed on the network for each frame error. Since we assumed that each frame has an average length of 1000 bytes, 1,000,000 frames × 1000 bytes per frame × 8 bits per byte, or 8,000,000,000 bits, are transmitted per frame error. This is equivalent to a BER of 1/8,000,000,000, or 1.25×10^{-8}, which is about what we would expect from a LAN that performs well, and that has properly connected cables routed a safe distance from sources of electromagnetic interference.

The alarm count interval can be used to generate an alarm when enabled and set to a specific time period. Then, if the number of frame errors specified by the frame error alarm occurs within the specified alarm period, an alarm frame count interval alarm will go off.

The intruder detection alarm operates by triggering an alarm when a new station enters the network that was not defined to the program by the assignment of a logical name. When we examine the Station Options screen, we will see how logical names are assigned to each station address. The last alarm shown in Figure 10.11 is Source Addr = Broadcast Alarm. Since all source addresses must be unique, this alarm occurs when a source address with its broadcast bit set is detected.

Station Options Display

Through EtherVision's Station Options display screen you obtain the ability to assign names, filters, and alarms to specific hardware adapter addresses. Figure 10.12 illustrates the display of the program's Station Options screen.

In examining Figure 10.12, note that the highlighted bar is positioned over the top address, which was previously assigned the logical name Sleepy. In this example, we are in the process of changing the station's name to Dumbo. By moving the highlight bar over different station addresses and/or pressing appropriate function keys, you can control the assignment of names, alarms, and filters to stations. For example, F2 permits you to add or change a name, F3 prompts you to delete the name currently selected by the highlight bar, and so on. When assigning names, you can specify a filter (Ftr) for each station. Then, during monitoring, only those stations marked for filtering

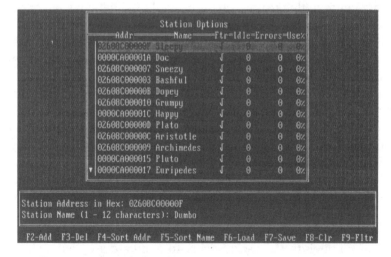

Figure 10.12 EtherVision station options display.

will be displayed on the program's monitoring screen. For a large network, filtering enables you to examine groups of stations, such as the accounting department's workstations. In addition to station filtering, you can use the Station Options display to set an idle alarm from 1 to 9,999, an error alarm of 1 to 9,999, and a usage alarm based on a percentage of network activity for each station. Thus, you can use the Station Options display to isolate a problem condition on a specific station or group of stations.

Network Event Logging Display

Figure 10.13 illustrates EtherVision's Network Event Logging screen. From this screen, you can enable and disable the logging of events to the program's log file and select the logging of error frames and peak utilization data. In addition, from this screen you can view the event log.

Figure 10.14 displays a portion of the network event log, which can be scrolled through a window on your display. Since we previously enabled the logging of both frame errors and peak utilization, the contents of the log reflect both types of activities. In examining Figure 10.14, note that "Frame Short" refers to any frame shorter than the minimum length of 64 bytes—a condition usually caused by a collision. Although collisions normally occur on an Ethernet/IEEE 802.3 network, a situation in which one station has a large number of collisions associated with its transmission may indicate a faulty adapter. Thus, from an examination of Figure 10.14 it appears that the

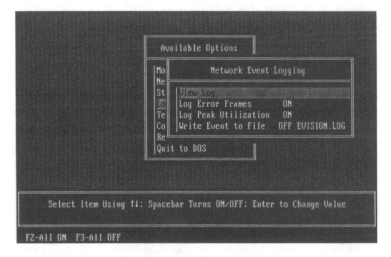

Figure 10.13   EtherVision network event logging screen.

Figure 10.14   EtherVision network event log.

adapter used on the station whose logical address is Sleepy may be in need of an awakening action, during which the adapter is tested, and if it continues to generate short frames, replaced.

As indicated by our short review of EtherVision, it permits you to perform most of the major functions associated with network management. Regardless of which management tool you use, you should always ensure that you have one available. The periodic use of an appropriate network management tool provides you with a detailed view of network activity, which can be invaluable in performing your network management functions.

Cinco Network's WebXRay

As previously discussed in this chapter, it is important to note that Ethernet is a layer 2 transport protocol that operates at the data link layer of the ISO Reference Model. This means that different types of protocols can be transported over Ethernet, which is both a key advantage of the network as well as the cause of many network-related problems. In this section we will turn our attention to the use of Cinco Network's WebXRay network monitoring and troubleshooting tool, which can be of considerable assistance when looking at IP traffic. As noted earlier in this chapter, Cinco Networks was one of several companies acquired by Network Associates over the past few years. WebXRay is now marketed as Sniffer Basic by Network Associates. Due to the growing role of the Internet and corporate intranets, most Ethernet

LANs carry a considerable amount of IP traffic, and the use of this program can provide a valuable tool for examining the state of different IP machines and the traffic they transmit and receive.

Overview

Figure 10.15 illustrates the WebXRay Dashboard, which provides a meter gauge view of IP statistics when the program is initialized. The top gauge displays the IP versus network load in terms of the number of packets per second. The next gauge indicates IP versus network utilization. In examining Figure 10.15 note that at the time the display was captured IP was contributing 39 percent of network utilization, with all traffic resulting in a network utilization level of 42 percent. This indicates that IP is the predominate protocol transported on the monitored network and any need to restructure the network due to high levels of utilization will have to consider the architecture of IP and its addressing.

Autodiscovery

One of the key features of WebXRay is its autodiscovery capability. Through the use of this feature you can use the program to identify all hosts on a segment as well as the IP services they are currently configured to support.

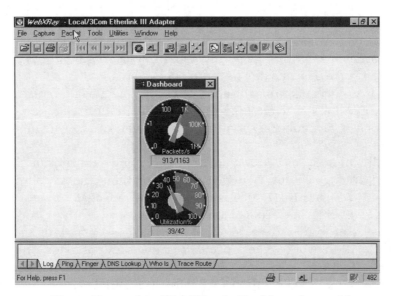

Figure 10.15 Cinco Network's WebXRay's Dashboard provides a meter or gauge display, which enables the role of IP traffic on a network to be visually noted.

Figure 10.16 Through the Topology Discovery dialog box you can configure WebXRay to search for a specific range of host addresses.

Figure 10.16 illustrates the WebXRay Topology Discovery dialog box. Into this box you enter the IP subnet address and the range for the last digit of the IP address you wish to search for. Since the WebXRay program uses the Ping application to locate hosts, it also provides you with the ability to set the timeout value for each ping. In the example shown in Figure 10.16, we will search the entire segment by using the last digit address range of 1 through 254 since 0 means this net and 255 is a broadcast address. A word of caution is in order concerning the entry of a Ping timeout value and host search range. If you set a very large Ping timeout value, a full search of a network segment for a large number of services per host can take a considerable amount of time.

To specify the services you wish to discover, you would click on the service tab of the Topology Discovery dialog box, generating a display similar to the one shown in Figure 10.17. In Figure 10.17 the selected services for DNS, FTP, HTTP, SNMP, and Telnet are shown checked. This means that the autodiscovery program will search each possible host address on the segment for the range of network values specified to determine if a host supports the services of interest.

Once you click the OK button in Figure 10.17 the autodiscovery process commences. As each node on the segment is discovered, its domain name will be displayed. If the domain name cannot be found, the IP address of the discovered node will be shown. Figure 10.18 illustrates a portion of the

Figure 10.17   Through the Service tab in the Topology Discovery dialog box you can select the TCP/IP services you wish the WebXRay program to scan for during its autodiscovery process.

Figure 10.18   During the autodiscovery process WebXRay displays the domain name or IP address of each host discovered.

autodiscovery process at a point in time when 17 nodes were discovered on the segment being monitored. As you might surmise, the autodiscovery feature represents a valuable mechanism to discover unknown machines users may have set up without informing management as well as services on those systems that might require a reconfiguration of a router's access list or firewall. Thus, a periodic autodiscovery process is usually a very valuable procedure for employing on a large network.

Once the autodiscovery process is completed you can determine the status of each service for each node discovered. To do so, you would click on the status tab at the bottom of the map window shown in Figure 10.18. This action will result in the display of the service window which is shown in Figure 10.19. In examining Figure 10.19 note that a happy face means the node or service is up and available, a question mark indicates that the status of the service is unknown, while a minus sign enclosed in a circle means that the service is not available for the network node. Since we previously indicated we wanted to restrict our service queries to specific types of services, those services with question marks primarily represent services we did not have the program query.

Figure 10.19 The WebXRay Service window indicates the status of different TCP/IP services or applications for each autodiscovered node on a segment.

As indicated by our examination of WebXRay, this program is well-suited for determining the effect of IP on your LAN and discovering nodes and the services they are configured to support. As such, WebXRay provides an additional insight into the activity on an Ethernet network that can be of considerable assistance in obtaining information on the operations and utilization of the network.

Wildpackets EtherPeek

In this concluding section of this chapter focused on network management, we will turn our attention to one of the most feature-packed Ethernet network monitoring and analysis programs. That program is EtherPeek, a product of WildPackets of Walnut Creek, CA. that was formerly known as the AG Group.

Overview

EtherPeek represents a full featured network monitoring and analysis software program. Unlike EtherVision, which is restricted to layer 2 monitoring, Ether-Peek has the ability to look deeper into a frame and determine and analyze information contained in each frame. For example, EtherPeek can read IP, UDP and TCP headers being transported in Ethernet frames. This enables the program to construct tables of data concerning source and destination IP address packet flows, tables concerning the distribution of protocols flowing on the network and similar information.

Operation

Figure 10.20 illustrates the EtherPeek main window with its two gauges shown in the lower portion of the display. The left gauge indicates network utilization while the right gauge indicates the packet rate. By checking on the tab labeled "value," you can display digital information in place of the analog gauges or you can close the lower window by checking on the X in the lower window's top left corner.

The top portion of the EtherPeek main window contains a series of menu entries that can be used to perform a variety of functions. You can capture data to a buffer, store captured data and analyze previously captured data at a later time or send captured data via email to a vendor's help desk for review. Because modern Ethernet LANs operating at 100 Mbps or 1 Gbps create a significant packet flow, you will probably want to use filters to restrict the type of packets to be captured, which represents another feature or EtherPeek we will examine later in this section.

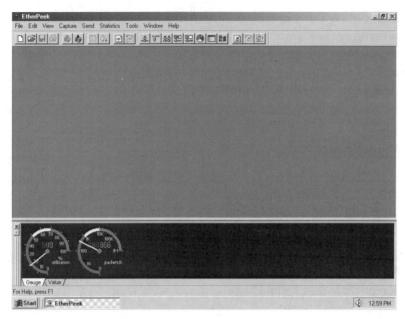

Figure 10.20   The EtherPeek main window with the network activity gauge shown in the lower portion of the display.

Packet Capturing

Through the File menu you can initiate the capturing of packets. To do so you would select the New entry in the File menu, which would generate the display of a dialog box labeled Capture Buffer Options. You would use this dialog box to set the buffer size that controls the amount of data that can be captured, as well as other data capture options.

Figure 10.21 illustrates an in-progress data capture operation. As data is captured, EtherPeek displays key information about each packet captured. Such information includes the source and destination address of the packet, its size in bytes, the time it was captured, the protocol used to transport the packet, and other information. To facilitate packet reference EtherPeek displays a packet number, which is shown in the left column in Figure 10.21. In addition, EtherPeek provides the ability for a user to perform a series of packet captures and to display the packet in each packet capture operation. In Figure 10.21 a portion of the packet captured during a second packet capture operation is shown displayed.

As a packet capture operation progresses EtherPeek updates the number of packets received, filtered and processed. While all three values are shown to

Figure 10.21   An EtherPeek in-progress packet capture operation.

be the same in Figure 10.21, this is because no filtering was performed and the processor of the computer operating EtherPeek was sufficiently fast to keep up with the flow of packets.

In Figure 10.21 the screen capture occurred when the capture buffer was 46 percent filled. In Figure 10.22 the capture buffer was completely filled, which is indicated by memory usage being shown as 100 percent. A total of 7401 packets were captured based upon the use of a 4 Mbyte capture buffer, which represents the default setting of the size of the buffer. Because RAM memory has become relatively inexpensive, most readers acquiring modern PCs to run an Ethernet monitoring and analysis program would more than likely select a large buffer size for packet capture.

Packet Decoding

One of the key features of EtherPeek is the ability to decode packets of interest easily. To illustrate this capability, let's assume you wish to decode the packet that flowed from IP source address 157.130.74.98 to destination address 205.131.176.11. This is the third packet shown in Figure 10.22 and is highlighted in the display.

Figure 10.22 Using EtherPeek to select a packet for decoding.

Double-clicking on an entry in the packet capture window results in EtherPeek automatically decoding the packet. Figure 10.23 illustrates the decoding of the third packet captured that was summarized in Figure 10.22. In examining Figure 10.23 you will note that the beginning of the packet decode provides summary information about the packet, such as its length and timestamp.

The actual beginning of the decode follows the summary information. As you will note from Figure 10.23, information about the Ethernet frame transporting the IP packet indicates the destination and source MAC addresses in the frame. This is followed by the value in the Type field, which indicates that IP is being transported.

The Ethernet header decode is followed by a decode of the IP header. If you go back to our earlier coverage of the IP header, you will note that the packet decode indicates the value of each field in the IP header. If we scrolled down further, we would also note the decode of the TCP header. If you focus your attention on the window above the gauge window, you will note that it consists of a sequence of hex characters. As you move the highlight bar from one entry to another in the top window, the applicable hex character that corresponds to the value of a field is highlighted. Thus, the hex characters

Figure 10.23 Using EtherPeek to decode a packet transported in an Ethernet frame.

00-A0-C9-E9-1E-09 are shown shaded, which corresponds to the Ethernet destination address header field.

Statistics

In addition to providing the ability to decode packets, EtherPeek includes a statistical display capability you can easily use to determine who is using your network and how it is being used. Figure 10.24 illustrates the EtherPeek main window showing the pull-down of its statistics menu in the foreground. In the background the node statistics display is shown for previously captured data, which resulted from the selection of the first entry in the Statistics menu.

If you focus your attention upon the background display in Figure 10.24, you will note that one IP address (205.131.176.11) is responsible for a majority of the traffic monitored. That address represents a Web server, which explains its high level of activity. Because four IP addresses are flowing through a LAN switch, EtherPeek indirectly alerts you to this by showing four IP addresses directly under the first MAC address on the display.

Continuing our examination of EtherPeek, Figure 10.25 illustrates the distribution of packets by their length. Note that, as you move you cursor

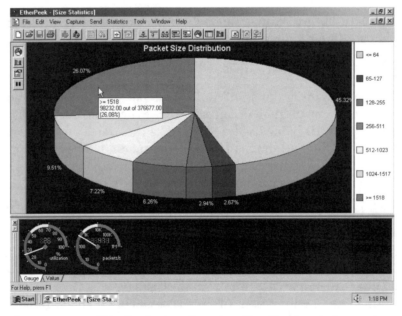

Figure 10.24 EtherPeek provides the ability to display several types of statistics concerning a monitored LAN.

Figure 10.25 Displaying packet size distribution information.

over each slice of the pie, the program displays specific statistics concerning the slice.

You can display the packet size distribution, as well as other statistics, in several ways when using EtherPeek. As noted in Figure 10.24, you can select "size" from the statistics menu or press Ctrl + 6. You can also click on the pie icon to display the pie chart.

Filtering

In concluding our examination of EtherPeek, we will focus our attention upon the program's filtering capability. EtherPeek's filtering capability can be applied to real-time as well as previously captured packets. Through the use of the program's packet filtering capability you can focus on an area of particular interest, such as a certain IP address or protocol.

Figure 10.26 illustrates the Edit Filter dialog box. In this example the filter was set to filter on the IP protocol, while the address to be filtered is shown as 205.131.176.11. In this example we want to filter packets with that IP source address but do not care about the destination address. In the lower portion

Figure 10.26 Using the EtherPeek filtering capability to focus on specific types of packets.

of Figure 10.26 we will filter on source port 80 but do not care about the destination port. If you examine the background of Figure 10.26 you will note the large number of protocols EtherPeek supports, ranging from AppleTalk to NetWare. Thus, EtherPeek provides a significant capability for monitoring Ethernet networks that transport a wide range of higher-layer protocols.

chapter eleven

The Future of Ethernet

When a book is devoted to a well-defined technology, it is always important to discuss the future of that technology. This is especially true with respect to Ethernet, since many readers are employees of organizations that have invested or plan to invest tens to hundreds of thousands of dollars or more in acquiring network adapter cards and hubs or switches, installing cabling, obtaining software, and teaching employees to use a network operating system. Thus, a logical question readers may have involves the safety of their current or planned investment in Ethernet technology. That is, what can you expect in the evolution of Ethernet technology, and will the introduction of new technology result in the obsolescence of your existing or planned Ethernet network? Although there is no simple answer to this multifaceted question, since the effect of technological advances is highly dependent on organizational communications requirements, we can examine trends in networking and Ethernet technology. This will provide us with a foundation of knowledge from which we can express some general observations about a previous or planned investment in an Ethernet network.

11.1 Ethernet Trends

In attempting to project the future of Ethernet, we should consider a variety of variables in addition to technological developments. Some of the major variables we must consider are the cost of technology, the performance it provides, and the potential to use existing technology in a more productive manner. The latter may minimize or reduce a requirement to migrate to new technology. In this section, we will focus our attention on the cost and performance of existing and evolving Ethernet technology.

Network Adapter Card Cost

Just a half-dozen years ago, the average price of an Ethernet adapter card was approximately $1000, while the cost of a personal computer was between

$3000 and $4000. Excluding the cost of cabling and a network operating system, an Ethernet adapter card represented an approximate 25- to 33-percent increase in the cost of a personal computer. By early 2002 you could acquire an Intel Pentium IV–based personal computer with 256 M of RAM, SVGA support, and an SVGA monitor for approximately $1000. At the same time, the average cost of a 10-/100-Mbps dual-speed Ethernet adapter card was under $50, so the additional cost to network a personal computer was only approximately 5 percent of an organization's hardware budget. Clearly, the cost of obtaining an Ethernet network communications capability was extremely nominal by 2002.

Future Price Direction

Not only has the cost of Ethernet hardware significantly declined over the past few years, but advances in chip fabrication technology indicate that price declines are far from being over. In 1992 Zenith Data Systems introduced several notebook computers with a built-in Ethernet communications capability on the computer's motherboard. Additional computer manufacturers now provide a built-in Ethernet networking capability for their products, enabling portable computer users to simply plug a dual-speed 10/100BASE-T jack into their computer's plug upon return to the office to obtain access to the corporate network.

According to several trade press articles, the inclusion of an Ethernet chip set on nonportable personal computers adds less than $20 to the cost of the computer. This can be expected to make an Ethernet networking capability on personal computers as pervasive as the inclusion of a parallel port. In comparison, alternative network adapter cards, such as Token-Ring and FDDI, range in cost from $150 to $200 for a 16-Mbps Token-Ring adapter to $400 to $550 for an FDDI adapter. Ethernet can thus be expected to continue to hold a significant cost advantage over competing local area network adapter cards. This should extend the use of Ethernet networks far into the foreseeable future.

In the area of desktop personal computers, it is almost a common occurrence to note approximately 25 percent of all advertisements now include either a built-in NIC or a 10-/100-Mbps adapter bundled with memory, an SVGA video adapter, and other computer features. Thus, not only is Ethernet recognized as the de facto network of choice, but, in addition, a significant number of PCs are now being bundled with Ethernet adapters.

Although the cost of Gigabit Ethernet adapter cards was relatively expensive in comparison to 10-/100-Mbps adapters, the cost of the former is rapidly declining. First introduced at prices above $2000, by early 2002 some Gigabit Ethernet adapters were priced below $1000. However, it is important to note that currently available Gigabit Ethernet adapters are based upon relatively expensive optical technology. As more vendors produce recently standardized 1000BASE-T network adapter cards, you can reasonably expect production of adapters using that media to achieve significant levels of production that can result in economics of scale, which lowers the cost of production. This in turn will eventually result in declining prices for 1000BASE-T adapter cards as the market for this product grows.

Although 10 Gigabit Ethernet is primarily expected to be used by large organizations and communications carriers in a metropolitan networking environment, we can also expect the cost of such equipment to decline as production increases. Thus, the cost per port of $20,000 or more for many 10 Gigabit switches entering the market during 2002, while out of reach for small to medium-size organizations, can be expected to become more nominal for use by large organizations. In fact, one of the most promising uses for 10 Gigabit Ethernet is as a supplement or replacement for Synchronous Optical Networking (SONET) equipment in a metropolitan networking environment, so let's turn our attention to this potential use of a developing Ethernet technology.

10 Gigabit Ethernet in the Metro

During 2002 the IEEE 802.3ae Committee's draft standard for 10 Gigabit Ethernet LAN and WAN implementations should be ratified. As a dominant LAN protocol a 10 Gbps standard could result in 10 Gigabit Ethernet becoming price competitive for use in the WAN at distances up to 40 km, in effect a metropolitan area networking capability.

To understand the rationale for the potential use of 10 Gigabit Ethernet in the WAN it is important to note that most metropolitan area networking currently consists of SONET-based technology. Under SONET, data is transported in frames that have a high amount of fixed overhead, with overhead bits used to convey many types of administrative data between nodes, as well as to support voice calls of repair personnel. SONET was developed in a pre-wireless communications era. It was also deployed prior to the development of optical switching and dense wavelength division multiplexing. While SONET includes the capability to have redundant rings with cutover from one to another in milliseconds when a fiber is out, there are less expensive evolving solutions today that provide a similar capability. One of those evolving solutions is the use of 10 Gbps Ethernet in the WAN.

In comparison to SONET, which represents a complex technology with complex framing, 10 Gigabit Ethernet represents a scalable extension of a well-understood technology. Prices per port of all types of Ethernet equipment routinely decline 20 to 30 percent per year, with 10 Gigabit Ethernet per port cost expected to decline to $10,000 to $15,000 by the end of 2002. In comparison, packet over SONET interfaces cost over 20 times that amount. In addition, the mapping of Ethernet to ATM that is also commonly used in the WAN represents another well-known technology. Thus, it probably will become practical for some large organizations to use a 10 Gigabit Ethernet connection to a carrier's ATM backbone in place of a SONET local loop.

Table 11.1 provides a comparison of Gigabit Ethernet and 10 Gigabit Ethernet. Note that the maximum drive distance of 10 Gigabit Ethernet is 40 km, which makes it well suited for both high-speed local loop and metropolitan area transmission.

To illustrate the potential use of Gigabit and 10 Gigabit Ethernet in a metropolitan area networking environment, consider Figure 11.1. In this example a Gigabit Ethernet and 10 Gigabit Ethernet local loop flow into a communications carrier's central office. That office routes metro transmission via Ethernet switches or SONET equipment to their applicable destination. Thus, if the destination is within the metro area, the data would be carried via a 10 Gigabit Ethernet switch infrastructure to the central office serving the destination local loop.

TABLE 11.1   Gigabit Ethernet vs. 10 Gigabit Ethernet

Attribute	Gigabit Ethernet	10 Gigabit Ethernet
Physical media	Single-mode fiber, multimode fiber, widewave division multiplexing, twisted-pair copper	Single-mode fiber, multimode fiber
Drive distance	Up to 5 km (3.11 miles)	Up to 40 km (24.86 miles)
Media Access Control	Full and half duplex	Full duplex
Coding	8B/10B	64B/66B and Sonet framing
Physical-media dependent	805 nm; 1300 nm, 1550 nm WWDM	850 nm; 1300 nm; 1550 nm

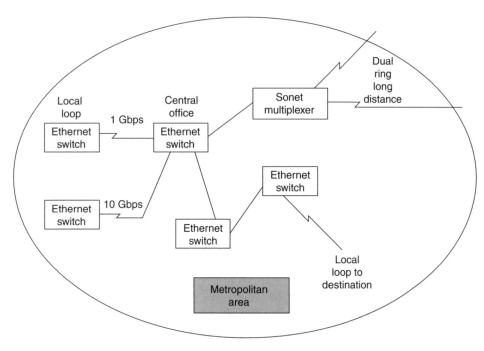

Figure 11.1   Potential use of Gigabit and 10 Gigabit Ethernet in the metropolitan area.

11.2 Network Performance Considerations

At the time this book was written there were a wide range of options available for supporting what some persons refer to as legacy 10-Mbps Ethernet LANs. Today you can consider using LAN switches, a faster backbone infrastructure, or a combination of switches and a fast shared backbone. In addition to pure Ethernet solutions you can consider the use of ATM and FDDI as a backbone. With all these potential solutions a logical question readers may wish to ask themselves is whether they need a 100- or 1000-Mbps or even a 10 Gbps local area network to satisfy their current and future data transmission requirements. Even if the answer is yes, this answer, as we will soon note, may not mean that your previous investment in Ethernet technology is obsolete.

Supplementing an Existing Network

To demonstrate how more modern and higher operating rate local area network technology can be used to supplement existing Ethernet equipment, let us assume that your organization previously installed a series of Ethernet networks on floors within a building, using 10BASE-T bridges and wiring through floor risers to interconnect users on each "floor"-based network. Under this networking scenario, it is quite possible that the initiation of a file transfer operation by two or more network users accessing a server on a third network via a 10BASE-T bridge would adversely affect other internet transmission until the file transfer operations are completed.

To see this potential for internet congestion, consider Figure 11.2, in which three "floor" LANs are connected with three 10BASE-T bridges wired together, perhaps using the riser within the building. Let us assume that stations A and C initiate file transfers to the server S_n located on network C. If each network operates at 10 Mbps, the traffic offered to the middle bridge is 20 Mbps. However, since each network operates at 10 Mbps, the best performance possible for the middle bridge is to route the file transfer data at 10 Mbps to the server. Now suppose that station D on network B attempts to access the server S on network C. Frames generated by that station must contend with frames generated by workstations A and C for service by the bridge. It is thus quite possible for interactive queries, as well as file transfer operations across networks, to be adversely affected by existing file transfer operations.

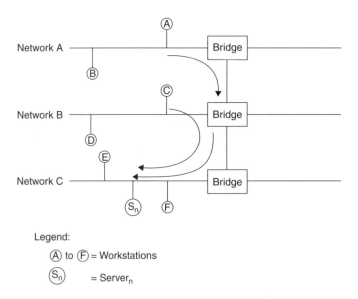

Figure 11.2 Potential for internetwork congestion. The initiation of file transfer operations from two or more workstations to a server on a third workstation can create network congestion.

Using a Backbone Network

Although one potential solution to internet congestion is to install new networks capable of supporting higher data transfer operations, doing so might require both new adapter cards and new network wiring. A far less expensive potential solution to internet congestion is to use a higher operating rate local area network to serve as a backbone net.

Figure 11.3 shows the use of an FDDI backbone network to interconnect the three previously installed Ethernet networks. Since the FDDI network operates at 100 Mbps, its use is equivalent to a high-speed interstate highway linking country roads together. That is, inter-LAN traffic is facilitated by a high-speed backbone LAN in the same manner that interroad traffic is facilitated by an interstate highway. Once a frame is bridged onto the FDDI network, it flows at 100 Mbps, enabling more frames to be carried between linked local area networks per unit time than possible when a 10BASE-T network is used as a backbone network.

Unless your organization is already using FDDI, its installation cost can be relatively expensive in comparison to 100BASE-T technology. Thus, many organizations will more than likely consider the use of a 100BASE-T shared media hub or even a 1-Gbps buffered distributor to form a network backbone.

In early 2002, the cost of an 8-port 100-Mbps shared Ethernet hub was under $100, providing a most economical method for creating a higher-speed

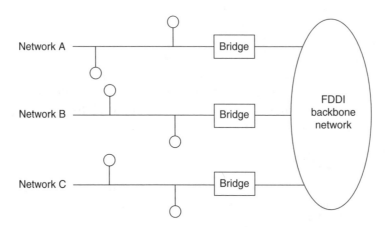

Figure 11.3 Using a high-speed backbone network. The use of a 100-Mbps FDDI network as a backbone to connect separate Ethernet LANs can remove a large degree of potential internet congestion while permitting the previous investment in Ethernet networks to be maintained.

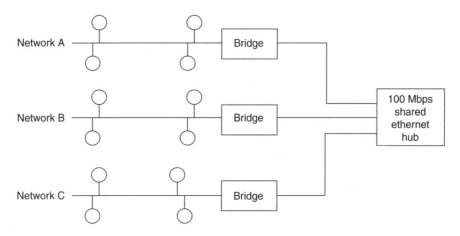

Figure 11.4 Using a 100-Mbps shared Ethernet hub as a backbone provides a very low-cost mechanism for supporting inter-LAN communications.

backbone network for bridging between LANs. Figure 11.4 illustrates how you could use a low-cost 100-Mbps shared Ethernet hub as a backbone for connecting legacy 10BASE-T networks. Note that this network configuration also preserves your investment as all cabling and network adapters to the left of each bridge remain as is. Since the cost of a 100-Mbps shared Ethernet hub is equivalent to the cost of a single FDDI adapter, this represents a low-cost mechanism to retain your network infrastructure.

In examining Figure 11.4, note that transmission from any bridge port to the 100-Mbps shared Ethernet hub is regenerated onto all other hub ports. However, the use of bridges on each network connection serves as a filter, barring repeated frames from flowing onto networks they are not intended for. Thus, although each network could be directly connected to a hub port, the use of bridges can significantly enhance network performance by limiting repeated frames from destination networks they are not actually directed to.

Using a Switching System

Another solution to network congestion can be obtained through the use of a 100BASE-T Fast Ethernet switch or creating a tiered hub-based switching network.

Figure 11.5 illustrates the use of a Fast Ethernet hub-based switch. In this example, network servers are connected to the 100-Mbps Fast Ethernet ports, while existing 10BASE-T hubs are connected to the switch using 10BASE-T adapters operating at 10 Mbps. Note that the switch can provide

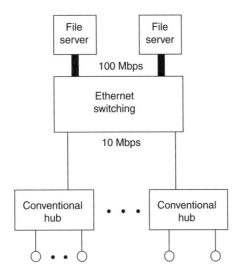

Figure 11.5 Constructing a tiered network.

two simultaneous cross-connections to the two file servers, boosting available bandwidth in comparison to the situation where file servers are located on a common network. In addition, through the use of a 100-Mbps connection each query response is completed quicker than if communications occurred on a shared 10-Mbps network.

The configuration illustrated in Figure 11.5, which this author labeled as a tiered network, can also be considered to represent a collapsed backbone. Although a switch using two Mbps Fast Ethernet port connections to two file servers is shown, there are many other network connections that can be considered to protect your investment in 10-Mbps Ethernet technology while providing a mechanism to reduce network congestion. You can consider the use of a switch with a fat pipe or full-duplex capability, or the use of a router as an alternative to the use of a switch.

Although the use of a switch or router can provide a mechanism to alleviate network congestion, another method you can consider is the bottleneck between workstations, servers, and the network. That bottleneck is the LAN adapter card. Many times the use of an enhanced adapter card may solve a network congestion problem many consultants would have you believe requires the use of a more expensive solution.

Using Enhanced Adapter Cards

One of the key limits to the ability of a workstation to transfer large quantities of data is the type of network adapter card used in a workstation. A typical low-cost Ethernet adapter card may have a data transfer rate of only 200,000 to 400,000 bytes per second. Such adapters are capable of transmitting and receiving data at only approximately 10 to 20 percent of the transfer rate of a 10BASE-T network. While this transfer rate is usually more than sufficient for most client/server operations, it becomes a bottleneck for long file transfers and for devices such as bridges, routers, and gateways that may require a higher transfer rate capability. The selective use of enhanced Ethernet adapter cards may provide you with the ability to increase network performance and reduce or eliminate network bottlenecks.

Two types of Ethernet adapter cards you may wish to consider for workstations that have a large amount of file transfer operations or for bridges, routers, and gateways are bus mastering and parallel processing adapter cards.

Bus Mastering Cards   A bus mastering card is designed to perform I/O data transfers directly to and from the memory of the computer in which it is installed. To accomplish this, a bus mastering card includes circuitry known as a *direct memory access* (*DMA*). The adapter card can initiate a DMA transfer, which permits data to be moved directly to or from memory, while the processor on the adapter card performs other operations. The net effect of bus mastering is to increase the transfer capability of the adapter card by 50 to 100 percent.

Parallel-Tasking Cards   Standard Ethernet adapter cards perform networking operations in a fixed sequential manner. Although a bus mastering adapter permits memory access operations to be performed in parallel with some network operations, greater efficiencies are obtainable with the use of parallel-tasking Ethernet adapters. One such adapter is Etherlink III, manufactured by 3Com Corporation, which has the capability to transfer data at approximately 500,000 bytes per second.

To demonstrate the efficiency of parallel-tasking, the top portion of Figure 11.6 shows the operation of a pair of standard Ethernet adapters used to transmit and receive data. As indicated, each operation has to be completed before the next can be begun.

The lower portion of Figure 11.6 shows the tasks performed for the transmission of information between two parallel-tasking Ethernet adapter cards. As noted by the time chart, the performance of many tasks in parallel reduces the time required to transfer information, which enhances the transfer rate of the adapter card.

100-Mbps Adapter Operations   Although the use of appropriate 10BASE-T adapter cards may by themselves prolong the ability to operate at 10 Mbps,

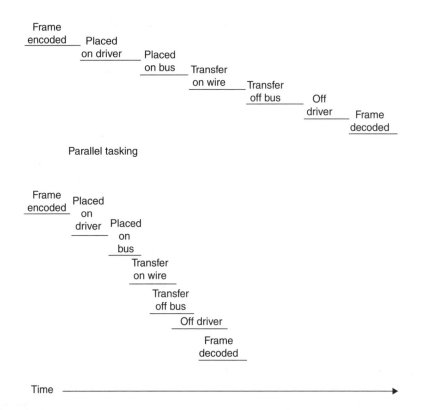

Figure 11.6 Serial-tasking versus parallel-tasking Ethernet adapters. The use of parallel-tasking Ethernet adapter cards permits the overlapping of many operations, thus reducing the time needed to transfer information and increasing the data transfer capability of the adapter.

when upgrading to 100-Mbps Fast Ethernet or another network, you must also carefully consider the capability of adapter cards. For example, assume your organization's 10BASE-T network is heavily saturated and additional applications to include multimedia are on the horizon. Although upgrading to a 100BASE-T network might initially satisfy your organization's networking requirements, it is quite possible that access contention to a video server, even at 100 Mbps, could result in delays that distance the delivery of video. In this situation you might consider installing a full-duplex 100BASE-T adapter card in the video server and connecting the server to a 100-Mbps switching hub.

1000-Mbps Adapter Operations When considering the use of Gigabit Ethernet the methodology of the manner by which data is moved between the computer and adapter as well as the bus supported by the adapter are extremely important design features you must consider. Today you can consider two types of PCI bus. One bus has a 32-bit width, while the other has a 64-bit width. Both can operate at a bus speed of either 33 or 66 MHz. Multiplying the bus width in bytes by the bus speed provides an indication of the raw or theoretical byte transfer rate of the adapter, while multiplying the bus width in bits by the bus speed provides an indication of the theoretical transfer rate of the bus. However, from a practical standpoint the overhead associated with frame copying, buffer alignment, checksum computations, and other overhead functions commonly reduces the efficiency of an Ethernet adapter to approximately 60 percent of its theoretical transfer rate. Using the preceding as a guide, Table 11.2 indicates the realistic bit transfer rates you can expect from the use of four types of PCI bus adapters. In examining the entries in Table 11.2, it is important to note that if you are using a 32-bit PCI card in a computer with a 33-MHz bus, at best you will probably achieve a data transfer capability approximately 63 percent of the transfer supported by Gigabit Ethernet.

Since the 60-percent efficiency previously used to compute the probable bit rate column entries in Table 11.2 is a representative average of different vendor products, one way to enhance the capability of the use of Gigabit Ethernet is to use more efficient adapters. However, this is normally only true if you are using a 32-bit PCI card in a computer whose bus operates at 33 MHz. If you are using a computer whose bus operates at 66 MHz or you are using a 64-bit PCI card from Table 11.2 you will note that the probable bit rate can be expected to be 1.273 Gbps or 2.534 Gbps. Even if the manufacturer of the Gigabit Ethernet NIC uses a highly inefficient buffering method that reduces throughput by 20 percent, the data transfer capability of the adapter should be more than 1 Gbps. Thus, when considering a Gigabit Ethernet adapter it

TABLE 11.2   Gigabit Ethernet PCI Bus Considerations

Bus Width (bits)	Bus Speed (MHz)	Theoretical Byte Transfer Range (MB/s)	Theoretical Bit Rate (Gbps)	Probable Bit Rate (Gbps)
32	33	132	1.056	0.634
32	66	264	2.112	1.273
64	33	264	2.112	1.273
64	66	528	4.224	2.534

is probably more important to consider the bus width and bus speed than vendor claims of design efficiency.

Summary

Ethernet represents a scalable networking technology that provides an operating rate support from 10 Mbps to 10 Gbps. As the LAN networking technology of choice, it represents the de facto winner of consumer acceptance with a market share hovering over 90 percent. During 2002 we can expect both Gigabit Ethernet and 10 Gigabit Ethernet to move into the WAN, with Gigabit Ethernet being used for local loop access while 10 Gigabit Ethernet can be expected to support both local loop and metropolitan area networking. Due to this we can safely observe that Ethernet represents a data transportation vehicle that will support organizational networking requirements for the foreseeable future.

index